# OXFORD STUDIES IN ANCIENT PHILOSOPHY

# Oxford Studies in Ancient Philosophy

## Volume III

### 1985

Edited by
## Julia Annas

CLARENDON PRESS · OXFORD
1985

Oxford University Press, Walton Street, Oxford OX2 6DP
Oxford New York Toronto
Delhi Bombay Calcutta Madras Karachi
Kuala Lumpur Singapore Hong Kong Tokyo
Nairobi Dar es Salaam Cape Town
Melbourne Auckland
and associated companies in
Beirut Berlin Ibadan Nicosia

Oxford is a trade mark of Oxford University Press

Published in the United States
by Oxford University Press, New York

© except where otherwise stated,
Oxford University Press 1985

British Library Cataloguing in Publication Data

Oxford studies in ancient philosophy.——3
1. Philosophy, Ancient
180'.938    B505
ISSN 0265-7651
ISBN 0-19-824911-X
ISBN 0-19-824910-1 Pbk

Set by Joshua Associates Limited, Oxford
Printed in Great Britain
at the University Press, Oxford
by David Stanford
Printer to the University

# ADVISORY BOARD

# CONTENTS

*Editorial*                                                                          viii

Meno's Paradox and Socrates as a Teacher
ALEXANDER NEHAMAS                                                      1

The Sea-Battle Reconsidered: A Defence of the
Traditional Interpretation   DOROTHEA FREDE        31

Permanent Happiness: Aristotle and Solon   T. H. IRWIN   89

Separation in Aristotle's Metaphysics
DONALD MORRISON                                                      125

Separation: A Reply to Morrison   GAIL FINE                159

Separation: A Reply to Fine   DONALD MORRISON    167

Epicurean *Prolēpsis*   DAVID K. GLIDDEN                    175

Logic and Omniscience: Alexander of Aphrodisias and
Proclus   MARIO MIGNUCCI                                             219

Professor Vlastos's Analysis of Socratic Elenchus
RONALD M. POLANSKY                                                 247

The Beautiful and the Genuine: A discussion of Paul
Woodruff, *Plato, Hippias Major*   CHARLES KAHN   261

Nature and Regularity in Stoic Ethics: A discussion of
Anna Maria Ioppolo, *Aristone di Chio e lo Stoicismo
Antico*   NICHOLAS WHITE                                             289

Demarcating Ancient Science: A discussion of G. E. R.
Lloyd, *Science, Folklore and Ideology: the Life Sciences
in Ancient Greece*   JAMES G. LENNOX                      307

*Index Locorum*                                                              325

# EDITORIAL

*Oxford Studies in Ancient Philosophy* has had a warm welcome, and it is gratifying that readers and reviewers alike seem agreed that there is indeed a place for a publication where articles can be, if necessary, expansive. In this issue we publish some longer pieces, including a revised and updated version in English by Dorothea Frede of her magisterial monograph on Aristotle's notoriously difficult Sea-Battle passage. We also continue to encourage reactions to and debate on articles, and reviews which engage with a book at length. We do not intend to stick to a single format; *Oxford Studies* will spring some surprises and try out new ideas. But we are happy that so far our major distinguishing features have all been popular; many thanks.

Next year we break our format for the first time, for the pleasantest of reasons. The 1986 issue of *Oxford Studies* will be a Festschrift for Professor J. L. Ackrill, to honour his sixty-fifth birthday. The Editor for this issue will be Michael Woods, of Brasenose College, Oxford. We are most happy to honour John Ackrill, and look forward to a very special issue.

Because the Festschrift will constitute the 1986 issue, no contributions will be accepted during 1985. The Editor will be happy to accept contributions again in 1986 for the 1987 issue.

*St Hugh's College, Oxford*                    JULIA ANNAS

# MENO'S PARADOX AND SOCRATES AS A TEACHER*

## Alexander Nehamas

Meno has always been considered as one of the least gifted and co-operative characters in Plato's dialogues. Commentators have disdained him generally, but their greatest disdain is reserved for the argument he introduces to the effect that all learning is impossible at *Meno* 80d5-9. Shorey, who had no patience for the view expressed in the paradox itself, referred to it disparagingly as 'this eristic and lazy argument'.[1] Taylor liked neither the argument nor Meno's reasons for bringing it up: 'Meno', he wrote, 'again tries to run off on an irrelevant issue. He brings up the sophistic puzzle . . .'.[2] Klein thought of the negative influence of the paradox on all desire to learn anything new and wrote that Meno himself 'was conspicuously reluctant to make the effort Socrates requested of him. It seems that his behaviour throughout the conversation was in agreement with the consequence that flows from the argument he has just presented'.[3] Bernard Phillips, who with many other writers takes the argument itself quite seriously, nevertheless insists that for Meno personally 'it is merely a dodge'.[4] Even Bluck, who is slightly more sympathetic to Meno than other writers are, cannot approve of him in this instance: 'So far as Meno is concerned, this question may be regarded as a convenient dodge, an eristic trick; but for Plato, it had important philosophical implications.'[5]

Plato himself certainly took Meno's paradox seriously, as we can see from the care with which he develops his own

* © Alexander Nehamas 1985.
[1] Paul Shorey, *What Plato Said* (Chicago, 1983), 157.
[2] A. E. Taylor, *Plato: The Man and His Work* (London, 1937), 137.
[3] Jacob Klein, *A Commentary on Plato's Meno* (Chapel Hill, 1965), 92.
[4] Bernard Phillips, 'The Significance of Meno's Paradox', in *Plato's Meno: Text and Criticism*, ed. Alexander Sesonske and Noel Fleming (Belmont, 1965), 78.
[5] R. S. Bluck, *Plato's Meno* (Cambridge, 1964), 8. Bluck's mixed view of Meno can be found on pp 125-6.

controversial and complicated solution to the problem (*Meno* (*M.*) 81a5-86c2) and from the intimate connection of that solution, the theory of recollection, to the theory of Forms when the latter eventually appears, as it does not in the *Meno*, in Plato's texts.[6] But does Plato take only the argument, and not Meno himself, seriously? Is Meno merely dodging the issue and trying to win a debating point from Socrates? Is his paradox simply a pretext for Plato to present his own, recently acquired, epistemological ideas?

This view is invested with considerable authority, but does not seem to me to be true. To see that it is not, we must first examine the general situation that prompts Meno to present his paradox as well as the precise wording of his statement. If we can show that Plato thinks that Meno himself has good reason to raise this difficulty then we shall be able to connect this passage with certain other issues, some of which were of considerable importance in Plato's philosophical thinking.

I

The question whether *aretē* is teachable, inborn, or acquired in some other way, with which Meno so abruptly opens the dialogue (71a1-4), was a commonplace of early Greek speculation. That it concerned not only Socrates but also, more generally, the sophistic movement is already indicated by the Gorgianic style of Meno's question.[7] More traditionally, the issue applied not only to *aretē* but also to *sophia* (wisdom); this may appear surprising in view of the fact that Socrates finds it uncontroversial to claim that if *aretē* is *epistēmē* (knowledge or understanding, often used interchangeably with *sophia*) then it is surely teachable (*M.* 87c5-6). Already by the end of the fifth century, the author of *Dissoi Logoi* (403-395 BC) can refer to the 'neither true nor new argument that *sophiē* and *aretā* can neither be taught

---

[6] The contrary views of Cherniss and Guthrie have been recently discussed by Michael Morgan, 'Belief, Knowledge and Learning in Plato's Middle Dialogues' (unpublished manuscript), 8-9, with full references.

[7] Cf. also G. B. Kerferd, *The Sophistic Movement* (Cambridge, 1981), 131-8.

[8] Cf. *Protagoras* (*Pr.*) 371a5-b3 and contrast *Euthydemus* (*Eud.*) 282c1-8.

nor learned' (6. 1).[9] In a famous passage of *Olympian* II.
86-8, Pindar had already claimed that the wise (which in this
case refers to the poet) is so by nature, the rest being to him
like cacophonous crows in comparison.[10] Isocrates was to
argue that *aretē* and *dikaiosunē* (justice) are not purely teachable, without, that is, the proper nature (*Contra Sophistas*
14-18, 21)[11]—a position with some affinities to Plato's view
in the *Republic*. Finally, a similar position in regard to
*andreia* (courage) is attributed to Socrates by Xenophon
at *Memorabilia* III. 9.

But though this question was commonplace, there was
little, if any agreement as to the nature of what it concerned,
the nature of *aretē*. What concerns me is not the specific
debate over the distinction between 'quiet' or 'co-operative'
and competitive virtues. Mine is the much simpler point that
*aretē* has an immensely broader range of application than its
conventional English translation 'virtue', while the more
recent 'excellence' strikes me as too weak and vague. *Aretē*
not only applies to more human qualities than 'virtue' does,
but it also covers features that are in no way specifically
human. This is, of course, perfectly clear from *Republic*
352d-354a, where Plato discusses explicitly the *aretē* of
instruments and, by implication, that of animals. But this
usage is not found only in Plato. Already in Homer, horses
are said to possess *aretē* (*Iliad* XXIII. 276, 374). Even inanimate objects can have their characteristic excellence: fertile
soil (Thucydides I. 2. 4) and fine cotton (Herodotus III.
106. 2) are cases in point. If it were not for this, we might
do well to construe *aretē* as 'success' or as the quality that
constitutes or that accounts for it. If nothing else, this would
show that the ancient debate is relevant to the many contemporary promises to ensure success, for an appropriate fee, in
all sorts of fields and endeavours and which prompt Socratic
and Platonic responses from all those who look down upon
the notion of success implicit in these promises and upon the

---

[9] On the date of the *Dissoi Logoi*, cf. T. M. Robinson, *Contrasting Arguments:
An Edition of the Dissoi Logoi* (New York, 1979), 34-41.
[10] Cf. *Nemean* III. 41.
[11] Cf. *Antidosis* 186-92, 274-5. For further references, cf. Klein, above n 3,
39 n 18.

endeavours themselves. We may thus be able to answer
Jowett, who, construing *aretē* as virtue, claimed that 'no one
would either ask or answer such a question (as Meno's) in
modern times'.[12]

In order to account for the application of *aretē* to animals
as well as to inanimate objects, it might be better to construe
it as that quality or set of qualities, whatever that may be,
that makes something *outstanding* in its group. We might
even consider it as what accounts for an object's *justified
notability*. Both suggestions concern not only intrinsic
features of such objects but also, in one way or another, their
reputation. And this is as it should be. For from the earliest
times on, the notion of *aretē* was intrinsically social, sometimes almost equivalent to fame (*kleos*). That this was so even
in late periods is shown by Hypereides, who in his *Epitaph*
wrote that those who die for their city 'leave *aretē* behind
them' (41). Also, an epigraph commemorating the Athenians
who fell at Potidaea states that 'having placed their lives onto
the scale, they received *aretē* in return'.[13]

The question, therefore, whether *aretē* can be taught is the
question whether one can be taught what it takes to have
a justifiably high reputation among one's peers.[14] But this, of
course, leaves the prior question unanswered; the term is not
non-controversially connected with any particular set of
human qualities. We still do not know the proper domain
within which one is supposed to be outstanding or, even
more importantly, in what being outstanding itself consists.

This last reasonable doubt, expressed in appropriate Socratic
vocabulary, suggests that Socrates' own response to Meno's
opening question makes rather good sense. In the persona of
an imaginary Athenian, Socrates tells Meno not only that he
does not know whether it can be taught but also that he

[12] B. Jowett, *The Dialogues of Plato*, 4th edn by D. J. Allan and H. E. Dale
(Oxford, 1953), 252.

[13] W. Peek, *Griechische Versinschriften*, vol i (Berlin, 1955), 20. 11.

[14] The question of the public aspects of *aretē*, though very complicated, has
not been widely discussed. My suspicion, though highly speculative and in need of
extensive support before it can be taken seriously, is that Plato was centrally
concerned with it. Part of his purpose in the *Republic*, I would want (and
have) to argue, is to ensure that *aretē* will always have a proper audience, and that
those who possess it will necessarily be recognized as such by everyone in their
social group.

doesn't know 'in any way at all (*to parapan*) what *aretē* itself is' (71a5-7).[15] Now as long as we think of *aretē* as virtue we have enough intuitions about what that is to think that Socrates' reply must be prompted by metaphysical or epistemological considerations. He, too, we suppose, has a pretty good idea of what virtue is, but insists that he does not in order to make a purely philosophical point about the priority of definition. Yet, though not without important metaphysical implications, Socrates' response to Meno's precipitate question is quite independently reasonable. Meno asks without preamble a commonplace question which none the less depends on many disputable presuppositions. Socrates' reaction is, simply, to try to slow Meno and the discussion down.[16]

In light of this, I follow Bluck (209) in taking *to parapan* at 71a6 closely with *oude*. Socrates is disclaiming all knowledge of the nature of *aretē*, and he does exactly the same at 71b4: *ouk eidōs peri aretēs to parapan*. I also take it that his very next point, that one cannot know whether Meno is beautiful, rich, or noble, if one does not in any way (*to parapan*) know who Meno is, is strictly parallel. Socrates is not appealing to a distinction between knowledge by acquaintance and knowledge by description as Bluck (32-3, 213-14) among others, has claimed, nor is he introducing, at least implicitly, a technical distinction between knowledge and belief and claiming that though one can have all sorts of beliefs about the object of one's enquiry, these beliefs cannot become knowledge unless they are supplemented by knowledge of the definition of the nature of the object in question.[17] His point is simple and intuitive: if he has *no* idea

[15] There is considerable irony in putting this reply in the mouth of an imaginary Athenian, since Anytus is later shown not to have any doubts about the fact that any good Athenian citizen can make another better (92e ff).

[16] The abrupt opening of the *Meno* concerns both Bluck (above n 5, 199) and Klein (above n 3, 38). The discussion above may offer an adequate dramatic justification for it.

[17] This view has become popular recently. It is supported for example, by Terence Irwin, *Plato's Moral Theory* (Oxford, 1977), 40-1, 63; by Gerasimos Xenophon Santas, *Socrates* (London, Boston, and Henley, 1979), 118-22, 311 n 26; and by Paul Woodruff, *Plato: Hippias Major* (Indianapolis, 1982), 138, 141. The issue is much too complicated to be discussed here, and it will occupy me on a further occasion. A careful examination of the passages cited in this connection (*Laches* 190b8-c2; *Pr.* 361c3-6; *Charmides* 157e7-159a3; *M.* 100b4-6; *Lysis*

who Meno is, how can he answer any questions about him? That this is so is shown by the fact that Meno immediately accepts Socrates' general view, as he should not on either of the two interpretations above. What he cannot believe is that Socrates is quite as ignorant as he claims to be about the nature of *aretē*.

Nevertheless, and in characteristic fashion, Socrates insists on his ignorance and asks Meno, who claims to know, to tell him what *aretē* is. Meno makes three efforts (71e ff, 73c ff, 76b ff). But in each case he can only produce many *aretai* instead of the one that Socrates wants in answer to his question. Meno is originally unwilling to agree that *aretē* is one (73a1-5). He then agrees to go along with Socrates without necessarily accepting his view (*eiper hen ge ti zēteis kata pantōn*, 73d1). He finally appears to accept Socrates' arguments to that effect (79a7-e4). Willing as he is to co-operate with Socrates, Meno is led from thinking that he knew what *aretē* is to being unable to say anything satisfactory about his topic, each time unexpectedly, and in a different way, being shown to make the very same error.

It is only after the failure of his third effort that Meno begins to lose his patience. Even so, he very politely concedes that Socrates seems correct in what he says (cf. 79d5, e4) and rather ingenuously confesses that he cannot answer the question. Through his famous comparison of Socrates to the torpedo-fish, he claims that though he had earlier spoken at length and well about *aretē* his contact with Socrates seems to have robbed him of all ability to do so now (79c7-80b3).

It is very important to notice the exact expression Meno uses at this point:

*nun de oud' hoti estin to parapan echō eipein*                              (80b4)

He admits that he is unable to say even in the most general terms what *aretē* is, that he is totally lost and confused. And by the repetition of the crucial term *to parapan*, through which Socrates had earlier disavowed all ability to lead the

---

223b4-8; *Hippias Major* 286c8-d2, 304d4-e3; *Republic* (*R.*) 345b3-c3) has convinced me that Socrates does not, and need not, appeal to the distinction between knowledge and belief in order to justify his views on the priority of definition. The present case is, I think, even more straightforward.

discussion, Plato now places Meno, even if against his will, in the very same position which Socrates had eagerly taken up at the opening of the dialogue. Socrates refuses to return Meno's compliment and offers a simile in his turn (80c3-6). If he has reduced Meno to perplexity, he says, it is only because he is himself perplexed.

καὶ νῦν περὶ ἀρετῆς ὃ ἐστιν ἐγὼ μὲν οὐκ οἶδα, σὺ μέντοι ἴσως πρότερον μὲν ᾔδησθα πρὶν ἐμοῦ ἄψασθαι, νῦν μέντοι ὅμοιος εἶ οὐκ εἰδότι.

(80d1-3)

This passage is important. We should notice, for one thing, the irony of the final phrase, in which Socrates, despite his earlier disclaimer, does after all offer a simile for Meno; though, of course, to say as he does that Meno is 'similar to someone who does not know' is literally true.[18] We should also notice that in saying that Meno may have known earlier what *aretē* is, Socrates suggests, equally ironically, that something that is known can actually be forgotten. In one sense this is quite true and it forms the central point of the theory of recollection. But once something comes to be known, once (in Plato's terms) it is recollected, then it becomes more difficult to forget it or to be persuaded to change one's mind about it. This, after all, is how Socrates distinguishes *doxa* from *epistēmē* at 97d6-98b5. True beliefs, he claims, like Daedalus' statues, are always escaping from the soul. But when they are bound down by an 'account of the explanation', which, 'as we earlier agreed, is recollection' (98a3-5), they are transformed into *epistēmē* and become permanent. There is a serious question here about the sorts of things that, once learned, become permanent. Does Plato believe, for example, that if you know the road to Larissa (97a9-11) you cannot ever forget it? Or would he more plausibly be willing to allow gradations of permanence which would prevent geometrical or ethical truths from being forgotten but which would allow lower-level truths to escape the soul either through forgetfulness or through contrary argument? We shall return to this question toward the end of this essay.

Our present passage, 80d1-3, is finally important because it completes the stage-setting for the raising of Meno's

---

[18] Cp. 80d3 with *homoiotatos . . . narkēi*, and cf. Bluck, above n 5, 271.

paradox. Since Meno has now admitted that he is totally lost with respect to *aretē* and since Socrates has repeated his earlier complete inability to say anything about it, neither of them can even know where to begin the investigation. It is only at this point and faced with yet a further exhortation by Socrates to say what *aretē* is (80d3-4) that the much-maligned Meno raises the not unreasonable question how, if this is indeed their situation, they can possibly go on with the enquiry. In stating the paradox Meno once again repeats Socrates' word *to parapan*: 'In what way', he asks, 'can you search for something when you are altogether ignorant of what it is?' (80d5-6). Plato has gone to great lengths in order to emphasize Socrates' ignorance and to strip Meno of all claims to knowledge. Given this situation, and far from being a contentious move, Meno's raising of the paradox of enquiry is natural and well motivated.

## II

Plato takes Meno's paradox, that you can't look for what you don't know and don't need to look for what you know, very seriously in its own right.[19] In addition, he provides Meno with good reason to raise it. He uses the paradox not only in order to discuss serious epistemological issues, but also to resolve a number of dialectical difficulties to which Socrates' practice had given rise.

Of course, Meno's paradox could easily be put to contentious use, as it was, in two related versions, in the *Euthydemus*. At 275d3-4, Euthydemus asks Cleinias whether those who learn are the wise or the ignorant; at 276d7-8, he asks him whether one learns things one already knows or things one does not. In each case Cleinias is made to contradict himself. Having claimed that it is the wise who learn, he is forced to admit that it has to be the ignorant instead (276b4-5) and immediately following, he is made to concede that in fact those who learn are, after all, the wise (276c6-7). Having claimed that one learns what one does not know, he is forced to agree that what one learns one actually knows

---

[19] Cf. Nicholas White, 'Inquiry', *Review of Metaphysics*, XXVIII (1974), 289 with n 1.

(277a8-b4) and, at that point, Dionysiodorus enters the argument and argues that one learns only what one does not know (277c6-7). Socrates replies on Cleinias' behalf that such paradoxes depend merely on verbal trickery. They equivocate between two senses of *manthanein* (to learn), one involving the acquisition at some time of knowledge that was not at all possessed previously and the other involving the exercising of knowledge that has already been acquired in the past (277e3-278b2). In this he is followed to the letter by Aristotle, who, in *Sophistici Elenchi* 4 (165b30-4), classifies this as a paradox due to verbal homonymy.

When such paradoxes, therefore, are offered contentiously, Plato is perfectly capable of giving them a short and easy reply. His reply in the *Euthydemus* depends crucially and unselfconsciously on the notion of the absolute acquisition of knowledge. But, in the *Meno*, Plato finds this reply deeply problematic. At the very least, he does not think that the paradox to which he can also supply a merely verbal solution has merely verbal force. What, then, accounts for this difference in attitude?

We have already said that Meno uses the term *to parapan* in stating his paradox. Some commentators have taken it that Meno simply overstates his case, and that Plato solves the problem by pointing this out. Their case depends primarily on the fact that Socrates omits this qualification in his restatement of Meno's problem (80e1-5). Thomas, for example, writes:

This immediately destroys the thrust of the original puzzle for, lacking 'parapan,' the crucial premise reads 'if a man does not have some knowledge' rather than 'if a man has no knowledge whatsoever.' The reformulated dilemma is consistent with the possession of some knowledge. . . . Plato is not making much of an effort to meet the eristics in their . . . own terms. How could he, since to do so would be to concede them victory? Why should he, when the dilemma proscribes the possible? One is not obliged to take seriously intellectual chicanery that prohibits us from doing what we already do.[20]

But to assume that this is chicanery and that we can perfectly well do what the paradox denies, being a begging of the

[20] John E. Thomas, *Musings on the Meno* (The Hague, 1980), 123, 128-9.

question, is itself a prime case of chicanery. Despite the similar views of Moravcsik[21] and Scolnicov,[22] it does not seem to me that Socrates refutes Meno by changing the terms of the argument. He may try to show that we do all possess some knowledge already but he cannot begin from that fact. In this respect, at least, White is correct in writing that there is no substantive difference between Meno's and Socrates' statement of the paradox: 'What Socrates does is simply to make clear that Meno's puzzle can be cast in the form of a dilemma' (290 n 4). The function of *to parapan* is important and ineliminable.

Discussions of this passage often claim that Plato is only concerned with one among the many species of learning. Gregory Vlastos, for example, writes that:

*Manthanein* . . . is being used in this context in the restricted sense of *learning to have propositional knowledge*. The acquisition of inarticulate skills, though well within the scope of the word in ordinary usage, is tacitly excluded.[23]

Moravcsik also believes that the paradox concerns only 'learning taking the form of inquiry' (53). Plato, he continues, is not concerned with the learning of non-intellectual skills, with learning by being told, or with learning by imitation (54).

This is in a way correct, since the *Meno* does discuss only learning by enquiry.[24] But we must avoid the implication, which perhaps these writers themselves do not want, that Plato acknowledges many ways of learning but discusses only one in this context. Instead, Plato seems to hold the view that any learning and *epistēmē* worth the name must be achieved through enquiry and that therefore all learning, not just one particular form of it, must, in Moravcsik's words, 'be given direction by the learner himself' (54). Plato is not simply excluding the learning or inarticulate skills from his discussion. Rather, he seems at least implicitly to be denying

---

[21] J. M. E. Moravcsik, 'Learning as Recollection' in *Plato: Metaphysics and Epistemology*, ed. Gregory Vlastos (Garden City, 1971), 57.

[22] Samuel Scolnicov, 'Three Aspects of Plato's Philosophy of Learning and Instruction', *Paideia* V (1976), 52.

[23] Gregory Vlastos, '*Anamnesis* in the *Meno*', *Dialogue* IV (1965), 143 n 1.

[24] Cf. White, above n 19, and Irwin, above n 17, 315 n 13.

that inarticulate skills are acquired through learning and that they are therefore, strictly speaking, objects of *epistēmē*. Similarly, he appears to deny that being told or imitation can, in themselves, constitute learning and produce understanding. But if learning can proceed only through enquiry and if neither Socrates nor Meno know how to go on, then their impasse is very serious indeed. Where can the elenchus even begin? In addition, Gorgias, who had been earlier mentioned as a possible teacher of *aretē* and who might have helped the discussion, has already been disqualified. Since Meno accepts his views, it was agreed that to include him in the discussion would have been superfluous (71c5–d5). And in any case, his account of what *aretē* is (71e1–72a5; cf. Aristotle, *Politics* I. 13. 1260a20–8) did not survive Socrates' arguments.

## III

It would seem, then, that for the discussion to proceed, Socrates and Meno are in need of another teacher who might guide them out of their impasse. Such teachers are mentioned later on in the *Meno*. Why does Plato not bring them into the discussion now? Is it simply because he is not interested in the case of learning by being told by another or is the matter, as I shall now try to suggest, considerably more complicated?

Three classes of possible teachers of *aretē* are brought up in the *Meno*: sophists, notably successful citizens, and, in a rather cursory way, poets (89e–96b). The sophists are disqualified because they cannot agree among themselves whether *aretē* can or cannot be taught (95b–c); also because, unlike the case of any other subject, those who claim to teach what *aretē* is are not acknowledged as proper teachers of their subject by others and are even claimed to lack that which they profess to teach (96a6–b1; cf. 91c1–92c5). Good and noble citizens, men like Pericles, Themistocles, Aristeides, and Thucydides, are disqualified because not one of them has been capable of teaching his own sons what *aretē* is (93b–94e); also because they, no less than the sophists, cannot agree on whether this is a teachable topic (95a–b, 96b1–3).[25]

---

[25] Similar arguments can be found at *Pr.* 319e–320b, *Alcibiades* 118c–119a.

Finally, the poets, through a quick examination of Theognis, are summarily dismissed because they cannot even produce internally coherent views on the subject (95c-95a). These arguments against particular sorts of teachers of *aretē* are common, indeed, commonplace.[26] In addition to them, however, Plato offers a more subtle and much more far-ranging argument against any self-professed teachers of success. The argument is implicit in a not very widely discussed passage of the *Protagoras* (313a1-314c2). In this passage, Socrates is warning Hippocrates against going to the sophist for instruction without first thinking the matter through very carefully. In addition, however, his warning involves an important paradox with some serious implications for our own discussion.

Socrates, we said, warns Hippocrates not to rush into Protagoras' company. He describes the sophist as 'a merchant or peddler of the goods by which the soul is nourished' (313c4-5). The soul, he continues, is nourished by what it learns (*mathēmata*, 313c7). He then offers an analogy between sophists, so construed, and those who sell any sort of food for the body (*ponēron ē chrēston*) but praise everything they sell indiscriminately (313d1-3). The buyers of such food also lack the necessary knowledge, unless they happen to be experts on such issues, gymnasts or physicians (313d3-5). The same is at least possible in the case of the peddlers of mental nourishment: some of them, too, may well be 'ignorant of whether what they sell is harmful or beneficial to the soul' (*chrēston ē ponēron pros tēn psuchēn*, 313d8-31). And the analogy holds further true of their clients, unless one among them happens to be 'a physician with regard to the soul' (*peri tēn psuchēn iatrikos*, 313e1-2). Now if, Socrates continues, 'you happen to be an expert regarding which of those things are beneficial or harmful, then it is safe for you to buy learning from Protagoras or from anyone else' (313e2-5). But if not, the danger is great, much greater indeed in this case than in the case of physical nourishment. Physical food can be taken away from the peddlers in a separate vessel and examined by an expert

[26] Cf. *Dissoi Logoi* 6. 3, 4.

before it is consumed (314a3-b1). But this is not possible
with food for thought:

> You cannot carry learning away in a jar. Once you have paid for it you
> must receive it directly into the soul and having learned it you must
> leave already harmed or benefited.                                    (314b1-4)

The discussion is at least cautionary, but it makes an additional point. Buying, or more generally receiving, learning
presents some special difficulties of its own. When buying
food one can always ask a third party, an acknowledged
expert, for advice before the fact and act accordingly. But
when buying learning the expert cannot be consulted, so to
speak, after the initial transaction. One must determine in
advance of all contact whether listening to the sophist or to
any other professor of *aretē* is likely to help or harm one's
soul. But at least part of the additional problem in regard to
learning is that in this case there are no acknowledged experts.
And therefore the same difficulty that applied to the sophists
will also apply to such putative experts: how is one to tell
whether their advice is itself harmful or beneficial?

The predicament gets worse. The dangers involved in
approaching the sophist, concerning as they do, what is
most dear and precious to us, the soul, are immense. The
implication, though it is not explicitly drawn in the text, is
that one should not approach such a professor unless one is
certain that one knows that what is offered will be beneficial.
Now to benefit or harm the soul, is, obviously, to make it
better or worse (cf. 318a6-9, d7-e5). And a discussion in the
*Laches* adds a special urgency to this connection.

In the *Laches*, Lysimachus and Milesias ask Socrates,
Laches, and Nicias whether they should train their sons in
armed combat. The two generals having disagreed on this
issue, Socrates questions whether any one of them there is
an expert (*technikos*, 185a1) on the issue at hand. In typical
fashion, he immediately generalizes that issue to apply not
only to fighting but to the large question whether the boys
will or will not become good (*agathoi*, 185a6). This in turn
he construes as the problem of how to make the boys' souls
as good as possible (186a5-6). But to know how to accomplish this, he continues, they must know what it is that

makes the soul better when it is present in it. And to know this, of course, is to know what *aretē* is (189d--190a).

In order to know whether a course of learning, therefore, will harm or benefit the soul, the expert (*iatrikos, epaiōn*) of the *Protagoras* must, like the expert (*technikos*) of the *Laches*, know what *aretē* is. But if the expert knows this, why bother to go to the sophist at all, why not learn instead from one who has already been determined to know? But the point is that there are no such acknowledged experts. Therefore, learners can only be certain that their soul will not be harmed by the sophist (or by the expert) if they themselves can tell whether such advice or instruction will be beneficial or harmful. But to know this, we have just shown, is to know oneself what *aretē* is. Therefore, unless one already knows what *aretē* is, and thus precisely what sophists claim to teach, one should never approach any professors of *aretē*. The sophists, and all who claim to teach what *aretē* is, are quite useless!

## IV

None of the problems discussed here, of course, could ever be problems for Socrates, since he never claimed to teach what *aretē* is. It is true that in *Alcibiades* I Socrates makes some startlingly extravagant claims about his importance to Alcibiades and his political ambitions (105d ff). But his point there, I should think, is to satirize the wooing practices of Athenian men.[27] In general, Socrates steadfastly refuses the teacher's role or function in Plato's early dialogues.[28]

These problems, therefore, could not have seriously disturbed Socrates. But they did become very serious indeed for Plato, who gradually, in the very process of portraying him as refusing that role, came to see Socrates not only as

[27] On which see Kenneth Dover, *Greek Homosexuality* (Cambridge, Mass., 1978), 81-100. In the course of the dialogue Socrates insists that he is not telling Alcibiades anything as their discussion proceeds (112d ff) and he readily admits that he, no less than Alcibiades, is in need of an education (124b1-c2). In a final ironic reversal, moreover, the dialogue ends with Alcibiades assuming the teacher's role and assigning to Socrates the student's position (135d-e).

[28] Socrates often describes himself as a willing disciple of someone who claims to know something about *aretē*; cf., e.g., *Euthyphro* 5a3-b7.

'the best, the wisest, and the most just' man of his generation (*Phaedo* 118a16–17) but also as the ablest, thus far,
teacher of *aretē*. For Socrates' sons, like the sons of Pericles,
Aristeides, and Themistocles, did little to distinguish themselves in their city. His friends and companions, like the
friends and companions of Protagoras and Gorgias, remained
mediocre, like Crito, or became vicious, like Charmides,
Critias, or especially Alcibiades. Though perhaps ironically
motivated, his views on whether *aretē* can be taught did not
remain stable. And he certainly was not universally acknowledged as an expert on *aretē*. On the contrary, his life no less
than his reputation suffered worse in the hands of the
Athenians than the lives and reputations of many who, in
Plato's eyes, had no claim to *aretē* whatsoever compared
to him.

How, we should finally ask, could Socrates be exempt from
the paradox that the teacher of *aretē* is useless? How could
Plato, the disciple who may have thought he learned something from him, believe that Socrates could be approached
even if one did not already know what was good and what
was bad?

The answer to this question goes to the heart of Socrates'
personality as well as of his method. It is that Socrates,
unlike all other teachers of *aretē* does not constitute a danger
to his students precisely because he refuses to tell anyone
what *aretē* is, especially since he denies having that knowledge in the first place. Whatever claim Socrates has to the
teaching of *aretē* lies exactly in his disclaiming any such
ability. The contrast around which the *Protagoras* and many
other early Platonic dialogues revolve is a contrast between
a method that depends on telling one's students what *aretē*
is, on transmitting information to them, and one that
does not.

But if Socrates' refusal or inability to offer positive views
makes it safe to approach him, it generates another problem:
how does the elenctic method result in any learning? How do
two people who are ignorant of the answer to a given question
discover that answer and how do they realize that they have
discovered it? If the elenchus presents a serious methodological question, this is it. And this is the very question

that Meno raises in the paradox with which we have been concerned.

Plato tries to answer this question in the *Meno* through the examination of the slave and the theory of recollection, though his views on these issues never remain unchanged. In claiming that Meno's paradox is well motivated and that it goes to the heart of Socratic dialectic, I find myself in agreement with Irwin, who writes that 'the examination of the slave is a scale-model of a Socratic elenchos, with a commentary to explain and justify the procedure' (139). However, I cannot agree with Irwin on the question of the resolution of the paradox. He thinks that the paradox depends on the view that if I know nothing about an object, I cannot identify it as the subject of my enquiry and I cannot therefore enquire into it at all (138-9).[29] According to Irwin, Socrates rejects this view and claims that

> though the slave does not know, he has true beliefs about the questions discussed. . . . To inquire into *x* we need only enough true beliefs about *x* to fix the reference of the term '*x*' so that when the inquiry is over, we can still see we refer to the same thing.                                   (139)

To support his view, Irwin relies crucially on 85c6-7, where Socrates asks whether one who does not know does not still possess true beliefs about the things he does not know (316 n 14). But, for one thing, the position of the passage announces it more as an intermediate step of the argument rather than as a conclusion to it.[30] More importantly, the question of identification does not seem to me so crucial to Plato's resolution of the paradox. It is quite true that Plato writes that before the enquiry begins the slave has true beliefs concerning the geometrical problem discussed. But these beliefs were in no way available to him as such at the time. They were mixed together with all sorts of false beliefs, some of which were both elicited and eliminated by Socrates during his questioning. These true beliefs are recovered by the slave at the end of his examination by Socrates; they could not therefore play the identificatory role Irwin asks of

---

[29] White (above n 13) offers a related account, more concerned with identifying the object enquired into throughout the enquiry, on 294-7.

[30] Cf. Michael Morgan, 'An Interpretation of *Meno* 85b8-86b4' (unpublished manuscript, 1982), 8.

them, and which requires them to be there consciously at its very beginning. Further, the knowledge that the slave is said to be eventually able to recover is also said to be in him, just as those true beliefs are (85d3-7). But if this is so, it is not clear that true beliefs are possessed in a particular manner, different from that in which knowledge is possessed and which therefore would enable them to have the different function Irwin's account assigns to them.

For true belief to secure the stable identification of the object of enquiry, it is necessary for it and for knowledge to be independent of each other. But this does not seem to be the case. Plato writes that the slave who now has only belief will acquire knowledge through repeated questioning (85c9-d1). This statement is not by itself very explicit, but it becomes a bit more clear when we connect it to the later discussion of 'the reasoning out of the explanation' at 97e-98a. Once this is achieved, Plato writes, true beliefs 'become *epistēmai*'. That is, these beliefs do not simply fix the object of which knowledge is to be acquired or, in Plato's terms, recovered; rather once acquired (recovered) themselves they become that knowledge when they have been properly organized and systematized.[31]

But before we offer some tentative remarks about Plato's resolution of the paradox we must raise one further, rather complicated problem. What exactly does recollection cover for Plato? Does it apply to the whole process of learning or only to part of it? Or, not to beg any questions about learning, which part of the slave's examination actually involves him in recollection?

The manner in which Socrates introduces the theory of recollection and his rather general statements at 81d2-3, d4-5, and 82a1-2, suggest that recollection applies to all the different stages that may be, however loosely, associated with the process of learning. Accordingly, we expect that everything that takes place during the slave's examination constitutes an instance of recollection. Socrates strengthens this expectation when he prefaces his examination by urging

---

[31] I have discussed some of the issues involved in this transition in '*Epistēmē* and *Logos* in Plato's Later Thought', *Archiv für Geschichte der Philosophie*, LXVI (1984), 11-36.

Meno to see whether the slave will be recollecting or learning from him (82b6–7), and by saying at the end of its first stage that he is only asking questions of the slave and not telling him anything (82e4–6). But doesn't Socrates teach or tell the slave all sorts of things during their discussion? How else can we construe the questions of 82c7–8 and d1–2 or the leading (that is, misleading) question of 82d8–e2 that prompts the slave to offer one of his many wrong solutions to the geometrical problem? In addition, we must not forget the passages 83c8–d1 and d4–5, where Socrates does not even bother to ask a question but himself draws the inference, marked in each case by *ara*, for the slave.

Bluck, who was exercised by this problem answered, that Socrates does not teach the slave 'in the sophistic way, by merely presenting him with propositions that he must accept'. He gradually 'leads' the slave to the correct solution and at that point the slave is 'able to "see" that what was said was true. The argument is simply that such "seeing" or comprehension would not be possible if the slave had not had previous acquaintance with the truth . . .' (12).

But is it so clear that there was such a thing as 'the' sophistic way of teaching? And if there were, is Bluck's description of it accurate? Some sophists, Hippias and sometimes Protagoras (*Protagoras* 320c2–4), may have taught in this manner. But Euthydemus and Dionysiodorus used a questioning method which, at least superficially, did not differ so drastically from the elenchus.[32] Bluck's appeal to 'seeing', in addition, seems to me rather empty. The point is not simply that, especially in the *Meno*, the text gives little warrant to the identification of the slave's understanding with 'his feeling of inner conviction' (12). More importantly, it is not clear that, even if such a feeling exists, the slave has it only when he 'sees' the right answer and not also when he gives the wrong one. On the contrary, Socrates' comment at 82e5–6 to the effect that the slave now thinks he knows the solution suggests that subjectively there is no difference between merely thinking one has knowledge and actually having it. If there were, and

---

[32] For some material on sophistic teaching methods, cf. Kerferd, above n 7, 59–67.

assuming that everyone knows at least one thing, learning should proceed on its own until this feeling of inner conviction is acquired.

In the course of questioning the slave, Socrates produces in him, or elicits from him, a number of false geometric beliefs. In the present case, he continues to clear them out and to replace them by true ones instead. But what if he had not? What if, in particular, their conversation concerned *aretē*, of which Socrates is himself ignorant, and thus the very soul of the slave? Would Socrates not be capable of causing at least as much harm to the slave as the sophists have earlier been said to cause their students unless these already know the answers to their questions?

It is at this point that we should take Socrates very seriously, if rather liberally, when he insists that he does not teach anyone anything. He does not mean that he will ask no obvious or leading questions, or that he will not make statements or even sometimes long speeches.[33] He does mean that he requires his interlocutor to assent only to what he thinks is true, nothing more and nothing less. This is what Vlastos has recently called the 'say what you believe' requirement of the elenchus.[34] Socrates' practice is in stark contrast with the method of Euthydemus, despite their apparent similarity. For Euthydemus insists that Socrates answer his questions in ways with which he is deeply dissatisfied, dropping a number of essential qualifications, in order to prove to him that (again in a way superficially and perhaps deliberately reminiscent of the *Meno*) he has always known everything, even before he or the whole universe came into being, provided Euthydemus 'wants it that way' (*Eud.* 295e-296d).

If knowledge consisted in a feeling of inner conviction, Socrates would have been quite dangerous to his interlocutors. For since knowledge and belief, true or false, do not differ subjectively, there might in fact be no way of telling, from the inside, whether a particular answer reached to

---

[33] For example, despite his insistence on short questions and answers at *Gorgias* 448e-449a, 449b4-c7, Socrates makes many longer speeches than Gorgias in the course of their conversation (451a3-c9, 452a1-a4, 455a8-e5, 457c3-458c8).

[34] Gregory Vlastos, 'The Socratic Elenchus', *Oxford Studies in Ancient Philosophy*, vol i (Oxford, 1983), 27-58, with full references.

a problem is true or false. But, of course, Socrates never ends his questioning when he has simply elicited a statement. The major burden of the elenchus is to *test* such statements and Socrates assumes that no false statement can survive these tests. Whether he is engaged in the more negative elenchus of the earlier dialogues or in the more positive investigation of the *Gorgias*,[35] Socrates consistently makes his interlocutors answer for their beliefs. What determines whether a belief is true or false has nothing to do with how the respondent feels and everything to do with that belief's dialectical impregnability.

The elenchus, therefore, depends solely on a dialectical test for truth: a belief is true if it cannot be overthrown by sound, non-contentious argument. To which, of course, one might be tempted to reply: but how can we know that a belief will not be overthrown? Socrates, I think, had no clear answer to this question. Plato may have tried to devise one: we can know this to be the case when we master the whole interconnected set of truths to which our particular belief refers. We have *epistēmē* when we have learned the axiomatic structure of the system in question and can prove any one of its elements.[36]

But even though Socrates' leading questions may be harmless to the slave, his claim that the whole examination involves recollection is misleading for the readers of the *Meno*. The slave only produces a false belief in the first stretch of the argument (82b9-83e3). Are we to infer that coming to have (or recovering) false beliefs is a case of recollection?[37]

By opening the second stretch of the examination by asking Meno to watch how the slave will now properly engage

[35] Vlastos's evidence, in 'The Socratic Elenchus', for his construal of the elenchus as a method for reaching positive ethical conclusions mainly comes, as he himself admits, from the *Gorgias*.

[36] This view is supported in '*Epistēmē* and *Logos* in Plato's Later Thought' (above n 31).

[37] Theodor Ebert, *Meinung and Wissen in der Philosophie Platons* (Berlin, 1974), 83-104, and 'Plato's Theory of Recollection Reconsidered: An Interpretation of *Meno* 80a-86c', *Man and World*, VI (1973), 163-81, thinks that it is because he thinks that Plato believes that learning is only analogous to recollection, and not an instance of it. But, I think, Plato's view is much stronger than that, and it would be very strange of him to consider that both the recovery of knowledge and the recovery of false beliefs are equally cases of recollection.

in orderly recollection (82e11-12), Socrates again suggests that the slave will be actually recollecting in what follows. What occurs here, of course, is that the slave is made to realize that he does not know the answer to Socrates' question (82e14-84a2). Are we to infer that recollection applies to the realization that one's beliefs about a topic are false?

Part of the answer to this question depends on the interpretation of Socrates' next question, which occurs in his summary of this second stretch of argument:

Ἐννοεῖς αὖ, ὦ Μένων, οὗ ἐστιν ἤδη βαδίζων ὅδε τοῦ ἀναμιμνῄσκεσθαι;
(84a3-4)

Thompson construes this as asking 'what point on the track of reminiscence he has now reached', and believes that recollection has already begun.[38] On the other hand, we could take the question to concern 'what point on the track *to* reminiscence he has now reached', in which case Socrates would be saying that the path to recollection is now open, not that recollection has already begun. In that case, we may take his earlier remarks about the slave's recollecting to apply not specifically to the first part of the discussion but, more generally and programmatically, to the whole examination. Recollection may be more restricted than is sometimes supposed.

This impression is reinforced by Socrates' summary of the last section of his questioning. He and Meno agree that the slave has only replied with beliefs that were his own (85b8-9) and that he has true beliefs about what he does not yet know (85c2-7). Socrates now claims that if 'someone asks him the same question many times and in many ways' he will finally have as much knowledge about these topics as anyone else (85c9-d1).[39] From this it is clear that the slave still does not have *epistēmē* of the subject and Socrates drives the point home by locating the slave's knowledge in the future in his very next question (*epistēsetai*, 85d3-4). He then goes on to say that it is just this recovery of knowledge which is still

---

[38] E. S. Thompson, *Plato's Meno* (London, 1901), 137.

[39] Plato radically qualifies this extremely optimistic view, of course, in the *Republic*. The myth of *Er* and the theory of recollection as presented in the *Phaedrus* provide a rationale for his more cautious claims about the ability of people to reach *epistēmē*.

all in the *future* for the slave, that is recollection (85d6–7). Recollection thus seems limited to a very small part of the process of learning.

Despite the tension it creates with the general statement at 81d4–5, such a restricted interpretation of recollection fits well with Socrates' later distinction between *doxa* and *epistēmē*: the former, he says, 'is worth little until it is tied down by reasoning about the explanation' (98a3–4). And it is *this* (*touto*, 98a4), he continues, that, 'as we agreed earlier, is recollection' (98a4–5). But the *aitias logismos*, as far as I can see, corresponds to nothing in the first stages of the slave's interrogation. The only process to which it can be connected is the repeated questioning that will eventually lead to the recovery of *epistēmē* (85c–d) and which we were just now, on independent grounds, considering as a candidate for recollection.

Suppose now that we restrict recollection in this way. Since we are explicitly told that the slave does not yet have any *epistēmē* does it not follow that he has not engaged in recollection in the dialogue? And if this is so, what is the point of his long examination? What has Plato succeeded in demonstrating by its means?

It is quite possible that recollection, strictly speaking, is not shown to occur anywhere in the *Meno*. Nevertheless, I think that the last stage of the slave's questioning, in which Socrates elicits the correct solution to the problem from him, is deeply representative of the process. It represents it, that is, because it is a part of it. The slave, Socrates says, will come to have knowledge 'if one asks him the very same questions [or: questions about the very same things] many times and in many ways' (85c10–11). What brings about the *aitias logismos* and transforms *doxai* into *epistēmē* is not a new operation, additional to the eliciting of true *doxa* but rather the eliciting of enough true *doxa* about the subject to make having them *constitute* the *aitias logismos*. The very same true beliefs the slave now has, Socrates claims at 86a7–8, 'having been aroused by questioning, become knowledge' (*epistēmai*).

Plato does not explain how this transformation is to occur, and it is very difficult to know what is involved in the transition. Certainly, simply having many *doxai* about geometry cannot be itself sufficient for *epistēmē*. One must also acquire the ability to organize them systematically, to become able to move from one of them to another properly and on one's own, to know how they are supported by one another. This is one of the reasons Plato emphasizes the role of questioning in the recovery of knowledge. Having the answers to as many questions as one pleases does not constitute *epistēmē* unless one is also capable of answering ever new questions as well as of formulating questions of one's own. The *aitias logismos* and recollection, strictly speaking, consist in this ability, which transcends merely having answers to different questions but which is acquired (or revealed) only in the course of learning them.[40]

Implicitly, true beliefs are in one in just the way that knowledge is supposed to be; explicitly, they enter the process of learning and recollection midway. It is therefore unlikely that Meno's paradox is resolved by appealing to them in order to secure, from the very beginning of the enquiry, reference to the object which the enquiry concerns. Plato seems to deny the claim, on which the paradox depends, that 'one cannot search for what one does not know for one does not even know what to search for' (80e5), on slightly different grounds. One does know what one does not know because questioning and the inability to answer continued questions determine that knowledge is lacking. Conversely, the continued ability to answer such questions suggests that knowledge has been reached and that 'you have happened upon' what you did not know (80d8). On the other hand, he also denies the claim that 'one cannot search for what one knows—for one knows, and one who knows does not need to search' (80e3-5). For one need not know what one knows since knowledge may be, and usually is, forgotten and is

---

[40] Restricting recollection in this way may help account for Socrates' argument of 96d ff that though *aretē* is beneficial it may still not be *epistēmē* but *orthē doxa* instead and thus not teachable. For recollection provides Socrates' alternative account of teaching and learning. If it applied to the recovery of a single true belief (or to a small number of them), then this recovery would definitely be a matter of teaching, and Socrates would have no grounds for arguing that *aretē* cannot be taught. But if recollection only follows the recovery, or mere possession, of true belief, he may have just such a reason: teaching produces orderly recollection.

brought out only by questioning. Knowledge is reached when what one knew that one does not know is matched with what one did not know that one knows. The role of questioning in bringing this matching about is crucial: Plato's resolution of Meno's paradox is dialectical rather than logical.

## V

The dialectical resolution of Meno's paradox, even when supported by the non-dialectical explanation offered through the theory of recollection,[41] does not by itself account for Socrates' continued insistence that he is not, in this or in any other case, engaged in teaching. We have seen that part of this account is that had Socrates been willing to offer positive views on the nature of *aretē*, he should not have been approached any more than the sophists should. But in the *Meno* the question does not concern *aretē* and Socrates is quite aware of the correct answer. Why does Plato insist that the slave must come to it on his own? Why is he so eager to point out that even when Socrates is transmitting information to the slave (which he has him do on a number of occasions) the slave is still only recovering knowledge from within himself?

Plato appears to believe that even in matters that do not concern the soul's welfare as directly as *aretē* does, *epistēmē* cannot and must not be reached through the transmission of information. But knowledge depends essentially on the transmission of information and is itself transmissible. What is crucial to knowledge is that the information in which it consists has been acquired in the proper way, no less and no more. As Bernard Williams has written, in regard to knowledge in general

not only is it not necessary that the knower be able to support or ground his belief by reference to other propositions, but it is not necessary that he be in any special state in regard to this belief at all, at least at the level of what he can consciously rehearse. What is necessary . . . is that one or more of a class of conditions should obtain . . .

[41] On the question whether the paradox is resolved primarily by the examination or by the theory of recollection, I agree with Irwin (above n 17, 139 and n 13; *contra* White, above n 19, 289, and *Plato on Knowledge and Reality* (Indianapolis, 1976), 40-1): the paradox is disarmed in the examination, and recollection explains how that is possible.

conditions which can best be summarized by the formula that, given the truth of p, it is no accident that A believes that p rather than not p.[42] Though this formulation, as Williams himself admits, needs much further refinement, it seems to me quite true. However, Williams's conditions are remarkably weaker than Plato's and even explicitly exclude what Plato considers most crucial to *epistēmē*: the ability to 'support or ground (a) belief', to give an account, a *logos* of the object of *epistēmē*.[43]

We might want to say that Plato insists upon an unduly restrictive notion of knowledge; but we would do better, I think, to say that when he is discussing *epistēmē* he is not producing unreasonable conditions on knowledge, but rather, quite reasonable conditions on what it is to understand something. For unlike knowledge, understanding involves, in rough and ready terms, the ability to *explain* what one understands. By contrast, many items of knowledge, for example, particular facts, are not even the sorts of things to which explanation is applicable in this context.[44]

In the case of mathematical knowledge, at least so far as non-elementary propositions are concerned, Williams accepts 'the Platonic view' that such knowledge involves *aitias logismos* which he glosses as 'a chain of proof'. But he goes on to claim that whether or not having such proof makes true beliefs more permanent, as Plato believes, is irelevant to the main point

that the access to mathematical truth must necessarily be through proof, and that therefore the notion of non-accidental true belief in mathematics essentially involves the notion of mathematical proof (the points which the Platonic model of *recollection* precisely serves to obscure).                                                                (9)

But Plato's emphasis on the permanence of *epistēmē* is anything but irrelevant. For one thing, the permanence of one's understanding of a topic is in itself a measure of the

[42] Bernard Williams, 'Knowledge and Reasons' in *Problems in the Theory of Knowledge*, ed. G. H. von Wright (The Hague, 1972), 5
[43] I have presented a full case for that claim in '*Epistēmē* and *Logos* in Plato's Later Thought' (above n 31); cf. also Jon Moline, *Plato's Theory of Understanding* (Madison, 1981), 32–51.
[44] This is not to say that the fact, which I know, that it is raining cannot be explained. It is only to say that my knowledge of that (meteorological) explanation has no bearing on whether I know the fact in question. Most people know the latter, when it is the case, and ignore the former.

degree to which one understands it. At some earlier time, I was capable of dealing with quadratic equations; my present total inability to do so strongly argues that I never understood that subject very well. For understanding the nature of quadratic equations is not an isolated act concerning an isolated object; it involves, at least in principle, the understanding of a vast number of mathematical propositions and operations, perhaps of all of algebra. And the more of a field one understands, the more systematically one's abilities with respect to it are organized, the less likely it is that the relevant beliefs will be forgotten: the more likely it is that they will be, in Plato's word, permanent (*monimoi*, 96a6). It is very easy, it is in fact inevitable, to forget whether it rained here three years ago today or to be persuaded that my recollection is wrong. It is also easy to forget how to get from one part of one's country to another. It is easy to forget how to determine the circumference of the circle, if you were only taught it once at school. But it seems more difficult to say that one has forgotten geometry, and almost totally absurd to claim to have forgotten what *aretē* is.[45] The broader and more encompassing the field to which a proposition belongs, the more permanent beliefs concerning that field, once mastered, are likely to be. The more worthy, therefore, that field is, in Plato's eyes, as an object of *epistēmē*.

Plato's model of recollection, though it may obscure Williams's points about knowledge, is crucial in emphasizing the necessity of working out a proof or of reaching any sort of understanding through and for oneself. Knowledge of fact, we have said, is transmissible and the

mechanism by which knowledge is transmitted is *belief*. More precisely . . . it is sufficient and necessary for the transmission of your knowledge that *p* to me that I *believe you* when, speaking (or writing) from knowledge, you tell me that *p*.[46]

But, as Augustine also saw and argued in the *De Magistro* (40), understanding cannot be handed down in this manner.

---

[45] Cf. Hesiod, *Works and Days* 293–4: 'He is the very best who understands everything having considered it himself and knows what is good later and to the end' (quoted by Moline, above n 43, 19; the translation is different).

[46] Michael Welbourne, 'The Transmission of Knowledge', *Philosophical Quarterly*, XXIX (1979), 3.

In an important discussion of this dialogue that connects it to Plato's concerns, Burnyeat describes its main thesis, 'that no man can teach another knowledge (*scientia*)', as

the claim that no man can teach another to understand something. The argument will not be that information cannot be transmitted from one person to another, but that the appreciation or understanding of any such information is something that each person must work out for himself. . . . The conveying of information is not enough for teaching in the sense of bringing the learner to know something.[47]

Burnyeat wants to connect Augustine's view that learning comes about through 'first-hand learning, by the intellect or by my own sense-perception' with a number of cases discussed by Plato. He mentions in particular Plato's insistence that the slave in the *Meno* can learn mathematics only through reasoning and with his claim that only someone who has actually gone on the road to Larissa knows the way there (97a–b). He also brings in the view of the *Theaetetus* (201b–c) that only an eyewitness to a crime can have knowledge about it (16). My own view is that Plato considers the examples of the traveller and of the eyewitness not as instances of *epistēmē* but as indispensable analogies by which to explain his view of it. Their function is to highlight the crucial condition that *epistēmē* must be acquired first-hand; and in so far as they satisfy this condition, they may be, catachrestically, considered as cases of *epistēmē*. But in a stricter sense,[48] *epistēmē* applies only to cases which in addition to first-hand acquisition also involve systematization, proof, explanation, or account: this is the *aitias logismos* of the *Meno* and the *logos* of the *Theaetetus* (202d5). Neither the case of the traveller nor that of the eyewitness seems to me capable of satisfying this additional constraint.

What, then, is the difference between *epistēmē* and *orthē doxa*? According to Burnyeat, the case of the eyewitness shows that if he tells me I may come to know much of what he knows himself (though not, of course, on his grounds); still, there will 'typically' be other things I will not know

[47] M. F. Burnyeat, 'Augustine *De Magistro*' (unpublished manuscript, 1982), 9, 11.
[48] This stricter sense, as I proceed to suggest, can be found in the *Meno* and in the *Theaetetus*, contrary to Burnyeat's suggestion, above n 47, 16.

because eyewitnesses 'nearly always' know more than they tell. What marks the difference between us is the eyewitness' synoptic grasp of something of which I at best know some isolated elements. And Burnyeat concludes that

the important difference between knowledge and understanding is this, that knowledge can be piecemeal, can grasp related truths one by one, but understanding always involves seeing the connections and relations between the items known.                                              (17)

The conclusion itself is quite correct, but I doubt that the case of the eyewitness testifies in its favour. First, I am not sure that it would be correct to say that the eyewitness does have understanding of what occurs. More importantly, the manner in which Burnyeat constructs his case (through the qualifications 'typically' and 'nearly always') suggests that he may think that eyewitnesses can on occasion tell all they see. But the difference between the eyewitness and me (if we attribute understanding to the eyewitness) cannot be, as this construal implies, merely one of degree. For if it depends simply on the amount of the information transmitted, then teaching may be after all, at least in principle, a matter of degree: what we would need would simply be a *very good* eyewitness. I think that the problem is caused by taking this case to constitute for Plato an actual instance of *epistēmē*. If, as I suggest, we take it only as a partial illustration of what *epistēmē* involves, then we will not feel it necessary to locate the difference between *epistēmē* and *orthē doxa* through it.

Instead, we can turn to the case of the slave and of mathematical knowledge. For here, the difference between belief (or even knowledge) and understanding is more clearly qualitative. Here, the connections and relations between the objects of knowledge, which were not easy to discern in the previous case, are much more central. For it is these relations and connections that produce understanding, and this limits understanding to fields which, unlike empirical low-level matters, involve them crucially. And it is precisely the mastering of these connections and relations that cannot be transmitted (cf. *R.* 518b6-7) because these connections are methods and rules for proceeding in a properly justified manner, from one item of knowledge to another. And even if such rules and methods can be formulated, and in that sense, transmitted, what cannot be transmitted in the same manner is the ability to follow the methods and to apply the rules.[49] And if we can formulate methods and rules for following the previous set, we will again face the question how these new rules and methods are to be correctly applied. The notion of recollection provides Plato both with an account of the inward, first-hand nature of all *epistēmē* and with a way of ending this regress: its power lies in its double contribution to Plato's philosophical purposes.[50]

In relation to *aretē* the connections we have been discussing are what allows one to do the right thing on all occasions and not only sometimes or capriciously. Unless it is in order to fool someone, the geometrician will not consciously produce a fallacious proof of a theorem. And unless it is in order to harm someone, the *agathos* will not willingly do the wrong thing. But part of being *agathos* of course, is never to want to harm anyone, as Socrates consistently argued in Plato's dialogues. The *agathos*, therefore, will never do the wrong thing.

Socrates, in Plato's eyes, never did the wrong thing and thus seemed to him to be the best man of his generation. But Socrates steadfastly refused the role of teacher: he claimed not to know how to make people good, and not even to understand at all what *aretē* itself consisted in. For practical and ethical reasons, Socrates had never wanted to tell his students (for students he certainly wanted, and had no less than any of the distinguished sophists) anything about the subject which they wanted to learn from him. For epistemological reasons, Plato came not to want Socrates to have believed that he was capable of doing so. Meno's paradox brought together Socrates' immediate concern with not harming his friends (a rather old-fashioned conception of *aretē* in its own right) with Plato's theoretical interest in the nature of understanding. The theory of recollection, whatever its ultimate shortcomings, succeeded in accounting

---

[49] The problem is discussed, but not resolved, by Gilbert Ryle, 'Teaching and Training' in *Plato's Meno*, ed. Malcolm Brown (Indianapolis, 1971), 243–6.

[50] Recollection does not perpetuate the regress, for the requisite abilities have, according to Plato (85e–86b), always been in the soul.

systematically for both, even if in the process some of the mystery of Socrates gave way to the mysticism of Plato.[51]

*University of Pittsburgh*

[51] For comments on an earlier version of this essay, I am grateful to M. F. Burnyeat, Rosemary Desjardins, Steven Strange, and Gregory Vlastos. I must also thank Paul Kalligas, who discussed these issues exhaustively with me and who gave me extensive and helpful comments. The generous support of the Guggenheim Foundation is gratefully acknowledged.

# THE SEA-BATTLE RECONSIDERED: A DEFENCE OF THE TRADITIONAL INTERPRETATION*1

Dorothea Frede

One of the most intriguing chapters in the *Corpus Aristotelicum* is chapter 9 of the *de Interpretatione*. Commentators of all times have tried their hands on it to work out a plausible interpretation, but no real consensus has been reached so far, not only with respect to the details of the text but even as far as the general intentions Aristotle was pursuing are concerned. The controversy in recent years has centred around the question whether Aristotle does or does not suspend the validity of what has been called after Lukasiewicz the 'principle of bivalence', or whether the text should be read in a different way.[2] Already the Greek text itself presents us with many obstacles because it is, even for Aristotle, unusually compressed and ambiguities abound—both logical and grammatical—unfortunately in the most crucial sentences. In his commentary Boethius complains about the unusual subtlety of the doctrine, the brevity of style, and adds that for these reasons the *de Interpretatione* 'gives rise to

* © Dorothea Frede 1985.

[1] In recent years I have repeatedly been encouraged to publish an abridged version of my book, *Aristoteles und die Seeschlacht* (Göttingen, 1970) in English since even scholars nowadays seem to read German only under duress and, in addition, my interpretation is inaccessible to the Greek- and Latin-less reader. I have been hesitant to follow this advice because I was afraid that—given the length of articles—I could merely render a re-statement of the traditional interpretation. Since *Oxford Studies in Ancient Philosophy* accommodates longer discussions I started to review my monograph and also the literature that has been published since 1970. The present article contains no major revisions, but various clarifications and short-cuts. In order not to exceed even the liberal space I have had to confine the discussion of differing opinions to the footnotes most of the time. The translation of the text of *de interpretatione* is John Ackrill's, all other translations are my own.

[2] *Aristotle's Syllogistic from the Standpoint of Modern Formal Logic*, 82. (See Bibliographical References for full details of publications mentioned in the footnotes.)

more sweat for the commentators than (even) the *Categories'*
(cf. *in Aristotelis de Interpretatione commentarius (in de
Int.)* 4. 9–14).

Traditions sometimes become a burden and beaten tracks
not only become worn out and boring to follow but may also
lead nowhere. It is, thus, a challenge for every innovative
spirit to try to read the text with 'fresh eyes', to find a new
solution for the old problem, and to point out that the
authorities old and new have so far been on a wild-goose
chase.[3] The traditional interpretation has therefore been
treated as something like an old hat one should get rid of if
one can, evidently on the understanding that the limitation
of the validity of the principle of bivalence should be considered a solution of last resort. When one looks more closely
at the present discussion, however, there seems to be an
almost paradoxical situation. While the *logicians* who are not
concerned mainly with the question of the *Aristotelian*
standpoint have considerably mellowed with respect to the
possibility of assigning a special status to 'future truth',[4] the
*classical scholars* are engaged in ever new efforts to read the
text in non-standard ways to avoid the limitation of the
validity of the principle of bivalence (called PB from now
on). I found none of those attempts really convincing, interesting though they may be. Their main drawbacks are that
they don't do justice to the text as a whole, and though one

[3] Most noteworthy are the contributions (cf. Bibliographical References) of
Albritton, Anscombe, Kneale, Hintikka, McCall, McKim, Rescher, Ryle, Sorabji,
Strang, Taylor, Weidemann, C. J. F. Williams, Waterlow, and, most recently, Fine.
[4] After Lukasiewicz (1) and (2) various other Polish logicians discussed problems connected with 'future truth'; cf. *The Polish Review (PR)* (1968) with
articles by Kotarbinski, Lesniewski, and Lukasiewicz. Especially, *A. N. Prior's*
work has stimulated new interest in the logical problems of determinism in the
English-speaking world. Various philosophers of different provenience have
reconsidered questions of determinism, time, and certainty in the last years. The
reason for this mellowing has been explained by Burgess (whose article is an
excellent introduction into the various problems) as an attempt 'to modify the
syntax of tense-logic to bring it into closer connection with the actual working of
the tense-system of English verbs. . . . As new work in linguistics is assimilated by
logicians, more "realistic" tense-logics will doubtless be constructed' (573). 'The
indeterminists want an interpretation that accounts for *one* past but many equi-
possible futures: Time is a "garden of forking paths" ' (574–5). For further
reading see Geach, Jeffrey, Mackie, McCall, McTaggart, Schick, Sellars, Thomason,
von Wright, M. J. White, and C. J. F. Williams (the list is, of course, far from being
complete).

may say that no stone in chapter 9 of the *de Interpretatione* has been left unturned, no clear picture has emerged, mainly because no painstaking analyses of the whole chapter have been carried out.[5] In fact, the chapter has often been treated like a stone-quarry where everyone takes what he thinks most interesting, leaving aside what does not fit the interpreter's intuitions. In addition there are some important misunderstandings about the traditional interpretation, its meaning, its preconditions and implications. If properly understood, the traditional interpretation is far from being worn out; it is in fact rather fascinating to follow the development of the discussion of future contingents throughout antiquity and into the middle ages. This I cannot do here, but I want to look at both the text and the traditional interpretation with 'fresh eyes' and point out *contra omnes murmurantes* that the most 'natural' reading of the text is also the best one. It has to be admitted, however, that no claim to certainty can be made. All I am trying to do is to tell a 'likely story', but some stories are more likely than others.

The text of the chapter falls into three parts:[6] I will discuss them in that order.

I: 18a28-18b25   The problem of future truth
II: 18b26-19a22   The consequences of determinism
III: 19a23-19b4   Aristotle's solution of the problem of future truth

## I The problem of future truth

As mentioned before, many of the difficulties that stand in the way of a clear and convincing interpretation arise from the brevity of the text. The introductory lines that contain the exposition of the problem are, however, comparatively speaking, quite elaborate. They contain a concise summary of

[5] Ackrill's commentary provides us with a very good survey of the possibilities and their strength and weaknesses. I have not discussed the whole text of ch 9 here. For a fuller discussion see my monograph *Aristoteles und die Seeschlacht*, hereafter referred to as *Seeschlacht*.
[6] Different interpretations have used different divisions, but I think that there are good reasons to make the cuts where I did. For a discussion of problems with the Greek text see *Seeschlacht* § 20 and § 21.

what has been discussed in chapters 6–8, that is, of what in later tradition has been called the *quaternio oppositorum*, the square of opposite assertions and negations. Since a decision about the meaning of the introductory lines precludes certain lines of interpretation we have to look at them carefully. I follow Ackrill's translation:[7]

> With regard to *what is and has been* it is necessary for the affirmation or the negation to be true or false. And with universals taken universally it is always necessary for one to be true and the other false, and with particulars too, as we have said; but with universals not spoken of universally it is not necessary. But with *particulars that are going to be* it is *different*. (18a28-33)

The grammatical construction of the text suggests that what is asserted in the first clause for all propositions, that they are true or false $T[p] \ v \ F[p]$, is denied in the last clause for the singular contingent propositions in the future (i.e. PB). In the second clause Aristotle reminds us that, as pointed out in 7. 17b24 ff, it has been denied for indefinite propositions what was asserted of all other cases, that in every pair of contradictory propositions one must be true, the other false $T[p] \ v \ T[\sim p]$ (I call it the law of alternation, LA).[8] Yet, it has been asked, how strong is the claim that 'particulars that are going to be are *different—ouch homoiōs?*'[9]

---

[7] Most of the *italics* are mine.

[8] The case of indefinite statements has been dealth with in 7. 17b29. Ackrill (129) thinks that Aristotle should better have left them out entirely but I think Aristotle wanted to include *all* forms of statements, and indefinite statements are used frequently in ordinary language. Nothing hinges on the difference between PB and LA, cf. n 10. That Aristotle includes the reference to *time* here (17b36) indicates that he has not forgotten what he holds elsewhere, i.e. that propositions can change their truth-values (cf. de Caelo (*Cael.*) I. 12. 283b6 ff; *Metaphysica* (*Met.*) Θ. 10. 1051b13–16; *Categoriae* (*Cat.*) 5. 4a21 ff). Singular propositions without reference to a definite time are then indefinite in a way. On the question whether propositions like 'Socrates sits' are incomplete see Prior, *Past, Present and Future*, 15–16.

[9] Cf. Ackrill 134–5. S. Waterlow stresses that the beginning of the chapter with the connecting particle '*oun*' suggests a close connection between ch 9 and what went on before, 'closer than the traditional interpretation makes it out: . . . indicates continuance of thought' (97). Her own solution, however, that what Aristotle denies is not PB in its ordinary sense but 'truth-in-opposition-to-falsity' is so idiosyncratic that one wonders how there should be *any* continuity between ch 8 and 9. I do not quite understand what she means when she contrasts Aristotle's 'naïve' sense of truth with our 'denaturalized quasi-technical' one (102, 106, 109). Her main point is that a speaker should not commit himself in an assertion to calling the opposite of what he expects to be 'false'. The commitment

Does this really mean that for them PB is suspended or is some other exception possible?

Let us look at the argument or arguments Aristotle uses to demonstrate the necessity for whatever exception he may have in mind, for there are really two 'determinist arguments', 18a34-b9 and 18b9-16, each terminating in the conclusion that unless PB (in what form remains to be seen) is modified, everything that comes about happens of necessity. Since the language suggests that the two parts are independent, though related (19b9 *'again'*—*'eti'*), we shall treat them separately and then regard their relationship to each other. The first argument goes as follows:

> For if every affirmation is true or false it is necessary for everything either to be the case or not to be the case. For if one person says that something *will be* and another denies this same thing, it is clearly necessary for one of them to be saying what is true—if every affirmation is true or false; for both will not be the case together under such circumstances.[10] For if it is true to say that it is white or not white, it is

would be a *psychological*, not a *logical* one, and the problem according to her focusses on the asserter and his willingness to *act* (99-104) in spite of the fact that Aristotle explicitly explains that no assertion need be made and if PB is valid it would hold a thousand years ahead of time (18b36-19a1). I do not see how Waterlow can handle Aristotle's own example in 18a39 ff. Is the question whether the asserter and agent intends to stay pale rather than get a tan? Regardless of the merits of her approach to Aristotle as a whole, I find her suggestions concerning ch 9 quite unconvincing since it suggests a very muddled sense of truth not to be found anywhere else in Aristotle. (For her general approach see the review by L. Judson in *Oxford Studies in Ancient Philosophy*, vol. i (1983), 217-55.)

[10] That Aristotle uses both PB and LA has confused some interpreters. It is clear that in the case of future *singular* contingents there is no real difference between them; because he wants to emphasize the difference between them and the *indefinite* propositions (18a37) he uses LA at times where one would expect PB (18b4, 18b29, 19b2). He has reason to stress the difference because it is tempting to regard future contingent propositions as *indefinites* of some kind. Hintikka, e.g., has succumbed to that temptation, see Hintikka (1), 472-3). He claims that Aristotle, due to the fact that he does not use dated propositions, mixes them up with indefinite ones (hence the 'Once and Future Sea Fight'). Since Aristotle insists in ch 7 that the *indefinite* statements are exceptional since they do not necessarily refer to the same *subject* or the same *time* we should grant him that if in ch 9 he says *'kath' hekasta'* (*singular*) then he *means kath' hekasta*. As *Met.* ⊖. 10. 1051b13 and *Cat.* 5. 4a21 ff show, Aristotle was well aware of the changing truth-values of undated contingent propositions. In ch 9 the example 'this coat' seems to stand for a rigid designator and I find it unlikely that Aristotle confuses his 'once and future coat'. The same must hold for the example of the 'sea-battle'. Since even in Greece sea-battles were not as frequent as car-accidents are nowadays Aristotle must have a definite situation in mind (like the one on the

necessary for it to be white or not white; and if it is white or is not white then it was true to say this. If it is not the case it is false, if it is false it is not the case. So it is necessary for the affirmation or the negation to be true. It follows that nothing either is or is happening, or will be or will not be, by chance or as chance has it (since either he who says or he who denies is saying what is true). For otherwise it might equally well happen or not happen, since what is as chance has it is no more thus than not thus, nor will it be.          (18a34–b8)

This argument has baffled the commentators and rightly so, because it is very unclear how Aristotle arrives at the conclusion that the assumption of truth values for statements about the future 'carries along' the necessity of the events in question. The *preliminary thesis* merely states that the validity of PB somehow implies that of the corresponding facts one or the other must obtain (I call the law that of two contradictory *states* one or the other must hold, the law of excluded middle, LEM).[11] Grammatically this preliminary thesis can be read in two different ways: We can have the weak thesis

$$(1) \quad T[p] \; v \; F[p] \to N(p \; v \sim p)$$

that merely states that LEM 'follows' from PB. There is nothing formally objectionable in this since LEM is indeed a necessary condition of PB but one wonders why Aristotle mentions it here and what could be supposed to follow from it. Why should Aristotle point out that the necessity of the disjunction is implied by PB? Or, we can take it in the strong sense

$$(2) \quad T[p] \; v \; F[p] \to Np \; v \; N\sim p$$

But would this not be a blatant *petitio principii*? We have to ask ourselves here whether it is possible that Aristotle did not notice the ambiguity and by mistake passed from (1) to (2).

day before the Battle of Salamis) where there is a clear *likeliness* of a battle. Ammonius (90. 18) reports a clarification by Theophrastus concerning this matter: '*tēn kath' hekasta horismenēn kalei*', as opposed to the '*merikē*'. That the token-reflexive form is not decisive has been pointed out by Sorabji (98 n 24).

[11] It is at first confusing to use PB/LA for *propositions* and LEM for the corresponding *facts* or *events*, especially since Aristotle passes freely from the one to the other but it helps to clarify and shorten the discussion, especially in Aristotle's 'solution' cf. below 68 ff. On the question of how truths imply facts see Ryle's criticism on p 13.

I find it very unlikely that Aristotle is simply confused or exploits the ambiguity, for Aristotle is usually quite conscious of the difference and he stresses it later in our chapter (19a27–32). The two comments Aristotle makes within the argument do not seem to be helpful either. The first one is merely a reminder that for the future singulars there cannot be the same exception as for the indefinite propositions, that is, that they can both be true (18a38);[12] the second one (18a39-b3) just repeats the preliminary thesis (with the same ambiguity), this time using the example of something being white or not white, and contains an addition of what seems, at least at first, irrelevant implications where no mention is even made of *necessity* nor of *future* truth:

| | |
|---|---|
| 18a39-b1 | $T[p] \ v \ T[\sim p] \rightarrow N(p \ v \sim p) \ or \ N \ p \ v \ N \sim p$ |
| 18b1-2 | $p \ v \sim p \ \rightarrow T[p] \ v \ T[\sim p]$ |
| 18b2-3 | $\sim p \ \rightarrow F[p]$ |
| 18b3 | $F[p] \ \rightarrow \ \sim p.$ |

It seems, then, that we have to stick to the preliminary thesis itself if we want to explain how Aristotle arrives at his deterministic conclusions. 'To distribute or not to distribute', seems then the most important decision an interpreter has to make for Aristotle. Since the thesis in its innocuous sense (1) may be 'useless' for Aristotle's purposes we have to ask ourselves whether Aristotle may not rather have presupposed the stronger thesis in the first place. I have claimed that Aristotle later on (9. 19a31 ff) does make the explicit distinction between (1) and (2), but it should be added that he is not very tidy in the way he *expresses* himself even there. One can also point out other passages elsewhere that display a similar carelessness. In *de Interpretatione* 13. 22b21, for example, it is only clear from the context that the 'necessary' is to be understood in the distributed sense: 'if it is necessary to be or not to be both will not be possible . . .' must be understood there to mean: 'if it is necessary to be the case or it is necessary not to be the case then both will not be possible'.

---

[12] There is the possibility that the 'was' (*ēn*) in 18b2 anticipates the recourse to 'infinite past truth' in the second argument. Since Boethius has 'est' and it does not seem likely that Aristotle anticipates what is not intelligible at this point I suggest that the sense is non-temporal.

38    *Dorothea Frede*

A similar unclarity is to be found in *Categoriae* 10. 13a12. And in *de Interpretatione* 7. 7b27 we find that Aristotle deals in the same cavalier way with the formulation of what ought to be read as *LA* but is expressed as if *PB* were meant; three lines later he uses the correct expression.[13]

If Aristotle's way of expressing himself is ambiguous we will have to use other considerations to determine whether he has the stronger or the weaker alternative in mind. On the hypothesis that Aristotle is not confused the stronger version of the initial thesis would mean that for Aristotle it is to be understood as the summary of the two implications

$$T[p] \rightarrow N p \text{ and } F[p] \rightarrow N{\sim}p.$$

This, however, would mean that for Aristotle the assumption of truth itself implies a necessity of some sort. This necessity would not be confined to future truth but to propositions in all tenses; but while he may have regarded it as harmless when it refers to the present and past, he must have regarded it as upsetting when applied to the future. If we rule out the explanation that Aristotle simply was confused,[14] there are two ways of explaining this implication of necessity:

(1) Aristotle may have regarded 'future truth' in a way that was later exploited in the so-called 'mower argument' (*therizōn logos*). Ammonius in his commentary cites it as an explanation for the difficulty Aristotle sees implied in 'future truth' (*in de Int.* 131. 25 ff), 'If you will mow you will not perhaps mow or not mow but you will mow in any case'. The point of the argument rests on the fact that one can understand the implication in two ways. If you look at it as a mere hypothesis then the necessity is purely hypothetical.

---

[13] Cf. *Seeschlacht* 16-17.

[14] For a discussion of the 'confusion theory' see Fine. She claims that Aristotle is working out the difference between *necessitas consequentiae* and *necessitas consequentis*. Since she 'plays the chapter backwards', starting with 19a23 ff, this has at first some plausibility. When one reads the whole chapter over, however, the interpretation does not seem convincing. On her reading of 19a23 ff see below 69 f. I also do not think that in all cases of conditions the 'logical structure is the same' (26), especially the '*anagkē ex hypotheseōs*'—e.g. 'if a house is *to be* built' is logically (and practically) different. Aristotle himself in *Physica* (*Phys.*) II. 9 establishes only an *analogy* between the two cases and does so in an awkward enough way (200a15 ff).

If you regard the condition as *fulfilled*, that is, you *will* mow, then the consequence is *guaranteed* and the possibilities are no longer to be regarded as *open*.

Now, Aristotle may have regarded the assumption of truth values for future contingent as just such a *commitment* to a fulfilment of the condition of the hypothetical; that is, 'Since it is true that you will mow you will mow in any case *(pantōs)*'. The advantage of such an explanation is that it would make it intelligible that Aristotle takes the problem of future truth seriously, as it seems he does.[15] He wants, then, to point out what the assumption of definite truth values means.

(2) Another possibility of explaining the kind of necessity in the implication 'if true that [*p*] then necessary that *p*' becomes apparent if one interprets them as correlates in a two-sided *relation*. It is true that Aristotle often treats them almost as synonyms (*Analytica Priora* (*An. Pr.*) 48b3, 49a6, 52a32; *Met.* Δ. 7. 1017a31: ' "to be" and "is" mean that it is true'; cf. also 29. 1024 ff), so one would rather think of an *equivalence*. On the other hand Aristotle treats them also as categorically distinct and like relatives (cf. *Met.* E. 4. 1027b25–8, Θ. 10. 1051b1 ff). In *Categoriae* 12 he treats them as relata and describes their relationship in such a way that it seems as if they differ from some other relative terms just because in their case there is also a priority asymmetry (*proteron—husteron*) because the *facts* are prior to—and the *cause* of—the truth and falsity of the proposition (cf. also *Met.* Θ. 10. 1051b7-9). Apart from this special characteristic (that they have in common with certain other relative concepts cf. *Cat.* 7. 7b22 ff) they are treated like ordinary relata: 'they reciprocate as to implication of existence' (*Cat.* 12. 14b12, 14, 27).[16]

This reciprocity explains then that though truth and facts are not simply to be regarded as equivalent and cannot

[15] Most interpretations assume that the chapter's overall strategy is, as I have tried to maintain, to prove in a long *reductio ad absurdum* that if PB (or something analogous) holds the concept of the contingent has to be given up, and that the solution contains an appropriate modification of PB. (Some interpreters, however, do not share this view, cf. Fine.) More will be said about the so-called binding force of truth further below.

[16] On the reciprocity in *Cat.*, see Oehler 245.

be substituted for one another they do 'necessitate' each other (cf. *Cat.* 7. 6b28) and satisfy the definition of relatives in Aristotle: 'We call *relatives* all such things as are said to be just what they are (*hoper estin*), *of* or *than* other things' (*Cat.* 7. 6a36). This reciprocity does not create a problem in the case of propositions about the present or past since the facts are in each case settled. That there is a problem in the case of future contingents for Aristotle is understandable, for in their case according to his conception of contingency by *definition* nothing is settled, they are indeterminate, '*aorista*'. In other words, future truth and contingency collide. For the status of the propositions must be 'borne out' by the facts (cf. Ammonius, in *de Int.* 154. 16-20). The necessity in question, according to this interpretation, is not a causal but a logical one, and the 'fact' in question is not necessitated in any absolute or causal sense but relative to the assumption that the corresponding proposition is true. In everday language we usually do not refer to a relative necessity of that kind; but if the relationship is questioned we express ourselves in such terms 'if someone. is a slave, he necessarily has a master'.

If this is the model of Aristotle's explanation of future truth then it explains the otherwise redundant implications in 18b1-3, that I called 'irrelevant' above because no *necessity* seems to be implied nor is a reference to the future made. This way Aristotle avoids the impression that any factual or absolute necessity is implied here.[17] Since normally the term 'relative *logical* necessity' is used to designate the necessity of the conclusion relative to the premises I have here adopted the term 'relative *semantic* necessity' for the relationship between propositions and the corresponding facts.[18] It means no more than that a definite truth value requires definite facts and vice versa.

One objection that has frequently been raised against the traditional interpretation is that such a limitation of the

[17] Aristotle seems to think, however, that one cannot leave matters with an uninterpreted hypothetical necessity. We have to treat it as an 'as if' causal or absolute necessity. Cf. Lukasiewicz show call the 'cause the factual counterpart of the proposition' (*PR* 57).

[18] The expression has been suggested to me by G. Patzig. I leave open the question of its relationship to other kinds of relative necessity, e.g. that of syllogistic necessity.

validity of **PB** is unlikely because Aristotle nowhere else
mentions such a restriction for future contingents. There is,
however, at least one passage where Aristotle does distinguish
between necessary and contingent events in the future even
though he expresses himself in a more cautious way. In the
*de Generatione et Corruptione* II. 11. 337a34 he defines the
distinction between absolutely necessary and contingent
future events by referring to the truth value of the relevant
proposition.
For our purposes two features are most noteworthy.
(*a*) Aristotle refers to the absolutely necessary future event as
'what will be' (*to estai*) and distinguishes it from what is
'about to come' (*to mellon*). Seeing a need to clarify the
distinction Aristotle adds: 'for what it is true to say that it
will be, it must one day be true to say that it is . . . while for
what is merely about to happen this is not so'.[19] This passage
not only teaches us that Aristotle was willing to limit **PB** but
also that he saw the necessity in question as a purely *logical*
one, for he does not say that future truth makes the *events* in
question causally necessary or anything of that sort. It is
merely claimed that the assumption of a truth-value for
a proposition in the future indicative implies that this proposition will one day have to be true in the present tense, hence
the necessity of the event is implied only indirectly. (*b*) The
*qualifications* Aristotle introduces for propositions about
what is merely 'about to happen' are significant for our
problem: 'of what it is now true to say that it is about to
happen (*hoti mellei*)[20] there is nothing preventing its not
happening (*ouden kōluei mē genesthai*)', for this implies that
in the case of a definite proposition there *must be* something
preventing its not happening. Furthermore, we can see how
Aristotle can avoid the problem of future truth if he wants to
do so: he can 'banish' assertoric statements about contingent

---

[19] For a more extensive discussion see the commentary by C. J. F. Williams
197–9, who accepts the distinction as valid but thinks that the problem in *de Int.*
9 is based on a fallacy that 'Aristotle never quite mastered' (198), i.e. $N(T[p] \rightarrow p) \rightarrow Np$.
[20] Aristotle refers to the distinction between *esomena* and *mellonta* elsewhere.
Cf. *de Div. Somn.* 463a28; *Meteorologica* 327b27. Most interesting is his use in
*Rhetorica*, esp. 1392b33–93a8, where he advises the orator to treat future possibilities as if they were *definite facts*.

future events. So the semantic necessity can be avoided if one adopts the appropriate linguistic conventions. The passage in the *de Generatione et Corruptione* seems to presuppose the discussion in *de Interpretatione* 9 and it is very possible that once the semantic distinction was canonized no further discussion was deemed necessary. In the *de Interpretatione*, however, the problem was unavoidable since all contradictory assertions and negations and their truth and falsity were under discussion.[21]

The interpretation I have advocated so far agrees mostly with the so called traditional one as it has come down to us in the commentaries on the *de Interpretatione* by Ammonius and Boethius.[22] It is useful to look at least briefly at these our sources themselves because the exact meaning of their testimony is not always clear and has given rise to some misunderstanding. The discussion of the problem of future truth in Ammonius varies in clarity and explicitness. He does, however, give something like an 'abstract' of his interpretation of chapter 9 at the beginning (CAG *in de Int.* 128–31) that makes it clear how he sees the problem of future truth: that is, that if with regard to future contingents the PB is not modified everything will come about with necessity. But while the general trend of his interpretation is clear it is not immediately obvious what, precisely, the modification is that Aristotle suggests for the PB. Ammonius claims that contradictory propositions about future contingents do not *divide the true or false* in a *definite* but in an *indefinite* way (*aoristōs*), while all other genuine contradictions divide it definitely (*aphorismenōs*), 131.3–4 *et passim*).[23]

---

[21] This accounts for the fact, it seems, that Aristotle can touch the problem of future contingents with a lighter hand in *de Generatione et Corruptione*. Circumlocutions with '*mellei*', on the other hand, are much more difficult to handle in a context like that of *de Int.* because of the vagueness of the meaning of the colloquial phrase.

[22] Besides his commentary Boethius discusses the problem of future truth in a more dramatic way in book V of the *Consolatio Philosophiae*.

[23] For the expression '*aphorismenōs*' see the discussion in *Cat.* 10. 12b26 ff about the necessity of possession *or* privation, where 'determinately one or the other' is used: 'Thus it is not necessary for one or the other of them to belong to everything capable of receiving them, but only to things to which the one belongs by nature, and in these cases it must be *definitely* the one and not as chance has it (*aphorismenōs anagkaion thateron hyparchein* . . .)' (12b39). Cf. the curious discussion of '*aphorismenōs–horismenōs*' and '*aoristōs eidenai*' in *Cat.* 7.

This diplomatic way of expressing himself avoids a clear decision whether we are to take it that according to Ammonius Aristotle merely 'temporarily suspends' PB or whether this is a definite limitation. The unclarity goes back, of course, to Aristotle himself, for in the final summary of chapter 9 Aristotle also somewhat hides behind a diplomatic terminology—'it is necessary for one or the other to be true or false —not this one or that one, but as chance has it . . .' (19a39). So the answer to the question whether PB is still generally valid sounds somewhat like Radio Erewhon 'In principle yes, but . . .'. This accounts then for the fact that the commentators who must have known the problem of *de Interpretatione* 9 all along, do not usually refer to it when discussing the general validity of PB or LEM elsewhere (cf. Alexander of Aphrodisias, *in Analytica Priora* 400. 34; *in Topica* 183. 24; *in Metaphysica* Γ; Philoponus, *in Analytica Priora* 376. 35, 436. 6; Simplicius, *in Categorias* 195).

The question *why* definite truth-values present a problem is, by contrast, discussed fairly extensively. The problem is, according to Ammonius, a logical one (cf. 130. 28): the truth of a proposition implies with necessity the definite existence of the fact in question so that '. . . there the elimination of the contingent follows on the basis of what has been said before' (141. 31 ff; cf. 143. 15-20). The paraphrase Ammonius gives for the preliminary thesis in Aristotle makes it clear that he sees the necessity functor as distributed: 'since the truth of the propositions is followed necessarily by the existence of the state of affairs and the falsity by the inexistence . . .' (139. 29). How Ammonius sees the relationship between statements and state of affairs can be seen even more clearly in one of his examples—'Now if the one says what is true who claims that he (sc. the sick person) is going to recuperate, it is *necessary* that he will recuperate (since it was presupposed that the truth of the statement is followed in any case (*pantōs*) by the events); while if the one says what is true who makes the opposite statement then it is *impossible* that he will recuperate' (140. 17-21; cf. 139. 2, 140. 19, 141. 16).

The interpretation we find in Ammonius is certainly much

8a33-b19. This must have been the phrase that inspired the *commentators* in their need to specify the limitation of PB.

older, as far as the general line of the arguments and the envisaged solution are concerned. Unfortunately the commentary on the *de Interpretatione* by Alexander of Aphrodisias (*fl.* AD 200) which would be our most reliable source is not extant; but since Boethius (died AD 525) in his commentary to *de Interpretatione* is in agreement with Ammonius (fifth century AD) in the most relevant points while their commentaries are different in outline and method, we can be fairly confident that their testimony represents something like the consensus of the Aristotelian school prior to their time. A short remark which is to be found in Simplicius' commentary on the *Categoriae* confirms this; he there compares the Stoic doctrine of future contingency with that of the Peripatetics and declares with respect to the latter that 'what is said about the future is not yet true or false, but it will be of this kind or that kind *(toia ē toia)*' 407. 12-13. We do find remarks in the *Scripta Minora* of Alexander of Aphrodisias that show that this is also his basic assumption 'since about what one says truly that it will be the case, that must with necessity occur' (*Quaestiones* I. 4. 11. 9 ff).[24]

The expression 'definitely true' *(aphorismenōs alēthēs)*, in Ammonius, and even more the phrases '*determinate verum*' and '*indeterminate verum*' in Boethius, can be misleading since the reader is tempted to see here a distinction between a weaker and a stronger sense of the truth value.[25] But in spite of some misleading passages in Boethius it becomes clear after a careful scrutiny of the text that only the *distribution* of the truth values is at stake:

those things are contingent that are equally prone to exist as not to exist, and just as they have *indefinite being* or *not being*, so the assertions and negations concerning them have *indefinite truth or falsity* in

[24] On Alexander's interpretation of the problem of future contingency see R. Sharples 11 f. He also printed and translated the relevant passages of the *Quaestiones*. I hope to finish an article on Alexander, *de Fato* X, 'Alexander's Mini-Sea-Battle', in the not too distant future.

[25] Cf. Sorabji 92 ff (followed by Fine 41 n 4). Sorabji (104-5) is quite wrong in his claim that ' "definite" should always be understood according to Boethius II,125,15'. What Boethius is saying there is merely that Aristotle rightly *defines* the noun prior to defining the verb in *de Int.*, '. . . postea vero definitum est verbum'.

the sense that while one is always true and the other false, which is true and which is false is not yet known in the case of the contingent events.[26]

There is no question of Boethius wanting to distinguish between definite and indefinite kind of *being* as an actual state.[27] The misleading formulation is clearly due to the vagueness in Aristotle's own way of expressing himself, especially at the end of chapter 9, where he asserts that 'we should not divide' (19a29). This is taken by the commentators to apply to the distribution of truth values so that they repeatedly suggest that 'we should not divide and treat one of the alternatives as definitely true and the other as false' (cf. Ammonius 130. 23-4, 154; Boethius 208. 1).

To sum up the results of the first determinist argument: the necessity of the future contingents is not derived from the false distribution of the necessity functor over the disjunction but from the assumption of definite truth-values. That the problem arises from future truth is only indicated in 18a3—'if someone says that something *will* be . . .' (*esesthai*). That the *consequences* of the determinist argument are not confined to future contingents but upset the whole realm of

---

[26] Boethius 200. 11 ff: 'contingentia autem sunt quaecumque vel ad esse vel ad non esse aequaliter sese habent, et sicut ipsa indefinitum habent esse et non esse, ita quoque de his adfirmationes et negationes indefinitam habent veritatem vel falsitatem, cum una semper vera sit, semper altera falsa, sed quae vera quaeve falsa sit, nondum in contingentibus notum est.' Cf. ibid 'veritas et falsitas ex eo quod est esse rei et ex eo quod est non esse rei sumitur' (200. 22); 'sicut ipsum esse et non esse instabile est, esse tamen aut non esse necesse est . . . veritas vel falsitas in incerto est (ibid.); indiscretum est quae una harum vera sit, quae altera false' (247-8); 'in his quamquam totius contradictionis in qualibet parte veritas inveniatur aut falsitas, non tamen ut aliquis dividat et dicat hanc quidem veram esse, illam vero falsam' (246. 2); 'eventus autem ipsorum indiscretus est . . . non est ex antiquioribus quibusdam causis pendens rerum eventus, ut quaedam quodammodo necessitatis catena' (246. 14 ff). Cf. Ammonius 130. 23: '*ou gar eti horismenōs estin eipein potera men autōn alētheisei potera de pseusetai*'. Alexander does not use a phrase like 'definitely true' or 'indefinitely true' in the *de Fato*; he does so, however, in *Quaestiones* (*Quaest.*) I. 4. 12. 13 ff. There is, then, no *split* in the traditional interpretation but just more or less emphasis on the point that PB is just suspended, not discarded. Upon reflection it is clear quite generally that if one divides something (like an inheritance) in an *indefinite* way then there just *is* no actual division!

[27] That Boethius does not have an epistemic indeterminateness in mind is clear from 208. 17. The question of the 'knowability' played an important role in the Stoic concept of determinism.

the contingent is emphasized by Aristotle in his conclusion of the argument (18b6-9):

It follows that nothing either is or is happening, or will be or will not be, by chance or as chance has it (since either he who says or he who denies is saying what is true). For otherwise it might equally well happen or not happen, since what is as chance has it is no more thus than not thus, nor will it be.

Once again it is clear that only the validity of PB can be what upsets the whole realm of the contingent in *all* tenses (*esti . . . gignetai, estai, an . . . egigneto*). And if Aristotle himself wrote the text in this order it must have been clear to him that only the most subtle minds would be able to follow him here. The second argument seems, then, to be designed to dispel our doubts about what is crucial in the determinist argument. But before we can turn to that I want to discuss a rival interpretation and some criticism of the first argument.

*E. Anscombe* (in her article 'Aristotle and the Sea Battle') has suggested an interpretation that has been adopted by various scholars and would indeed change the whole story. She claims that Aristotle in our chapter does not suspend the validity of PB but rather introduces the distinction between *necessary* truth and *simple*, contingent, truth. According to this interpretation the necessity functor is to be distributed over the truth and falsity of the propositions right at the beginning of the chapter, so we have to read: 'With regard to what is and what has been the affirmation is necessarily true and the negation necessarily false . . .'. Anscombe does not think that for Aristotle this should be immediately apparent to the reader but that there is an ambiguity which is eventually unveiled. The reason for this procedure according to her lies in the fact that there is a kind of *factual necessity* that Aristotle maintains for what is present and past, in opposition to what is contingent in the future, and that the kind of truth-value assigned to the propositions respectively is supposed to mirror the difference in the ontological state of affairs. The main justification for this interpretation lies in the fact that Aristotle in his *solution* to the problem maintains that '. . . statements are true according to how the actual things are . . .' (19a32-3).

I have to refrain from going into the details here[28] but can just indicate the main weaknesses of this interpretation. An ambiguity at the beginning of our chapter is, of course, possible. I do not find it likely, however, because Aristotle there merely sums up what had been said about the truth or falsity of *all* kinds of affirmations and negations in chapters 6–8, where no 'necessary truth' can have been implied (modalities are not mentioned in *de Int.* till ch 12). Furthermore the subordinate clause in 18a29–31 that specifies the exception to be made for the *indefinite* propositions depends on the first 'necessary'—that is, it would have to be first read as distributed then as not distributed. Very similar problems arise at the various other places where the Anscombian version presupposes ambiguity and distribution; especially *Rescher*'s claim that 'The context is invariably such that what appears prima facie as an argument against the truth (or falsity) of future contingents can equally well—or better— be construed as directed against their NECESSARY truth (or NECESSARY falsity),' cannot be maintained, most of the time for simple grammatical reasons.[29] More importantly, while a camouflage of the ambiguity at the beginning of the text still makes sense it should later on be removed. But even at the most crucial points Aristotle does not speak of 'necessarily true', for example at 19a38–9: '. . . not, however this one or that one, but as chance has it; or for that one to be true *rather* than the other but not *already* true or false'. We would urgently need a 'necessarily' here (at least an ambiguous one) to make the interpretation work. The same is true for other places (cf. 18a39, b2, b7, b10, 19a19–21); that

---

[28] For a more detailed discussion see *Seeschlacht* 27–32. I have, incidentally, given a paper on this subject at the University of Pennsylvania in Spring 1977. Anscombe and Geach were in the audience and participated in the discussion. They both felt that the odds and the textual evidence were very much against the 'true'/'necessarily true' distinction.

[29] Rescher has called this interpretation the 'Farabian' since he claims that it is to be found in Al-Farabi's *Commentary to de Interpretatione*. If, however, the translation and notes by F. W. Zimmermann are to be trusted Al-Farabi followed the traditional interpretation and claimed that truth and falsity cannot definitely be distributed. 'Saying that they distribute truth and falsity indefinitely means that they are, by their own modes of existence and to our minds alike, in an indefinite state' [81. 16]. Rescher's interpretation, at any rate, needs so many supplementations and unwarranted textual changes that I cannot share his optimism as far as *de Int.* 9 itself is concerned.

a 'necessarily' is missing is crucial at places where not even
an ambiguity is possible because Aristotle speaks of *one*
proposition only, instead of the pair of opposites (cf. 18b3,
18b10-12).

It should be added that nowhere else do we find a distinction between truth and necessary truth or any other
modalization of true or false in Aristotle. Such locutions are
conspicuously absent in the *Prior Analytics* where, if anywhere, one would expect them; but only the propositions
themselves are modalized. There are some passages where it
might seem at first that Aristotle at least implies such modalization but a closer look dispels that impression. In *Metaphysica* Γ. 5. 1009b14 Aristotle reports someone else's
argument; in *Analytica Priora* B. 4. 57a35-40 he does say
'. . . the conclusion can nevertheless be true but not necessarily . . .', but the context shows that this means that the
conclusion *may* be true but does not *have to be* true.

There is one passage where Aristotle does indeed use the
phrases 'necessarily true' or '—false'; in *Metaphysica* Δ.
12. 1019b23 ff he explains as one meaning of 'impossible'—
'impossible is that whose opposite is necessarily true . . . for
that the diagonal should be commensurable is not only false
but necessarily false'. But the subject here is different; for in
Δ. 12 Aristotle does not use 'true' and 'false' as truth functors
of *propositions* but as synonyms for 'to be' and 'not to be',
that is something is impossible if its opposite is necessarily true
(= necessarily the case). Later on (*Met.* Δ is regarded as rather
early) Aristotle seems to have dropped this kind of expression and rather *contrasts* 'impossible' and 'false', using 'false'
as a modal operator: something is *false* but not impossible
(*Cael.* I. 12. 281b2 ff; *Met.* Θ. 4. 1047b13; *An. Pr.* 34a25-9).

The error of assuming that Aristotle distinguishes between
'true' and 'necessarily true' is quite widespread. Ross, for
example, writes in his commentary to Aristotle's *Metaphysics*
(ii, p 244): 'Diodorus in his famous *kurieuōn logos* used the
principle that "everything that is past is necessarily true" (an
Aristotelian dictum, *EN* 1139b7-9, *Rhet.* 1418a3-5).' Now,
it is debatable what Diodorus' *logos* means,[30] but in the

---

[30] The question of the relationship between the Aristotelian and the Megarian
conception of possibility has received quite some attention. I have devoted

two Aristotelian passages there is no mention of 'necessarily true': what Aristotle does say in *Ethica Nicomachea*, is rather: 'one does not deliberate about what has happened but about what is in the future and contingent; what has happened cannot not have happened'.

Since neither in chapter 9 nor anywhere else in Aristotle is there an explicit distinction between truth and necessary truth I do not think that the Anscombian interpretation is tenable,[31] and the same verdict applies to other kinds of interpretation that presupposes that distinction.[32]

This takes us to the *philosophical criticism* of the determinist argument. The many attempts to disprove Aristotle's argument in one version or another have a common source, that is, the suspicion that in spite of Aristotle's philosophical acumen the problem of future truth in the last analysis is, nevertheless, a '*Scheinproblem*'. The kinds of suspicions that befall the student of Aristotle have been summed up very lucidly by *G. Ryle* in his paper 'It Was to Be'.[33] I want to discuss here only two points of criticism that Ryle ventures against the determinist argument:

(1) that the determinist seems to presuppose that there is not just a *logical* necessity connecting proposition and fact but a kind of *causal* necessity. From what has been said earlier we have no reason to suppose that Aristotle committed that kind of mistake, especially since it is explicitly stated in the passages quoted above,[34] that for Aristotle the fact is rather the cause for the truth.

a chapter to a comparison of the two doctrines and to a reconstruction of the *kurieuōn logos* in *Seeschlacht* 93–112. My interpretation agrees to a large part with Prior's except that I use a different auxiliary premise.

[31] A remark in Alexander's *de Fato* (177. 3 ff) suggests that the Stoics modalized 'true' and 'false', so that '*ex anagkēs alēthes*' gradually became common use; we find it frequently in the later commentators.

[32] Cf. Hintikka (1) 478–83; cf. Fine 32.

[33] Ryle does not address himself to Aristotle, but it is clear that he has the Sea-Battle in mind. Since he confines himself to the discussion of the philosophical problems he avoids taking a stand as far as Aristotle himself is concerned.

[34] That Aristotle does not discuss the question of the connection of truth and fact in *de Int.* 9 while he does it elsewhere shows that here, as Ackrill put it (136), 'His arguments do not presuppose a principle of universal causation but rely on purely logical moves'. It has wider consequences, however. This is also Ammonius' understanding: '*Touto to theōrēma dokei men einai logikon, kata alētheian de pros panta ta moria tēs philosophias estin anagkaion*' (130. 27).

(2) more to the point, that in the determinist argument the fundamental difference between facts and propositions is not taken into consideration, so that the truth of a *proposition implies* the existence of a *fact*. In Ryle's words, 'But in this way in which one truth may require or involve another truth, an event cannot be one of the implications of a truth. Truths can be consequences of other truths, but they cannot be causes of effects or effects of causes' (22). This mistake is based, as Ryle points out, on the determinist's failure to notice the distinction between what is 'logically necessary' and what is 'practically necessary'. 'But in the way in which some truths carry other truths with them and make them necessary, events themselves cannot be made necessary by truths. Things and events may be the topics of premisses and conclusions, but they cannot themselves be premisses or conclusions' (24).

This is a serious objection, and one may feel that Aristotle's habit of not always distinguishing carefully whether he is talking about a fact or a statement about it makes him liable to such a mistake. Indeed the assumption that there is an *equivalence* between fact and proposition where the one can be substituted for the other seems to presuppose that kind of mistake. The 'relativity-theory' mentioned above suggests, however, that Aristotle, careless though his language often may be, does not commit this obvious mistake; the distinction between what lies definitely in the future (*esomena*) and what is merely 'about to happen' (*mellonta*) shows that he is concerned with the commitment concerning the ontological status of future events, as we also saw in *de Generatione et Corruptione* II. 11. The *relation* between the status of an event and the way in which we *describe* it is the main concern in our chapter in *de Interpretatione*; I take it that what Aristotle has in mind here is that the assumption of a fixed truth value for a proposition in the future necessitates the *assumption* that the event is certain too.

According to my interpretation, Ryle's criticism of the determinist argument does not apply to Aristotle because Aristotle's relative semantic necessity is not a practical necessity at all. It may be questionable whether the concept of truth necessarily carries along such implications but we should grant Aristotle for now that it is not implausible to think so. Ryle's own further discussion shows that he is at least sympathetic to Aristotle's point of view. For he grants that we cannot deal with future events as we deal with present and past ones, in the sense that they are not *individuals*. The battle of Waterloo was not 'the battle of Waterloo' before 1815; nor was Gilbert Ryle 'Gilbert Ryle' before he was born; nor can we use demonstrative pronouns and talk of 'this accident' but only of 'an accident of this or that kind that may be prevented . . .' (25-7).

What becomes apparent in Ryle's criticism of the determinist argument and his observations about our linguistic habits concerning future events is that there are certain difficulties caused by the asymmetry between present, past, and future. That the distinctions are not purely linguistic can be seen from the fact that we find it strange to talk about tomorrow's ('this') traffic accident but natural to talk about tomorrow's eclipse. The latter is an *esomenon*, a definite event, while the former is not.

Let us see whether the *second determinist* argument confirms or modifies what we have said about the meaning and function of the first one:

Again, if it is white now it was *true to say earlier* that it would be white; so that it was *always true* to say of anything that has happened that it would be so. But if it was always true to say that it was so, or would be so, it *could not be so*, or not be going to be so. But if something cannot not happen it is impossible for it not to happen; and if it is impossible for something not to happen, it is *necessary for it to happen*. Everything that will be, therefore, happens necessarily. So nothing will come about as chance has it or by chance; for if by chance, not of necessity. (18b9-16)

This argument in a way supplements the first one, but the strategy seems to be quite different. For while so far Aristotle has merely pointed out what consequences follow from the assumption that a proposition is true the second one contains a real argument; Aristotle demonstrates step by step that everything is necessary if PB obtains. Since Aristotle here no longer starts with a *disjunction* no ambiguity is possible and none is apparent. Let us follow the argument to see what the crucial steps are and what possible flaws there are. The first sentence consists of two implications the first of which seems acceptable since it merely states what PB entails, that is, that if something is the case now it was earlier true to say so. The consequence that is drawn from this however, already gives reason to pause, especially since for Aristotle omnitemporality is closely tied to necessity. 'Eternal truths' reek of determinism. It is clear, however, that no time limits can be imposed, that is, on the basis of PB the rule *once true always true* must hold. That we encounter a kind of (psychological?) insecurity here explains why Aristotle has taken the detour via an example of something that holds *now*: it seems less problematic at first to admit the truth of the proposition prior to the event *ex pòst facto*. The three steps that lead from 'eternal truth' to necessity are simple:

(1) $(t) \{ T[p] \} \rightarrow \sim\Delta\sim p$
(2) $\quad \sim\Delta\sim p \rightarrow A\sim p$
(3) $\quad\quad A\sim p \rightarrow N p.$[35]

All critics of Aristotle's determinist argument have tried to point out a false step here.[36] Let us see what its weaknesses are. There seems to be nothing wrong with steps (2) and (3), since the modal operators are treated as equivalent by Aristotle elsewhere (cf. *de Int.* 12, 13). This leaves us with step (1) as the critical point. Why does Aristotle want us to infer that infinite truth in the past precludes the event's contingency?[37] It is clear that the procedure from 'true' via 'true earlier' to 'always true' formally should make no difference. Nevertheless it seems as if Aristotle wants to put considerable weight on the 'omnitemporality' in the second argument. That for him there may even have been a formal difference between plain truth and omnitemporal truth can be seen when we compare

[35] I have consciously avoided the symbols used in modern modal logic; *N* stands for necessary (*anagkē*), *A* for impossible (*adunaton*), $\Delta$ for possible (*dunaton*). I refrain from an attempt to interpret the modals. By 'possible' in ch 9 Aristotle means two-sided possibility. On his difficulties with one- and two-sided possibility see *Seeschlacht* 54–9.

[36] I omit here the lengthy discussion of the second argument by Taylor, Albritton, Anscombe, Strang, and Kneale. Cf. *Seeschlacht* 41–52.

[37] On the 'argument from past truth' see Sorabji 91–113.

the contraposition of (1) with that of the simple implication (*):

(1) $(t)\{ T[p] \} \to \sim\!\Delta\!\sim\!p \Rightarrow \Delta\!\sim\!p \to \sim(t) \{T[p]\}.$
(*) $\qquad T[p] \to \sim\!\Delta\!\sim\!p \Rightarrow \Delta\!\sim\!p \to \sim T[p].$

While (1) seems at first an acceptable equation, (*) does not.
This question needs a closer scrutiny. A modern logician may
wonder, of course, why even the right side of (1) should be
taken for granted, but for an Aristotelian it is justifiable
because according to his concept of contingency every possible
event must be capable of coming true eventually, so that
[*p*] cannot have been 'true forever' while *not-p* was still
*possible*. But if this is the justification for (1) then (*) must
also be acceptable for the Aristotelian because the implication on its right side is just: 'if it is contingent that *not-p* then
it cannot be true that [*p*]', in other words, 'If it is contingent
that there will be a sea-battle tomorrow it cannot be true that
there will not be one'. But if the addition of 'true forever'
formally should not make any difference then the validity of
the second argument hinges on the same point as the first one
did, that is, that Aristotle simply regarded the assumption of
fixed truth-values for contingent propositions as incompatible
with the assumption that the events are contingent.

It is all very well, the critics of this interpretation may say,
that there should be no formal difference between (1) and
(*) from our point of view, but can we be sure that Aristotle
saw the matter in the same light? The way Aristotle usually
depicts the relation between *necessity* and *omnitemporality*
seems to speak against it. This is the crucial point Hintikka
has fastened upon in his interpretation of the Sea-Battle:
'Aristotle's problem is thus primarily that of omnitemporal
truth—or more accurately—that of infinite past truth'
(467). According to Hintikka, 'necessary' and 'always true'
are equivalent in Aristotle.[38] This, however, is not quite

---

[38] Hintikka's interpretation(s) suffer from his preoccupation with his
'statistical' interpretation of Aristotle's concept of modality. His observations
about the 'statistics' and their importance for the determination of the modal
status of things and events are not mistaken, but there is no simple *identity* of the
meaning of necessity = always–, contingent = sometimes–, impossible = never the
case. If this were so Aristotle need never have written the *Analytica Posteriora*
where he goes into great lengths to determine what constitutes the necessity of

accurate. For Aristotle, and this is a small but decisive difference, treats what always *exists* or always is the same way
when it is as necessary, and apart from our chapter he hardly
ever uses the phrase 'always true'.[39] He has good reasons not
to do that, because even singular propositions about future
necessary events change their truth value as the example
'there will be an eclipse tomorrow' shows.

If the switch from 'simple' truth to eternal truth is not the
decisive step in the second argument we have to explain its
relationship to the first one. Has it been added for dialectical
reasons in the sense that it *looks* more like a proper proof
since it contains several steps, and is the switch to eternal
truth just a psychological manoeuvre? Furthermore, could

the premisses of the scientific syllogism and says in so many words that omnitemporality is not enough (cf. *Analytica Posteriora* (*An. Po.*) I. 6. 75a1–37)! That
omnitemporality is so important in Aristotelian *natural* science (though of course
not in mathematics) is due to the fact that besides the manifestation of a *dunamis*,
statistics is often the only thing we can go by, since the questions of attributes
*per se* or of the '*dioti*' are difficult to decide. Hintikka's later work (e.g. 'Aristotle
on Modality and Determinism') shows that he has become aware of the fact that
the metaphysical considerations are at the centre of Aristotle's modal theory.

[39] I have found only two passages where 'always' is used in connection with
'true' but neither speak of 'eternal truth'. In *Met.* Γ. 5. 1010b24 Aristotle says
that what is sweet as such does not change but '*all' aei alētheuei peri autou*', but
this only means that one cannot be wrong about it; the other passage might at
first sight speak in favour of Hintikka's interpretation since Aristotle in *Met.* Θ.
10. 1051b16 states that statements about things that do not change are not
'sometimes true and sometimes false, but always the same is true or false'. This,
however, as the word order shows, only means that always the *same* proposition
is true or false. I do not deny that propositions about what is necessary are always
true (if properly formulated, i.e. *hen kath' henos*), but claim that the reverse is
not true. Hintikka's reference (481–2) to 18a30 does not support his interpretation either: 'it is always necessary for the one to be true and the other false' does
not mean that one is *always* true and the other always false, but that the law of
alternation always holds, as a comparison with 7. 17b27–30 shows (where there is
no question of 'eternal truth'!) and is confirmed by Ackrill's translation. The
reason why Hintikka's interpretation goes wrong is that he falsely assumes that by
'universal statements' Aristotle means only *genuinely* (i.e. necessary) universal
sentences (482 and n 6). This, however, is clearly not the case, as Aristotle's
examples show, i.e. 'all men are white'/'all men are not white' (17b18). The complexity of the modals in Aristotle and the many functions they fulfil simply *defy*
the attempt to give a unifying definition. The same criticism that applies to
Hintikka's interpretation also applies to Waterlow where she follows him. ('Aristotle equates contingency as such with RT contingency' (84); 'all necessity is
tense-relative'). She does not realize that this does not, e.g., apply in mathematics.
It is then no accident that she nowhere mentions the *An. Po.* I cannot further
discuss her interpretation in general since I would have to go into the intricacies
of her interpretation of *Cael.* I. 12.

Aristotle have thought that such a bolstered-up argument would throw the indeterminist who is an adherent to PB off track? I doubt that this can have been Aristotle's strategy because it is unlikely that he wants to distract us from realizing what he had stated so baldly in the first argument, that is, that it is the notion of future truth itself that causes the problem.

The second argument is, I want to suggest, a supplement of the first one and adds or clarifies three important points. (*a*) Since there is no longer a disjunction there can be no question of an erroneous distribution of the necessity operator. (*b*) The detour via 'if true . . . then not possible that not' shows that Aristotle does not simply confuse the *necessitas consequentiae* with the *necessitas consequentis* by misplacing the necessity operator. (*c*) The addition of the 'infinite past truth' draws to the reader's attention what he in all probability had not realized yet, that is, that a commitment to definite truth-values not only rules out the contingency of a certain event at a certain point of time but that the determinist argument entails that there never was nor ever will be any truly contingent event. For, as stated earlier, once 'future truth' has been admitted, no time limit can be proferred and so it does not matter (as Aristotle points out in part II) when a prediction is made or whether it is actually made at all—as long as it is assumed that propositions can be ascribed definite truth values. An enlightened indeterminist may, of course, simply reject both (1) and (*) and claim that contingence and future truth are quite compatible, that is, he may presuppose a different concept of proposition and of the meaning of truth. In this case the truth or falsity of propositions in the future are purely hypothetical and the prospective event remains untouched. This, however, does not seem to be Aristotle's conception of truth.

Does the assumption of a *relative semantic* necessity provide a satisfactory explanation for the relation between fact and proposition? Since this necessity applies to all those relations, regardless whether the propositions are about the past, present, or future, we would have to find an explanation why the necessity of 'future truth' presents a problem.

This question has already been raised by Ryle: 'Why does the fact that a posterior truth about an occurrence *requires* that occurrence not worry us in the way in which the fact that an anterior truth about an occurrence does worry us?' (l.c., p. 21). Ryle himself sees the reason for the worry in the temptation to regard the necessity as a *causal* one. This association certainly contributes to the confusion but I do not think that this is all; the relative semantic necessity is certainly the same in all tenses, that is, if a proposition is true the corresponding fact must obtain—*in fact*—not of (absolute) necessity. In the case of present and past events this causes no problems since they do obtain and possess what one may call 'factual' necessity. In the case of future events the contingency is eliminated if one hypostasizes them as 'facts', thus the distinction between relative and absolute necessity gets blurred.[40] The main reason for the worry about future contingency is, thus, a conceptual one; it arises from the need to assign, for theoretical reasons, an ontological status to future events to which nothing corresponds *in rerum natura*: yet, so it seems to Aristotle, the status of propositions must somehow be 'borne out' by the facts.

Our 'relative semantic' necessity is usually not conspicuous since normally we do not pay attention to the dependence of facts from truths but presuppose the reverse dependence, just as Aristotle himself does in *Categoriae* 12. Sometimes, however, such a dependence does come into relief, for we occasionally make use of the fact of a 'semantic commitment'. Person A may have to explain to person B that if he does not want to break his promise he *has to do* what he promised to do, he cannot bona fide regard the matter as still open. The same is true for telling the truth or taking an oath; in these cases there is a *bind* because the person has made a commitment and it avails him nothing to try to maintain that there is no connection between words and facts, or that truths do not imply actions. The assumption of definite truth-values is just such a bind. The attempt to avoid the problem of future contingency by changing to timeless propositions and timeless

---

[40] It seems as if Aristotle wants to point his finger to the dilemma: that the determinist argument *starts out* with a relative logical necessity but leaves the reader with a free-floating (temporally unlimited) one.

truth may seem like an easy way out of the whole difficulty. It is all too easy because it eliminates meaningful predictions and promises alongside with a genuinely open future. More about this will be said in what follows.

## II The consequences of determinism

The lengthy discussion in the middle of chapter 9 (18b26–19a23) points out the dire consequences of the determinist arguments.[41] Some of the problems that later dominated the discussion of determinism (like freedom of the will) are here only indicated (cf. 18b31–3). Other questions like the concepts of fate, providence, or determinism in nature are not discussed at all. Aristotle's concern is here mainly the theoretical problem of the compatibility of contingency with fixed truth-values. Since chapter 9 as a whole is staged as a *reductio ad absurdum* the theoretical (practical) consequences are pointed out in detail.

That the decision about 'future truth' affects the existence of the class of the contingent as a whole is not only indicated by Aristotle's repetition of the condition of the problem in 18b26–31 and the summary (cf. 19a9, 'and in general', *holōs*) but also by his painstaking definition of contingency:

> For we see that what will be has an origin both in deliberation and in action, and that, in general, in things that are not always actual there is the possibility of being and of not being; and, consequently, both coming to be and not coming to be. (19a9–11)

This definition is exemplified with the case of a coat where there is the possibility that it will be cut up but also the possibility that it will be worn out (19a12–16). Aristotle then indicates that nothing hinges on the particular conditions of

---

[41] I have left the section 18b17-25 out of the discussion since it poses textual problems unrelated to the rest of the chapter. I have made suggestions concerning the Greek text of this part in *Seeschlacht* 85-9. It is clearly out of place, since it supplements the determinist argument by showing that for future contingents it also cannot be the case that both propositions are *false*. Aristotle, perhaps misleadingly, uses the expression 'neither is true—that it neither will be nor will not be so' (18b18). But *Cat.* 10. 13b21 ff uses the same phrase to express that both are false, and *de Int.* 4. 17a4 and *Cat.* 10. 13b6 suggest that for 'neither true nor false' we should expect the expression '*oute alēthes oute pseudes*', or '*oudeteron oute alēthes oute pseudes*'—against Strang (452-4) and Hintikka (465).

the example; for the conclusion is quite general: the whole realm of the contingent would be eliminated if such propositions were true or false (19a16–22).

So it is the same with all other events that are spoken of in terms of this kind of possibility. Clearly, therefore, not everything is or happens of necessity: some things happen as chance has it, and of the affirmation and the negation neither is true rather than the other; with other things it is one rather than the other and as a rule, but still it is possible for the other to happen.

The fact that the notion of the contingent, and of generation in general, are referred to, and precise conditions are indicated shows that Aristotle takes the commitment of future truth very seriously and that he does not see it as a logical problem only.

We should at this point take a step back and ask ourselves whether, regardless of Aristotle's position, the assumption of fixed truth-values does imply the certainty of the respective facts. This question has been discussed by various logicians— and has been answered in quite diverging ways. It is, for example, almost comic to see the three Polish logicians (in the articles contained in the *Polish Review*, XIII) Kotarbinski, Lesniewski, and Lukasiewicz disagreeing with one another, each one expressing the firm conviction that future truth does or does not have deterministic implications (the score is 2 : 1 in favour of Aristotle). Lukasiewicz, the father of multivalued logic, is quite explicit about the reason for such divergence by insisting that we ultimately have to resort to our *intuitions* in this question (cf. 48, 49, 51, 58: 'We have accepted the assumption a) [sc. PB] on entirely intuitive grounds') and reached the conclusion that 'Since it [PB] is a fundamental law it cannot be proved. One can only believe in it and only a person who thinks it is evident will believe in it. I myself do not think it is evident' (60).

Are we, then, confined to exchange intuitions, putting up flags that show whether we are adherents of the *'therizōn logos'* or not, that is, 'mowers' or 'anti-mowers'? A closer look at the discussion of present-day tense-logic would reveal that our predicament is not that bad even if not all problems have been solved. As Prior expressed himself: 'The formation-rules of the calculus of tenses are not only a prelude to deduction but a stop to metaphysical superstition.' Especially *von Wright* has worked out a careful analysis and an evaluation of the problem of future truth that clarifies the issue and can help us to 'shape up' our intuitions. I can only indicate here what seems to me most relevant to our discussion. What concerns us most is the question of the 'binding-force' of the truth-value. As von Wright points out in his article 'Determinismus, Wahrheit und Zeitlichkeit',[42] there are two main issues that need to be clarified: (1) our conception of the nature of time, especially the future, and (2) the relationship of truth to time.

(1) Concerning the future we have to make one major decision: whether we assume that it is an open tree-like topological system or whether we see it as a closed linear system in the same way as the past and present.[43] To be able to point out the most important difference von Wright modifies the axioms of classical modal logic to accommodate the logic 'of the past' and 'the future', the logic of 'tomorrow' and 'yesterday' (cf. 167 ff). The difference between (*a*) an open tree-like future (that allows for genuine contingency) and (*b*) a linear one (where necessity and possibility coincide because there is always just one possibility) is that we can maintain LEM in (*a*) only in a non-distributive sense, that is, (if $N$ stands for 'it is true already today that') $N\ (p\ v \sim p)$ but not, as in (*b*), $Np\ v\ N \sim p$. This does not mean, however, as von Wright explains, that logic can help to demonstrate determinism; determinism is already presupposed when we chose (*b*) rather than (*a*). A determinist argument that is based on the move from (*a*) to (*b*) would therefore be based on a *petitio principii* (174).

(2) What imports determinism, as the formalizations show, is the *temporalized* concept of truth, that is, $N$ = 'it is true already today that . . .'. There is no need to accept this

---

[42] The application of the relevant distinctions to Aristotle's Sea-Battle is further discussed in his later article 'Time, Truth and Necessity'.

[43] What different choice there is concerning the notion of *time* can be seen in the articles by Thomason, Jeffrey, and Burgess. Jeffrey introduces two different operators, $F$ and $P$, to make the distinction between what is and what is not predetermined, i.e. a baldly factual '$F\ p = finally\ p$' and a non-modal '$I\ p = ineluctably\ p$' (253).

semantic notion; we may just as well presuppose a *timeless* meaning of truth, where 'it is true that there will be a sea-battle tomorrow' means no more than 'there will be a sea-battle tomorrow'. As von Wright points out, in the case of 'timeless' or 'atemporal' truth (later in *Time, Truth, and Necessity* he calls it 'plain' truth (246)) the inclusion of the truth-factor is redundant; this is not so when the *temporalized* truth-value as in (*b*) is presupposed since there 'is true already today' implies certainty. This certainty is neither epistemic nor derived on the basis of logic but imported with the semantic interpretation of truth that ties it to a *linear* future. If we make the distinctions that von Wright suggests we will not have 'to drive a wedge' between LEM and PB in Lukasiewicz's sense or to resort to ultimate beliefs and intuitions.[44]

Is this a solution Aristotle could have envisaged? Von Wright thinks that it is possible that Aristotle may have been confused since he did not see the distinction between temporal and atemporal truth (177–8). My suspicion is that even though that may be true, Aristotle was quite aware of the *petitio* but thought the deterministic implications inevitable—for genuine singular propositions about the future. For it is *senseless* to make such predictions and to call them true or false if one does not commit oneself to what one says. What sense does it make if I make a prediction about a contingent fact in the future such as 'There will be a sea-battle in the Persian Gulf tomorrow, and this is true in the plain sense but it is quite open and there may not be a sea-battle?' Without wanting to turn Aristotle into an ordinary-language philosopher, I assume that for him we have to choose between a commitment or 'idle talk'.

To return to Aristotle: though the determinist argument itself is based on logico-semantical considerations it has metaphysical consequences. The problem that chapter 9

---

[44] To judge from the two unpublished papers mentioned in the bibliography that are part of a larger project that deals with problems of time and necessity von Wright seems to have arrived at a much more differentiated picture on the basis of the distinction between temporalized and atemporal truth in terms of synchronic and diachronic modalities and an appropriate limitation of the validity of LEM and PB. I do not feel authorized or qualified to discuss these questions any further here, however.

continues to present to the student of Aristotle, that is how the truth of a statement can affect the existence of facts, has to be seen on that background: certain laws Aristotle adopted in one part of his philosophy, in this case that every proposition (if properly formulated) is either true or false, do not fit certain tenets in another part, in this case that there are cases of genuine two-sided possibility which are not predetermined one way or another.[45] The result is that the Aristotelian can admit that e.g. it is true that your prediction that my coat will be cut up does not bring its destruction about; the scissors do that. Yet my spiteful hanging on to it 'makes' your prediction wrong; just as your prediction 'made' me hold on to it.

We now have to take a closer look at the concept of contingency in Aristotle. The relatively elaborate way in which Aristotle goes into the question why future truth and contingency are not compatible relies on a specific concept of the contingent—'so it is with all other events (*genesis*, 19a17) that are spoken of in terms of this kind of possibility'. Concerning 'this kind of possibility' Anscombe claims that 'We have here the starting-point for the development of Aristotle's notion of potentiality' (6). I do not find this explanation plausible, since our chapter seems to presuppose the rather differentiated notion of contingency we find discussed in *Met.* Θ.[46] We cannot go into a discussion of the whole conception of *dunamis* and *energeia* here but will just take a look at the criteria for the distinction of the contingent which affects 'future truth'.

Of the various characteristics in *Metaphysica* Θ the one in Θ. 8. 1050b8 is especially relevant, namely that every potentiality is 'at the same time of opposites' (*pasa dunamis hama tēs antiphaseōs estin*). In this way the truly contingent differs from what is possible in a different sense, that is, the one-sided

---

[45] When discussing contingency Aristotle usually discusses chance and what happens spontaneously, i.e. rare exceptions of the regular course things take. This seems to be due to Aristotle's conception of science. That the class of what is ('quantum in se est') not predetermined one way or another is *vast* does not become apparent. When Aristotle discusses the notion of *dunamis* and *energeia*, however, it is clear that the world is full of unrealized possibilities at any moment, see esp. *Met.* Θ. 1047a17 ff.

[46] See esp. *Met.* Θ. 1050b10-12 and *de Int.* 9. 19a9-11.

possibility of what always is or always is the way it is when it is (Θ. 8. 1050b10-12). This distinction not only plays an important role in Aristotle's *physical* writings (e.g. as an explanation of the eternity of the circular motion of the heavenly bodies, as in *Met.* Θ. 8; or, on the other hand why everything that comes to be must perish again (*Cael.* I. 11-12)), but also in the writings dealing with problems of logic: in *de Interpretatione* 12 and 13 Aristotle tries to work out the distinction between one- and two-sided possibility by establishing the logical equivalences of all modal functors. One  and two-sided possibility have in common that the corresponding fact/event is *not impossible*; while the contingent (two-sided possible) in addition is not *necessary*.[47]

As it is easy to see, the one-sided possibility poses no problem with 'future truth' since the event in question is necessary anyway; while in the case of two-sided possibility there is not just a metaphysical (or physical) problem but a logical one as well. As Aristotle stipulates in *Analytica Priora* (A. 13. 32b18-20; cf. *Met.* Θ. 3. 1047a24: 'Something is possible if it is not necessary and nothing impossible results from the assumption that it is the case.' The circumspect description for 'not impossible' indicates that quite different cases can fall under it. Something may be impossible because there is a conceptual incompatibility as in the concept of 'married bachelor': something may be impossible because one can demonstrate a contradiction, as in the case of the incommensurability of the diagonal (cf. *Cael.* I. 12.281b6; *Met.* Θ. 4; *Physica* (*Phys.*) H. 242b72; *et al*); and something may be impossible because external conditions make it impossible as in the case of the combustibility of a piece of wood at the bottom of the sea.[48]

---

[47] The distinction between one- and two-sided possibility has caused some problems for Aristotle, as can be seen in *de Int.* 12 and 13. Aristotle gets into difficulties there with his table of contradictory modal affirmations and negations (22a14 ff). He starts out with the two-sided possibility but then corrects it and uses one-sided possibility. It is hard to say whether Aristotle saw what the difficulty he incurs is: that 'neither necessary nor impossible' is a complex expression that cannot be negated in a simple way (see *An. Pr.* I. 3 and 13).

[48] That Aristotle would call this kind of event 'impossible' (*adunaton*) is claimed by Alexander (*in A. Pr.* 184. 10 ff) who makes use of this example to distinguish between the Aristotelian, Diodorean, and Philonean concept of

The case of future truth must present for Aristotle just such an impossibility. Now, in the case of my coat it is clear that there is no conceptual incompatibility in its being cut up nor is there any factual definite impediment that stands in the way. If we assume the truth of the proposition that the coat is going to be cut up this contradicts the assumption that it *will* be worn out. There is then a genuine impossibility. This very *reductio* is carried out by Aristotle in *de Caelo* I. 12 at great length to show the incompatibility of omnitemporality and the possibility of generation and destruction. Alexander of Aphrodisias also refers to this proof: if on the basis of the assumption that [*p*] is true the possibility of *not-p* is maintained and the truth of ∼[*p*] assumed also, the affirmation and denial will be true at the same time (cf. *Quaest.* I. 4. 13. 2–8).

It is, of course, not obvious whether Aristotle had this kind of *reductio* in mind in *de Interpretatione* 9. The text favours such an explanation, however, because it makes intelligible why Aristotle keeps repeating that both possibilities must remain *open*. In addition, there is at least one passage in *Metaphysica* Θ where Aristotle seems to prescribe quite generally that it cannot be maintained that something is contingent but will not be the case (1047b4).[49] Though the context is somewhat different there we can assume that Aristotle finds it illegitimate to say of *whatever* kind of events (including particular contingent ones) that 'this is possible but it will not be the case'; the expression 'this' (*todi*) seems to be quite neutral and the case of *de Interpretatione* 9 'this coat' (*touti to himation*, 19a12) seems to fit into that category very well. Once a particular event is taken to be certain the opposite possibility is no longer open

possibility. For further discussion see my article 'The Dramatization of Determinism'.

[49] The text at *Met.* Θ. 4 seems somewhat corrupt, but it is clear that Aristotle is fending off the Megarian concept of possibility. His remarks need not be restricted to *types* of events but can, as in ch 9, include particular events. The battle about the *kurieuon logos* deals extensively with *futura* and the definitions of the Stoic modals contained references to what 'is and/or will be'. Cicero, *de Fato* 13: 'Ille autem [sc. Diodorus] id solum fieri posse dicit, quod aut sit verum aut futurum sit verum . . . Tu autem [sc. Chrysippus] et quae non sint futura, posse fieri dicis'; cf. *Seeschlacht* 99 ff.

but has become an impossibility in the sense indicated in *Metaphysica* Δ. 4. 1015a35.

Since only future events are 'open' possibilities it would certainly not do for Aristotle to make the whole problem of future truth disappear by transforming all statements in the future tense into dated propositions in a timeless present, according to Quine's suggestion,[50] as, for example, in 'coat A is cut up on 18 July 1988'. Not only will there be no formal distinction between present, past, and future propositions; there will also be no distinction between the respective *events*. This may be a welcome solution for someone who holds that there is no need of any distinction because the future is just as full of facts as the present and past.[51] But Aristotle would not have accepted that and need not: the logical-semantical difficulties incurred are evidently not sufficient to compel him to do so; he would have regarded the undesirable consequences from such a solution as incompatible with his physics and metaphysics and therefore rejected such transformations.

While up to 19a18 Aristotle's explanation why and in what sense contingency must be preserved is clear and supported by other Aristotelian texts the passage that concludes the second part of chapter 9 (19a18–22) presents us with various problems:

> Clearly, therefore, not everything is or happens of necessity: some things happen as chance has it, and of the affirmation and the negation neither is *true rather than the other*; with other things it is one rather than the other and as a rule but still it is possible for the other instead.

Why does Aristotle all of a sudden discuss differences among the various kinds of contingent events while up to now no such distinctions had been made? It seemed, after all, that the problem of future truth would apply to all kinds since the logical qualification (neither necessary nor impossible)

---

[50] Cf. W. V. O. Quine, *Elementary Logic* (Boston, 1941), 6; the idea that dated propositions are the solution to the problem has been accepted by many philosophers. Tense-logic has argued against this levelling out of the temporal distinctions.

[51] This position has been taken by D. C. Williams, it is one of the main issues in the Williams–Linsky debate. Cf. also the criticism ventured by Schick against Shackles and his 'book of history' (225).

itself is what creates the difficulty of 'future truth'. So far no mention has been made of any import of the kind of *causal* determination which might be at work in the different kinds of contingent events. Ackrill therefore rightly points out that the distinction between what happens for the most part, as often as not, or by chance, cannot have an impact here (loc. cit., 136). For in all cases the necessity derived from PB must be the same. In addition, the qualification added here between what is 'true rather' and what is not is difficult to understand. Is there a difference in the *degree* of truth?[52]

The Greek phrase '*mallon alethēs*' that Ackrill rendered as 'true rather' can have at least two meanings. It could mean (*a*) that there are different degrees of truth, that is, we would then here have at least an indication that Aristotle contemplated something like a many-valued logic. The expression can also be meant in a loose sense (*b*) that it is *more likely* in one case than in another that a proposition is (will be) true. Interesting as it would be to find traces of a many valued logic in Aristotle, it does not seem to be plausible. I have found the phrase 'more true' only in four places at two of which he reports some other philosopher's opinion (cf. *Met.* Γ. 5. 1009b10, K. 5. 1062a24), at the other clearly no 'degrees of truth' are meant but what we render by the colloquial phrase that something is 'closer to truth' or, the opposite, even 'further away from the truth'.[53] It should also be noted that such an interpretation would have to meet the main difficulty for the traditional interpretation with much less ground to stand on, namely that Aristotle, apart from chapter 9, insists on the validity of both LEM and PB (esp. *Met.* Γ. 7). We will have to come back to this question later.

If, on the other hand, (*b*) Aristotle is just trying to establish an analogy between the *probability* of the realization of an event and the *likeliness* of the truth of the correspondent proposition in the future then it is easy to see why Aristotle resorts to the phrase 'true rather': it is the analogue to the

---

[52] On the 'statistical' interpretation cf. Fine 34; Waterlow 107–8.

[53] Since Aristotle attributes *mallon* (more) both to facts and to propositions it is very difficult to give a precise meaning to it (18b9, 19a19, a33). The meaning of 'rather this than that' must vary depending on the subject matter. If types of events are meant the statistical, 'more often' is more appropriate, with particulars 'more likely'.

qualification Aristotle had used in 18b9 for the kinds of *things* that happen 'not this way rather than the other' (*ouden mallon houtōs ē mē houtōs* . . .). So what is said here, then, is that there is no greater *likeliness* that a proposition will be true than that it will not. Since Aristotle in the next sentence in (19a20-1) switches back to talk about the *event* in question (as far as one can see from his somewhat loose way of speaking),[54] it does not seem to matter much to him whether the 'more likely' refers to the events or to the propositions.

This does not, however, answer the question why Aristotle distinguishes between the *probability* of the different kinds of future contingent events. Since he later on in his 'solution' at a crucial point refers back to this distinction (19a38-9), it is important to find an explanation for this use here.

Two observations are helpful at this point.

(1) In all places where we find the expression 'more likely' Aristotle does not speak of particular future contingent events but of the different *classes* of such events (and the characteristics of these classes) and their relative frequency (here the statistics are quite in order) thereby reinstalling what had been refuted in the determinist argument (18b5-9).[55]

(2) Up to 19a18 only *two* kinds of contingent events have been mentioned, the case where the chances are not greater one way or the other (*hopoter' etuchen*) and what happens by chance (*apo tuchēs*) or rarely (cf. 18b5-9, b15-16, b24, b29-30). But in 19a20-1 Aristotle all of a sudden includes 'what happens for the most part and as a rule' (*hōs epi to polu*), and to this kind he seems to refer again in the formula that sums up the result of the discussion in 19a38-9.

That Aristotle did not mention the events that happen 'as a rule' earlier in the determinist argument can be explained by the special status they usually have in Aristotle, that is, that they are considered as 'almost necessary'. In fact, often

---

[54] On Aristotle's loose way of switching between propositions and facts see Ross ad loc *Met.* Θ. 10. 1051b23: 'Aristotle's carelessness of language has made his meaning seem more obscure than it really is' (ii, 278).

[55] About this kind of necessity I have said more in my article in the forthcoming Festschrift for D. Balme, *Aristotle on the Limits of Determinism.*

they are subsumed under that class without any difficulties since *a fortiori* what happens of necessity happens for the most part and if there were no rare exceptions such events would not differ from what is necessary at all.[56] This affinity to what is necessary unqualifiedly usually allows Aristotle to group them together and contrast this group with what happens 'accidentally and as chance has it'. Only of the former can there be any science, the latter are, as the name already indicates, incompatible with what happens of necessity and cannot be used as premisses in the scientific syllogism. In the context of chapter 9, however, the almost-necessity is not enough; as long as there is even a faint chance of an irregularity in nature or of an interference in human actions a prediction of such an event cannot (yet?) be true or false, otherwise an impossibility would result in case the unexpected should come about. The addition of a reference to what happens most of the time is then *not* a further argument against the deterministic conclusions, as one might feel tempted to infer from the connecting particles at the beginning of the sentence, 'Clearly, therefore, not everything happens of necessity . . .', but an expansion and clarification of what the realm of the contingent includes.[57]

*G. Fine* regards the distinction between what happens for the most part, what happens either way and what happens by chance as the main point (besides the logic lesson that starts in 19a23) that Aristotle is trying to make to refute determinism. As indicated earlier she does not acknowledge any asymmetry between past, present, and future in *de Interpretatione* 9 and does not see 'future truth' as the central issue either (cf. 24, 34). I find this suggestion highly implausible because it presupposes the existence of a very dumb determinist who denies the difference in the relative frequency of events. Nor would a not so dumb determinist who does acknowledge the difference give up the claim that even the rare occurrences are necessary. The Megarians, Aristotle's most likely opponents

[56] Cf. *Met.* Δ. 30. 1025a15, 20; *Phys.* 196b11 ff; *An. Pr.* 25b4, 32b10, 43b33–6; *An. Po.* 79a21, 87b22, *et passim.*

[57] There is a tension in Aristotle's attitude towards necessity and regularity. The scientist Aristotle pleads for as much necessity and regularity as possible, the logician recognizes the need for the notion of the contingent, and the moralist wants as much freedom as possible.

in questions of determinism, are dealt with on quite different grounds in *Metaphysica* Θ. 3 and 4.

### III  Aristotle's solution of the problem of future truth

The interpretation favoured by me so far is, as I stated at the beginning, only 'a likely story'. The only kind of confirmation we can hope for must come from a careful scrutiny of Aristotle's own solution as envisaged in 19a23-39. Unfortunately the last part of our chapter presents us with as many difficulties as the first one, so we cannot expect absolute certainty but will, again, have to be satisfied with a high degree of plausibility. What makes the task easier is the fact that the 'solution' consists of three clearly recognizably different steps so one can treat them separately and then decide what 'progress' is made in the sequence:

(1) 19a23-7:  Aristotle distinguishes between things that are *unqualifiedly* and things that are only *conditionally necessary*.

(2) 19a27-32: This distinction supposedly also applies to the *contradictory possibilities*.

(3) 19a32-9:  It is decided what consequences should be drawn from (1) and (2) concerning the validity of the *principle of bivalence*.

We will follow the text step by step to see what is the most likely interpretation.

(1) 19a23-7: What is, necessarily is when it is; and what is not necessarily is not, when it is not. But not everything that is, necessarily is; and not everything that is not, necessarily is not. For to say that everything that is, is of necessity, when it is, is not the same as saying unconditionally that it is of necessity. Similarly with what is not.

At first sight it might seem as if Aristotle addresses himself to the same question we have looked at in the discussion of the first determinist argument, that is, whether Aristotle tries to warn us from somehow falsely attributing the necessity functor of the implication $N(p \rightarrow p)$ to its consequence $p \rightarrow Np$. This, however, is not quite what the first argument did start with. Whether we take the strong or the weak version, the initial implication established a relationship between the *truth* or falsity of propositions and the corresponding *facts*

$N(T[p] \to p)$ or $T[p] \to Np$, while here Aristotle decidedly and conspicuously speaks of *onta*, of what exists; the question of truth comes in only in step (3). That he has *some* kind of distinction between relative and absolute necessity in mind is agreed by most interpreters.[58] As the traditional interpretation has it, the distinction is between 'temporary' (at the time *when* something is) and absolute necessity.

Some comment on 'temporal necessity' is now due.[59] What is meant is *not* the necessity of paying my rent on the first day of every month or that New Year's Eve is 31 December. It is rather the 'Nixonism' (Burgess, 567) that at a 'point of time' (cf. *Cael.* 283a11 *'epi tōde tō semeiō'*), given the situation, that is, external and internal circumstances (which in the case of Watergate included the given ethical standards and political practices), something is inevitable. Such temporal modality is at stake in the debate about the Megarian concept of possibility (cf. *Met.* Θ. 3-4), that is, whether something is possible only when it actually exists.

In 19a23, on the other hand it has to be admitted, there is also the possibility that the conditional (*hotan*) does not carry its usual temporal sense but that, rather, the mistake Aristotle is trying to warn us of is the one of *logically* inferring that if something is the case then it is necessary. Ackrill is, on the whole, more in favour of the traditional interpretation but cautions that the temporal conditionals (*hotan*, 19a23; *hote*, a26) may be used in a non-temporal sense just as the corresponding 'not already' (*ēdē*) in the conclusion may be (141).

In my monograph I have argued that the most plausible assumption is that Aristotle does have the temporal interpretation in mind and I still think it is the most natural and likely one (cf. 65-6). But Fine has ridden a spirited attack against this claim and tried to argue that the whole last section contains a lecture on logic and how to avoid basic

[58] Ackrill gives a very concise summary of the two most likely general approaches to the 'solution' (139-42). The traditional interpretation largely takes his second line. I do not share some of Ackrill's scruples and think one does not have to attribute any confusion to Aristotle.

[59] 'Temporal' necessity is sometimes also used in the discussion of Aristotle to denote that something must come about at *some* point of time or other (cf. *Cael.* I. 12 *et al*).

mistakes therein, and she refers to other distinguished scholars who share her iconoclastic views.[60] So I came to realize that expressing confidence is not enough at this point. I can only put in a nutshell what speaks against Fine's claim that only the mistake of *distribution* of the necessity functor is at stake here. It is (*a*) the language and (*b*) the context.[61]

(*a*) It is true that the conditional in 19a23 'when/whenever' (*hotan*) is used very often by Aristotle in a non-temporal sense. But the same is not true of 'when' (*hote*) in 19a26. At the three passages to which Fine refers to support her claim it is much more natural to read '*hote*' in the temporal sense than in the logical sense, and, worse, no necessity is even mentioned (neither *consequentiae* nor *consequentis*).[62] Furthermore, if Aristotle had wanted to teach us some elementary logic he would have used the normal terminology with 'obtains' or 'does not obtain', that is, *huparchein ē mē huparchein*, as he had done earlier in the *de Interpretatione* (cf. 5. 17a24, 6. 17a26 ff, b2) and still does at the beginning

---

[60] Fine mentions unpublished papers by T. Penner and A. Code (40 n 1).

[61] Without being able to go into the details I just find it not plausible that the lengthy middle part is supposed to establish merely the tripartite distinction between everlasting, chance, and usual things (34). That distinction is certainly *presupposed* but the goal is to show what consequences for the future contingents we should envisage.

[62] Fine, 24-7 and n 10-14, 31 and n 18. In *An. Pr.* 34a14 Aristotle explains that 'what has come to pass, once it has come to pass, is' (*to gar gegonos, hote gegonen, estin*). The temporal meaning of *hote* is most likely, especially since the temporal condition of possibility is discussed three lines earlier. In *Cael.* I. 12. 281b16 Aristotle explains why it is the case that though one possesses at the same time (*hama*) the capability to stand and sit one cannot sit and stand at the same time. There is clearly no *logical* implication or simultaneity at stake: 'when he has the one (capacity) he has the other (*hoti hote echei ekeinēn, kai tēn heteran*) but not so that he can sit and stand at the same time but at a different time'. The whole chapter *Cael.* I. 12 deals with the question of the temporal conditions for the realization of *dunameis* (i.e. generability and destructibility). At the end, in a passage Fine seems to have overlooked, the 'temporal restriction' is repeated, this time unequivocally—'it will later also have the ability not to be, except not not-to-be at the time when it is (*plen ou tote mē einai hote estin*)'—and Aristotle makes it clear why there is a necessity—'*huparchei gar energeia on*' (283b8-11). In *Sophistici Elenchi* (*SE*) 166a23-31 we have the same example as in *Cael.* and the same point is made, i.e. that the two possibilities cannot be realized at the same time, in *SE* 166a3 Aristotle explains 'that someone who is sick does or suffers something does not mean *one thing* but that at one point (*hote men*) that 'he who is sick now', at another (*hote de*) that 'he who was sick earlier'. The claim that at all of these passages the *necessitas consequentiae* is what is at stake must be due to some disarray in Fine's *Zettel*.

of chapter 9 (18a35, 18a38–b3) as long as the mere logical mutual implications between truth and fact are under discussion.[63] The language changes significantly in chapter 9, when Aristotle discusses the ontological consequences of determinism on what is or comes to be.[64] The same language remains in use throughout the final argument. It sounds very odd (even if it is not impossible) to translate 19a23 '*To men oun einai to on hotan ē*' by 'That what is is *whenever* it is . . .' as if there were recurrent *onta* under discussion (cf. Fine, 24).

(*b*) The context and the continuity of Aristotle's arguments seem to make it very improbable that, as Fine claims, *no asymmetry* between present, past, and future is maintained and that no special treatment is given to future contingents. Even if we leave out the introductory period of chapter 9 with reference to which she expresses some discomfort (I would find it *very* difficult to disregard it as *the* exposition of the basic question in ch 9), all the examples seem to be chosen to illustrate the problem of the truth of contingent statements about the future (cf. 18b35; also the coat, 19a13; and, not to forget, of course, the sea-battle tomorrow, 19a28).[65]

It seems to me, then, that it is not likely that Aristotle in 19a23 is warning against committing a simple logical mistake which, according to what was said earlier, is not even contained in the determinist argument. For Aristotle's solution according to Fine would, thus, start with a refutation of a faulty position only a bad logician and/or an over-eager determinist would hold. Aristotle's enlightenment about the

---

[63] The only exception is 18b17–25; but as said above, it properly (if at all) belongs in the determinist argument.

[64] Even though both future being *and* becoming are the subject-matter of future truth, the emphasis is on *genesis*, cf. 18b8, 14, and 15, 30 ff, 19a3–6; '*hōste kai epi tōn allōn genese ōn, hosai kata dunamin tēn toiautēn . . .*' (19a17).

[65] I do not understand why Fine (42–3 n 18) claims that the traditional interpretation needs to presuppose the 'necessity of the past' and that *gegonos* would be appropriate to express that. Aristotle speaks from the beginning to the end in very general terms of what is and has come to be, of '*epi tōn ontōn kai genomenōn*', cf. 18a30; *genesthai*, *huparchein*, esp. 19a1–5, '*gegonos*' would be rather unusual in that context (that is why Aristotle explains in *An. Pr.* 34a12 that it *is*, too!). In addition: a failure to use an expression cannot militate against anything (43 n 18).

simple logical mistake, it has to be added, would be unduly
elaborate, for he would say the same things twice over: it is
necessary that everything that exists exists (and what does
not exist does not exist) but not everything that exists is
necessary (nor is what does not exist necessarily not), for it is
not the same that everything that exists is necessary when it
is and that it is unqualifiedly necessary.

The elaborateness makes sense, however, if more is implied
than just that p does not imply that necessarily p. If, by
contrast, we respect the *temporal* conditional, the second
sentence unfolds what is merely indicated in the first one:
that is, that once something has come to be it exists necessarily (the *'ex anankēs'*, 19a25-6, incidentally, modifies
*exists* and not the implication as a whole). That there is
something like a *factual* necessity according to Aristotle has
been argued above and is also attested elsewhere; what makes
an event necessary when it comes about is the concurrence of
potentialities as described by Aristotle in *Metaphysica* Θ.
5. 1047b35 ff (cf. also *Cael.* 283b8-11). If there is an ambiguity
in *de Interpretatione* 9 this is due to the fact that the determinist argument in 18a34-b16 has left entirely open *how* the
event comes about, it just requires that it should.[66]

But, so we have to ask ourselves, why does Aristotle make
this elaborate distinction between conditional and uncon-
ditional necessity here? It does not seem to be yet another
refutation of the determinist; that refutation has been ended
with fanfare in 19a18-22 ('so it is clear that not everything is
or comes about of necessity . . .'). It seems to me that in
19a23 Aristotle wants to clarify what has to be modified and
what is left intact—in what sense 'necessity' has been refuted
and in what sense even contingent events are, nevertheless,
necessary, namely once they come to be. The reason why
Aristotle introduces the temporary qualification of necessity
at the beginning of his own solution becomes clear once the
solution is unfolded: that is, that the PB must be adaptable
to the *ontological status* of the particular kinds of events.

[66] *How* events come about is indicated in *Met.* Θ. 5 (where Aristotle describes
that the active and passive *dunamis* 'get together' and then (with a nice temporal
*'hotan'* 1048a6!) interact. Aristotle is remarkably uninterested in describing how
processes actually work. This accounts for some of our uncertainty as to what
kind of determinism we should ascribe to him.

This is what the very last sentence of chapter 9 confirms 'For what holds for things that are does not hold for things that are not but may possibly be or not be'.

What application does Aristotle make of the 'temporal' (it should better be called 'eventual')[67] restriction of necessity in what follows in step (2) for the members of a contradictory disjunction? At first sight it seems, none! Let us take a closer look:

(2) 19a28-32: And the same account holds for contradictories: everything necessarily is or is not, or will be or will not be; but one cannot divide and say that one or the other is necessary. I mean, for example: it is necessary for there to be a sea-battle tomorrow; but it is not necessary for a sea-battle to take place tomorrow, nor for one not to take place—though it is necessary for one to take place or not to take place.

Since earlier in the chapter there had been at least an ambiguity with regard to the kind of necessity that Aristotle wants to attribute to the disjunction '$p \ v \sim p$', the 'friends of a logic-lesson' in step (1) have argued that he now wants to point out that there is yet another logical fallacy to be avoided. As has been seen by other interpreters too, however, this is not, as the introduction of step (2) lets one expect, the 'same account' (*ho autos logos* 19a27-8) at all. And all the philosophical subtlety one can try to throw into the battle here does not seem sufficient to justify the claim that the mistake in the implication in step (1), that is, $p \rightarrow Np$, and the mistake in the distribution in the disjunction in step (2), that is, $N(p \ v \sim p) \rightarrow N p \ v \ N \sim p$, could both be called 'mistakes of distribution'.[68]

What, on the other hand, can be said to be the same '*logos*' if one tries to justify the 'temporary necessity'-thesis? I do not think there is any need to ascribe a possible confusion to Aristotle at this point, as Ackrill seems to think.[69] One just

---

[67] Cf. 'The Dramatization . . .', 286 'omne quod fit quando fit necesse est fieri'.

[68] 'The misplacing of the operator' seems to me not at all similar, especially since Aristotle almost certainly did not use our kind of notations; cf. Fine, 30-1, 43-4 n 23. Fine speaks of 'distribution' (of necessity functors) but that is hardly what Aristotle means by 'dividing'. For such division (splitting up the conjunction) see *Met*. E. 4. 1027b20 '*merismos antiphaseōs*'.

[69] Cf. Ackrill, 138.

has to take Aristotle's words literally here, and to respect the *ontological status* of each of the members of the disjunctions, that is, to take into account whether they are of the absolutely necessary or the contingent kind of *onta* that are necessary only when they come about. (That Aristotle is concerned here with the *events* and not the contradictory propositions, in spite of the word 'antiphasis' (19a27) is clear and has been granted by most interpreters.) But why, then, does Aristotle stress that the law of excluded middle is effective nevertheless and introduce the famous example of the sea-battle to point out that though the antithesis is necessary, the distribution of the necessity is wrong, that is, that: $N (p \, v \sim p)$, but not: $N p \, v \, N \sim p$?

I do not deny that Aristotle warns us not to make that kind of mistake, I just want to claim that this is not what Aristotle is really concerned with. We, rather, have to make the application of the differentiation prescribed in step (1) in the cause of an antithesis ourselves! That is to say, we must not regard one of the members (the one we take to be or become real) as absolutely necessary (and its opposite as impossible) when it is only conditionally necessary. We are advised in this way not because we are bad logicians and tempted to commit logical fallacies, but because we treat what is contingent as if it were determinate. This seems to me to be what Aristotle has in mind when he says that 'one cannot divide and say that one or the other is necessary' (19a29). Is there any justification for the claim that the warning 'one cannot divide' is to be taken in the not-distributive sense?

I have found only one parallel that is close enough (for any interpretation) to be of significance. In *Metaphysica* Γ. 4. 1008a18–22 Aristotle asks whether the extreme Heracliteans would maintain their contradictions only in conjunction, that is, 'something is white and not white', or whether one could take them apart and maintain them separately, that is, that 'something is white' and 'something is not white'. The passage suggests that Aristotle means by 'dividing and calling one taken by itself true' that the complex expression can be split up and each conjunct be called true—not because there is a 'truth-value' that can be distributed over the conjuncts, but for the reasons Aristotle refers to afterwards, that is, that otherwise all subjects would end up being one and the same. I want to claim that the same scheme applies in step (2) in the solution. We should not divide the complex and take one of the alternatives to be unqualifiedly necessary, or to take the other one and take that as unqualifiedly necessary. What remains *intact*, however, is the law of excluded middle, that in each case one or the other has to be the case or not to be the case, or come to be or not come to be. This is also how Ammonius understands step (2) 'We should not divide and by asserting one of the parts of the antiphasis *alone* point out indubitably that it *will* come to be in any way (*pantōs*) or it *will not* come to be'.[70] The alleged 'warning' not to commit a logical mistake is then rather to be understood as yet another clarification of what is and what is not necessary, in *preparation* for the final and last point in the 'solution' of the determinist argument, that is, for the necessary modification of the validity of PB to which we can now turn.

(3) 19a32-9: So, since statements are true according to how the actual things are, it is clear that wherever these are such as to allow of contraries as chance has it, the same necessarily holds for the contradictories also. This happens with things that are not always so or not always not so. With these it is necessary for one or the other of the contradictories to be true or false—not, however, this one or that one but as chance has it; for one to be true *rather* than the other, yet not *already* true or false.

By indicating in what way the limitation of the PB is prepared in steps (1) and (2) I have to some extent anticipated what the result of Aristotle's final solution is going to be: since according to the determinist thesis at the beginning of the chapter the fixed truth-values necessitate the outcome of the respective event, the validity of PB must be modified to accommodate the ontological status of genuine contingent events in the future. That there is a need for accommodation is indicated by Aristotle's claim (19a33) that 'statements are true according to how the things are'. This expression can, however, be understood in at least two ways: Aristotle may have a strong correspondence in mind, namely that the *truth* itself is modified in accordance with the mode of the event

[70] Ammonius, *in de Int.* 154. 33 f.

(that would be the Anscombian version), or a weaker correspondence in the sense that if the facts are definite (for whatever reason) then the truth-values are definite too. I have indicated earlier why I do not find the stronger version likely: it lacks the final confirmation to be expected in line 19a38–9, (regardless whether the 'already' is to be understood temporally or not) the 'necessary' in line 36 simply cannot be extended in such a way that in line 38–9 we could read 'or for one to be true *rather* than the other, yet not already *necessarily* *true* or *necessarily* *false*'. The weaker version is, therefore, much more plausible.

How, precisely, Aristotle wants to modify PB is not easy to pinpoint, since the sentence is ambiguous. The sentence '. . . it is necessary for one or the other of the contradictories to be true or false—not this one or that one . . .' can grammatically mean (*a*) that it is one of the two *propositions* that is true or false but not decidedly one or the other or (*b*) both propositions would be true or false but not decidedly *true* or *false*. According to the traditional interpretation there is no real difference in meaning, but it is clear that the ambiguity aggravates the difficulty of deciding for *any* of the versions suggested. That the limitation of PB to accommodate the facts is Aristotle's solution according to the traditional interpretation, can be seen from Boethius' summary: 'Aristotle does not say that neither is true or false, but that in each one of them, whichever (*quaelibet*) is true or false but not in the definite way, as with what is past or present' (loc. cit., 208. 7 ff).

But why, if Aristotle wants to suspend the validity of PB (temporarily or not), does he express himself in such a way that the reader gets the impression that the truth values hang somehow 'over the heads' of the propositions? There are two explanations that are quite compatible with one another. Aristotle may have in mind that once the outcome in a particular case is inevitable the propositions do become true or false, since the propositions must match the facts (in this case the 'already' in 19a39 *is* to be taken in its temporary sense). Or Aristotle wants to indicate that *in principle*, that is *potentially*, PB is always valid. That this is not just a bad excuse becomes obvious when one thinks of the validity of the law of excluded middle in the case of future contingents.

LEM is also applicable *in principle* but not *in fact* as long as the outcome is open. The case of LEM is just not as obnoxious because its validity clearly is restricted to the time of the event in question. We do not ask ourselves whether it is now the case that there will be or will not be a sea-battle tomorrow.[71] Truth, on the other hand, is omnitemporal, and that causes the whole problem of chapter 9. This would, in short, imply that Aristotle treats PB and LEM on a par, that is, both are suspended in the same way but while LEM is harmless PB is not.

The solution Aristotle provides according to the traditional interpretation has been criticized time and again. The main point of criticism is what has been called by Quine, 'Aristotle's fantasy that "It is true that *p* or *q*" is an insufficient condition for "It is true that *p* or it is true that *q*" '.[72] We have to investigate whether Aristotle deserves this reproach. A closer look will show that the 'fantasy' *is* a misnomer because it is not to be found in our chapter in the way Quine (and others, e.g. M. Kneale) presuppose. For nowhere does Aristotle say that the disjunction—*p* v~*p*—is *true* (nor, incidentally that it is necessarily true). Aristotle in 19a27 asserts only the validity of LEM, that is, the necessity that *p* or *not p*. Nor does Aristotle call the disjunction containing PB true in 19a32-9.

But does not the necessity of the alternative *a fortiori* imply the truth of the antiphasis (19a35), the modern philosopher will ask? We have to take two things into consideration: (*a*) there is no such state of affairs as 'a sea-battle is taking place or a sea-battle is not taking place', that can be described by a true or false affirmation; in fact LEM excludes such 'states of affairs'; (*b*) neither LEM nor PB are propositions for Aristotle since his whole theory is based on—and limited to—the concept of 'assertion', the *logos apophantikos*, in the sense defined in *de Interpretatione* 6. 17a25: 'An affirmation is a statement affirming *something of something*,

---

[71] That is, however, how some determinists did want to treat future events. Cf. D. C. Williams 282 on radical determinism in antiquity.

[72] W. V. O. Quine, 'On a so-called Paradox', *Mind*, LXII (1953), 65. This has been invoked time and again against the traditional position, in spite of Lukasiewicz's protest against the anachronism.

a negation is a statement denying something of something.'[73] The whole of *de Interpretatione* is dedicated to the investigation of the various forms of affirmation and negation. An antiphasis, however, is not called a *logos apophantikos* anywhere. Lukasiewicz has already noted that 'only the Stoics later came to regard disjunctions and implications as propositions and came to realize that there exists a large class of propositions having no subject and no predicate, such as implications, disjunctions and so on' (cf. *Aristotle's Syllogistic*, 132 with reference to Alexander of Aphrodisias, *in An. Pr.* 11. 17).

This limitation is not confined to the *de Interpretatione*. In fact, I have not been able to find a single passage where Aristotle attributes truth to a disjunction or implication. The passage in *de Interpretatione* 8. 18a19 ff, where he calls a conjunction 'true' confirms rather than undermines this claim, for Aristotle points out there that a conjunction is nothing but the sum of two separate *apophantikoi logoi*, no truth-value is attributed to the conjunction as a whole. What then is the status of something like PB or LEM or, still more importantly, of *syllogisms*—are they not *logoi*? That can certainly be admitted, but so is the *Iliad*[74]—and as Aristotle stated earlier in *de Interpretatione* 4. 16b33: 'Every *sentence* is significant . . . but not every sentence is a statement-making sentence, but only those in which there is truth or falsity.' It seems, then, that Quine's reproach does not apply to Aristotle since he does not share our notion of what a proposition is, nor is his logic propositional.

Since Cicero in his *de Fato* ventured the same criticism as Quine against the attempt to limit PB in order to escape the deterministic consequences of 'future truth' he is often referred to as a witness that already in antiquity the faultiness of this solution was recognized. If this was generally recognized, the opponents of the traditional interpretation reason, how can we attribute such a mistake to Aristotle? Cicero

---

[73] I myself have committed the anachronism of using the term 'proposition' for '*apophantikos logos*' most of the time in this paper, mainly because of aesthetic reasons. 'Assertion' and 'statement' did not sound right. The German 'Aussage' is less assertive and stately.

[74] Cf. *Met.* Z. 4. 1030a7–10, H. 6. 1045a12: 'The definition is a *logos* that is one not only through conjunction like the *Iliad* . . .' (*ou sundesmōi hen*).

who, incidentally, does not seem to have known Aristotle's esoteric writings too well,[75] does not direct his criticism against Aristotle but against the Epicureans. Since they were not really interested in technical details of logic itself, it is to be assumed that they 'borrowed' the tools of logic from another school. It is, however, much more likely that they directly responded to the *Stoic* doctrine of universal determinism and simply denied the condition on which the Stoics argument was based.[76] This clearly does not warrant the conclusion that Aristotle already had adopted the same position as the Epicureans did. As Lukasiewicz has maintained, 'he [sc. Aristotle] did not know the logic of propositions which was created after him by the Stoics' (*AS* 205).

I have tried to point out that Aristotle in *de Interpretatione* 9 tries to limit the validity of PB while he asserts LEM (with qualifications, see above). There remains the question how likely such a solution is in view of the doctrine Aristotle maintains elsewhere. In connection with the problem of future truth it is often pointed out that nowhere else does Aristotle limit PB and that especially his rigorous defence of LEM in *Metaphysica* Γ makes it unlikely that he ever envisaged such a restriction. It has to be admitted that already the usual formulation of LEM in Aristotle seems at first sight to indicate that he envisaged no exceptions, that most of the time he does not even clearly distinguish between LEM and PB, since LEM is usually formulated in terms of *propositions*, not *alternatives of states of affairs* (i.e. instead of using 'is the case or not the case (*hyparchei ē mē hyparchei*)' the standard formulation is 'it is necessary to affirm or to deny one thing of another (*anangkē ē phanai ē apophanai*)'. In *Metaphysica* Γ we find only this phrasing of LEM and most of the time it is employed elsewhere, too.[77] The principle of non-contradiction,

---

[75] Cicero in *de Fato* seems unaware of the fact that the determinist argument came from Aristotle. He mentions him only once and counts him among the determinists, together with Heraclitus, Empedocles, and Democritus.

[76] Cicero's *de Fato* presents the struggle between the Epicureans and the Stoics very vividly; see III. 21: 'concedendum sit, fato fieri, quaecumque fiant— si enim alterum utrum ex aeternitate verum sit, esse id etiam certum, et si certum necessarium: ita et necessitatem et fatum confirmari putat.'

[77] Cf. *Met.* Γ. 1012b10, B. 996b26 ff; *SE* 171b3, 172b18, 174b38, 181a38, 181b23; *An. Po.* 71a13, 73b23, 77a22, 77a30, 88b1; *de Int.* 9. 18b27, 12. 21b20,

by contrast, is expressed either in terms of 'to affirm and deny' or in terms of 'to be' or 'to be the case'.[78]

If one studies the background and origin of the phrase *phanai ē apophanai* the impression vanishes that the formulation indicates that LEM and PB up to *de Interpretatione* 9 were really identical' in meaning. The expression 'necessary to affirm or negate' occurs most frequently in the *Sophistici Elenchi*, and from the way it is employed there we can conclude that it expresses the basic rule of the dialectic exercises, that one must either affirm or reject a proposition proferred by the opponent. In several of the passages in *Sophistici Elenchi* there is no question of truth or falsity implied but, rather, instructions are given how to lure the opponent into contradicting himself by making clever use of the fact that he can only *assent or negate* (cf. 171a17-27). Besides the various passages where cunning tricks for such refutations are recommended (cf. 171b18, 174b38, 175b17, 175b23) the rule is also used for more constructive purposes, that is, as a test whether a question has been adequately formulated, to avoid ambiguities etc. It seems that only gradually did this rule of dialectic acquire the meaning and function of the Law of Excluded Middle. This does not mean that LEM was not known or used beforehand, it only means that the formulation 'to affirm or negate' does not already imply the alternative of truth or falsity. Properly formed *assertions* are, of course, true or false. The old connection with the dialectic exercises is, incidentally, still alive in *de Interpretatione* 6. 17a36 '. . . together with all other such conditions that we add to counter the troublesome objections of sophists'.

This leads over to the question why Aristotle in chapter 4 of *de Interpretatione* does not mention any exception when he distinguishes the *apophantikos logos* from all other sentences by its 'possessing truth or falsity' (16b33). This passage is not the only one where Aristotle insists on this, in *Categoriae* 4. 2a8 and 13b2 (cf. *de Int.* 1. 16a11) he also does not envisage any exceptions.

12. 22b12; the expression using *'einai'* or *'genesthai'* I have found only *Phys.* VI. 235b15, *'pan gar anagkē ē einai ē mē einai'*.

[78] Cf. *Met.* Γ. 3. 1005b19, 1006a3, 4. 1008a4, 34, *et al*; cf. *'adunaton hama katēgoreisthai tas antiphaseis'* (1007b18).

The ancient commentators also firmly rely on the doctrine, in fact Alexander of Aphrodisias refers to *de Interpretatione* 4 to justify his definition of the difference between a *protasis* and an *apophansis* (*in An. Pr.* 10. 15 f). It is difficult to say when Aristotle first realized that there was a problem with the future contingents and why he does not mention it elsewhere. The *panacea* of calling a piece of text that does not quite fit into the context (or, worse does not fit according to the adopted interpretation) a later addition should not be used without clear 'medical' indication.

The style and composition of *de Interpretatione* as a whole, however, suggest strongly that at least its first chapters originate from a relatively early time. The distinctions made between noun and verb, their functions in sentences, the introduction of negation, and the study of the opposing assertions, remind one of the *Categoriae* and the also early *Metaphysica* Δ. The sentences are short, and no excursions into further logical or metaphysical questions are to be found. Chapters 10 to 13 continue the investigation of more complex contradictory statements and end with a discussion of the meaning and role of the modal functors in contradictory statements. It seems to be most likely that the *de Interpretatione* was originally written as a preparation for the *Priora Analytica*, as an instruction of how to form proper premisses, and as a study of the parts of speech in general. The original scheme is very simple (cf. chs 1–5) and it is not surprising that Aristotle encounters other difficulties there, such as that of the indefinite statements.[79]

Our chapter 9, by contrast, displays quite a different style and background. The sentences are much longer, and in the middle part we have the extended excursion into the problems of determinism. The chapter is, however, well worked into the text. The introduction and conclusion seem designed to give the impression that it contains a necessary excursion into a problem that has an impact on the rest of the treatise, that is, that of logical (semantical) determinism. Problems of

---

[79] In passages such as *An. Pr.* 38b21, *An. Po.* 72a11, or *Cat.* 10. 13a37 Aristotle seems to presuppose the knowledge of the meaning of '*apophansis*' and the distinction between *kataphasis* and *apophasis*; in *de Int.* 1 they are introduced ceremoniously.

determinism arise elsewhere in different parts of Aristotle's philosophy for different reasons and, presumably, at different times. The question of future truth may first have become apparent when Aristotle saw the need to clarify and modify his position in view of the Megarian challenge.[80] I do not want to go into a discussion of the relationship between the sea-battle and the *kurieuon logos* of Diodorus Cronus here, I have said more about that question in my monograph (cf. 93–112). But the philosophical relevance of the question of future truth does not end here.

We have seen at least an indication of Aristotle's awareness of the problem of future contingents at the end of *de Generatione et Corruptione* where Aristotle uses linguistic means to distinguish between what *is to be* and what *may be*. Let me turn to yet another text that indicates not only that Aristotle was confronted with this problem once in a while but that it concerns the centre of his philosophy.

Book Γ of the *Metaphysics* is often used as a witness that Aristotle regards LEM as a fundamental and exceptionless principle. He defends it there with great energy against the Heracliteans, or rather, he forces them to acknowledge it as the basis of all human thought. His strategy is to get them at least to the point of admitting definite meanings of words (cf. 1006a13 ff), and on that basis he tries to make them agree that they cannot maintain contradictions at the same time (1007b18). This is where the conception of the *antiphasis* comes in and the necessity that every proposition should be affirmed or denied (1008a12 ff). Since this is the function of LEM and/or PB in the argument it is, of course, not to be expected that Aristotle mentions any exceptions to the principle. The Heracliteans do not doubt PB, they want to maintain that both sides in an antiphasis are *true*.

Since it is Aristotle's aim to undermine that position it is all the more significant that at one point Aristotle does refer to an *exception* from LEM in *Metaphysica* Γ, namely in 1007b26–9 where he declares that the Heracliteans are mistaken in the nature of the object about which they are talking when they claim that everything '. . . is at the same

---

[80] Cf. *Met.* Θ. 3. This must certainly be the point from which the age-old debate about the meaning and implication of possibility/contingency originated.

time and is not . . .'. As if in exasperation he adds there 'they seem to talk about the *indefinite* (*to aoriston*), and though they believe they talk about what is (*to on legein*) they talk about what is not; for what is *potentially* and not in actuality is the indefinite'. This sounds like another version of the conclusion of our chapter 9: 'Clearly, then, it is not necessary that of every affirmation and opposite negation one should be true and the other false. For what holds for things that are does not hold for things that are not but may *possibly be or not be*; with these it is as we have said.'

If Aristotle has not been more cautious in the rest of *Metaphysica* Γ, this is for the simple reason that he confines himself in his attack on the Heracliteans to the discussion of things that are, *onta*. And all proper affirmations and negations in that case are true or false. With what is potentially it it is different, and there is the need of *indefiniteness* to account for contingency. Aristotle must therefore have encountered the problem of the Sea-Battle when he developed the distinction between *dunamis* and *energeia*, as witnessed both in his physical and metaphysical writings. As I have tried to maintain, the problem of 'future truth' itself for Aristotle is mainly a conceptual one, and the physical/metaphysical considerations prevail over the need to assert PB as a common axiom. If the Sea-Battle does not play a larger role in those writings and is almost hidden in the little treatise *de Interpretatione*, this finds its explanation in the fact that in science for Aristotle individuals and particular statements have (or ought to have) no place; but this does not allow the conclusion that the problem of future truth is an obscure question.

*Rutgers University*

# BIBLIOGRAPHICAL REFERENCES

## I Texts

### (a) Aristotle

*Aristotelis Categoriae et Liber de Interpretatione*, ed L. Minio-Paluello (Oxford, 1949).

*Aristotelis Organon Graece*, novis auxiliis adiutus recognovit, scholiis ineditis et commentario instruxit Th.Waitz (Leipzig, 1844).

*Aristotle's Prior and Posterior Analytics*, a revised text with introduction and commentary by W. D. Ross (Oxford, 1949).

*Aristotelis Topica et Sophistici Elenchi*, ed W. D. Ross (Oxford, 1958).

*Aristotelis De Caeolo*, ed D. J. Allan (Oxford, 1955).

*Aristotle On Coming-To-Be and Passing-Away*, a revised text with introduction and commentary by H. H. Joachim (Oxford, 1922).

*Aristotle's Physics*, a revised text with introduction and commentary by W. D. Ross (Oxford, 1936).

*Aristotelis Ethica Nicomachea*, ed I. Bywater (Oxford, 1894).

*Aristotle's Metaphysics*, a revised text with introduction and commentary by W. D. Ross (Oxford, 1953).

*Index Aristotelicus*, by von H. Bonitz (vol 5 Berliner Akademieausgabe, Darmstadt, 1955).

### (b) Other texts

*Alexandri Aphrodisiensis Praeter Commentaria Scripta Minora: Quaestiones, de Fato*, vol ii, Pars II, ed I. Bruns (Berlin, 1892).

*Anticii Manlii Severini Boetii Philosophiae Consolationis Libri Quinque*, ed R. Peiper (Leipzig, 1971).

*Ciceron, Traité Du Destin*, texte établi et traduit par Albert Yon (Paris, 1950).

## II Commentaries

*Commentaria in Aristotelem Graeca*, edita consilio et auctoriatate Academiae Litterarum Regiae Borussicae

II. 1: *Alexandri in Aristotelis Analyticorum priorum librum I commentarium*, ed M. Wallies (Berlin, 1883).

I: *Alexandri Aprhod. in Aristotelis Metaphysica commentarius*, ed M. Hayduck (Berlin, 1897).

IV. 5: *Ammonius, In Aristotelis De Interpretatione commentarius*, ed A. Busse (Berlin, 1897).

VIII: *Simplicii In Aristotelis Categorias commentarium*, ed C. Kalbfleisch (Berlin, 1907).

XVIII. 3: *Stephani In Librum Aristotelis De Interpretatione commentarium*, ed M. Hayduck (Berlin, 1885).

*Anicii Manlii Severini Boetii Commentarii In Librum Aristotelis Peri Hermeneias*, ed C. Meiser (2nd edn, Leipzig, 1880).

*Aristotle's Categories and De Interpretatione*, translated with notes by J. L. Ackrill (Oxford, 1963).

*Aristotle's De Generatione et Corruptione*, translated with notes by C. J. F. Williams (Oxford, 1982).

*Al-Farabi's Commentary and Short Treatise on Aristotle's De Interpretatione*, ed and translated by F. W. Zimmermann (London, 1981).

*Aristoteles, Kategorien*, übersetzt und erläutert von K. Oheler (Berlin, 1984).

## III Literature to *de Interpretatione* 9
### (and future contingency in general)

Albritton, R., 'Present Truth and Future Contingency', *Philosophical Review*, LXVI (1957), 29–46.

Anscombe, G. E. M., 'Aristotle and the Sea-Battle', *Mind*, LXV (1956), 1–15.

Baudry, L., *La Quérelle des Futurs Contingents (Louvain 1465-1475), textes inédits* (Paris, 1950).

Becker, A., 'Bestreitet Aristoteles die Gültigkeit des "Tertium non datur" für Zukunftsaussagen?', *Actes du Congrès International de Philosophie Scientifique VI, Philosophie des Mathématiques*, 69–74 (Paris, 1936).

Boehner, P., *The 'Tractatus de praedestinatione et de praescientia Dei et de futuris contingentibus' of William Ockham, with a Study on the Mediaeval Problem of a Three-Valued Logic* (New York, 1945).

Burgess, J., 'Logic and Time', *Journal of Symbolic Logic*, XLIV (1979), 566–82.

Burrel, D., 'Aristotle and Future Contingencies', *Philosophical Studies*, XIII (1964), 37–52.

Butler, R. J., 'Aristotle's Sea Fight and Three-Valued Logic', *Philosophical Review* LXIV (1955), 264–74.

Cahn, S. M., *Fate, Logic and Time* (New Haven, 1967).

Fine, G., 'Truth and Necessity in De Interpretatione 9', *History of Philosophy Quarterly*, I, no. 1 (1984), 23–47.

Frede, D., *Aristoteles und die Seeschlacht* (Göttingen, 1970).

Frede, D., 'Omne quod est quando est necesse est esse', *Archiv. f. Geschichte der Philosophie*, LIV (1972), 153–67.

Frede, D., 'The Dramatization of Determinism. Alexander of Aphrodisias' De Fato', *Phronesis*, XXVII (1982), 276–98.

Frede, M., *Die Stoische Logik* (Göttingen, 1974).

Geach, P. T., 'Some Problems about Time', in *Studies in the Philosophy of Thought and Action*, ed P. F. Strawson (Oxford, 1967).

Hamblin, C. L., 'The effect of when it is said', *Theoria*, XXXVI (1970), 249–63.

Hintikka, J., (1) 'The Once and Future Sea Fight: Aristotle's Discussion of Future Contingents in: De Interpretatione IX', *Philosophical Review*, LXXIII (1964), 461–92.

Hintikka, J., *Time and Necessity* (Oxford, 1973).

Hintikka, J. (in collaboration with U. Remes and S. Knuuttila), 'Aristotle on Modality and Determinism', *Acta Philosophica Fennica*, XXIX (1977).

Isaac, J., *Le peri Hermeneias en occident de Boèce a Saint Thomas, Histoire littéraire d'un traité d'Aristote* (Paris, 1953).

Jeffrey, R. C., 'Coming True', in *Intention and Intentionality, Essays in Honour of G. E. M. Anscombe*, ed C. Diamond and J. Teichman (Sussex, 1979) 251–60.

Kneale, W. and M., *The Development of Logic* (Oxford, 1962).

Kotarbinski, T., 'The Problem of the Existence of the Future', *The Polish Review*, XIII (1968), 7–22.

Lesniewski, S., 'Is Truth Eternal and Since Eternity?', *The Polish Review*, XIII (1968), 23–43.

Linsky, L., 'Professor Donald Williams on Aristotle', *Philosophical Review*, LXIII (1954), 250–2.

Lukasiewicz, J., (1) 'On Three-Valued Logic—Farewell Lecture at the University of Warsaw, March 7, 1918—On Determinism', *The Polish Review*, XIII (1968) 43–61.

Lukasiewicz, J., (2) *Aristotle's Syllogistic from the Standpoint of Modern Formal Logic* (Oxford, 1957).

Lukasiewicz, J., 'Philosophische Bermerkungen zu mehrwertigen Systemen des Aussagekalküls', *Comptes Rendus des Séances de la Societé des Sciences et des Lettres de Varsovie*, XXIII, 3 (1930).

Kretzmann, N., McCord-Adams, M., *William Ockham; Predestination, God's Foreknowledge, and Future Contingents* (New York, 1969).

McCall, S., 'Temporal Flux', *American Philosophical Quarterly* (1966), 270–81.

McCall, S., 'Time and the Physical Modalities', *Monist*, LIII (1969).

Mackie, J. L., *The Cement of the Universe* (Oxford, 1974).

McKim, V. R., 'Fatalism and the Future: Aristotle's way out', *Review of Metaphysics*, XXV (1972), 80–111.

Maier, H., *Die Syllogistik des Aristoteles*, 2 vols (Tübingen, 1896–1900).

Maier, H., 'Die Echtheit der Aristotelischen Hermeneutik', *Archiv f. Geschichte der Philosophie*, XIII (1899), 23–72.

Patzig, G., *Die Aristotelische Syllogistik* (Göttingen, 1961).

Prior, A. N., 'Three-Valued Logic and Future Contingents', *Philosophical Quarterly*, III (1953), 317–26.

Prior, A. N., *Time and Modality* (Oxford, 1957).

Prior, A. N., *Past, Present and Future* (Oxford, 1967).

Prior, A. N., *Papers on Time and Tense* (Oxford, 1968).

Rescher, N., *An Interpretation of Aristotle's Doctrine of Future*

*Contingency and Excluded Middle, Studies in the History of Arabic Logic* (Pittsburgh, 1963), 43-54.

Rescher, N., 'On the Logic of Chronological Propositions', *Mind*, LXXV (1966).

Rescher, N., 'Truth and Necessity in Temporal Perspective', in *The Philosophy of Time*, ed R. Gale (London, 1968).

Ryle, G., 'It was to Be', in *Dilemmas II* (Cambridge, 1954), 15-35.

Schick, F., 'Self-knowledge, Uncertainty, and Choice', *British Journal for Philosophy of Science*, XXX (1979), 235-52.

Seel, G., *Die Aristotelische Modaltheorie* (Berlin and New York, 1982).

Sellars, W., 'Fatalism and Determinism', in *Freedom and Determinism*, ed K. Lehrer (New York, 1966).

Strang, C., 'Aristotle and the Sea Battle', *Mind*, LXIX (1960), 447-65.

Taylor, R., 'The Problem of Future Contingencies', *Philosophical Review*, LXVI (1957), 1-28.

Thomason, R., 'Indeterminist time and truth-value gaps', *Theoria*, XXXVI (1970), 264-81.

Von Wright, G. H., 'Determinismus, Wahrheit und Zeitlichkeit', *Studia Leibnitiana*, VI (1961), 161-78.

Von Wright, G. H., 'Time, Truth and Necessity', in *Intention and Intentionality, Essays in Honour of Elizabeth Anscombe* (Sussex, 1979), 237-50.

Von Wright, G. H., 'Omne quod est quando est necesse est esse' (forthcoming).[81]

Von Wright, G. H., *Determinism and Future Truth* (forthcoming).[81]

Waterlow, S., *Passage and Possibility* (Oxford, 1982).

Waterlow, S., *Nature, Change, and Agency in Aristotle's Physics* (Oxford, 1982).

Weidemann, H., 'Möglichkeit und Wahrheit, Oskar Beckers modale Grundfigur und das Aristotelische Bivalenzprinzip', *Archiv f. Geschichte der Philosophie*, LVI (1979), 22-36.

Weidemann, H., 'Überlegungen zu einer temporalen Modalanalyse', *Zeitschrift f. Philosophische Forschung*, XXXIV (1980), 405-22.

White, M. J., 'Aristotle and Temporally Relative Modalities', *Analysis*, XXXIX (1979).

Williams, C. J. F., 'True Tomorrow, Never True Today', *Philosophical Quarterly*, XXVIII (1978).

Williams, C. J. F., 'What is, when it is, necessarily is', *Analysis*, XL (1980), 127-31.

Williams, D. C., 'The Sea Fight Tomorrow', in *Structure, Method and Meaning*, ed P. Henle (New York, 1951), 282-306.

Williams, D. C., 'Professor Linsky on Aristotle', *Philosophical Review*, LXIII (1954), 253-5.

Wolf, U., *Möglichkeit und Notwendigkeit bei Aristoteles und heute* (München, 1979).

Zeller, E., *Die Philosophie der Griechen in ihrer geschichtlichen Entwicklung*, II 2 (Leipzig, 1879).

[81] Professor von Wright kindly let me see two as yet unpublished manuscripts.

# PERMANENT HAPPINESS: ARISTOTLE AND SOLON*

## T. H. Irwin

## 1. Introduction

Satan answered the Lord, 'Has not Job good reason to be God-fearing? Have you not hedged him round on every side with your protection, him and his family and all his possessions? Whatever he does you have blessed, and his herds have increased beyond measure. But stretch out your hand and touch all that he has, and then he will curse you to your face.                                                                (Job 1: 9–11)

Many of Aristotle's arguments begin from common beliefs. He does not commit himself to agreement with them; but he recognizes an obligation to explain them—to show the partial truth in the beliefs he rejects, and the grounds for rejecting them (*Nicomachaean Ethics* (*EN*) 1154a22-5).

In his initial claim about happiness he attends closely to common beliefs. When he has defined happiness as an activity of the soul expressing complete virtue in a complete life, he introduces the common view that happiness is rather unstable because it is vulnerable to ill fortune, to external hazards that the agent cannot control. Aristotle remarks that if someone is well off for most of his life, but finally suffers disastrous ill fortune and comes to a bad end, no one counts him happy; this is what happened to Priam at the end of his life (1100a4-9).

Here Aristotle seems to raise a serious difficulty for himself. For he has just argued that if we want to be happy, we should cultivate and practise the virtues (1099b25-1100a4). Most of the *Ethics* is devoted to an account of the virtues that Aristotle regards as constituents of the happy life. But if he admits that happiness is vulnerable to external hazards, he cannot claim that virtue ensures happiness. How, then, can he advise us to be virtuous if we want to be happy?

This is a difficulty within Aristotle's theory. But we may think it is a more general difficulty about his whole approach

* © T. H. Irwin 1985.

to moral theory. We expect an account of moral virtues to prescribe some degree of inflexibility; for we expect an honest and reliable person to stick to his principles even when he is offered some attractive inducements to violate them, or faces some severe threat for sticking to them. We tend to agree with Satan's method for testing Job's virtue, by plunging him into severe misfortune. Job's wife was puzzled that Job remained inflexibly virtuous in disaster: 'Are you still unshaken in your integrity? Curse God and die!' (Job 2: 9). Though we may also be puzzled, we expect this integrity from a virtuous person. The Greeks expect it also. It is rather surprising to us, then, that Greek moralists advocate the pursuit of virtue by appealing to the agent's happiness, when it seems obvious that his virtue does not always promote his happiness. The problem about ill fortune is simply one expression of this general difficulty about virtue and happiness.

Aristotle sees the difficulty. He wants to solve it not by brusquely rejecting common beliefs, but by examining them to see what they imply, and how far they really conflict with a reasonable view of happiness. After the remark about Priam he adds: 'Then should we not count any one else either as happy, as long as he is alive? Should we follow Solon's advice and see the end?' (1100a11–12).[1] I agree with Aristotle's view that Solon's advice deserves discussion, and that it illuminates the problem about happiness and fortune. Before considering Aristotle's views we will find it useful to explore Solon's advice further.

## 2. Solon's problem

We learn most about Solon's advice from Herodotus' elaborate account of it (I. 30–3). The rich and successful Croesus gives Solon a conducted tour of the palace and treasuries, and then asks Solon to say who he thinks is the most prosperous of human beings. Solon mentions the winner and the runners-up, all utterly obscure people, and Croesus is predictably disappointed, since he could have bought and sold them all.

---

[1] For Solon's proverb see *Paroemiographi Graeci*, ed. E. L. Leutsch and F. G. Schneidewin (Göttingen, 1839), i, 315: *telos hora biou—touto to apophthegma Solon eipe Kroiso(i).*

Solon explains that the obscure people he favours were all permanently well off, though less rich and splendid than Croesus; we know they were permanently well off because they are dead, and so no longer liable to reversals of fortune. Croesus, however, is alive, and we cannot know that he is permanently happy, because we do not know that he will be spared reversals of fortune.

When Solon advises us to see the end of a person's life before deciding about the person's happiness, we see how he conceives happiness. He refuses to consider the apparently natural possibility that Croesus might be happy at one time and unhappy at another time in his life. He must, then, regard happiness as a condition of a person's life as a whole. It is reasonable for him to do this, if he conceives happiness as success. For the success that a person reasonably wants and pursues is not success for a day or two, but his success over his whole lifetime.[2] And that is the sort of thing that, as Solon reasonably observes, you can discover only when you contemplate a person's complete lifetime after it is over.

Solon's conception of happiness was widely shared. It is reflected in Aristotle's account in the *Rhetoric* of common views. Aristotle describes happiness as 'doing well combined with virtue' or 'self-sufficiency of life' or 'the pleasantest life with safety' or 'prosperity of possessions and bodies with the power to protect them and use them in action' (1360b14-17). Power and fortune are also parts of happiness because these are the best providers of safety (1360b28-9). It is because we aim at complete and secure success in life as a whole that we need fortune, and cannot be assured of happiness till we are dead; for the fortune that is needed for prosperity is unstable and variable (*EN* 1100b2-7). Not surprisingly, it becomes a Greek commonplace that no one should be called happy until his death.[3]

This shared belief that happiness requires fortune, and

---

[2] This demanding attitude is expressed in Sophocles (Soph.), *Antigone* 583-92. It explains the pessimistic conclusion about human happiness in Aeschylus (Aesch.), *Agamemnon* (*Ag.*) 553-4; Soph., *Oedipus Tyrannos* (*OT*) 1186-96.
[3] See Aesch., *Ag.* 928; Soph., *Trachiniae* 1-3, *OT* 1524-30; Euripides, *Andromache* 96-103, *Trojan Women* 505-10, *Heraclidae* 863-4, *Iphigenia at Aulis* 161-3.

fortune is unstable, provokes different reactions; and these set some of the problems for Aristotle.

Since Solon remarks that good and bad fortune can affect happiness, a sensible person might think he needs to be adaptable, so that he can act on reasonable predictions about the future and avoid too serious a loss if things turn out badly. The supremely adaptable Greek is Odysseus, both in Homer and in the tragedies in which he appears.

On the other hand, many find it hard to admire the astutely flexible person. One prominent type of tragic character refuses to be sensible and adaptable, and apparently harms himself and others by his inflexibility and wilfulness. None the less, these characters are presented as admirable, not always without reservation, but often as more admirable than the plastic and adaptable characters. Ajax is the traditional type of the inflexible hero to contrast with Odysseus; and Prometheus, Antigone, and Medea share this trait.

The contrast between the adaptable and the inflexible character is a particular interest of Sophocles, who explores it in the *Ajax*, *Antigone*, *Electra*, and *Philoctetes*. The bad aspects of inflexibility are prominent in the *Ajax*; the good sides in the *Antigone* and *Electra*; the *Philoctetes* is much less decisive.[4] The same sort of contrast much later forms some of Plutarch's antitheses in his parallel lives, and through Plutarch shapes some of Shakespeare's characters.[5] We are familiar with the inflexible character of Coriolanus and the adaptable character of Antony.

The contrast between adaptability and inflexibility points to an odd feature of Greek pre-philosophical reflection. Solon's view of happiness seems to support the adaptable person's strategy. Such a person foresees all that can be foreseen, and when something unforeseen happens he improvises suitably.[6] But some Greeks hesitate to advocate this sort of outlook, and find themselves admiring the inflexible

[4] Heroic inflexibility; B. M. W. Knox, *The Heroic Temper* (Berkeley, 1964), 10-27.

[5] See Plutarch, *Alcibiades* 16. 3, 23. 4-5; *Alcibiades et Coriolanus* 1. 3, 2. 1, 3. 2 (for *oikeiōs* cf. *EN* 1171a15), 4. 5, 5. 1. See D. A. Russell, *Plutarch* (London, 1973), 110-29.

[6] This adaptability and foresight is illustrated in Thucydides' presentation of Themistocles, I. 138. 3, and Pericles, II. 65. 6-6.

person, even though his inflexibility seems to destroy his prospect for happiness. Why should inflexibility seem so admirable? The common conception of happiness offers no answer to this question, and common sense offers no ground for admiration apart from happiness. A student as sympathetic and critical as Aristotle should be able to identify this conflict in common-sense reactions to Solon's advice; and he should be able to find the true or false beliefs underlying the conflicting views. In his discussion of Solon's advice Aristotle tries to do justice to both sides in the conflict.

### 3. Aristotle's agreement with Solon

Aristotle makes it clear that in his view happiness depends on fortune and external conditions, so that to this extent he has strong reasons for agreeing with Solon.[7] Since happiness is the highest good, it must be complete (*teleion*) and self-sufficient (*autarkes*). A complete and self-sufficient good is one that all by itself makes life choiceworthy and lacking in nothing. If it really makes life lacking in nothing, a complete good must be comprehensive; nothing can be added to it to make a better good (1097b8-21).[8] A comprehensive good must extend beyond conditions of the agent himself; Aristotle explains that it must include the happiness of family, friends, and fellow-citizens (1097b8-13).

---

[7] 'Auf jeden Fall ist er weit davon entfernt, Schicksalssichläge in ihren Auswirkungen zu bagatellisieren'; F. Dirlmeier, *Nikomachische Ethik* (Berlin, 1969), 288.

[8] Because of 1097b20 I take b16-20 to be an explanation of self-sufficiency, rather than a third condition. On the sense of b16-20 I follow J. L. Ackrill, 'Aristotle on eudaimonia', in *Essays on Aristotle's Ethics*, ed. A. O. Rorty (Berkeley, 1980), 21-4. I also agree with his explanation of *teleia arete*, 27 f. For a defence of the alternative view of 1097b16-20 (happiness is only the best single good) see A. J. P. Kenny, *The Aristotelian Ethics* (Oxford, 1978), 204, well answered in J. M. Cooper's review, *Nous*, XV (1981), 384 f. The alternative view, however, responds to a genuine problem in Aristotle's position, that he must allow the possibility of adding goods to happiness. Eustratius (discussed by Kenny and Cooper) seems to be aware of the problem; for he contrasts happiness, taken to include its more important (*kuriōtera*) parts, with the better good that results from the addition of the less important parts (*CAG* XX, 64. 34-65. 17, esp. 65. 3-8). This distinction allows him to cope with the problem of addition (cf. 98. 19-29). The problem, however, does not raise an insuperable difficulty for the first view of b16-20; see s 4 below.

If happiness is comprehensive, and goods dependent on fortune are genuine goods, then happiness must include them. If it did not, then their addition to happiness would produce a good better than happiness alone, which is impossible. Aristotle agrees that goods of fortune are genuine goods; hence he agrees that happiness requires them (1099a31-b8). He sharply rejects the Socratic and Cynic view that virtue alone is sufficient for happiness (1095b31-1096a2, 1153b14-25).[9]

This point needs no qualification when Aristotle defines happiness as activity of the soul expressing complete virtue. For both the acquisition and the actualization of complete virtue require goods of fortune. Some examples make the point obvious. We cannot be magnificent or magnanimous if we are not rich; and we cannot live with our friends if they die at the wrong times. The definition of happiness shows why it is subject to fortune.[10]

[9] J. M. Cooper, *Reason and Human Good in Aristotle* (Cambridge, Mass., 1975), 125, rightly stresses the importance of voluntariness in happiness, and concludes: 'On the view I am suggesting, to flourish is not actually to possess a full portion of all the basic good things, but rather to be living in accordance with principles that are rationally calculated to secure them.' In commenting on 1153b19-21 (the rejection of the Socratic position) Cooper remarks: 'But it is not easy to see exactly how he thought his own theory of *eudaimonia* could accommodate this insight' (126). It certainly would not be easy to see this, if Aristotle held the view Cooper ascribes to him. But the evidence Cooper cites (*Politica* (*Pol.*) 1323b24-9; *Eudemian Ethics* (*EE*) 1215a12-19; *EN* 1099b18-25) does not commit Aristotle to this view. (See n 19 below.)

J. McDowell, 'The role of eudeaimonia in Aristotle's ethics', in Rorty (ed), above n 8, 370 and n 26, argues: 'If we take seriously (a) Aristotle's contention that a person's eudaimonia is his own doing, not conferred by fate or other people, but also try to make room for (b) his commonsense inclination to say . . . that external goods make a life more satisfactory, we are in any case required to distinguish (c) two measures of desirability or satisfactoriness; one according to which (d) a life of exercise of excellence, being—as eudaimonia is—self-sufficient (1097b6-21) (e) can contain no ground for regret in spite of great ill-fortune; and (f) one according to which such a life would have been better if the fates had been kinder' (reference-letters added). There is no conflict between (a) and (b), since (a) does not imply that fortune has no influence on happiness; see n 19 below. Hence there is no need for (c). Aristotle does not claim (d); the virtuous activity that belongs to happiness must be 'in a complete life', 1098a18 (see s 5 below). Besides (e) is consistent with (f); the virtuous but unlucky person may not regret any of his actions (see n 25 below), but still may recognize that his life could have been better. McDowell's reasons for (c) are therefore insufficient.

[10] Aristotle discusses Solon's problem more fully and carefully in the *EN* than in the *EE*. Unlike the *EE*, the *EN* rejects the sufficiency of virtue for happiness at the outset, and explains this by an argument to show that happiness must be

Since happiness is an activity of the soul expressing complete virtue in a complete life, external goods have two distinct roles. Aristotle describes them as follows:

(*a*) In many actions we use friends, riches and political power as we use instruments; and (*b*) there are some things the lack of which mars blessedness. (1099a32-b2)

Among the remaining goods ⟨i.e. the external goods⟩, (*b*) there are some whose presence is necessary ⟨for happiness⟩, (*a*) others that are by nature co-operative and useful as instruments. (1099b27-8)

Great and numerous ⟨strokes of fortune⟩ that turn out well make his life more blessed; for (*b*) they themselves by nature adorn it, and (*a*) his use of them proves to be fine and excellent. (1100b25-8)

In each passage Aristotle distinguishes (*a*) the role of external goods as instruments of virtuous action from (*b*) their role as contributors to happiness apart from (*a*). The difference between the two roles needs to be explained. In one way all external goods are 'resources' (*chorēgia*; cf. 1099a32-3, 1178a26) that a virtuous person has to use properly; a vicious person will misuse the goods he has to his own harm (1129b1-4). But still, not all external goods are goods simply because they are used to do virtuous action. A temperate person's pursuit of sensual pleasure is regulated by his temperance, but his enjoyment of ordinary sensual pleasures is not good for him simply because it is what temperance prescribes; on the contrary, temperance prescribes it partly because it is the sort of thing that is good for him. Similarly, the instrumental goods that secure these sensual pleasures are not good because they help him to be temperate, but because they secure these pleasures. For similar reasons the magnanimous person values honour, and thinks he deserves it as the appropriate prize for virtue (1123b15-24, 34-6); it is an appropriate prize not because he needs it to act virtuously but because it is the greatest external good in its own right.[11]

complete (cf. *atelestera*, 1095b32). The *EE* mentions the completeness of happiness, 1219a35, but has not argued for it, or related it to the insufficiency of virtue. (H. Rackham, *Eudemian Ethics* (London, 1935), 238, suggests that *ēn*, 1219a35, refers back to 1218b7-12, which, however, does not include *teleion*. On *EE* 1219b4-7 see s 5 below.

[11] In 1153b17-25 Aristotle remarks that external goods are needed for happiness because it requires unimpeded activity and ill fortune impedes activities. This

Honour is simply the most important of the non-instrumental external goods needed to make a virtuous person's life complete. Aristotle suggests that someone who is physically repulsive (not merely undistinguished) or of low birth, or solitary or childless is a poor candidate for happiness; and remarks that it is even worse for someone who has bad children or friends, or has had good ones who have died (1099b2-6). He does not suggest that the absence or loss of these goods is bad because it causes pain or frustration, or because it prevents virtuous action (though no doubt it may have both of these effects). These are goods that are valued for their own sake, and therefore belong to a complete life.[12]

No external good is a part of happiness if it is isolated from virtue; a healthy, strong, handsome, vicious person has no part of happiness at all, since he will simply misuse the external goods he has (1129b1-4). The external goods that in

role of external goods is relevant in a discussion of the claim (not endorsed by Aristotle) of pleasure to be happiness; he does not imply that this is the only role of external goods. (He might, however, construe it as their only role, consistently with what we have said about Bk I; for the activities impeded by lack of external goods need not be only virtuous activities, and the goods whose absence impedes activities need not be purely instrumental goods; we cannot have the unimpeded enjoyment of honour without the intrinsic external good of honour.) Questions raised by J. L. Ackrill and Alan Fuchs have helped me to see some of these issues more clearly.

[12] A different view of the role of external goods is ably defended by Cooper, 'Aristotle on the goods of fortune', *Philosophical Review*, XCIV (1985), 173–96. I believe he underestimates the different between the two types of external goods, and gives insufficient grounds for denying that a large loss of external goods will by itself deprive a person of happiness (even apart from its effects on his capacity for virtuous action). Cooper rightly emphasizes that Aristotle thinks external goods are the normal consequences of virtuous action, 'so that they should not be counted as goods that he needs as *supplements* to virtue if he is to be happy (195). This does not seem to follow, however, since the normal consequence does not always result from the virtuous action; and when it does not, the virtuous person seems to gain one component of his happiness, but fails to gain another that is rightly described as a supplement to virtue. Cooper denies this, appealing to 'Aristotle's central conviction that what determines the character of a person's life is what he does' (195). I doubt if Aristotle believes this in a strong enough sense to secure Cooper's conclusion (see n 19 below, and text). Moreover, if the right action is sufficient for happiness and the results are no part of happiness, why should the virtuous person aim at them? This question raises an issue about Aristotelian and Stoic ethics that I discuss in 'Stoic and Aristotelian conceptions of happiness', in *The Norms of Nature*, ed M. Schofield and G. Striker (Cambridge, forthcoming). I have benefitted from reading Cynthia Freeland's comments on Cooper's paper.

the *Rhetoric* count as parts of happiness are refused this status in the *Ethics*, because they are not parts of happiness in their own right; it is the virtuous person's correct use of one of these goods, not the good by itself, that is a part of his happiness.[13] Still, the external goods are necessary for happiness, and some are necessary because they are intrinsic (i.e. not purely instrumental) goods.

## 4. Aristotle's disagreement with Solon

It is easy to see why Aristotle has reasons for agreeing with Solon's view that happiness is exposed to chance; and if he agrees this far, we might expect him to advocate flexibility. We might suppose that someone is best equipped for the pursuit of happiness if he is able to adapt himself and his aims to circumstances, minimizing the ill effects of misfortune. In fact, however, Aristotle defends a surprising degree of inflexibility, because he thinks Solon is quite wrong on one crucial point.

Solon's conception implies that happiness depends on conditions outside the agent; and Aristotle criticizes such conceptions. He rejects the life of honour as a candidate for happiness, because honour depends on the attitudes of other people, whereas 'we intuitively believe that the good is something of our own and hard to take from us' (1095b25). Our intuitive belief is partly satisfied if happiness is controlled by virtuous activities (1100b11-22), since these are our own, in our power and hard to take from us. The external goods are those that, in Job's view, 'the Lord gives and the Lord takes away' (Job 1: 21). The Lord does not in the same way take away Job's integrity; it is up to Job himself to retain his integrity, and Aristotle argues that this is what controls happiness.

Aristotle must reconcile these claims with his equally firm belief that happiness includes external goods, and hence

---

[13] The *EN*, unlike the *EE* and *Magna Moralia* (*MM*), actually avoids speaking of parts of happiness, probably to avoid the suggestion that an external good could be a part of happiness all by itself. See Ackrill, above n 8, 29; Cooper, above n 9, 123.

depends on fortune. His attempt to reconcile his different views is characteristically compressed and complex:

> Many strokes of fortune occur, differing in degrees of importance. Small strokes of good fortune or its opposite clearly will not tip the balance of his life. If many great strokes of fortune turn out well, they will make his life more blessed; for they themselves are of a nature to adorn his life, and moreover the way he uses them proves to be fine and excellent. But if things turn out the other way, they oppress and mar his blessedness, since they introduce pains and impede many activities. None the less, in these conditions also what is fine shines through, whenever someone bears with good temper many serious strokes of ill fortune, and does this not because he is incapable of feeling distress, but because he is noble and magnanimous. And if it is activities that control life, as we said, no blessed person could ever become miserable; for he will never do what is hateful and despicable.   (1100b23-35)

Aristotle makes two claims about the role of major gains or losses of external goods:

1. Major gains make a happy person happier.
2. Major losses deprive a happy person of his happiness, but do not make him unhappy.

Both claims need to be explained.

The first claim is difficult because it seems to conflict with the assumption that happiness is complete, and therefore can have no further goods added to make a better good. If external goods can be added, then apparently they make a better good, and so the person who lacks them cannot be happy. Aristotle raises the same puzzle for us in his remarks about how events after my death may affect my happiness. These events, in his view, may indeed affect me for good or ill, but only to a degree that neither makes someone happy when he would otherwise not be happy, nor takes away the happiness of someone who is otherwise happy (1101b1-9).[14] Aristotle needs to explain how the addition and subtraction of goods can make someone more or less happy without making him cease to be happy, if happiness cannot have any goods added to make a better good.

His claims are consistent if he explains completeness in the

---

[14] I do not think this passage implies post-mortem consciousness. Contrast K. Pritzl, 'Aristotle and happiness after death', *Classical Philology*, LXXVIII (1983), 101-11, and P. W. Gooch, 'Aristotle and the happy dead', ibid, 112-16.

right way. The goods that are components of happiness are determinable types of goods; these are exemplified in determinate types of goods and in determinate tokens of these types. My playing golf now is a token of the type playing golf, which is a determinate type of the determinable type physical exercise and the determinable type recreation.

Aristotle probably believes that the complete good is composed of a sufficient number of tokens of some determinate types of each of the determinable types of good. If recreation is a component of the good, and one afternoon's golf and one evening's bridge or bingo are equally good types of recreation, then I can achieve this component of the good either by playing golf one afternoon a week or by playing bridge or bingo one evening a week. It may not matter which determinate type of activity I prefer, as long as I include the right number of tokens of the right determinable types. In saying that no good can be added Aristotle means that no determinable type of good can be added to happiness to make a better good than happiness.

These distinctions certainly raise difficulties of application. How are we to choose the right level of generality to identify the appropriate determinable types? How are we to decide the right number of tokens to count as the realization of a given type? It is not only the problem about degrees of happiness that forces such questions on Aristotle. He must face them in any case once he defines happiness as a realization of human capacities in a complete life. If we count capacities perversely, the fulfilment of my capacities will be too difficult (if they are too specific) or too easy (if they are too generic). We must count them according to the right conception of a human being's physical and psychological nature; and this will not be an easy task. Moreover, Aristotle's demand for completeness seems both unsatisfiable and unreasonable unless it requires an acceptable number of tokens, rather than all the tokens, of a determinate type of action. For however complete someone's life may seem to be, we will be able to imagine some token good activity that could have been added; but Aristotle will not want to concede that such a life is not complete and not happy.[15]

`[See p 100 for n 15]`

Though further enquiry is needed to see if Aristotle can satisfy us on these questions, we can see how he might draw intelligible distinctions that would solve the problem about completeness. I am happy, he can claim, if my virtue and external conditions allow me to fulfil my different capacities in the right order and proportion—if, for example, I am virtuous, and also rich enough to make magnificent actions prominent in my life. To be magnificent in contributing to the public good I need enough money for the appropriate large expenses. If I am left a large legacy, I will be pleased; for I will be able to do more of the magnificent actions that I enjoy and value. As Aristotle says, the use of these extra goods will be fine and excellent (1100b27). But though they make me happier, they do not produce a greater good than the happiness I previously had; for they do not add any further determinable good, but only add further tokens of some determinate types of a determinable good.

Aristotle can therefore defend his first claim about fortune —that good fortune can make me happier, though it does not give me a greater good than happiness. The effects of ill fortune are more serious. The happy life requires a certain moderate level of external goods (1179a1-17); and if these are lost, the happy person ceases to be happy.[16] He does not, however, become unhappy.[17] Aristotle can defend this claim if he appeals again to the composite character of happiness.

If happiness has several determinable parts, I am happy if I have all these parts, and not happy if I lack at least one of them. But there is still a difference between having some parts of happiness and having none at all. In Aristotle's view this difference is crucial. For the virtuous person always retains one crucial part of happiness, without which none of the other goods is a part of happiness at all. The virtuous

[15] This objection to the more plausible interpretation of 1097b16-20 (see n 8 above) is raised by, e.g., S. R. L. Clark, *Aristotle's Man* (Oxford, 1975), 154.

[16] In I. 10, as elsewhere in the *EN* (contrast *EE* 1215a10, M. J. Woods, *Eudemian Ethics* (Oxford, 1982), 55), *eudaimōn* and *makarios* have to be used interchangeably. Unless they are, the argument of 1100b33-1101a11 is unintelligible.

[17] 'Unhappy' represents *athlios*, used as the contrary, not the mere negation, of *eudaimōn*. Cf. Plato, *Meno* 78a1-9; Soph., *OT* 1204, Seneca, *Epistolae Morales* 92. 22, mentions the appropriate distinction, between *non beatus* and *miser*.

person, then, always has some part of happiness, and the non-virtuous person has no part of happiness, however many other goods he may have. The virtuous but unlucky person is not happy; the lucky but non-virtuous person is unhappy.

Since Aristotle believes this about virtue, he regards it as the *dominant* good, and the dominant component of happiness; it is always to be preferred over any other component or combination of components of happiness, and over any other good or combination of goods.[18]

## 5. The stable and the unstable components of happiness

Aristotle's arguments imply that Solon's view is either wrong or else seriously incomplete. Solon assumed that because happiness depends to some degree on fortune, fortune can make someone miserable. He did not realize that the dominant component of happiness is stable and immune to fortune. Since Solon requires happiness to be permanent, lasting through a lifetime, he seems to make it unstable; for it is vulnerable to bad luck all that time. Aristotle suggests that happiness is more stable than Solon thought it was, because it is controlled by virtuous actions, and they are controlled by virtue, which is stable and not likely to be destroyed in our lifetime (1100b11-22). If virtue is stable, then happiness is stable to the extent that virtuous actions control happiness; and in so far as it is stable it is permanent.

Aristotle's position may appear to be inconsistent if we consider his claim that virtuous actions 'control' (*kuriai*)

[18] This notion of dominance is used by Antiochus in his defence of an (allegedly) Aristotelian view in Cicero, *de Finibus* V. 92. Passages such as 1100b25-6 might have suggested to Antiochus the distinction between being *beatus*, for which virtue is sufficient, and being *beatissimus*, for which external goods are also needed, and encouraged him to ascribe it to Aristotle. His mistake is to suppose that in these passages Aristotle thinks virtue is sufficient for the happiness that can be increased by external goods. On the relevance of these chapters to Antiochus see Cooper, above n 12, n 7.

In considering Aristotle's claims about the composition of happiness and the place of virtue in it, I have assumed that no revision is demanded by his advocacy of contemplation in *EN* X. 6-8. D. Keyt, 'Intellectualism in Aristotle', in *Essays in Ancient Greek Philosophy*, vol. ii, ed J. P. Anton and A. Preus (Albany, 1983), 364-87, offers a plausible account of Bk X. If, however, the account in X identifies contemplation with the whole of happiness, Aristotle is still more influenced by the demand for stable happiness than I allow.

happiness (1100b11-22); that someone is happy 'because of' (*dia*) himself and not because of fortune (*Pol.* 1323b24-9; cf. 1099b20-1); and that happiness is 'in' one's own character and actions (*EE* 1215a13-19; cf. 1100b8). These claims may seem to conflict with the admission that happiness depends on fortune. But Aristotle's use of the relevant causal concepts implies no conflict. In saying that virtuous actions control or cause happiness, he does not mean that they are sufficient for it, or that happiness consists only of them and their necessary consequences. He means that in the right circumstances virtuous actions make the decisive contribution to happiness; we are to assume a reasonable level of external goods and then notice the role of virtue and virtuous action. This causal claim is not easy to evaluate; but it shows how Aristotle's position is consistent, and why he insists in the same sentence both that virtuous actions control happiness and that human life needs external goods as well (1100b8-11).[19]

Since Aristotle's view insists that virtue controls happiness, it implies that we are right to admire inflexible people to some extent, and right to be somewhat suspicious of adaptable people. A virtuous character is stable; and someone who maintains that inflexibly will secure the dominant component of his happiness; inflexibility does not require a sacrifice of happiness.[20] The adaptable person who is ready to change his character and outlook to meet changing fortune does this to secure the aspects of happiness that depend on fortune. If he cares more about these than about having a virtuous and stable character, he chooses subordinate goods rather than the dominant component of happiness. His choice is futile; for without the virtues these goods are not components of happiness at all. In choosing subordinate goods over virtue he shows that he misunderstands the nature of virtue and the nature of happiness. It is better to be inflexible about virtue;

[19] For a clearer grasp of the causal claims I am indebted to Susan Sauvé and Gail Fine. Cooper and McDowell rely on the causal claims in ways that lead them to underestimate the role of fortune in happiness; see nn 9, 12.

[20] In stressing the stability of virtue as a reason for choosing it Aristotle agrees with Solon, who says he will not exchange virtue for wealth, because virtue is stable, *empedon aiei*, while wealth fluctuates. See Plutarch, *Solon* 3. 2 = *Anthologia Lyrica Graeca*, ed E. Diehl (Berlin, 1949), fr 4. 9-11. There is no evidence to show that Solon connected this claim with his advice about happiness.

and to that extent we are right to prefer the inflexible to the adaptable character.

Aristotle has explained why happiness is in some ways more stable than Solon noticed; why it is complete, though allowing addition; and why it is caused by virtue, though vulnerable to ill fortune. He can now evaluate Solon's advice to call someone happy only when he is dead. The advice rests on the assumption that happiness must be permanent, so that if I lack it at any time in my life, I never have it.

In the *Eudemian Ethics* and *Magna Moralia* this assumption about permanence seems to be accepted, and so Solon's advice is endorsed:

Since, then, happiness is a complete good and an end . . . it will also be in something complete. For it will not be in a child (for a child is not happy), but in a man, since he is complete ⟨i.e. mature⟩. Nor will it be in an incomplete time, but in a complete one; and a complete time is as much time as a human being lives. For the many are correct to say that we must judge the happy person in the greatest time of his life, on the assumption that what is complete must be both in a complete time and in a ⟨complete⟩ human being. (*MM* 1185a5-9)

And ⟨there is supporting evidence for us in the claim⟩ that a person is not happy for ⟨just⟩ one day, or as a child, or for each period of his life. Hence Solon's advice is right, not to count anyone happy while he is alive, but only when his life reaches its end. For nothing incomplete is happy, since it is not a whole.[21] (*EE* 1219b4-8)

In the *Nicomachaean Ethics*, however, as we have seen, Aristotle insists that complete happiness still allows addition. He is correspondingly careful when he explains that happiness, being complete, requires complete virtue and a complete life:

Further, ⟨the activity of the soul⟩ must be in a complete life; for one swallow does not make a spring, nor does one day; nor, similarly, does one day or a short time make one blessed and happy. (1098a18-20)

---

[21] The scope of 'Hence Solon's . . .' and 'For nothing . . .' is ambiguous; different views are reflected in Woods's and Rackham's translations. The *MM* passage suggests narrow escape for 'Hence Solon's . . .' (i.e. referring to 'for each period') and wide scope for 'For nothing . . .' (explaining that all the previous points rely on completeness). However, we would expect Solon's advice to explain 'one day' as well as 'for each period'; it should then also explain 'as a child', presumably as an example of 'for each period'; in that case the point about children and adults is different from that in the *MM*, which offers different explanations of this point and the point about an incomplete time.

This connection between happiness and length of time is explained later. A child, like an ox or a horse, is incapable of happiness because he is incapable of the right sort of activity, and if we congratulate him on his happiness it is because we expect that he will perform the right sort of activity when he is an adult (1099b32–1100a3). Aristotle adds:

> For, as we say, we need both complete virtue and complete time. For many variations and fortunes of all sorts arise in life, and it is possible for the most prosperous person to fall into great disasters in old age, as is told of Priam in the Trojan story; and if someone suffers such misfortunes and comes to a miserable end, no one counts him happy.[22]
>
> (1100a4–9)

As in the *Eudemian Ethics* Aristotle suggests some connection between happiness and length of time; and we might think he regards a 'complete time' as a lifetime. On this view, Priam's misfortunes in old age imply that he never was happy.

Eventually, however, Aristotle shows that this is not his view. For he recognizes that a happy person can lose his happiness if he suffers the misfortunes of Priam (1101a6–11). If happiness requires a complete life and a complete time, he must have had these before he suffered the misfortunes; hence a complete time cannot be a lifetime. Aristotle confirms this point when he remarks that someone who has lost his happiness can still regain it, 'not . . . in a short time, but, if at all, in some long and complete time, in which he has succeeded in great and fine achievements' (1101a12–13). Though 'if at all' suggests that the task of recovering happiness is not easy, it is plainly not self-contradictory, as it would be if a complete time were a whole lifetime.

The different claims in the *Nicomachaean Ethics* explain each other if we begin from the 'great and fine achievements'. Happiness is complete, and therefore requires a complete

---

[22] There is some difficulty in 1099b5, on which see especially J. A. Stewart, *Notes on the Nicomachean Ethics* (Oxford, 1892), i, 103. Aristotle supports the demand for a complete life by remarking that we can, like Priam, be unlucky in old age, and that if this happens no one counts us happy, *eudaimonizei*, 1100a9. If this means (1) 'no one thinks we *ever* were happy', then Aristotle takes the Solonian view. But perhaps it means (2) 'no one thinks we are happy *then*'. In that case the point might be only that we need some good luck, and that bad luck can destroy happiness. If only (2) is meant, the position in the *EN* is consistent and different from the one in the *EE*.

range of activities realizing human capacities. A complete time is a time long enough for such a complete range; and since the projects of a virtuous friend or of a magnificent and magnanimous person take some time to realize, a complete time will not be a short time. Moreover, since a child is incapable of the complete range of activities, it cannot achieve happiness. And yet, just as a complete good allows addition, a complete time need not be a whole lifetime; I may be happy if I have had a complete time and exercised the complete range of activities, and then lose my happiness, as Priam did. With enough time I may also regain happiness. When God 'blessed the end of Job's life more than the beginning' (Job 42: 12) Job lived another hundred and forty years, and saw his sons and grandsons to four generations. This is presumably rather above the minimum needed for Job's return to happiness; but at least he needed long enough for the restoration of his herds, flocks, and family, and of his standing with his neighbours. As we have seen, Aristotle has assumed that happiness is complete in a way that still allows some sorts of addition; and the same notion of completeness explains his view of a complete length of time. If the parts of happiness are determinable types of action, and I can realize sufficient tokens of all of them in less than a lifetime, then I am completely happy in less than a lifetime, even though I am even happier if my happiness lasts longer than the time needed for completeness.[23]

Aristotle's rejection of Solon's advice, then, is not a casual disagreement. He has looked for plausible assumptions about happiness that might seem to support Solon. He appeals to the correct assumption that happiness is complete; and he argues that the correct assumption, correctly understood, does not support Solon. In the *Rhetoric* Aristotle accepted the common view that happiness must be secure, and recognized this as a reason for including good fortune and power in happiness (1360b28-9). In the *Magna Moralia* and *Eudemian Ethics* the popular demand for security and permanence is defended by appeal to completeness. But in the *Nicomachaean*

---

[23] It is useful (as A. A. Long suggested to me) to compare the notion of a 'complete action' in *Poetics* 1451a30-5, which allows quantitative addition that does not increase the qualitative completeness of the complete whole.

*Ethics* Aristotle shows that the relevant sort of completeness needs more careful explanation than it receives in the other works; when we see that completeness allows addition we also see that it does not justify the belief that a complete time is a lifetime, and therefore does not justify the demand for security and permanence. Nothing else justifies these demands either; happiness need not be secure and permanent, and a stroke of ill fortune that ends my prosperity neither ensures that I never was happy nor necessarily deprives me of the prospect of future happiness. Contrary to Solon's view, I may be happy in some periods of my life and not in others.[24]

Though he rejects Solon's demand for permanent happiness, and suggests why he thinks it is wrong, Aristotle still thinks there is something right in the demand for permanence. Solon is wrong to demand that something as unstable as happiness should be permanent. It is better to demand permanence in a component of happiness that is stable and in our power; and virtue meets these conditions. If we are virtuous, we assure permanent success in securing the dominant component of happiness; for virtue is stable, not exposed to destruction by external circumstances, and hence we can count on it to be permanent. Once we recognize this, we

[24] Some difficulty has reasonably been found in reconciling this view with 1101a16-21. R. A. Gauthier, *Aristote; l'Éthique à Nicomaque* (Paris and Louvain, 2nd edn, 1970), ad loc, finds the difficulty so great that (following Rassow) he condemns the passage as an interpolation. It is unconvincingly defended by J. Burnet, *Ethics of Aristotle* (London, 1900), ad loc. The question 'ē prostheteon . . .' is asking 'Should we agree with Solon after all?' I. Bywater (*Ethica Nicomachaea* (Oxford, 1894)) punctuates so that 'epeidē to mellon . . .' gives a reason for agreeing with Solon. In that case what does the 'ei d' houtō . . .' clause mean? The question is whether 'kai huparxei' (a) concedes Solon's point, or (b) maintains some weaker condition. If (a), then this whole section conflicts with the previous admission that happiness can be lost, and with Aristotle's earlier criticism of Solon in 1100a34 ff. But if (b) is meant, what is the argument, when 'ē prostheteon . . .' seems to have given an argument for (a)? We might perhaps make better sense of the whole passage by reading 'epei dē' instead of 'epeidē' in 1101a17, and taking this to support what follows, not what precedes. Then the argument will be: 'Should we agree with Solon (ē prostheteon . . . logon)? No. Since we think happiness is complete but the future is unclear, we can't make happiness depend on a whole lifetime. We must insist that happiness can be complete without requiring a whole lifetime. Hence we will insist that it must continue *some* way into the future (kai huparxei), but should not require a whole lifetime of happiness.' If this is right, then the passage will reflect the modified view of 'complete life' that marks the disagreement between the *EN* on the one side and the *EE, MM*, and Solon on the other side.

can allow that happiness is impermanent, liable to come and go.

Aristotle's view on the relation between virtue and happiness is not an innovation. It is derived from Plato's *Republic*. Plato does not maintain the Socratic claim that virtue is sufficient for happiness.[25] In the *Republic* the unlucky just person loses external goods and suffers genuine harms by his loss. His justice does not ensure that he is happy, but only that he is happier than any unjust person would be.

Though Aristotle does not comment on this doctrine of the *Republic*, he refers in his verses on Plato to Plato's views on virtue and happiness: 'He alone, or first among mortals, showed clearly both by his own life and by enquiries in arguments that a man is becoming good and happy at the same time'.[26] Aristotle chooses his words carefully here. He does not ascribe to Plato the Socratic claim that the good person *is* happy, but the different claim that someone is becoming happy at the same time as he is becoming good; and this is a claim that Aristotle himself can accept. In saying that Plato is the first to have shown this Aristotle may be implying that Socrates had not shown it. Perhaps Socrates' life was beyond reproach; but he had not shown clearly by his enquiries in arguments that becoming virtuous is becoming happy. Socrates had argued unconvincingly for the sufficiency of virtue, which Aristotle thinks no one would maintain except as a philosopher's paradox. Plato had argued convincingly for the dominance, not the sufficiency, of virtue. This is the position that Aristotle himself defends.[27]

[25] I have discussed this in 'Socrates the Epicurean?', forthcoming, in *Illinois Classical Studies* (1985).

[26] Aristotle, *Fragmenta Selecta*, ed W. D. Ross (Oxford, 1955), 146. 'Is becoming' translates *gignetai*. If we take it to mean 'has come to be' Aristotle ascribes to Plato a position incompatible with the *Republic* (*Rep.*).

[27] W. Jaeger, *Aristotle* (English translation, Oxford, 1938), 110, finds 'tragic resignation' in Aristotle's praise of Plato because 'the fact is that Aristotle in his *Ethics* denies Plato's doctrine that man's happiness depends only on the moral power of his soul'. See also Jaeger, 'Aristotle's verses in praise of Plato', *Scripta Minora* (Rome, 1960), 339-45 (from *Classical Quarterly*, XXI (1927), 13-17). Here (342) Jaeger ascribes to the *Rep.* belief in the sufficiency of virtue, citing the *Gorgias* and *Rep.* I. Significantly, he offers no evidence from the rest of the *Rep.* Jaeger doubts if Socrates holds this thesis, but does not consider, e.g., *Apology* 41c-d, *Crit.* 48b9-10. Here Jaeger's position on Aristotle's view is not clear (344).

## 6. Virtue and reason

We have seen how Aristotle disagrees with Solon because he believes virtue is dominant in happiness. Why then does he believe this, and how good are his reasons? It will not be enough to argue that being virtuous and actualizing virtue as far as possible is a good in itself. It could be that and still be less than a dominant component of happiness. It is hard to find a direct and explicit argument for the conclusion Aristotle needs. Still, arguments can be found, reflecting different aspects of Aristotle's conception of virtue. In this section and the next two I sketch three lines of argument:

1. The rational agent will correctly value rational agency over its external results.
2. He will correctly value rigid states of character and attachment to particular goals over a flexible character adapted to external circumstances.
3. H will correctly regard as dominant those rational and rigid states of character that secure complete happiness in moderately favourable external circumstances.

Though I will speak of 'the virtues', and use examples of Aristotelian virtues at each stage of the argument, it is important to notice that only the third stage defines the specific Aristotelian virtues.

Aristotle defines happiness as activity of the soul expressing reason and virtue. Happiness will require the best activities that actualize the person's capacities; and the best ones will be those that best express practical reason. Hence the virtuous person guides his life most of all by practical reason.

Someone who guides his life by practical reason will want to develop and exercise practical reason in his choice of aims and goals. He will regard these as matters for rational reflection, not simply as the products of nature or environment or unalterable desires.

The same concern for the exercise of practical reason will encourage someone to choose goals that allow practical reason in their pursuit, in preference to goals that do not allow it. This means that a wise person will not choose as his primary goals those that leave little or no scope for practical reason because they depend heavily on fortune and external circumstances. If I see this, I will not choose success in winning lotteries, or any other sort of success that depends almost entirely on chance, as my ultimate and overriding end. I will prefer activities in which practical reason determines the end to be pursued, and the means that will successfully attain it.

If someone reflects in this way about preferable ends and activities, he will come to see good reasons for valuing states of character and the activities that express them. Being virtuous and acting as virtuously as possible are in a person's power; they can be developed and preserved by rational reflection. Evidently the virtuous person wants to succeed in doing virtuous action, and in achieving the end for which he does the action; it is a strange just person who does not care at all about whether a struggle against injustice succeeds or not. But since he cares above all about guiding his life by reason, he will want above all to be just and to do just actions, whether or not he succeeds in his further aims.

Character and action will be his primary, not his exclusive concern. He has other capacities than those that belong to him as a rational agent; and he will want to exercise them too. But he will want to be sure that his life allows the maximum development of practical reason; and it will allow this if his dominant aim is character and action, rather than their external results. If he preferred the external results over the character and action themselves, he would be forgetting that he is a rational agent. For he would be willing to subordinate the exercise of the rational agency that is essential to him to some good that is good for some less essential aspect of him. A rational agent who correctly identifies himself with his rational agency will have no reason to believe he could have been better off if he had been less virtuous; while he might have gained benefits that were good for some aspect of him, he could never have benefited himself more. Aristotle claims that the virtuous person will be 'just about with regret' (1166a29). This is not because he will always be successful in his aims, or because his failures do not distress him (cf. 1100b32-3). Rather, he will always be pleased that he did what a virtuous person would do, and will not wish that he had been a less virtuous person; for he sees that he would have been worse off if he had sacrificed the rational agency that is the dominant component of his good.

The argument for the dominance of rational agency and character relies on notoriously disputable (or at any rate disputed) Aristotelian claims about the human essence and its relation to the human good. I do not intend to examine these claims further. They deserve our attention here, however, to show that Aristotle's belief in the dominance of virtue is not an anomaly in his theory. His claims about the function and essence of a human being do not imply that rational agency is the whole of human nature; therefore they do not imply that virtue is sufficient for happiness. But they imply that rational agency is primary and essential in human nature; and therefore they support the dominance of virtue in happiness.

## 7. Virtue and stability

To say that rational agency and character are dominant over other goods is not to say much about the sort of character a rational agent will have reason to form. Perhaps we can agree that a rational agent will not want to abdicate his rational agency if (to take relatively simple examples) the abdication would increase his sensual pleasure or his wealth or his power over others. But still, we could apparently exercise rational agency in the prudent planning for these goods, adapting ourselves to external circumstances, and sacrificing our other aims and ends to secure these overriding ends.[28]

Aristotle, however, takes a different view of the proper sort of character. The virtues he describes are rather inflexible and rather liable to conflict with external conditions. Someone with the Aristotelian virtues does not have just one overriding aim, for example power or pleasure, to which he subordinates his other aims. Nor does he have simply the schematic end of happiness, waiting to be filled by different specific ends suited to particular circumstances. He has a series of relatively fixed specific ends that he pursues inflexibly

[28] In this section I have benefited from criticisms and suggestions by Richard Boyd, David Brink, Eugene Garver, Mark Fowler, and William Wilcox.

even when they conflict with each other and with external circumstances. He is expected to be brave, and so to risk his life and the other goods he values; he is expected to be just, and so to face the penalties of being just and to forgo the advantages of injustice.[29]

Someone with these rigid aims and virtues may seem to defeat his own ends; for he could apparently sometimes secure his ends more effectively if he had less of a virtue. Justice requires him to be concerned with the good of his neighbour and the common good of the community; but sometimes he might secure these results better if he were willing to be less concerned with them. Machiavelli remarks: 'Hence a prince who wishes to maintain his position must learn to be able *not* to be good, and must use or not use that ability according to necessity.'[30] Reflection on such bad results of virtue suggests that someone 'must have a mind disposed to bend itself (disposto a volgersi) as the winds and variations of Fortune command it, and must not depart from the good, when he is able ⟨not to depart from it⟩, but must know how to enter into evil, when he is necessitated ⟨to enter into it⟩'.[31]

In Aristotle's view, the virtuous person with rigid aims is not defeating his own ends. For he attaches dominant value to having this state of character and expressing it, not to the result he achieves by it. Though he has reason to be sorry that being just does not always achieve its anticipated results, he has no reason to think he should care less about being just; for he is better off being just and unsuccessful in achieving the results than he would be if he were successful and unjust.

But we may still wonder why Aristotle thinks the virtuous person should attach himself to these rigid aims and to the dangers of failure, when he could cultivate a more flexible state of character. Aristotle needs to answer that the appropriate sort of rigidity in states of character is itself an aspect of the virtuous person's happiness. When the virtuous person

[29] This aspect of the virtues is well explained by Cooper, above n 9, 83-5.

[30] Machiavelli, *Prince*, ch 15, ed S. Bertelli (Milan, 1960), 65. In such passages Machiavelli probably attacks rigid commitment to Aristotelian virtues. See Q. Skinner, *Foundations of Modern Political Thought* (Cambridge, 1978), vol. i, 121, 131.

[31] *Prince*, ch 18, 73 f.

cultivates stable and unchanging states of character (1100b12-22, 1104b32-3), he secures his own happiness. His stability distinguishes him from the vicious person, who is unstable (1172a9), and therefore lacks the benefits of stability. In saying that the vicious person is unstable Aristotle should not mean that he has a less constant and steady ultimate end and rational plan than the virtuous person's; he is unstable in so far as he is more willing to adapt and sacrifice his other ends to his overriding ends (1167b4-16). Aristotle must show that the vicious person's adaptability is itself a reason for preferring virtue.

Aristotle considers a rational agent planning for his own interest. As we have seen, such an agent attaches dominant value to the exercise of practical reason. He also considers himself as a temporally extended rational agent concerned for himself and for his persistence as the same rational agent. Aristotle wants to argue that the right plans for my future will prescribe the persistence, as far as possible, of the aims, concerns, and states of character that belong to my present self. The more adaptable and flexible my character is, the more readily I will destroy myself in trying to achieve the results I value. The adaptable person wants to adapt himself to secure his own interests. But in making himself flexible and refusing to form a fixed character, he allows less of himself to persist into the future. In adapting himself he partly destroys himself; and hence he will fail to secure his own interest.

To defend this argument Aristotle must agree that the persistence of a person depends in some way on the persistence of states of character. We can see that he agrees with this view if we consider three points in his account of persistence.

1. In a natural organism the form is what persists in the absorption and elimination of matter; hence the form is the primary subject of growth and shrinkage. It is compared to a pipe with water flowing through it, and to a measure that remains constant while different particular quantities and pieces of matter come and go (de Generatione et Corruptione (GC) 322a28, 321b24).[32] The particular organism persists as

[See opposite page for n 32]

long as the form keeps absorbing and eliminating matter in the right way; the form is 'a sort of capacity in the matter' (322a29). 2. The form of a living organism is its soul, the first actuality of the living body. The first actuality is, for example, the state of someone who knows French even when he is not actually speaking it, and the second actuality is the activity of speaking it (*de Anima* (*DA*) 412a22-8). A creature's form will not be its second actuality; second actualities are intermittent, but the creature itself is stable because it has the persistent state that is actualized in these intermittent activities. Hence the persistent state is the form and the soul. 3. To connect these general metaphysical claims about persistence with Aristotle's view of happiness we must attend to the role of states of character. The states of character that we develop when we acquire the virtues are first actualities realized in intermittent virtuous actions; and they are among the essential states whose persistence is the persistence of the same person. Aristotle's description of the best kind of friendship makes it clearest that he regards these states of character as essential to the person. A virtuous person loves his friend in himself by loving the friend's virtuous character, because the friend is good in himself (1156a7-9). His virtuous character is essential to him, and he is the person he is in so far as he has the virtuous character he has (1156a10-19). Since virtuous people are friends because of themselves and their character, and their character is an essential and persistent state of them, their friendship is also persistent, whereas the friendship of other friends is unstable and transient (1156a16-24, b9-12). It follows that if someone's character changes enough, he is no longer the person he was, and that if I was his friend because of his former character, that gives me no reason to continue the friendship when he acquires his later character. Aristotle accepts, indeed stresses, this result, to explain the dissolution of friendships; if we were friends, but my character changes for the worse, I am no longer the person you were friendly to, and you are released from the obligations special to friends (1165b20-36).

---

[32] G. E. M. Anscombe, in *Three Philosophers* (Oxford, 1961), 55 f, rightly draws attention to these passages.

These claims are reasonable only if Aristotle thinks that the persistence of the person includes the persistence of his states of character.

We are justified, then, in ascribing to Aristotle the claims about persistent characters and persistent persons that support his preference for stability and inflexibility. In his view, adaptability fails to secure my future interests, since it fails in some important way to secure my future persistence.

If Aristotle's claim is to be plausible it must be neither indefensibly strong nor uselessly weak. The adaptable person does not literally destroy himself; he still remains the same person. On the other hand, his choices are self-destructive; less of him persists in the future than would persist if he had been less flexible. His prudent planning frustrates itself if it requires the disappearance of many aspects of his present self.

Aristotle's claim requires us to think of an important aspect of prudence that is not always obvious. On his view, the prudent person will plan for self-preservation not only by ensuring the satisfaction of his future desires, but also by ensuring that as many as possible of his present aims and goals, and as much as possible of their present structure, remain in his future self; the more of them remain, the more of himself will persist. If I concentrate on some one overriding end, I may destroy some aspects of myself. A vicious person who regards his power or sensual pleasure as his overriding end will also have subordinate ends; though these are less important to him than his overriding end, they are not merely instrumental to it. He may, for instance, be somewhat attached to his family and friends, and somewhat reluctant to cheat innocent people. But his overriding end requires him to sacrifice those aspects of himself that are attached to his subordinate ends.

Aristotle rejects this degree of self-sacrifice, and urges a rational agent to form plans that allow him to be strongly attached to the same system of ends. The just person does not have to sacrifice his attachment to justice in order to achieve the good of his community; for the dominant component of his good is not the achievement of this result, but the state of character that is concerned with it. Though we cannot achieve incompatible results, we can retain states of character that include concern for incompatible results. By being rigidly attached to particular states of character and to their associated aims and sentiments the virtuous person secures his own interest better than he would if he were more flexible.[33]

These points about stability and self-preservation explain why a rational agent is better off if he cultivates stable and persistent states of character, and does not adapt himself entirely to circumstances. It does not follow that everyone is better off, everything considered, the more stable his character is. If I have a bad character, then I will be better off if I change it; but changing it will itself involve a loss, since less of my old self will persist in my improved character. This is no objection to Aristotle's view. On the contrary, he will argue that it is one further benefit of having a virtuous character; the virtuous person is the only one who can achieve happiness for the whole of the person who aims at it.

The claims about rationality and stability suggest why being virtuous seems to Aristotle to be a dominant component of happiness. Someone who pursues other goods when they require abandonment of goals dependent on rational activity, or when they require dissolution of a stable character, has forgotten that he was concerned with happiness for a human being and for himself as the human being he is. Finding what might be good for another sort of being or for someone other than himself is no answer to Aristotle's question. Since we could not secure happiness for ourselves by sacrificing rationality or stability, we could never have reason to prefer any other good over these, if we are choosing rationally and aiming at our own happiness.

## 8. Virtue and completeness

These arguments may show that rationality and stability are dominant in happiness. But they do not yet prove the

[33] The Aristotelian views about character and persistence that I have sketched here are evidently connected with issues discussed by D. Parfit, *Reasons and Persons* (Oxford, 1984), esp. 298–306, and B. Williams, 'Persons, character and morality', in *Moral Luck* (Cambridge, 1981), esp. 12–14. Not being sure exactly what the connections are, I leave them unexplored.

dominance of the Aristotelian virtues. It is not clear why these virtues are necessary for rationality and stability. For are there not rational and stable states of character that allow, for example, total indifference to the interests of others? Moreover, is it clear that the Aristotelian virtues are even sufficient for rationality and stability? They are defined by reference to the complete good. The complete good has other components besides rationality and stability. How do we know that the demands of Aristotelian virtue will not conflict with rationality and stability?

Someone who regards rationality and stability as dominant even in unfavourable external circumstances might suppose that his plans ought to assume the worst about external circumstances; then he will not be disappointed, and will not have to change his plans or his state of character when things go badly. But is this the rational attitude?

If two stable and rational agents both have good fortune, the optimist who uses the external goods will be happier than the pessimist who refuses to use them for fear that he will lose them. By using external goods the optimist will realize more of his capacities, will have a more complete and self-sufficient life, and will therefore be happier.[34] If both suffer ill fortune, the pessimist's assumptions will have been proved true. The optimist will fail in his more ambitious aims. But, like the pessimist, he regards a stable and virtuous character as the dominant component of happiness; and he still has this character. He is therefore no worse off than the pessimist.

This conclusion may be disputed. The optimist has suffered failures and the resulting pain from which the pessimist is free. Though each of them has the dominant component of happiness, the pessimist seems to have more of its other components, if both suffer ill fortune, and therefore seems to be better off on the whole. Still, we need not agree; perhaps the optimist is better off if he suffers the pain that results from failure in worthy projects than if he suffers no pain as a result of avoiding the projects. Aristotle claims that some

---

[34] I use 'optimist' loosely, for someone who is willing to plan on the basis of something more than the most pessimistic assumptions, not for someone who makes unrealistically optimistic assumptions. In this section I have benefited from Hilary Kornblith's criticisms.

pleasures are bad if they are taken in the wrong objects, even if the fact that they are pleasures is a good feature of them (1173b25-8). He might claim with equal justice that suffering some types of pains is on the whole good, even if the fact that they are pains is a bad feature of them. Aristotle can therefore defend the apparently paradoxical claim that when Priam's misfortunes are at their worst, even so (supposing Priam to be a virtuous person) Priam is better off than a pessimist would be who had neither attempted Priam's projects nor suffered Priam's failures.

Aristotle, then, must accept the view that Tennyson has made a commonplace, that failing is better than not trying.[35] His conception of the dominant component of happiness explains the truth of the commonplace. By attempting a worthy project the optimist has exercised his practical reason to make a desirable difference to the world; even if he fails and suffers pain for his failure, he is better off for having exercised his practical reason in this way than if, like the pessimist, he had decided not to exercise it at all. Pessimistic assumptions encourage the agent to narrow the area in which he can exercise practical reasoning; in deciding not to form a plan requring non-pessimistic assumptions about external conditions, he makes one rational decision, but denies himself the opportunity of making others. He would be justified only if the failure of his attempts would make him worse off than he would have been by not making them. But he cannot reasonably believe this if he attaches dominant value to character and practical reasoning; for in that case he cannot count the harm resulting from failure as greater than the benefit of having made the attempt.

If there were no practical possibility of moderately favourable external circumstances, the choice between optimism and pessimism would make no practical difference. But if there is any such practical possibility, the rational person has reason to be an optimist, and to choose the states of character

---

[35] 'I envy not in any moods / The captive void of noble rage, / The linnet born within the cage, / That never knew the summer woods; / . . . I hold it true, whate'er befall, / I feel it when I sorrow most; / 'Tis better to have loved and lost / Than never to have loved at all.' (*In Memoriam* XXVII.) The reference to noble rage suggests a reason fairly close to Aristotle's.

and the goals that make the best use of external circumstances. The Aristotelian virtues are intended to be those states of character that a rational person recognizes as virtues when he is optimistic. They never leave him worse off than he would be if he were pessimistic, and in moderately favourable external circumstances they leave him better off. They equip us both to use good fortune well and to face ill fortune without disintegrating.

We can be rational and stable in ill fortune even if we lack the specific Aristotelian virtues, but we cannot be well equipped for both good and ill fortune. Nor can we have understood Aristotle's defence of rationality and stability if we refuse to form plans that carry some risk of failure. Once we see why rationality and stability are dominant, we have no reason to fear failure enough to refuse risks.

## 9. Virtue and inflexibility

The Aristotelian virtues of character are intended to secure complete happiness, in the right external circumstances. At the same time these virtues include a commitment to inflexibility; they are stable states of character that the agent will retain even in ill fortune. Their inflexibility is beneficial both in good fortune and in ill fortune. To show that the individual virtues of character meet these conditions it would be best to examine them one at a time. But even without doing this we can suggest and illustrate Aristotle's general view. To illustrate it by reference to the Aristotelian virtues, however, we must grant one further assumption—that, as Aristotle says, the good for an individual includes the good for his family, friends, and fellow-citizens (1097b8–11). The direct benefits of the Aristotelian virtues are often benefits to the agent's community, and the agent himself benefits only in so far as Aristotle's assumption is correct. The assumption and Aristotle's grounds for it clearly deserve a full discussion; here I will simply try to show how Aristotle's argument works if the assumption is accepted.

Aristotle's doctrine of the mean applies to the use and pursuit of external goods. Two aspects of a virtue define the two errors to be avoided:

1. The virtuous person avoids the pessimistic attitude that refuses to be concerned with external goods or with any aim that requires successful use of them. He has friends, he takes and gives money, and he pursues honour and reputation.
2. He avoids the over-valuation of external goods that leads someone to be excessively adaptable; he will not compromise his virtuous aims and outlook to secure external goods, desirable though they are.

We have already seen why the first component of a virtue is better for securing complete happiness in moderately favourable external circumstances. Some people are ungenerous with money because they are afraid of losing it and being 'compelled' to do something shameful (1121b21-8). But they are wrong. If they fell on hard times, and did something shameful, they would be over-estimating the value of the external goods gained by the shameful action; and the virtuous person, recognizing the dominance of virtue, will never do this.[36]

We might think the second concept of virtue is an insurance policy that will pay off in adverse circumstances, but is unnecessary in reliably favourable circumstances; perhaps it is only our belief about the fickleness of external goods that makes it wrong to be too attached to them. Aristotle, however, denies this. He wants to show that in good times as well as bad it is better to be inflexible about virtue and hence reserved about external goods.

The point is easiest to see with bravery. The brave person willingly faces the loss of external goods when bravery requires him to sacrifice his life. His friends and fellow-citizens benefit if he is willing to make this sacrifice. Since his good includes the good of friends and fellow-citizens, he is better off being inflexible about bravery than he would be if he were more flexible.

The magnificent (*megaloprepēs*) person is not so concerned with honour and reputation that he spends his money in ostentatious and conspicuous displays; he wants to spend it

---

[36] 1110a4-8, 19-29, requires us to qualify this remark, by distinguishing what is shameful some things considered from what is shameful all things considered.

to benefit the community (1122b19-23), not merely to win admiration (1123a19-27). His reserve about external goods benefits the community; and a community of such people will be less likely to admire the ostentatious person, and so will collectively benefit from their collective reserve about external goods.

Aristotle claimed that the virtuous person will take the right attitude to misfortune because he is 'noble and magnanimous' (*megalopsuchos*) (1100b31-3); and his account of magnanimity explains that it is the appropriate virtue for these circumstances, since it controls the virtuous person's relative valuation of external goods.[37] The magnanimous person values external goods enough to pursue them vigorously on the right occasions. He wants to be honoured, but only for the right reasons by the right people, precisely for being virtuous and only secondarily for other things (1124a20-6). He is ready to press his own claims, and fear of failure does not restrain him; for failure cannot remove the virtue that is the dominant component of his happiness, and the value of a worthy attempt cannot be overridden by the harm resulting from failure. Even the greatest external good is small by comparison with virtue (1123b32, 1124a19). The magnanimous person pursues the complete good that the pusillanimous person denies himself; but his interest in external goods is not the excessive attachment of the vain person. Hence he is neither too pleased about good fortune nor too distressed about ill fortune (1124a12-20). He cares less about the goods of fortune than about being as virtuous as he can be, and hence he is not prone to lament about them (1129a9-10).

A community of people who lack magnanimity will be both selfish and self-sacrificing in the wrong ways. If they care too much about external goods, they will be ready to cheat each other, or ready to harm their friends for the sake of keeping up the friendship; for they live 'with an eye on another' (1124b31), an attitude that Aristotle condemns as

---

[37] A comparison between the *EE* and *EN* on this point is especially instructive. I hope to present it elsewhere. There are helpful suggestions in D. A. Rees, 'Magnanimity in the *EE* and *NE*', in *Untersuchungen zur Eudemischen Ethik*, ed P. Moraux and D. Harlfinger (Berlin, 1971).

slavish. At the same time they may be ready to harm themselves for inadequate reasons, when the magnanimous
person will refuse (1124b23-6); someone who cares a lot
about other people's opinion or about other external
goods may be ready for some foolish and dangerous exploit that the magnanimous person avoids. This sort of
person will be too ready to cultivate the adaptable character commended by Machiavelli. Such a person, Aristotle
suggests, may make a good mercenary soldier (1117b18-
20); but a community of such people will have mistaken
views about the dangers that should and should not be
faced.

In all these ways Aristotle argues that magnanimity pro-
motes complete happiness better than any different attitude
to external goods would promote it. This does not mean that
magnanimity always results in happiness. But its contribution
to happiness is inseparable from the virtuous person's attitude
to virtue when it does not promote happiness. If he did not
believe that being virtuous dominates the other components
of happiness, he would not secure the other components of
happiness. Aristotle believes that virtue should be chosen
when we cannot have complete happiness, and that it pro-
motes complete happiness; and each of these beliefs explains
and supports the other.

Aristotle needs this sort of argument if he is to show that
the demands of rationality and stability do not conflict with
the demands of the other components of complete happiness,
and to show that the rational agent's concern for his own
good does not conflict with his attachment to the good of
some larger community. If Aristotle's theory cannot avoid
these conflicts, then we have to face the possibility raised by
Machiavelli, that concern for the good of a community
requires an agent to cultivate traits that he rightly condemns as vicious. Aristotle will reject the cultivation of
such traits as unreasonable self-sacrifice for the benefit
of others; and he argues that the conflict that seems to
demand such self-sacrifice does not arise in moderately
favourable external conditions. In less favourable circumstances Machiavelli may be right to say that the conflict
arises; this is one consequence of Aristotle's claim that the

good person and the good citizen are identical only in the best political system (*Pol.* 1276b20–35).

The magnanimous person is inflexible in a way, and Aristotle sees that he may easily remind us of the stubborn and self-willed tragic character who refuses to adapt his views to accommodate external circumstances. When the magnanimous person despises something, he despises it justly, from a true sense of its worth (1124b5); but people easily confuse him with a contemptuous person (1124a20; *EE* 1232b9). To avoid this confusion it is important to see the difference between the inflexibility recommended by Aristotle and that displayed by Ajax or Coriolanus.[38] Ajax is stubborn and unyielding in ways that harm himself and others, because he is ashamed and afraid of dishonour. Though he despises other people, and seeks to display his superiority and independence, he is not independent after all; he is excessively attached to honour, which depends on external conditions, and especially on other people's opinion of him. Hence he is excessively afraid of failure and dishonour, and tries to escape it no matter what harm he does to himself and others.

The magnanimous person is different. He will not be like Ajax or Coriolanus, because he will not be so attached to honour or to any other external good. Since he sees that virtue is dominant, he will be inflexibly virtuous. But since he sees that other goods are subordinate to it, he will be flexible in his pursuit of them, and has no reason to be sullen or uncooperative or unforgiving as Ajax was. Though we are right to admire something about Ajax and about his reaction to Solon's advice, we are wrong to admire Ajax's inflexible and antisocial attachment to those particular values. When Aristotle accepts part of the common attitude he also corrects part of it.

Our discussion of the virtues of character may suggest how Aristotle tries to show that the Aristotelian virtues are a rational agent's best equipment when he faces good fortune and ill fortune. Hence they are the best stable states of character to acquire; and someone who has them has the dominant component of happiness.

---

[38] On Ajax see *Fragmenta* 147 (Ross); *Analytica Posteriora* 97b15-26.

10. Aristotle's solution

Aristotle is right to attend to Solon's problem; for his answer to the problem illuminates his own conception of happiness. Solon was right to suggest that happiness is unstable because it is vulnerable to chance and external circumstances. But we are wrong if we suppose that chance also determines whether we are unhappy or not; and we are wrong if we decide to make ourselves adaptable to external circumstances. The inflexible response is right, if we are inflexible about the right things. We should realize that the Aristotelian virtues are the dominant component of happiness, and that, though happiness itself is unstable, its dominant component is stable.

Aristotle's answer to Solon's problem is as complex as his answer to most of the traditional problems of Greek ethics that he discusses. He does not totally reject the common-sense outlook. He refuses to follow the Socratic and Cynic solution that ensures the stability of happiness by taking virtue to be sufficient for it. Still, his solution would appear to common sense to be much closer to the Socratic position than to common sense. Here as in his discussion of incontinence Aristotle first rejects Socrates' position, and then argues for one of its most counter-intuitive elements.

Aristotle's view did not convince his main Hellenistic successors, who generally agreed with Socrates. It has not convinced most modern moralists either. Even when they want to agree that a morally virtuous person has reason to prefer to be virtuous even at a severe cost to him, they do not normally rely on Aristotle's sort of argument. Many have thought that once Aristotle rests his defence of virtue on an appeal to happiness he cannot succeed. And even if he succeeded, many would reject this as the wrong sort of defence of morality, a defence that the moral person should not seek.

Once we understand Aristotle's argument, however, we may have some reason to resist both these criticisms. We should ask ourselves again more carefully whether his defence of virtue is relevant to the proper concern of the morally virtuous person. He argues that the virtuous person's proper degree of commitment to virtue is explicable and justifiable by reference to a plausible conception of the good of a rational agent. The conclusion is striking enough to make it worth our while to examine the premisses.[39]

*Cornell University*

[39] Versions of this paper were read at a meeting of the Southern Association for Ancient Philosophy in Cambridge; Cornell; the University of California, Riverside; Colgate; William and Mary; and the University of Vermont. I am grateful to the helpful critics mentioned in the footnotes above, to others who raised questions on these occasions, and especially to Susan Sauvé and Jennifer Whiting for detailed and useful written comments.

# SEPARATION IN ARISTOTLE'S METAPHYSICS*[1]

## Donald Morrison

## Introduction

Separation is among Aristotle's most important criteria of substance. At *Metaphysics* M. 10. 1086b16-19 he says: 'If one does not suppose that substances are separated, and in the way that particular beings are said to be ⟨separated⟩, one will destroy substance as we understand the term.' At Z. 3. 1029a28: 'But ⟨that matter is substance⟩ is impossible; for both separation and 'thisness' are thought to belong chiefly to substance.' At 1040b28: 'But those who say the Ideas exist in one respect are right, in giving the Ideas separated existence, *if* they are substances.'

This criterion is employed by Aristotle in his criticism of Platonic Ideas. The Ideas are conceived of by the Platonists as separate universals; but no universal can be separate; so Ideas as they are conceived of by the Platonists cannot exist. Separation also does work for Aristotle within his own theory. The three most promising candidates for substance, in Aristotle's view, are matter, form, and the composite of the two. Matter turns out not to be separate at all, and form turns out to be separate merely in a qualified way: form is 'separate in definition' (1042a29). The composite alone is separate without qualification. For that reason, so far as the criterion of separation is concerned, the composite has the best claim to be substance. Since other criteria of substance lead in other directions, the use of separation as a mark of

* © Donald Morrison 1985.

[1] An earlier version of this essay formed Ch IV of my PhD thesis, *Three Criteria of Substance in Aristotle's Metaphysics: Unity, Definability, Separation* (Princeton, 1983). Thanks are due to John Cooper, who advised the dissertation; to Peter King for his help on that chapter; and to Julia Annas, David Blank, Alexander Nehamas, Dan Warren, and Jennifer Whiting for their comments on later versions. Part of this essay was given as a lecture to the Columbia University Department of Philosophy in March 1984, whose audience provided a stimulating and helpful discussion.

substance leads to significant strains within the theory. An example: the form is prior in definition to both the matter and the composite; substance is thought to be primary in definition;[2] so by this criterion of substance, the form has the best claim to be substance.

Although the concept of 'separation' is important, detailed scholarly investigations of the concept have been rare.[3] In this paper I shall address the questions: What was Aristotle's conception of separation as a criterion of substance? What are its consequences, and how does it function?

Among the conclusions I argue for, two are especially controversial: (i) for substance to be 'separate' on Aristotle's view is for it to be separate from other substances; and (ii) Aristotle's use of 'separate in definition' as a means of saying that forms are after all 'separate' is indefensible—indeed it is a kind of cheat. The first claim sounds reasonable enough, but it is controversial. The separation of substance is sometimes held to be either 'separation in place' or else 'independence'. These views seem wrong, for reasons I explain. The alternative I argue for is that the separation of a substance is its separation from other substances. Views similar to this one can be found in the literature, but they are never worked out in detail. As I state the view, it has some tricky consequences. The second claim is one such consequence; and I wish I could avoid it. One reason to doubt my general view of separation, I admit, is that it makes Aristotle's use of 'separation in definition' in *Metaphysics* H. 1 seem to be a mere sophistical dodge.

### Some initial evidence

Aristotle says that substance is separate.[4] But separate *from what* and *in what way*? He never gives a detailed answer to

---

[2] *Metaphysics (Metaph.)* 1028a32, 1031a1-2, 10 ff.

[3] See A. Preiswerk, *Das Einzelne bei Platon und Aristoteles*, in *Philologus*, Supplementband 1939; C.-H. Chen, *Das Chorismos-Problem bei Aristoteles* (Berlin, 1940); E. de Strycker, 'La notion aristotélicienne de séparation dans son application aux Idées de Platon', in *Autour d'Aristote* (Paris, 1962), and now G. Fine 'Separation', in *Oxford Studies in Ancient Philosophy*, ii (1984), 31-87.

[4] See *de Generatione et Corruptione (GC)* 317b28; *Metaph.* 991b1, b3, 1029a28, 1040b28, 1070b36, 1077b3, b7, 1080a1, 1086b17, b19, 1087a23; *Physics (Ph.)* 185a31.

either question. He discusses whether matter and form are separate from each other and from the compound; whether parts are separate from their wholes; and whether Ideas, mathematicals, and immaterial movers are separate from sensibles and particulars. In all of these cases he specifies what the item is supposed to be separate *from*. But the separation of substance he never 'completes' in this way. Or at best, he may do so, obscurely, in just one passage. The passage is *Metaphysics* M. 10. 1086b16-19:

εἰ μέν γάρ τις μὴ θήσει τὰς οὐσίας εἶναι κεχωρισμένας, καὶ τὸν τρόπον τοῦτον ὡς λέγεται τὰ καθ᾽ ἕκαστα τῶν ὄντων, ἀναιρήσει τὴν οὐσίαν ὡς βουλόμεθα λέγειν.

(If one does not suppose that substances are separated, and in the way that the particular beings are said to be ⟨separated⟩, one will destroy substances as we intend the term.)

Following, for example, Ross and Annas, I have translated *tōn ontōn* as a partitive genitive: 'of beings' specifies the class within which the particulars fall. But a second construal is possible: *tōn ontōn* can be taken as completing *kechōrismenas*. The translation would then read: '. . . and in the way that particulars are said to be [separate] from the beings . . .'. The 'beings' of this alternative translation might be taken to signify either (i) all beings whatsoever, (ii) the other beings, or (iii) the other particulars. Of these, the third is most plausible. The first will not do, since particulars themselves are beings. The second is ambiguous, depending on the sense of 'other'. Surely a particular is not separate from its attributes (*Ph.* 216b6, b7, 217a24), yet its attributes are 'other' than it. If 'other' has the stronger sense 'not numerically identical with', then the second interpretation is equivalent to the third, since numerical identity *is* the kind of identity particulars have.

Thus, 'the other particulars' is an acceptable, though not a particularly natural interpretation of *tōn ontōn* at line 18. Certainly if Aristotle meant 'the other particulars', he could have said so in a much better way. The other reading, though far more natural, is also awkward, since as a partitive genitive *tōn ontōn* is almost intolerably vacuous. 'Of the beings' does not restrict the range of the particulars, *ta kath' hekasta*, at all. Since neither reading is very happy, it seems that *tōn ontōn* here cannot be relied on as evidence for what Aristotle thinks substances should be *chōristai* from.

On the other hand, M. 10. 1086b16–19 is interesting for a second reason: it is one of only two passages in which Aristotle explicitly tells us something about the *way* in which substances are separate. He says: 'in the way that particulars are separate'. This explanation is disappointing, since it only pushes the question one step back: how, one asks, are the particulars separate?[5] This new question is easier to answer if one does assume that the separation of particulars meant here is their separation from each other. Taking *tōn ontōn* as 'from the other particulars' is one way to justify this; but in any case it is hard to see what else 'the separation of particulars' might mean.

The second passage where Aristotle says something explicit about the way in which substances are separate is *Physics* 185a31: 'For none of the others is separate, except substance. For all things are said of substance as of a substratum.' This remark suggests that the way to be separate in the way that a substance is, is to be not said of anything else as of a substratum; and (combining this with the evidence of M. 10) that the way for two particulars to be separate is for them not to be said of a common substratum or of each other. In the next section I will amplify and defend this construal of separation

## The competing accounts

At least four explanations of the separation of particulars are worth considering: (1) their spatial separation—that is, separation in 'place'; (2) their existing independently of each other; (3) their being numerically distinct; (4) their being outside each other's ontological boundaries. I shall argue that (1) and (2) are mistaken accounts of Aristotle's theory, while (3) and (4) are equivalent, and correct.

---

[5] This disappointing explanation is exactly parallel to another, more famous explanation at *Metaph.* Δ. 1016b32. Why are things numerically one? Because their matter is one. But what makes matter one? To this question Aristotle nowhere gives an explicit answer.

The first account is that the separation of particulars is separation in place.[6] One might think this because of the contrast Aristotle draws at *Metaphysics* H. 2. 1042a30 between absolute separation (*haplōs*) and separation in definition (*logōi*). There he states that absolute separation is the separation of the composite, whereas separation in definition is the separation of the form. And, though he does not explain himself in this way explicitly here or elsewhere, it might seem natural to think that composites *are* spatially marked off from one another. Furthermore, there is undeniably a spatial metaphor contained in *chōrizein*, and the exclusion of special senses by *haplōs* might be thought to restrict 'separation' precisely to this spatial sense. However, even if one does assume that the separation of composites is *spatial* separation, the separation of the composite cannot automatically be identified with the separation of substance in general. Matter, form, and composite are all substance in a way. So even if the absolute separation of the composite were separation in place, this does not by itself establish that separation of *substance* is separation in place.

Separation *haplōs* is in fact mentioned only once in Aristotle's corpus, at the passage in H. 2 just cited.[7] The distinction between absolute separation and separation in definition is introduced there just because the three-way division of substance into matter, form, and composite requires a more sophisticated account of how substances are separate. Perhaps the separation of the composite is the kind of separation originally and more naïvely ascribed to all substances; in fact that is what I will argue. But without further defence, this cannot be assumed. Further, at 1042a30 separation in place is not mentioned: we are told only that the separation of composites is *haplōs* while the separation of form is *logōi*.

---

[6] I have heard this view attributed to Aristotle several times in conversation, though in print I have only found it suggested in H. Bonitz, *Index Aristotelicus* (Berlin, 1870), 860a24; and K. Bärthlein, *Die Transcendentalienlehre der alten Ontologie* (Berlin, 1972), 120. Many contemporary substance theorists place heavy weight on spatiotemporal continuity, so for that reason alone it is important to discourage the temptation to overemphasize that component of Aristotle's thought.

[7] *Sophistici Elenchi* (*SE*) 166a18 and *Metaph.* 1077b32 initially seem parallel, but they are not. At 166a18 *haplōs* depends upon *sēmainei*; and at 1077b32, on *legein*.

Separation in place and separation in definition are contrasted elsewhere[8] but only as two among various ways in which things can be separate. Hence the argument for equating separation *haplōs* and separation in place must be made on philosophical grounds.

The immediate objection to this view is that immaterial substances clearly have no place. Yet they are paradigmatic substances, they are particulars, and they are separate (1073a4, 1074a6).[9]

The substance composed of matter and form is separate in place from other substances, since the composite occupies a single place.[10] Even so, it would be a mistake to think that being separate *in place* is what makes even material substances separate, and hence substance. A finger is separate in place from the rest of the body, yet it is not 'separate' in the way necessary for it to be a separate substance.

The second account interprets being separate as being 'independent'.[11] The notion 'independence' is itself open to interpretation; I have some doubt that those scholars who use the word all mean the same thing by it. Fundamentally, however, there seem to be two different views. The first is that '*X* is *chōristos* from *Y*' means '*X* is independent from *Y*' in the sense that *X* can continue to exist after it has been separated from *Y*. (This separation may occur due either to *Y*'s destruction, or simply to the splitting off of *X* from *Y*.) The problem is that on this view 'independence' just amounts to 'separability'; and I have argued elsewhere on philological

---

[8] *de Anima* (*de An.*) 413b14-15, 429a11-12, 432a20; *GC* 320b24 (see 320b12-14); *Ethica Nicomachea* (*EN*) 1102a28-31; see *Ph.* 193b4-5; *Metaph.* 1048b14-15.

[9] For the objection generally, see H. Cherniss, *Aristotle's Criticism of Plato and the Academy* (*ACPA*) (Baltimore, 1944), 367-8. Further evidence: 1042a31 is an obscure sentence, but if one takes it in the most straightforward way (see Ross's translation), it expressly *says* that immaterial substances are *chōrista haplōs*.

[10] See *Metaph.* 1068b26 for a definition of togetherness and separation *topōi*.

[11] de Strycker, above n 3, 124, 138 (but he has reservations: see 132); Cherniss, *ACPA* 229; P. Aubenque, *Problème de l'Etre chez Aristote* (Paris, 1962), 36 n 2; Chen, above n 3, 175; Bärthlein, above n 6, 122; J. Annas, *Aristotle's Metaphysics: Books M & N* (Oxford, 1976), 136-7; M. Frede, 'Individuen bei Aristoteles', *Antike und Abendland* XXIV (1978), 32; Preiswerk, above n 3, 193; Fine, above n 3, s 2, and the additional references she provides.

grounds that *chōristos* must mean actually separate, not separable.[12] The second view is that *X* is independent from *Y* just in case *X* is able to exist without *Y*; that is, even when *Y* does not exist. *X* might be independent in this sense because it can exist even though *Y* be destroyed; or because it can exist even though no *Y* ever existed (or more strongly: ever could have existed or could exist). Irrelevant to the independence of *X* on this view (as opposed to the former view) is the case where *X* and *Y* are separated off from each other, both continuing to exist. This second version of 'independence' does correspond to an expressly identified technical concept in Aristotle's philosophy: Aristotle calls it 'natural priority'.[13]

The view that for Aristotle the separation of substance is the same as the natural priority of substance, and hence for substance *X* to be separate from *Y* is for it to be able to exist without *Y*, seems to be the most popular of all in the literature. Moreover, this view has recently been ably defended by Gail Fine in her article cited earlier, 'Separation'. Although I am about to argue against Fine's position, her article has the virtue of stating what seems to be the dominant interpretation of separation in Aristotle clearly and precisely, defending it in more detail than anyone else has done.[14]

Before discussing the textual evidence against the view that Aristotle's concepts of natural priority and separation of substances are identical, I wish to lodge three general complaints. The first concerns the meaning of *chōristos* in Greek. Some advocates of this interpretation (though they are by no means clear about this) seem to want to translate *chōristos*

---

[12] In 'Χωριστός in Aristotle', forthcoming in *Harvard Studies in Classical Philology*, LXXXIX (1985).

[13] At *Metaph.* 1019a1–4 Aristotle explains what it is to be *protera kai hustera kata phusin hai ousian* in just these terms; see also 1071a2, a33, 1077a36–b11; *Protrepticus* Ross fr 5, p 32; *Peri Ideon* Ross fr 5, Alexander, in *Aristotelis Metaphysica commentaria* (*in Met.*) 97. 18–19; *Eudemian Ethics* (*EE*) 1218a2 ff; *de Generatione Animalium* (*GA*) 736b22.

[14] Readers of her paper may wish to know something about the relative chronology of our work. The initial versions of Fine's paper and of mine were completed independently. Fine saw my paper (in the form of a chapter of my PhD dissertation) only in time to add a long footnote taking issue with my views. Due to her kindness in letting me see a copy of her paper in advance of publication, I, by contrast, have had the luxury of ample time to read and consider hers.

by 'independent'. But *chōristos* just does not mean 'independent' in Greek; it means 'separate'. Those who put forward the independence account of *chōristos* ought to put it forward as a philosophical reconstruction, or explanation, of Aristotle's idea; not as an account of the meaning of the word. Those who do simply translate *chōristos* as 'independent' are mistranslating the Greek.

Gail Fine is too sophisticated, and too clear about her own position, to make this mistake. She translates *chōristos* as 'separate', and goes on to claim quite properly that, for her, ' "Capable of independent existence" is an effort to give content to, to explain the force of, "separate"; and it certainly involves no mistranslation to suppose that that is its force.'[15]

However, Fine's view is subject to a related difficulty. For she, along with anyone who wishes to defend her view, owes us an account of why this Greek term should be used to express that concept. 'Separation' and 'independence' seem to be very different concepts; the one has primarily local and spatial overtones; the other does not. It is intrinsically implausible that a Greek word whose basic meaning is 'separation' should also be used to express the very different concept of 'independence'. Those who advocate the 'independence' interpretation of *chōristos* need to be able to explain how this word came to be used for that concept; but such an explanation is difficult to find.[16, 17]

The second general objection to Fine's view is that it would make Socrates an accident of the sun. Aristotle held, quite reasonably, that the sun is a sustainer of all life. If the

[15] Fine, above n 3, 36 n 19.

[16] The best suggestion that I know of remains quite unpromising. One could argue that whenever one thing is dependent on another, the two things are *ipso facto* connected in some way. They may not be next to each other, or connected physically, but they are *causally connected*, and that is connection enough. But the notion of causal connection is difficult to impute to Aristotle; and I doubt that a mere causal connection is connection enough.

[17] Fine might object that this argument weighs equally strongly against my own account of separation. True enough, my account must satisfy the same demand as hers; but in my case the demand is easier to satisfy. My explaining *chōristos* as 'being outside the ontological boundaries of' is no more a translation than Fine's 'capable of independent existence'; but as an explanation, it is much closer to the ordinary meaning of the term. The local and spatial overtones are plainly there; the extension of the concept of separation from a concern with spatial boundaries to a concern with ontological ones is a very natural one.

sun should pass out of existence, so too would Socrates. But this means that the sun is naturally prior to Socrates and he is not independent of the sun. Then, on this view, Socrates is not separate from the sun—so Socrates is not himself a substance, but rather an accident of the sun.

Fine has responded to this by saying that on the independence view the separation of substance is not from other substances—as on my view—but rather from accidents.[18] Substance is separate from, that is relative to, accidents, but not vice versa. That Socrates, a substance, is not separate from the sun, another substance, is beside the point. I respond that, on the contrary, this is exactly the point. On the independence view asymmetrical separation *constitutes* the distinction between substance and accident. So if the sun is separate from Socrates but not vice versa, then Socrates is not a substance, but an accident of the sun.

This argument has a further, more general consequence. Later I will argue that the separation criterial for substance is its separation from other substances, basing this on a reciprocal notion of separation. The independence theorist has a non-reciprocal notion of separation—$X$ can be separate from $Y$ without $Y$ being separate from $X$—but this non-reciprocal notion also requires that a substance be separate from other substances. On the independence view, substance must be separate from *everything*—since whatever it is not separate from, it will be posterior to and hence an accident of. What is distinctive of the view I defend is not that it requires substance to be separate from other substances as well as accidents, but that it requires substance to be separate only from other substances. As the reader will see, my view admits that a substance is not separate from its accidents. What is untenable on any version is that substance can be separate from accidents alone.

Perhaps defenders of the 'independence' interpretation of *chōristos* would aim to avoid this objection by appealing to an 'ontological' notion of independence that abstracts from any natural, 'causal' dependence or independence. The difficulty with this is to find a notion of 'ontological' independence

[18] In Fine, above n 3, 36 n 19.

that both does the job and could plausibly be attributed to
Aristotle. One example will illustrate the difficulty. The
classic medieval notion of independence relies on the following test: *X* is independent of *Y* if God could create (or
maintain in existence—here they come to the same thing)
the one without the other. This may do the job, *if* one
happens to believe in the God of the medievals; but Aristotle
did not. Aristotle did not believe that *anyone* could maintain
Socrates in existence after the destruction of the sun—let
alone the shape, colour, and taste of the wafer after the
transformation of its substance. For Aristotle, at least outside
of syllogistic contexts, 'possibility' is real, physical, causal
potentiality, and no doctrine of independence based on any
other notion of possibility can plausibly be attributed to him.

My third general complaint against the independence view
is that it has difficulty accounting for the passages in which
Aristotle insists that the Forms should be placed *in* sensible
things. As Fine points out (41), Aristotle never explicitly
equates Plato's separation of the Forms with his failure to
place them in sensible things—but given the native spatial
sense of *chōristos*, and the fact that Aristotle uses both
separation and failure to be 'in' to express his dissatisfaction
with the Forms,[19] a strong interpretive goal should be to find
an account of separation and of failure to be 'in' on which
they amount to the same thing, or at the very least are closely
related.[20] This the 'independence' interpretation cannot do.

[19] It is misleading of Fine to say (also 41) that *en* and *chōris* appear only a few
times in close proximity. In addition to the adverb *chōris*, verbs, adjectives, and
nouns formed on the *-chōris-* stem must also be considered. Passages containing
*en* and *-chōris-* in close proximity that are especially relevant to the separation of
substances include the following: *de An.* 403b6; *de Caelo (Cael.)* 278a11, 305a17;
*Categoriae (Cat.)* 1a24; *GC* 320a34–b9, 320b28, 324b19; *Magna Moralia (MM)*
1. 1. 12. 2; *Metaph.* 996a15, 998a9, a18, 1023a23, 1026a15, 1036a32, b4–7,
1038b32, 1039a27, b1, 1060b16, b25–8, 1065a23–7, 1068b26, 1076a33, b3,
1077b15 ff, 1080b1, 1085a26, 1090a24, a30; *Ph.* 192b28–30, 193b4, 203a6,
210b4; *de Sensu (Sens.)* 439a24; *de Xenophane* 980b11. Less directly relevant
passages in which *-chōris-* and *en* are contrasted include: *Analytica Posteriora*
93a13; *de An.* 416b24; *Cael.* 302a1; *EE* 1219b34; *EN* 1102a26; *GA* 715b29,
736b26, 739b30; *Historia Animalium* 555a16, 507b36; *de Juventute* 469a21;
*MM* 2. 12. 10. 2; *Metaph.* 1030b23, 1064a25; *Ph.* 186b22 ff, 209b24; *SE*
181b36; *Sens.* 446a12, a18. If paraphrases of *-chōris-* and related words such as
*morion*, 'part', were included, the list would be even longer.
[20] 'At the very least are closely related', because in *Metaph.* M. 3 Aristotle
seems to come to the conclusion that mathematicals are neither in things nor

Fine says that the list of senses of 'in' at *Physics* Δ. 3 reveals that 'in' can be used to indicate dependence of some sort. If this were so, then an Aristotelian sense of 'in' would be available to the independence theorist which would permit identifying separation with failure to be 'in': namely the sense in which 'in' means 'dependent'. The passages in which the Forms are said to be both separate from and not in the sensibles could then be interpreted in that light. But in *Physics* Δ. 3 Aristotle does not specify any sense of 'in' as 'dependence of some sort'. What he does is specify two senses of 'in' that are dependencies of two particular sorts. Neither sense transfers well into English: one is a sense in which an effect is 'in' its primary efficient cause, and the other a sense in which a thing is 'in' its good or end, that is its final cause.[21] If the independence theorist wishes to rummage *Physics* Δ. 3 for a suitable sense of 'in', he or she will need to interpret the issue of the separation of Forms from the particulars as concerning either the Forms not being efficiently caused by the particulars, or else their not being finally caused by them. I take it as obvious that neither interpretation is remotely plausible: at best it should be the other way around.[22]

separate from them, but have a third sort of status. That the problem in M. 1-2 by means of an opposition between separation and being in shows that the concepts are at least closely related. In fact, it suggests that this is how Aristotle normally views the problem—that is, apart from the dialectical trick which he is about to pull in M. 3. His solution there strikes one as a typical Aristotelian 'saving of the appearances' in a misleading way so as to make his view seem to have more in common with the losing side than in fact it does. Mathematicals may not be 'in' things in the way that some theorists would have them—as ghostly, coextensive quasi-bodies—but that does not mean they are not 'in' things in a perfectly good Aristotelian sense of 'in', for example as health is in what is hot and cold.

[21] Senses (6) and (7) as they are numbered in Edward Hussey's new translation and commentary, *Aristotle's Physics: Books III and IV* (Oxford, 1983), 24, 107-8. Senses (1) and (2), concerning whole and part, also indicate dependencies: since whole and part are correlatives, they are thereby mutually dependent. But since Fine is trying to avoid interpreting *chōristos* as local separation, these senses are not relevant here.

[22] *Ph.* Δ. 3 lists another sense of 'in' that immediately recalls his dispute with Plato over the status of Forms: '(5) In another, as health is in hot and cold things, and generally, as the form is in the matter' (210a20-1), Hussey trans.; see also *Metaph.* 1023a11-13). Just by itself, this sentence provides strong evidence that for Aristotle the separation of substance (the separation which forms do not have) is failure to be 'in', for some suitable sense of 'in'. But of course it does not provide much help toward explaining, philosophically, what that sense amounts to.

So much for the general arguments. Now, the textual evidence. One piece of textual evidence cited by Fine (35) in favour of the independence view is *Metaphysics* Z. 1. 1028a31-b2:

ὅμως δὲ πάντως ἡ οὐσία πρῶτον, καὶ λόγῳ καὶ γνώσει καὶ χρόνῳ. τῶν μέν γὰρ ἄλλων κατηγορημάτων οὐθεν χωριστόν, αὕτη δὲ μόνη . . . Generally substance is prior in all ways, in definition, in knowledge, and in time [or: in nature]. For of the other things predicated, none is separate, but only substance.

Aristotle goes on explicitly to give explanations of priority in definition and in knowledge, so that the first explanation, which I quoted, that 'only substance' is separate, must match up with priority in time. Scholars have found it difficult to see how separation could serve as an explanation of priority in time. The account of priority in time at *Metaphysics* Δ. 11 is no help. But there is an alternative solution available: the lemma, or citation, of this line in the late Greek commentator Asclepius adds 'in nature' (*phusēi*), to the list. Merely adding it to the original list of three creates a problem, for now one has only three explanations for four kinds of priority. But perhaps 'in nature' could be substituted for 'in time': then the separation of substance would explain its priority in nature. Since priority in nature, or 'natural priority', is defined by Aristotle as 'independence', this reading would provide a direct textual link between the ideas of independence and the separation of substance.

The trouble is that this reading of the text is highly implausible. First, a lemma in Asclepius, standing alone against all other evidence, has very weak authority. And second, as Ross suggests in his commentary, 'in nature' is just the sort of thing likely to be added as a gloss by a commentator who is puzzled by the meaning of 'in time'. So this reading in Asclepius *is* evidence that someone in the tradition of Asclepius interpreted the passage in the way the independence theorist wants: but it is no evidence that Aristotle himself meant it this way. *Metaphysics* Z. 1. 1028a31-b2 is famously a crux, a mystery: no one knows how to interpret it, and it can provide no evidence for the 'independence' interpretation of separation.[23]

[23] Fine claims that this passage supports her interpretation regardless of how

A second passage containing evidence for the 'independence' interpretation serves as a warning that one must be very precise in stating the implications of a text. The passage is *Eudemian Ethics* 1217b2–16:

> For they say that the good-itself is the best thing of all, and the good-itself is that to which it belongs to be both first among goods, and the cause by its presence, for other things, of their being goods. For, they say, . . . it is first among goods—since, if the object in which things share were taken away, with it would go all the things that share in the Form, and are called what they are called through sharing in it; and that is the way that the first stands in relation to what comes after. And indeed, like the other Forms, the Form of the good is separate from the things that share in it.                (Woods' translation)

This passage says that the Form of the good is first among the goods because it is naturally prior: if it were taken away everything else that is good would disappear as well. It concludes with a teaser: 'And indeed, the Form of the good is separate from the things that share in it.' One might think that Aristotle is here summing up his preceding point, and thereby identifying independence with separation. But this conclusion is unnecessary, and even unlikely. For the Greek words translated as 'And indeed' (*kai gar*) have a strong 'explanatory' flavour.[24] The sense I get from these words here is: 'and now I am going to remind you of a familiar fact, on the basis of which all that has gone before will seem naturally to follow'. The familiar fact: that this Form, like all others, is separate. To be explained by that fact: that this Form is naturally prior.

So it does follow from this passage that the separation of a Form should at least entail the natural priority of the Form. But this need not require that separation and natural priority are the same; in fact, the passage works better if they are not. If 'separation' is the same as 'natural priority', then it doesn't serve well as an explanation of natural priority.

Situations like the present one occur often: demonstrating that one of Aristotle's philosophical terms entails the other is

the text is read. I myself do not see this: without the word *phusei*, the text contains no link to the particular kind of priority which Aristotle uncontroversially defines in terms of 'independence'.

[24] On this sense see J. Denniston, *Greek Particles* (2nd edn, Oxford, 1954), 118, s (2).

fairly easy; a mutual entailment between the terms can also frequently be shown. But even mutual entailment is not yet enough to show identity of concept, though it is evidence in that direction.

This exhausts the direct textual evidence linking natural priority and the separation of substance.[25] Neither on general philosophical grounds nor on textual grounds can it be shown that the separation of substance *just is* natural priority according to Aristotle.

### The present account

The third interpretation of the separation of particular substances mentioned above (128) was their numerical distinctness from one another. This account seems to me both true to Aristotle, and genuinely explanatory. Substances are indeed separate because they are numerically distinct. However, this explanation is not fundamental. Two accidental entities can be numerically distinct, and thereby separate *from each other*, without thereby being substances. In the case of two objects, one large and one small, 'the large' and 'the small' are numerically distinct, but neither are substances. Numerical distinctness explains why a substance is separate, but it does not explain its having that sort of separation which is unique to and constitutive of substances. The notion of numerical distinctness presupposes the distinction between substance and accident, whereas we want an explanation of that distinction itself.

To find this deeper explanation, one must ask the question: What after all makes particulars numerically distinct? An adequate response to this question would require many pages; but a plausible short answer is this: Two things are numerically one just in case they have the same basic substratum (*hupokeimenon*). A thing is numerically one just in

---

[25] A passage in the *Peri Ideon* does mention both notions, but in a way that permits no inference about their relationship: 'On this showing, the Ideas would be destroyed along with the things in which they are. Nor would they have a separate existence, but only existence in the things which share in them' (fr 5 Ross). The connective 'nor' (*all' oude* in Greek) could signify either that the second sentence presents a new point, distinct from the first, or that it merely restates the first in other words.

case it has only one basic substratum. (A universal is not numerically one, just because it has many substrata.) Two things are numerically distinct just in case they are each numerically one, and have different substrata.[26] Numerical unity, so explained, coheres nicely with Aristotle's remark on the mode of separation of substances quoted earlier. Recall that at *Physics* 185a31 Aristotle says: 'For none of the others is separate, except substance. For all things are said of substance as of a substratum.' None of the other things—in the context, it is clear that Aristotle has in mind qualities, quantities, and so on—is separate, because they are not separate from substance. And he explains that they are not separate from substance because they are said of it as of a substratum; that is, they inhere in the substance, they have it as their basic substratum. Having substance as their basic substratum, they are numerically one with substance, hence not numerically distinct from substance, hence not separate from substance.[27] If numerical unity, inherence in a substratum, and separation are connected in this way, then this passage provides positive evidence that in Aristotle the separation of a substance is equivalent to its numerical distinctness from other substances.

The account of separation as numerical distinctness coincides with the fourth account mentioned on page 128, 'being outside of each other's ontological boundaries', provided that having something as a basic substratum is one way of being within the ontological boundaries of that thing. Aristotle does not use the term 'ontological boundaries', but the idea is useful for understanding what he has in mind. For that purpose, 'having as a substratum' or 'inhering in' should be seen as one way of 'being within the ontological boundaries of'.

---

[26] For the purpose of these definitions, 'having a substratum' must be taken loosely, so that 'being' a substratum is one way of 'having' a substratum. This is not quite Aristotle's usage, but it will do for the present purpose.

[27] In his early works, Aristotle allows that attributes inhere in universals— e.g. substance in general, man in general—and that this inherence is distinct from their inhering in particulars. In these early works, Aristotle also allows that universals are numerically one. What I say in this paper about the relations between inherence and numerical unity is not quite adequate to handle the doctrine of the early works.

The notion of ontological boundary needs elaboration. Consider a man in a box; or perhaps better, a man hidden inside the trunk of a large old oak. In this situation there are what both Aristotle and we consider two substances, yet one is inside the other. If being in something, in *any* sense of 'in', were sufficient to disqualify separation, then the man would not be separate from the oak. Yet the man is separate from the oak, because, in some way needing to be specified, he is outside of its 'ontological boundaries'. The man may be within the oak spatially, but the territory of the oak itself ends at its inner surface. The man, although inside the place created by that inner surface, is still outside that volume which goes to make up the oak.[28]

The reason the man and the oak are ontologically distinct is primarily, on Aristotle's view, that they lack unity of motion in place and time.[29] They lack unity of motion because the oak is stationary whereas the man can leave: he can climb out, walk around, and so on. Unity of motion is the basic criterion because it holds whether there is a form involved or not. To take Aristotle's example from Δ. 6, a conglomeration of bits of wood randomly glued together *has* no form, and therefore it cannot be the same or distinct in form with anything. None the less, if it were placed inside the hollow of an oak, it would be distinct from the oak.

The man and the oak in the earlier example not only lack unity of motion. They also lack specific unity, since the man is an organized whole different in kind from the organized whole that is the oak. The parts of the man are governed by one principle of organization, his soul, and the parts of the oak are governed by another principle of organization, *its* soul. However, their lack of specific unity is not the cause of their ontological distinctness. A tiny young oak, potted

[28] Anatomists use a similar principle in considering the contents of our digestive tracts to be outside of our bodies.

[29] *Metaph.* I. 1. 1052a25-8; see also Δ. 6. 1015b36-1016a17. *Ph.* V. 4 discusses unity of motion at length, although not unity of motion 'in place and time'. An adequate account of unity of motion in place and time would be a long and subtle business, especially since the interpretation of unity of motion in general is notoriously vexed. A short discussion that ignores the more general problems can be found on pp 65-6 of my *Three Criteria of Substance*; a recent extensive discussion of unity of motion in general can be found in David Charles, *Aristotle's Philosophy of Action* (Ithaca, 1984), esp. Ch. 1.

and set inside the hollow old one, would still be numerically distinct.

Though specific unity is not the sole cause of ontological distinctness, the immanent form or soul *is* basic in a way, because it is the difference between the souls of the man and the oak which explains why they do not have unity of motion. The souls of the man and of the oak function like the glue which holds together the bits of wood. What counts is that the souls are different souls, not that they are different in kind.

Having unity of motion, and having unity of form in addition to unity of motion, are grades of numerical unity for substances.[30] For things that have a form, the spatial extent of the thing, its ontological boundaries in the spatial dimension, are determined by the range of influence of the form. For Aristotle the form of something is, among other things, its principle of organization and the source of its characteristic behaviour. My soul is responsible for the fact that my body and all of its parts act in ways radically different from the ways of a corpse. Further, the extent of the influence of this animating factor, the form, is the extent of the substance which is me.

'The extent of the influence of the form' may sound vague and metaphorical, but the metaphor can be cashed out in very precise Aristotelian terms. Suppose that to be a substance for Aristotle is to be a first cause and principle of the being of something, and that the various criteria of substance are the various ways of being this sort of first principle and cause.[31] If that supposition is right, then underlying Aristotle's metaphysics is a conception of the world as organized into clusters, where the principle of clustering is one of priority relations, and at the core of each cluster is *ousia*. My soul is

[30] Aristotle does not quite say this at Δ. 6 and 12, but it is clearly implied. Otherwise, having unity of form without contiguity and unity of motion—as universals have—would be included there in the list of *per se* unities.

[31] For convenience, in what follows I will drop the qualification 'of the being of a thing', and speak just of 'first principle and cause'. Not all priority relations carry with them priority of the *ousia* sort. For example, efficient causality does not. Nor does final causality, at least not always: the Prime Mover is not the *ousia* of the cosmos, though it is undeniably primary. Sorting out the various priority relations into those which count towards substancehood and those which do not, and attempting to justify Aristotle's choices in this matter, is a difficult business.

prior to my body and all of its parts, and your soul is prior to your body and all of its parts. My soul is not prior in the same ways to any of the parts of your body; therefore the parts of your body are outside of the 'sphere of influence' of my soul, and hence they are outside the boundaries of my substance, and hence they are separate from me. The boundaries of a substance are determined by the priority relations it enters into. Everything to which a certain substance is prior as first principle and cause is 'in' that substance and not separate from it; all things to which it is not prior in the relevant ways[32] are outside of its boundaries and are separate from it. To return to metaphor: one can think of priority-relations as the metaphysical glue whose holding-power gives structure to the universe. To be separate from something is to be *not* attached to it with this sort of glue; to be 'in' something and not separate is precisely to be attached to it in this way.

To be the substance of something is to be its first principle and cause. Since to be a substratum is to be a first principle and cause, all things which inhere (*huparchein*) are within the ontological boundaries of the substrata in which they inhere, and are hence not separate from them. The substrata in which they inhere, *qua* substrata,[33] are their substance. Thus things which inhere are in a substance; thus they are not separate from substance; thus they fail the separation criterion for being substances themselves.

The parts of this interpretation fit together as follows. The essence of substance is to be a certain sort of first principle and cause. If one takes the boundaries of a substance to be determined by the extent of its priority relations, and separation from a substance to be existence outside of those

[32] For example, according to Aristotle, parents, though causally prior to their children, are not prior in the relevant way; nor is the Prime Mover prior in the relevant way to the rest of the cosmos. Both of these opinions are, or ought to be, controversial: one could claim that a tribe is a thing, a substance, and that its substantial unity is due to its common ancestor; and on a cosmology not far from Aristotle's own, the cosmos is a substance—indeed the only substance, since no substance is composed of substances—and the Prime Mover, as first cause, is the source of its substantial unity.

[33] The qualification, as always, is necessary because the substratum criterion can come into conflict with other criteria, causing difficulties about which sort of priority relations *really* determine substance.

boundaries, one is then able to understand how separation can be a criterion of substance. For example, material parts and 'logical parts'—accidents—are both posterior to, and hence not separate from, something which is for that very reason their substance. In so far as they are posterior, they fail to be substances themselves.

Finally, viewing substances as the *prius* in this way, and its ontological boundaries as encompassing precisely the *posteriora*, explains how these three views of the separation of substance can be equivalent: (1) its numerical distinctness from other substances; (2) its being outside the ontological boundaries of other substances; and (3) its separation from other substances.

Views of Aristotelian separation somewhat like the one I am proposing are found in the literature. For example, a similar view is suggested by Mabbott when he says:

We must first find out what Aristotle meant by 'separation'. There can be no doubt that he meant a severance which was complete and absolute.

Another example is Ross:

It seems, therefore, that Aristotle must mean not that substance can exist without the other categories, but that it can exist apart while they cannot. The substance is the whole thing, including the qualities, relations, etc. which form its essence, and this can exist apart. It implies qualities but these are not something outside it which it needs in addition to itself.[34]

In addition, passing reference to separation as 'existing apart' are common in the literature, too common to document. These people all seem to have in mind something like the doctrine I propose: for something to be separate is for it to be existing apart from, that is be outside of and external to,

---

[34] Mabbott, 'Aristotle and the ΧΩΡΙΣΜΟΣ of Plato', *Classical Quarterly*, XX (1926), 77; Ross, *Aristotle's Metaphysics*, vol i, p xci. Ross seems confused here in claiming that qualities, relations, etc. are components of the 'essence' of a substance. Also I disagree with Ross's claim that the substance is the whole thing: I believe that the compound of matter and form does *not* include the accidents. Therefore in its details my account would be quite different from Ross's. Ross's reliance on the notion of what the substance 'needs in addition to itself' shows how the 'independence' interpretation can insinuate itself even when someone is trying to dissociate himself from it. For other comments about separation that resemble mine, see E. Ryan, 'Pure Form in Aristotle', *Phronesis*, XVIII (1973), 213, and Preiswerk, above n 3, 193 ff.

whatever it is separate from. In the case of ideas and universals, what is at stake is their being external to the particular substances, and in the case of accidents, existence outside of the substances in which they in fact inhere.

The shortcoming of such remarks is that they need elaboration. What is it for one substance to be 'outside' of another? What is 'existence apart'? Without further explanation, the word 'apart' is no more informative than the word 'separate'. One of my aims in this essay is to turn these hints by Mabbott, Ross, and others into a defensible interpretation, by providing a theoretical background and support for the intuition they express. Defining 'ontological boundary' in terms of such Aristotelian concepts as priority, numerical unity, inherence, and substratum adds determinate content to the notions of 'separation' and 'existence apart', and this content has consequences. One consequence, for example, is this: since universals inhere in many particulars and inherence is one way to be 'within the ontological boundaries of', each universal is within the ontological boundaries of many things. If the present account of separation is correct, Aristotle's description of universals as *koina*—common—must be taken literally.

Earlier I claimed that for a substance to be separate is for it to be separate from other substances. That account of separation coincides with accounts (3) and (4) just in case for one substance to be separate from others is for it to be numerically distinct from them and outside of their ontological boundaries. This seems to be exactly what Aristotle believes.

The explicit evidence concerning Aristotle's notion of the separation of substance has now been exhausted; hence the further evidence can only be implicit and indirect. Either interpreting the separation of substance as separation from other substances helps one to understand and reconstruct Aristotle's arguments that involve the separation of substance, or it does not. To the extent that it does, the interpretation is plausible; to the extent that it does not, less so. In what follows I attempt to show that this interpretation does indeed meet that test.[35]

[35] A note about strategy. In the following sections, I assume that Aristotle's

## No substance is composed of substances

The doctrine that a substance is separate just in case there is no other substance that it is in seems to lie behind Aristotle's doctrine that no substance is composed of substances (1038b28; 1039a17). If one substance could be composed of substances, one substance could be inside another. But then the contained substance would not be separate. Since separation is a criterion of substance, there cannot be any such contained substance, and so no substance can be composed of substances. This thought also seems to be behind his statement that 'actuality separates' (1039a7). Aristotle says this in support of the claim, made at 1039a3-4, that no substance can consist of two actual substances present in it. The reason this is impossible, he says, is that the substance would then be *two*, not one. What is actually one can be potentially two, but not *actually* two: because 'actuality separates'. This passage is additional evidence for the claim that two items are separate if and only if they are numerically distinct.

Aristotle's claim is that nothing can be two substances at once. There is only one king of the hill; only one *ousia* in power. Either the parts are separate substances *or* the whole is; but not both. Either the accidents are all separate substances; *or* the essence is; but not both. I speculate (such matters can never be proved) that one source of this doctrine is the Socratic *ti esti* question. Socrates assumed that whenever the *ti esti* question can be asked, there will be a single answer: the *logos*, a single phrase, not more. This Socratic assumption, enormous though it may seem to us, quietly conditioned the whole of classical Greek metaphysics.[36] For

metaphysical discussions involving separation—those concerning the separation of Platonic Ideas, mathematical entities, the separation of accidents, the separation of matter, the separation of immanent Aristotelian forms and of their composites with matter—all concern 'separation' in the same sense. My reasons for this assumption are simple. If Ideas are separate, then they are substances; if mathematical entities are separate so are they. If matter is separate, it is substance; if accidents are separate, I argue, so are they. At issue in all of these cases is the kind of separation that a substance is supposed to have, whether that kind of separation is being affirmed or denied. Whatever account one gives of Aristotelian separation, it must be adequate to cover all of these contexts equally, or else it should be accepted for none of them.

[36] But this need not mean that the assumption was not doubted or denied—just that, when doubted or denied, it was present in the background as something

Aristotle substance is paradigmatically definable; it is paradigmatically the sort of thing of which the *ti esti* question
can be asked. This entails that substance cannot be composed
of substances: else the *ti esti* question could receive a double
answer.

### Accidents

When Aristotle denies the separation of accidents, he usually
has in mind the suggestion that accidents could exist where
no substance exists. Could there be 'blue' or 'three-feet tall'
without there being something that is blue or is three-feet
tall? Aristotle, reasonably enough, says no.[37] Such passages
are easily compatible with the view that *chōristos* means
'capable of separate existence'; but they are also compatible
with the view that *chōristos* means 'separate from another
substance'. For if a person were destroyed in such a way that
nothing was left but the 'blue' of him or her, that blue would
be separate from any substance, so it would be a substance
itself. Aristotle thinks that this kind of survival is manifestly
impossible, so he rejects the notion that attributes could be
separate as absurd; from this it follows that they cannot be
substances.

Aristotle also considers another type of case. Suppose that
you did not destroy the person, but merely did some re-
arranging. Imagine segregating the weight over here, the skin
colour there, the cheerfulness up where the nose used to be,
and so on. This, too, Aristotle finds absurd, again reasonably
enough; but he thinks some of his precedessors (notably
Anaxagoras) did hold such a view;[38] therefore he discusses
the case.

Aristotle never does discuss a somewhat different case, one
which is important and which his theory ought to equip him

to be *struggled against*. In '*Episteme* and *Logos* in Plato's Later Thought', *Archiv
für Geschichte der Philosophie (AGPh)*, LXVI (1984), 11–36. Alexander Nehamas
has argued that the assumption was indeed denied by Plato in the later dialogues.

[37] *GC* 316b3, 317b11, b33, 320b25; *de Longitudine* 465b15; *Metaph.* 989b3,
1028a23, 1038b29; *Ph.* 188a6, 201b23.

[38] *Metaph.* 989b2–4; *GC* 327b17–22. H. Joachim, in his commentary on this
passage (*Aristotle on Coming to Be and Passing Away* (Oxford, 1923), 179),
thinks that Aristotle has in mind the 'Sphere' of Empedocles as well. The re-
arranging of accidents in the thought experiment corresponds to the 'original
mixture' of the Presocratics.

to handle. What if someone were to accept Aristotle's basic views about the constitution of objects, cosmology, and change, *except* for the priority he gives to substance? Such a person would insist that 'all predicates are equal': none of the properties of a thing 'inhere' in any others, none is 'essence' or 'substratum' to the rest. This sort of 'bundle of qualities' theory of objects is common enough in modern and recent philosophy. What would Aristotle have had to say in response to it? My view is that Aristotle's response would have been to say that such a theory makes each of the properties into a substance of its own. Since the accidents no longer inhere in anything, they are separate;[39] and *qua* separate, they are substances.[40] Since the accidents are separate substances, the 'bundle' made out of them cannot be a substance. (Recall the doctrine that no substance can be made out of substances.) A complex object would be a mere congeries of its accidents. There would be no *single* thing that it is, and correspondingly there would be no single answer if the question should be posed of it, *ti esti?* The price of destroying the substance/accident distinction is, among other things,[41] eliminating the substantial unity of items like Socrates. And that is too high a price to pay.

Now the application of Aristotle's doctrine of separation to the theory of things as 'property-bundles' is not one that Aristotle makes himself. Either the essence/accident distinction is too firmly entrenched in his thought, or else his discussion of the issue has simply not survived. But if I am right about how the application works out, neither the 'place' nor the 'independence' interpretations of Aristotle's notion of separation can be correct. First, many properties within a given bundle will share the same place. And second, nothing prevents several groups of these properties from always passing in and out of existence simultaneously, as a matter of natural law (in Aristotelian language, from being propria of each other). On the 'independence' interpretation of

[39] The relation between non-inherence and separation is relied on by Aristotle at *Metaph.* 1087b1 in connection with the separation of attributes.

[40] As before, the caveat is required because other criteria of substance might conflict.

[41] Such as being unable to solve logical puzzles concerning accidents and puzzles about change.

separation, all mutually independent groups of such lawfully coinstantiated properties would constitute separate substances. Both the 'place' and the 'independence' interpretations require that Aristotle respond to the bundle theory by saying that it divides the substance into smaller substances made up of groups of properties—either groups sharing the same 'place', or groups that are lawfully coinstantiated. But by denying the essence/accident distinction, one denies inherence. This ought to put all properties on an equal footing—making either all of them substances, or none of them—rather than splitting them up into substantial subgroups, as these other interpretations require. The connection between non-separation and inherence does require the account of 'property-bundles' that I have given, and both the 'place' and 'independence' interpretations must be wrong.

## Parts

The separation of parts from the whole provides another test case.[42] If the parts of a whole are separate, then each part is by itself a substance, and the whole is not a whole: the 'whole' is then no single thing at all, but a mere collection of parts. This counterfactual reasoning does not depend on any imagined chopping-up of the object. Take Socrates, whole and living as he once was. *If* his thumb were separate, then it would be a substance by itself, and hence no part of Socrates. If all of Socrates's organs were separate, then he would be no object, no whole, no substance, but a mere collection of pieces. If Socrates is an actual substance, then none of his parts can be substances.

The question of the status of a part of Socrates after that part has been separated from him, that is chopped off, is a different but related question. A finger is not a separate substance; rather it is a part of a substance, part of the larger whole that is Socrates. To be a finger is to be a certain part of a man. When the finger is chopped off, it is no longer what it was. It is no longer a finger, because it is no longer a part of a man. Now it is something else: perhaps a coherent lump of particular chemical compounds. Once chopped off, the

[42] See *de Motu Animalium* 703b22; *Metaph.* 1035b23, 1039a7, 1040b7; *de Partibus Animalium* 644b29, b31, 654b4, b8, b10; *Ph.* 210b3, 212b6, 257b31.

'finger' is, to be sure, a separate substance of a kind, but it is no longer a finger.

### The Platonic theory of Ideas

Aristotle's criticisms of Platonic Idea theory also support the hypothesis that, for Aristotle, separation is separation from other substances. Aristotle conceives Platonic Ideas, in brief, as separate universals.[43] The trouble with postulating separate universals, Aristotle thinks, is that separation and universality are incompatible. The framework presented here makes it easy to see why Aristotle should think this. To be a universal is to be predicated of many; but if something is predicated of many, it is *in* that many. To be predicated of is to inhere, and to inhere is to be in. And if the thing is in the many, then it is not separate from them. Earlier I quoted *Physics* 185a31, where Aristotle explains the non-separation of something by its non-inherence. On Aristotle's view, a universal is a paradigmatic example of something that inheres.[44] If the universal is separate, then it cannot inhere, but if it did not inhere, then it could not be a universal. Of course, the many that the universal inheres in are the sensible particulars, and 'the sensibles' and 'the particulars' in Aristotle's usage refer to the sensible and particular *substances*. The trouble with the Ideas is that they cannot be separated from the particulars, on pain of losing their status as universals.

My own view is that most of Aristotle's many different

---

[43] *Metaph.* 1078b31, 1086a35; *MM* 1182b13, b15; *peri Ideon*, Alexander, *in Metaph.* 80. 14, 85. 22.

[44] One might object that although accidents inhere according to Aristotle, substantial genera and species do not. Being two-footed does not inhere in me, nor does being a man, though having brown hair does. This view is plausible, and here I can only sketch my reply. The inherence of accidents is certainly more obvious than that of substance universals. At a philosophical stage where one is still taking universals seriously as substances, but has realized, e.g., that weight inheres in body and colour in surfaces, the inherence of accidents will be more plain than the inherence of substance universals. This is the stage that is represented both by Aristotle himself in the *Categories* and by the Platonists he attacks at *Metaph.* A. 9. 990b22–991a8. On the other hand, once one shifts viewpoints and comes to see the substantiality of universals as untenable in any case, then the differences between the two kinds of universals become less important. Universals in categories other than substance may inhere twice over (both in 'man' and in Socrates), but universals in the category of substance inhere (in Socrates) just the same. Inherence is the crime, and both kinds of universals stand condemned.

arguments against the Ideas do rely on this single objection.[45] However, at present I can only put this forward as a suggestion: to show that most of Aristotle's arguments against the Forms are in fact based on this one objection is much too large a task to be attempted here.

Aristotle himself believes in universals, although, in the *Metaphysics* at least, he does not believe that they are either separate or that they are substances. This is why he so often complains against the Ideas that they are held to be *separate*. The Platonists were right to believe in universals; they went wrong in separating them.

To this basic objection the Platonist's response is this. Perhaps Aristotle is mistaken about the relation between the universal and the particulars. In fact, the universals, the Ideas, are the *real* substance. The particulars constantly change, and they are not definable, so they cannot be substances in the strict sense, as the Ideas are. Therefore the Ideas *are* separate from other substances, even though they inhere in the particulars, because the particulars are not substances in the first place. In fact, just because the particulars are not substances, 'inherence' is a misleading concept to use in describing their relation to universals. The very phrase 'the inherence of the universal in the particular' makes it seem as if the particular is prior. But the Form, as the only substance in sight, is in fact prior to all of the 'non-substantial' particulars. This being so, a better concept to employ is 'participates'. 'The particulars participate in the Ideas' places the emphasis in the right place: the Ideas are what is prior.

To this Aristotle has two replies. First, of course, he would deny that the Ideas are prior.[46] Second, even if the Ideas are prior and the only real substances, still it is wrong to claim that they are separate from particulars. If particulars are not substances, then the Ideas must be the substance *of* the particulars named after them.[47] The Platonists held that the

---

[45] For a supporting view, see Mabbott, above n 34, 73.

[46] See esp. *Metaph.* Z. 13

[47] This assumption is not so odd as it might seem. In fact, in the philosophical context of the time it was perfectly sound. The way one arrives at Ideas is by asking the *ti esti* question of particulars. What this question yields is the being— the *ousia*, the substance—of the thing about which the question was asked. For

Ideas are the substances of things, yet also that they are separate from what they are substances of. But that is absurd. How can something be the substance—the *ousia*, the being —of another thing which is separated from it? A particular cannot be separate from its *ousia*, its very being. Nothing can. Aristotle himself takes the argument up to this point; and taken that far, his argument is sound. A criterion of *ousia* from Socrates onwards is that the *ousia* of something be what is given in answer to the *ti esti* question asked of that thing. And it is indeed absurd to suppose that what is given in answer to that question is separated from that of which the question is asked. How could a thing be separate from its very being?

A sufficiently daring Platonist, however, could revise his doctrine and make what seems to me a satisfactory reply. 'Certainly, Aristotle,' the Platonist might respond, 'the Idea is not separate from the particulars, any more than on your theory the particular substance is separate from its accidents. The correct way to view the relation between an Idea and the particulars falling under it is just the way that you view the relation between a substance and its accidents. Participation is in a way *just* like your inherence, only with the priorities reversed. The Idea is the ontological core—the "substratum", if you wish—for the many particulars that fall under it, just as your "substance" is the ontological core for its many accidents. On my view the Idea Red and all the bits of red throughout the world have a status analogous to the one that Socrates and all of his accidents have for you. The universal "red" causes you trouble, because it is scattered across many substances and hence is not a substance, and does not have the strong numerical unity that either Socrates or his particular accidents have. You cope with this by appealing to "unity of definition", which the universal has even though it is scattered across the many. My problem lies with items like Socrates. On my view, *he* is scattered across many substances: the Idea Wise, the Idea Man, and so on. But like you, I can appeal to another sort of unity—numerical unity, perhaps, or unity of motion—as *my* lower grade of unity that pseudo-, or anyway "troublesome", entities like Socrates have. Using

more on the conceptual continuity of *ousia* as essence and *ousia* as substance, see the Introduction and Ch IV of *Three Criteria of Substance*.

the philosophical tools that you provide me, I can match you step-by-step. Whatever you do, I can do too, while simply assigning the priorities in a different way.'

This Platonist reply seems to me cogent. A Platonist willing to steal from Aristotle can live off his adversary in good health. The dialectic is not over yet, however, and other issues remain to be examined. In particular, a defender of Aristotle might think that such a Platonist would face far more serious problems with the identity and individuation of Ideas than Aristotle faces with his substances. None the less enough has been said to indicate how Aristotle's disputes with the Platonists about the separation of Ideas, universals, and mathematical entities can be seen as disputes about their separation from other substances.

### Complex substances

Substance must be separate in the sense of being separate from other substances. This absolute statement will suffice so long as the internal complexity of substance is left out of account. A more sophisticated theory of substance, one which takes internal complexity into account, demands a more sophisticated theory of separation as well.

One stage of sophistication occurs when substance is divided into matter and form. The matter, the form, and the composite are all substances in a sense (e.g. 1029a2, 1042a25–32); the enquiry in *Metaphysics* Z has as a result that these three 'substances' should be ranked thus: form is more substance than the composite, which is in turn more substance than matter (1029a22–33). Though both are controversial, I believe that Aristotle never wishes to deny that either matter or the composite are substance,[48] even though form turns out to be the 'primary substance' for which he is searching. All three are substance, though in different ways and to different degrees. Aristotle's view is that form and matter together constitute the composite; moreover the form is *in* the matter (*Ph.* 210a20; *Metaph.* 1023a12, 1037b6). This inherence of the form in the matter[49] causes problems

[48] See esp. *Metaph.* H. 1.
[49] On this doctrine, see J. Brunschwig's excellent article, 'Forme, Prédicat de la Matière?', in *Etudes sur la Métaphysique d'Aristote*, ed Aubenque (Paris, 1978),

for the doctrine of separation. Form is in matter; form is substance; matter is substance; therefore one substance, form, is in another substance, matter. So primary substance, form, is not 'separate' full stop (*haplōs*), because it is not separate from substance of every kind and degree: it is in matter. True, form 'is *more* substance than matter; but still, both are substance, so the rule that no substance is in another substance is broken. Perhaps this does no harm, since the status of the two substances is so unequal. A new rule is called for. Let us try this one: 'No primary substance can be in another primary substance'.[50] To be separate absolutely is to be separate from substance absolutely. The composite is separate in this way. Primary substance, however, need not be separate absolutely; it need only be prior to all of the substances from which it is not separate absolutely. Matter loses on both counts: it is not separate absolutely, because it is in the composite; and it is posterior to both the composite and the form.[51] The form is in the matter in one way, but the form is also in the composite, in a different way.[52] So even if matter is not itself substance, form is still in a substance.[53]

An additional notion is needed in analysing the relation between form and composite: that of 'substance of'. The form is in the composite; the form is not separate from the

and also J. Kung, 'Can Substance be Predicated of Matter?' (*AGPh* LX (1978), 140–59.

[50] This is a more general form of the rule that is suggested at 1039a3: 'no substance can be composed out of actual substances'.

[51] At 1029a31–2 Aristotle implies that the matter is prior to the composite in one way, as an 'element' of it. But in the end, matter's lack of definability, actuality, and 'thisness' combine to make it, all things considered, posterior to the composite. Aristotle never says this directly; but it seems clear that his doctrine works itself out in this way. He comes close to saying it at 1029a29–30, where he says that both form and composite are 'more substance' than matter is.

[52] The issue whether matter is substance comes down to this: Aristotle believes that matter is potentially a substance—i.e. a compound. Is being potentially a different kind of substance one way of being a substance, or is it a way of not being a substance at all? Both textual and philosophical considerations make it hard to choose.

[53] The matter is in the composite in the same way that the form is; the matter may also be in the form, in a sense described by Aristotle at *Metaph.* Δ. 23. 1023a8 ff.

composite; as the primary substance in and of the composite, the form is the substance of the composite. One of Aristotle's main complaints against the Platonist theory of Ideas is that although the theory claims the Ideas are the substances of things, it also insists they are separate from what they are substances of. Aristotle's forms are in their composites; they are not separate from what they are substances of. A form is a substance; the composite is a substance; a form is the substance of the composite; hence a form is the substance of a substance. Aristotle never actually uses the phrase 'ousia tēs ousias', but that is clearly what he has in mind.[54]

### The form as separate in definition

The form is not separate *haplōs*, because it is *in* a substance. Instead, the form is separate *logōi*. Something is separate in logos or definition if its definition does not include reference to anything else. The definition of white is, say, 'penetrative colour in a surface'. Since this definition includes reference to surface, which is distinct from white, white is not separate in definition.

Separateness in definition is the same as unity of definition, which in turn is the same as priority in definition.[55] The topic 'being separate in definition' need not be treated in detail here. None the less this much must be said: if I am right about Aristotle's original notion of the separation of substances, his claim that primary substance, form, is separate because it is separate in definition, is a philosophical dodge that borders on being a cheat.[56] Being separate in definition is not one way for a thing to be separate. Even if the definition of the thing should be separate, the thing itself remains

[54] *Ousia* is followed by the genitive case of the definite article in the following places in Aristotle: *Cat.* 3b36, 3a21, 8a13, a31, b21; *de An.* 406a17, 415b11; *Cael.* 293b15; *Metaph.* 1002a4, 998a18, 1035b15, 1038a19, b12, b21, 1039b16, 996a3, 1002a28, 1050b7, 1088a23; *EE* 1219b36; *GC* 321a34; *GA* 731b34; *Ph.* 193a10, 225b11. Many relevant passages are not on this list, but it does give one a start.

[55] For more on this, see Ch III, 'Definability', of *Three Criteria of Substance*. Separation in definition appears in Aristotle at: *de An.* 403b10, 413b14, 429a12, 432a20, 433b25; *GC* 320b25; *Metaph.* 1016b3, 1025b28, 1030b25 (see 1038b29), 1042a29, 1064a24 (see 1078a17, a22), 1077a31; *Ph.* 186b21, 193b4, 194a1.

[56] The crucial passages are: 1016a33-b7, 1052a30-4, 1042a30.

non-separate (in another substance) all the same. The situation Aristotle has gotten himself into is this: he has argued himself into the view that the form is primary substance. The form is not separate, yet a part of his goal is to show that whatever is substance satisfies all of his initial criteria of substance. Ready to hand is the criterion 'unity of definition', another name for which is 'separation in definition'. This latter criterion, form satisfies. Thus by appealing to the notion 'separation in definition', Aristotle is able to *say* that the form is separate, after all. However, if I have been right about the way separation was supposed to function as a criterion of substance, Aristotle's victory is only verbal. 'Separation' has become ambiguous, and form has been shown to be 'separate' in a sense quite different from the original sense in which substance was held to be separate.

In the end, this face-saving dodge does not even save face. Aristotle believes that the definitions of all enmattered forms include reference to their matter (1025b30 ff, 194a1 ff). Therefore, all forms which are not separate *haplōs*, which are in matter, are also not separate *logōi*: their definitions are not separate from the matter that they are in. Immaterial substances are not in any substance, and their definitions reflect the fact. Immaterial substances are separate both *haplōs* and *logōi*.

On the other hand, in Aristotle's favour, one should realize that so far as the criterion of separation is concerned, the only thing at stake here is face. If the modified rule presented in the last section is accepted as Aristotelian doctrine, namely that it is all right for substances to be in substances, so long as no *primary* substance is in any *primary* substance, then the criterion of separation has lost its stranglehold on substance and form may be substance, even primary substance, without being separate in the relevant sense at all. Accepting this modified rule is a drastic step, certainly a debatable and perhaps an unwise one. But having accepted it, one has abandoned the criterion of separation for a crucial class of cases, and admitting that form, though substance, is not separate in those cases should cause one no shame.

Conclusion

I have argued that the separation which is criterial for substance in Aristotle's metaphysics is 'separation from other substances', and that this separation in turn is best explicated using the notion 'outside of the ontological boundaries of', which itself, admittedly, is not an Aristotelian notion but an interpreter's term of art.

The leading alternative interpretation of Aristotle's separation of substance construes it as 'independence'. Against this interpretation I have argued that the word *chōristos*, whose basic meaning is 'separation', is a very peculiar choice for expressing the notion of 'independence', and that no explanation is available of why this Greek term should have been used to express that concept. Further, the independence view would make Socrates an accident of the sun, since he is not independent of the sun. And finally, the independence view gives insufficient weight to those many passages in Aristotle in which being *chōristos* is contrasted with being 'in'.

One interpretation of the separation of substances which I endorsed as both true and genuinely explanatory is their 'numerical distinctness' from one another. This account is not fundamental, however, because it presupposes the distinction between substance and accident, while the notion of the separation of substance is meant to help *constitute* that distinction. Explicating numerical distinctness by means of the notion 'being outside of the ontological boundaries of' avoids presupposing the distinction between substance and accident, but this new notion, an interpreter's invention, itself needs explication and defence.

In this way the most fundamental level of my account of Aristotle's separation of substance is reached. I sketch a conception of Aristotle's universe as ordered by priority relations and organized by those priority relations into clusters, each cluster containing one first cause and principle, its substance, and many posterior entities: accidents, matter, and so on. The 'edges' of these priority clusters are the ontological boundaries definitive of separation.

To fully explore this conception of Aristotelian metaphysics would require at least a book. Here I apply the conception to several test cases for the notion of separation of substance: the doctrine 'no substance is composed of substances'; accidents; parts; the Platonic theory of Ideas; complex substances; and Aristotelian immanent form. Two surprising conclusions emerge. Since form, matter, and the compound of the two are *all* substance, at least in some way or other, the rule that 'no substance is composed of substances' is broken. A new, more sophisticated rule is called for: 'No primary substance can be in any primary substance'. The second surprising conclusion is that Aristotelian immanent form is separate only in a Pickwickian sense: it is separate in definition all right, but that sort of separation is totally different from the sort of separation that is criterial for substance. On the other hand, if the more sophisticated rule is adopted, form does not need to be separate in the (otherwise) criterial sense: it can be in another substance, hence not separate, yet still be both substance and primary.

A final word remains to be said about the relation of separation as a criterion of substance to other criteria: 'thisness', substratumhood, definability and knowability, unity, and being *per se*. On the account presented here, separation is not one criterion of substance among the others, each serving to help establish the priority relations that structure Aristotle's universe into substances. Instead, separation is the result of, and expresses, the priority relations established by all the other criteria. For two things to be separate is for them to be on opposite sides of an ontological boundary; such boundaries are created by the world's being organized into clusters by means of priority relations; and these priority relations are just those established by the remaining criteria of substance. Thus, one may say that separation as a criterion of substance has no independent force; but on the other hand, separation is eminently suited to serve as the *major* criterion of substance, as the one that *sums up* all the rest— for example in the debate with the Platonists over the Ideas.

*Harvard University*

# SEPARATION: A REPLY TO MORRISON*

## Gail Fine

In his paper 'Separation in Aristotle's Metaphysics',[1] Don Morrison takes issue with the account of separation I advanced in my paper 'Separation'.[2] In this brief reply I shall attempt to rebut some of the charges Morrison levels against me. I shall resist the temptation to level charges of my own against his more positive claims.

I must first note that Morrison misdescribes my view. He characterizes my view as 'the view that for Aristotle the separation of substance is the same as the natural priority of substance';[3] or, again, he says that on my view, 'Aristotle's concepts of natural priority and separation of substance are identical'. But this is not my view. On my view, $A$ is separate from $B$ just in case $A$ can exist without, independently of, $B$. $A$ is naturally prior to $B$ just in case $A$ is separate from $B$, but not conversely. If $A$ is naturally prior to $B$, then $A$ is separate from $B$. But $A$ can be separate from $B$ without being naturally prior to $B$; for $A$ and $B$ might be separate from one another, in which case neither is naturally prior to the other. The natural priority of $A$ to $B$ implies the separation of $A$ from $B$; but the separation of $A$ from $B$ does not imply the natural priority of $A$ to $B$.[4]

Now I cited *Eudemian Ethics* 1217b2-16 as evidence of my interpretation of separation. Morrison argues that this passage does not support me. All it shows, he claims is that separation entails natural priority, not that they are identical.[5] However, I deny that natural priority and separation are

* © Gail Fine 1985.
[1] See pp 125-57.
[2] *Oxford Studies in Ancient Philosophy*, vol ii (Oxford, 1984), 31-87.
[3] p 131. The quote that follows is from the same page.
[4] I distinguished separation and natural priority in 'Separation', nn 5 and 19, and on p 35.
[5] p 137.

identical; so if *Eudemian Ethics* 1217b2-16 fails to establish their identity, that hardly counts against me.[6]

Or again, Morrison claims that '[o]n the independence view, substance must be separate from *everything*—since whatever it is not separate from, it will be posterior to and hence an accident of'.[7] But this claim is false. On my version of the independence view, if a substance *A* fails to be separate from something else, *B*, it does not follow that *A* is posterior to *B*. There might be mutual dependence, in which case neither *A* nor *B* is prior or posterior to the other. This would of course not be possible if, as Morrison thinks I believe, natural priority and separation were the same. But since they are not the same, this is possible.

On my view, then, to say that *A* is separate from *B* is to say that *A* can exist without, independently of, *B*. To say this, however, is indeterminate in two important ways. First, there is a temporal indeterminacy: can *A* exist whether or not *B* ever exists? Or, is it just that *A* can exist at *t1* whether or not *B* exists at *t1*? In my paper, I took no stand on this question. I did argue that, according to Aristotle at least, Platonic Forms are separate from sensibles in that they can exist whether or not sensibles ever do. But I did not argue—nor do I believe—that for any item *A* that is separate from some other item *B*, *A* must be able to exist whether or not *B* ever does.

Separation is also indeterminate as to range. To say that substance is separate, for example, implies that it is separate from something; but it does not imply anything about what it is separate from. 'Independence' explains what separation consists in; it is another question entirely what a given thing is separate from. In my paper, I argued that, according to Aristotle at least, Platonic Forms are separate from sensible particulars. But I also suggested that each Aristotelian substance is supposed to be separate—not from any or all other substances, but—from non-substances.[8] To say that a given

---

[6] I also, of course, deny Morrison's claim that the passage infers natural priority from separation. '*kai gar*' can, of course, be used inferentially in the way Morrison suggests; but it need not be so used. And we should be reluctant to see such a use here, if the claim in my paper, that Aristotle believes natural priority implies separation but not conversely, is correct.

[7] p 133.           [8] See my n 19 in 'Separation'.

entity is separate is not, by itself, to say anything about what it is separate from; and different sorts of entities might be separate from different ranges of things.

Now Morrison is concerned to argue that for a substance to be separate, is not for it to exist independently, but rather 'for it to be separate from other substances'.[9] But this is a false dichotomy. A proponent of the 'independence' interpretation can, but need not, argue that each substance is separate from every other substance. In my paper, I rejected this account of the range of the separation of substance. But one could accept it, and still accept the 'independence' interpretation of what separation consists in. In fact, I now think I was wrong to deny that, for Aristotle, each substance is separate from every other substance; as I point out below, Aristotle can— even on my independence interpretation—satisfy this demand. As I shall also point out below, he can also satisfy the demand I imposed on him—but one Morrison apparently wishes to lift[10]—that substance is (in a way to be explained) separate from non-substance.

These preliminaries out of the way, I now turn to Morrison's three general objections to my interpretation:[11]

(1) Morrison's first general objection is that ' "Separation" and "independence" seem to be very different concepts; the one has primarily local and spatial overtones; the other does not. It is intrinsically implausible that a Greek word whose basic meaning is "separation" should also be used to express the very different concept of "independence".'[12] I confess that I find this objection implausible. Aristotle clearly uses 'separation' (*chōris*) in contexts having no 'local or spatial overtones'. He speaks, for example, of separation in definition. *A* is definitionally separate from *B* just in case *A* can be defined without mention of (the definition of) *B*.[13] There are

---

[9] See, e.g., p 126.  [10] p 133.

[11] Morrison also argues that various texts I adduce in my support do not in fact support me. One of these texts is *Eudemian Ethics* 1217b2-16, discussed above.  [12] p 132.

[13] Morrison rather explicates definitional separation as: 'Something is separate in *logos* or definition if its definition does not include reference to anything else' (p 154). I take it that this is sufficient but not necessary for definitional separation. Morrison also incorrectly claims (same page) that definitional separation is the same as definitional priority; this mistake parallels his mistaken assimilation of the independence interpretation of separation to natural priority.

no local or spatial overtones here. But if Aristotle uses
'separation' in contexts having no local or spatial overtones,
my account of separation need not, in principle at least,
convey such overtones. Nor do separation and independence
seem so very different to me as they do to Morrison. If $A$ is
definitionally separate from $B$, it can be defined independently
of $B$: plainly this' is what Aristotle means, and it is a very
natural thought.

(2) Morrison's second general objection is that my view
makes 'Socrates an accident of the sun',[14] since on my view
Socrates is not separate from the sun, since he cannot exist
without it. The gist of this objection is that on my account of
separation, some of Aristotle's main candidates for substance
—spatio-temporal particulars such as Socrates—are not
separate; yet separation is one of Aristotle's main criteria for
substance.

This objection rests, in part, on the assumption that when
Aristotle says that substance is separate, he means that each
substance is separate from every other. In 'Separation'
I rejected this view. I now believe that rejection was wrong:
if the temporal qualifiers are correctly construed, then
Socrates is separate from the sun. It is of course true that
Socrates could not exist if the sun never existed, just as he
could not exist had his parents never existed, or had oxygen
or food never existed. But Socrates can exist at $t1$ even if
none of these things exist at $t1$. Of course, he could not exist
for very long without some of these things also existing; but
he could exist at any given (though not at every) moment
without any of these things existing at that moment. So if
the temporal qualifiers are correctly construed, Socrates is
separate from the sun.

One might object that even if so, Socrates is not separate
from every other substance. For, matter is substance, but
Socrates cannot exist at $t1$ if no matter exists at $t1$; he at
least needs the matter that constitutes him to exist. But to
this one could reply in turn: Socrates needs some matter or
other, but not any given bit of matter in particular. He can
exist at $t1$ even if the matter that happens to constitute him
at $t1$ does not exist—so long as some other suitable matter

[14] p 132.

constitutes him. If to say that every substance is separate from every other substance is only to say that every substance is separate from any given other substance (rather than from all substances as such), then Socrates—even on my independence interpretation—is separate from every other substance.

Morrison argues not only that each substance is separate from every other substance (a claim with which I now agree, if the claim is interpreted as above), but also that no substance is separate from its attributes.[15] In my paper, I claimed that each substance is separate from non-substances. I still believe that claim. But since it was left unexplained in my paper, perhaps it would be useful to spell out what I had in mind: Socrates (to take a sample substance) can exist independently of any piece or quantity of matter, and independently of several sorts or types of exact matter. That is, his continued existence does not depend on his having just these cells, or on his being made of flesh and bones (any functionally equivalent matter would do). Similarly, Socrates can exist independently of any given non-substance attribute he has (though not independently of all of them), and independently of some general non-substance attributes. Thus, for example, he can exist without having this (or any) instance of tan, and without continuing to be 160 lbs—though, to be sure, he cannot exist without having some colour or other, or without having some weight or other. Socrates is, then, separate from matter and non-substance attributes, if the range of these is spelled out as I have just spelled it out.[16]

(3) Morrison's third general objection to my view is 'that it has difficulty accounting for the passages in which Aristotle insists that the Forms should be placed in sensible things'.[17] This is because (I insert letters for ease of reference) 'given

---

[15] p 133.

[16] Why does Morrison deny that each substance is separate from its attributes? Because, I think, he sometimes explicates separation—not as separation from other substances, but—as 'outside the ontological boundaries of', a metaphor he explicates so that it is equivalent to being numerically distinct from (139), where two things 'are numerically one just in case they have the same basic substratum' (138), and where 'being a substratum' is a way of having a substratum (n 12). Since Socrates and his attributes have the same substratum, they are numerically one, and so are not separate from one another.

[17] p 134.

(*a*) the native spatial sense of *choristos*, and (*b*) the fact that Aristotle uses both separation and failure to be 'in' to express his dissatisfaction with the Forms, (*c*) a strong interpretive goal should be to find an account of separation and failure to be "in" on which they amount to the same thing, or at the very least are closely related'. This sentence is a conditional with a conjunctive antecedent. I have already argued that one conjunct of the antecedent—(*a*)—is irrelevant; but even if it were not, I fail to see how it contributes to (*c*) (even in conjunction with (*b*)). Nor does (*b*) provide any support for (*c*). Aristotle mounts a variety of objections to Forms; there is no presumption that any 'two' of them ought to be the same or even closely related. So Morrison's conditional is false.

But suppose we concede the consequent none the less. Is Morrison correct to say that on the independence interpretation, there is not a close connection between the failure of Forms to be in things, and their separation? I think not. As I noted in my paper,[18] 'in' can be used to indicate dependence. If Forms are separate from sensibles, they are not dependent on them, and so are not, in that sense of 'in', in them.

Morrison objects that *Physics* IV. 3 does not, as I alleged, use 'in' to indicate dependence of the relevant sort. He allows that its senses (6) and (7) indicate some sort of dependence —but not ones useful for my purposes. I agree. But I take it that its fifth sense does indicate a sort of dependence relevant to my purposes: 'as health is in hot and cold things, and, generally, as the form is in the matter'. Morrison cites this sense in note 22; but he seems to believe that it is unhelpful to me, since Aristotle does not, here, say how form is in matter. To be sure he does not. But elsewhere, Aristotle seems to claim that form is in matter in that (sensible) forms cannot exist without some matter or other. If this is right, then this is just the sort of dependence my interpretation requires.

But I need not rest my suggestion, that Aristotle sometimes uses 'in' to indicate a sort of dependence that contrasts relevantly with separation, on a reading of *Physics* IV. 3. To take just one other example, at *Categories* 1a24–5, Aristotle says: 'By "in a subject" I mean what is in something, not as

---

[18] Cf. my paper, 41; and Morrison, 135.

a part, and cannot exist separately from what it is in.' Here, I take it, if $A$ is in $B$, $A$ cannot exist without $B$;[19] this is just the sort of 'immanence' that offers the relevant contrast to separation as I construe it.

I conclude, then, that none of Morrison's general objections to my interpretation of separation as independent existence succeeds. Morrison is right, however, to say that each substance is separate from every other (if that is interpreted in the manner suggested above). But he is wrong to think that this claim is incompatible with my claim that separation consists in independent existence, or that substances cannot be separate from one another if separation is construed my way.

*Cornell University*

[19] The interpretation of this passage is, of course, disputed. I generally follow Ackrill's view, as against Owen's, that Aristotle here means that if $A$ is in $B$, $A$ cannot exist independently of $B$.

# SEPARATION: A REPLY TO FINE*[1]

## Donald Morrison

I am grateful to Professor Fine for the clarifications of her view. One of those clarifications corrects a mistake of mine: I should not have claimed that Fine identifies separation and ontological priority, since she does distinguish them explicitly in note 5 of her original paper.[2] My comments in this reply will be directed at her view that for Aristotle $A$ is separate from $B$ just in case $A$ can exist without $B$, that is even if $B$ should not exist. By contrast, on this view $A$ is ontologically prior to $B$ just in case $A$ is separate from $B$ but not conversely.

Fine's view turns separation into a necessary condition for ontological priority. But presumably the more important trait for substance to have is ontological priority itself, and not its mere necessary condition, separation. If Fine's view were correct, the notion of ontological priority should have the major role in Aristotle's *Metaphysics*, and the notion of separation be brought in only occasionally to help establish or cast doubt on ontological priority. But the facts are the reverse: ontological priority is mentioned only a few times, chiefly in connection with the Ideas, while separation recurs constantly as a major criterion of substance. If separation is as Fine's view has it, separation should not be as important to Aristotle as it clearly is.[3]

Fine's view has difficulties with those passages in which

* © Donald Morrison 1985.

[1] I wish to thank Dr Walter Cavini of the University of Florence for his kindness and hospitality in allowing me the use of his scholarly library, without which this 'Reply' could not have been completed in time to be included here. I also thank Cynthia Freeland and Andreas Teuber for extremely helpful comments.

[2] 'Separation', *Oxford Studies in Ancient Philosophy*, vol ii (Oxford, 1984), 31–87.

[3] Why the concept of ontological priority plays such a minor role in the *Metaphysics* is a puzzling and important question. After all, the words used to label the concept—'priority in being' (*prōtē ousiai*)—make it seem absolutely fundamental. My guess is that ontological priority is a criterion Aristotle took over from the Platonic Academy as having been very important to them, and which he continued to be willing to use, but whose importance for him lessened as his distinctive views took shape.

Aristotle writes either of '*A* being separated from *B*', or '*A* being able to be separated from *B*'.[4] On her view, these must be interpreted as '*A* being rendered such as to be able to exist without *B*', or as '*A* being able to be rendered able to exist without *B*'. In both cases, the interpretation seldom fits the context, and the sense of the second interpretation is obscure. A passage quoted by Fine herself (164-5 above), *Categories* 1a24-5, illustrates the problem. I translate the passage, substituting her account of separation for the Greek word *chōris*: 'By "in a subject" I mean what is in something, not as a part, and is not able to be able to exist without what it is in.'[5] This cannot be what Aristotle intended *Categories* 1a24-5 to mean.

Fine says that on her view substance need not be separate from everything, since mutual dependence establishes non-separation without priority or posteriority. True; but I think that on Fine's view substance will still be separate from *virtually* everything, since mutual dependence is rare and mostly negligible. (The most important case of mutual dependence is essence and propria.)

It follows from my view of what the separation of substance involves that substance is both (1) separate from other substances and (2) not from accidents.[6] Moreover I believe that the first fact, that substance is separate from other substances, is *explanatory* in a special way: what *makes* something separate in the way that substances are separate is that there is no other substance that it is 'together' with. The special explanatory character of this fact motivated me to call it a 'view' of the separation of substance (126 above). Of course, one can believe that substance is separate from other substances (as Fine now does) without believing that this fact has the special explanatory role that I give it (and Fine does not). However, it should be clear that even for me

---

[4] Those passages which involve *theories* separating *A* from *B*, either mentally or in the sense of claiming that they are separate, will of course present no difficulty.

[5] For readability, I use 'be able to' where Fine uses 'can'. Surely this does no harm, and perhaps brings out overtones of Aristotelian potentiality even better than her word does.

[6] I distinguish the issue of what separation itself involves from the issue of what substance is separate *from* (what Fine calls the 'range') on pp 126-7 above.

this 'view' of the separation of substance as separation from other substances is not fundamental. My aim in the section 'The present account' (esp. 138–146) was to argue that the fundamental account of the separation of substance is 'being outside of the ontological boundaries of', and the other two accounts follow from it.[7]

Fine's reply to my first general objection reveals a basic disagreement between us. I think that 'separation' and 'independence' are very different concepts, and she does not. I believe that Fine owes us an account of how the Greek word which normally expresses the first came to be used for the second, whereas she feels that no such account is needed.

Fine is wrong to say that Aristotle *clearly* uses 'separation' in contexts having no local or spatial overtones. There *are* local and spatial overtones present in definitional separation, for example. *A* is definitionally separate from *B* just in case the definition of *A* does not contain within it (the definition of) *B*; in other words, just in case one string of words (or its ontological correlate) does not contain another string of words (or its ontological correlate) as a part. Now I admit that it is possible to view Aristotle's definitional separation as concerned simply with whether something is 'mentioned' in the definition. This places the emphasis on theoretical reduction and the elimination of theoretical terms, in a spirit with which we are all nowadays familiar. But it is also possible, and more true to Aristotle's philosophical context, to understand the basic intuition behind definitional separation in the more graphic way that I have just described.

My response to Fine's reply to my second general objection is that she is not as free to specify the temporal qualifiers as she would like. Fine is correct that if the temporal qualifiers of separation are construed in such a way that the existential dependence must be instantaneous, then Socrates is separate from the sun. But Aristotle's metaphysical outlook, and in particular the breadth of his notion of cause (*aitia*) prevent narrowing the temporal qualifiers in this way. And if the

---

[7] For this reason I now realize that it was misleading for me to present 'being separate from other substances' so prominently in the fourth paragraph of my article (126 above). The account of separation which should have been featured in that paragraph is 'being outside of the ontological boundaries of'.

causal dependence need not be instantaneous, then Fine's view does run afoul of examples like Socrates not being separate from the sun.

Destroying the sun destroys Socrates, and if ontological posteriority is established by being destroyed when the prior thing is destroyed but not conversely (*Eudemian Ethics* (*EE*) 1218a2 ff), then Socrates is posterior to the sun, and it should not matter that the process takes time. Stated more generally: causal dependence is dependence. Some causal processes take time, and there is no special reason to suppose that merely taking time should invalidate dependence. If separation is understood in terms of existential independence, then existential independence resulting from causal processes taking time should be sufficient to establish separation.[8]

Fine argues that Socrates is separate from his matter because of the truth of the following counterfactual: if Socrates had come to be constituted at moment *t1* by some matter other than that which did constitute him at *t1*, he might have existed none the less. However, since questions of dependence and independence for Aristotle ought to be construed in terms of real, causal potentiality, the criterion of independence ought to be construed, not counterfactually, but as a subjunctive conditional: if Socrates' matter were to pass out of existence, could Socrates survive?

This subjunctive conditional criterion of independence does not yield an unambiguous result. If Socrates' matter were destroyed chemically by a bath of acid or a blast of intense heat, Socrates could not survive. If Socrates' matter were destroyed gradually, say by metabolic processes over many years, in such a way that other matter satisfactorily replaces it, then Socrates could survive. Socrates is *not*

---

[8] In my brief remarks here I have only been able to begin to suggest a defence of this position, and there is surely room for further debate. First, since existential dependence shows up explicitly in Aristotle most often in connection with the ontological priority of Ideas, where the question of destruction in time hardly arises, direct textual evidence on either side is hard to find. Second, one might try, as some have, to distinguish *logical* from *causal* dependence (in our, not Aristotle's, sense of 'cause'), where logical dependence is instantaneous and causal dependence need not be, and say that for Aristotle the dependence relevant for substantiality is logical dependence. This view is worthy of respect, but my reaction is that it is an ingenious revision of Aristotle's system, one which a medieval philosopher might well embrace but which is untrue to Aristotle himself.

dependent on his matter because if you destroyed it in a certain way, he would survive. On the other hand Socrates *is* dependent on his matter because if you destroyed it in a certain other way, he would not. If one accepts the subjunctive conditional criterion of independence (and hence separation), then either one must simply say that Socrates is in a way independent (and hence separate) from his matter and in a way not, or else one must find some good reason to ascribe to Aristotle a preference for one 'sense' of independence over another as constitutive of separation. Finding cogent textual evidence for one preference or the other seems to me very difficult, but fortunately I can leave that task to the independence theorist.

Fine argues that Socrates is separate from his attributes because he could exist without any particular non-substance attribute that he has. However, whether Socrates is independent of his particular non-substance attributes depends on what particular non-substance attributes there are. If either 'weighing more than a gram' or 'metabolizing' is such an attribute, then he is not. Many other such properties could be mentioned. Perhaps individually their status as genuine particular non-substance attributes could be questioned. But the problem here is a structural one: no theory of separation should be accepted which makes the answer to the question whether substances are separate from attributes dependent on the complex and uncertain details involved in deciding exactly which putative properties are genuine and exactly how specific the various infimae species are.

Fine recognizes that on her view Socrates is not independent of certain general non-substance attributes that he has. I am surprised that she does not find this consequence unsatisfactory. If Socrates is not separate from colour, then so far as this criterion of substance is concerned (*a*) Socrates and colour are equally substantial, and (*b*) *both* are more substantial than his particular shade of colour at a given moment. One might possibly think Aristotle would accept (*b*), but surely he would not accept (*a*).

Concerning Fine's reply to my third objection, perhaps it would clarify my reasoning if I add a third conjunct to the antecedent. In between her (*a*) and (*b*), add '(*a'*) and given the native spatial sense of "in" '. When I wrote the sentence she quotes, I was assuming $(a')$ as understood; but I now realize that Fine looks at these matters so differently from the way I do that she would probably either deny $(a')$ or deny that it is at all applicable to the present context.

Aristotle does mount a variety of objections against the Forms, but my sense when reading them is that the separation of the Forms and their failure to be 'in' things are employed by Aristotle in such a way as to make it clear that they are very closely related. Unfortunately this 'sense' is largely a matter of judgement, one for which straightforward arguments are hard to give. I can only hope that the list of passages I gave in note 19 of my original paper (134 above) will help others to make up their minds.

If Fine can find evidence for a sense of 'in' in Aristotle that indicates dependence of the relevant sort, and if that usage fits the contexts where 'separation' and 'in' are used together, then she can avoid my objection. It did not occur to me that in citing *Physics* IV. 3 she might have had the fifth sense in mind, because I understand the metaphor underlying 'as the form is in the matter' to be 'as the impression of the seal is in the wax', which metaphor has precisely the local-and-spatial overtones that I have been arguing for. Perhaps one could also interpret the 'form in matter' sense of 'in' at *Physics* IV. 3 in Fine's way, as indicating dependence. But Fine has given us no good reason why one should. She says that 'elsewhere, Aristotle seems to claim that form is in matter *in that* (sensible) forms cannot exist without some matter or other' (italics mine). Unfortunately, Fine does not say what other texts she has in mind here. By itself, the fifth sense of 'in' at *Physics* IV. 3 is at best compatible with her view and does not provide any positive evidence in its favour.[9] If there are any passages in which Aristotle clearly does present the dependence of form on matter as an *explication*[10]

---

[9] *EE* 1217b2-16 presents a similar circumstance. Fine is correct to point out (160 above) that when her view is correctly interpreted, this passage is not counterevidence to her view. But it is not favourable evidence, either. The last sentence of *EE* 1217b2-16 is indeterminate enough to be compatible with either her view or mine, as well as many others.

[10] The words 'in that' which she uses are quite strong, and the textual evidence given must be sufficient to support that strength.

of form's being in matter, then *these* are the passages which Fine should bring forward to support her position.

Fine cites *Categories* 1a24–5 as another example of Aristotle's using 'in' to indicate dependence. Read in accordance with my interpretation of separation, *Categories* 1a24–5 states that $A$ is in $B$ as 'in a subject' if $A$ is within the ontological boundaries established by $B$ and $A$ cannot exist outside of those boundaries. But even if 'separately' in this passage should be understood in Fine's way as equivalent to 'without', the phrase 'cannot exist separately from what it is in' does not explicate $A$'s being 'in'. That is done, rather vaguely, by 'in something, not as a part'. Instead, 'cannot exist separately from what it is in' explains what it is for the thing which $A$ is in, namely $B$, to be its subject.

A concluding remark. Separation is a crucial metaphysical concept for Aristotle. Why does he never tell us what he means by it? Aristotle defines plenty of other metaphysical concepts, some of them much less central than separation. The bulk of his surviving metaphysical writings is large enough that the accidents of transmission are not a sufficient explanation. Perhaps there is some deep philosophical ground, one to which neither Fine nor I have yet penetrated, that would explain why Aristotle uses the notion of separation so often without ever elucidating it.

*Harvard University*

# EPICUREAN *PROLĒPSIS*\*

## David K. Glidden

Sextus brings his attack on definitions to a close with the remark that definition is useless, even if someone should say that definition was just an account which acts as a brief reminder, bringing us to conception of the things which underlie our utterances (λόγος εἶναι . . . διὰ βραχείας ὑπο-μνήσεως εἰς ἔννοιαν ἡμᾶς ἄγων τῶν ὑποτεταγμένων ταῖς φωναῖς πραγμάτων, *Outlines of Pyrrhonism* (*P.*) II. 212). Of course one wants to know who might have originally said this and what his motive was in saying it, but the text is interesting enough.

One can take the entire phrase 'conception of the things which underlie our utterances' in two ways. On the first reading the things which underlie our utterances are constrained by how we conceive them to be, so that what we refer to with our speech is what we meant to refer to. Here conception, or *ennoia*, signifies the intended description of the facts we refer to. And the passage is saying that a definition is a kind of mnemonic device designed to trigger the full recollection of that *ennoia*. What we are led to is not the way things are, however we might describe it, but rather the way things are only as we describe it. Consequently, if my definition of tigers—namely, that tigers are large striped furry animals—triggers my conception of what it is I refer to when I say 'tiger', then what I refer to cannot be *Felis tigris*, because that is not what I meant at all. Although I refer to something with my speech I do so only under one particular viewpoint, that of my own *ennoia*. The things which underlie our utterances are, as it were, governed by the *ennoia*.

'Conception of the things which underlie our utterances' is also open to a second interpretation, signalling an achievement by linking some psychological act of recognition with some actual state of the world, regardless of how the speaker

\* © David K. Glidden 1985.

or listener might characterize his state of mind or that state of affairs. The emphasis here is on 'conception of the *things* which underlie our utterances': viz. recognizing with the mind's eye what those real things are which our utterances name and label. Here *ennoia* represents not a determining mental content, but the fruition of the mental act of recognition. It is the tiger I recognize when I say or hear 'Tiger!' regardless of what I happen to know about tigers—that they are striped and furry—or do not know—that they are in the species *Felis tigris*. On the former interpretation it is '*conception* of the things which underlie our utterances' which is all determining. On the latter interpretation it is rather the world which triggers *our recognition*. It is the difference between *de dicto* and *de re*.[1] It is also the difference between a psychological reading of the line, concerned with the way in which the subject represents the world to himself, and an ontological reading, concerned with the state of the world which we happen to recognize.

It is clear from the context Sextus provides that the psychological reading of the line is the one intended by the defender of definitions. It is also clear from Sextus' own viewpoint that his objection against the value of definition requires an ontological reading of the line. Now the proponents of definition as a mnemonic device are approximating the modern view that 'perception may be regarded as primarily the modification of an anticipation'. One recognizes what one expects to see. Similarly, one is able to conceive of what it is the speaker or listener is referring to, because one already has an idea of the kind of thing that is meant—specifically a conceived definition of what that kind of thing is like. And it is this precise psychological position that Sextus ridicules with his objection that if someone were asked if he had passed a man on the road riding a horse and leading a dog, it would be beside the point and ridiculous as well to trigger the person's memory by reminding him of the definitions of 'man' and 'dog' (*P*. II. 211-13). The important point is the

---

[1] Interestingly enough, it is also the difference between what Descartes means by 'idea' and what Locke means by 'idea': cf. Ashworth (1981). For contemporary guidance concerning this distinction I have turned to Burge (1977), Putnam (1979), Fodor (1981), and Kim (1982).

ontological one: had he met the man on his horse with a dog. It is beside the point to explore the mental state of the witness—specifically, his conceptual apparatus. One wants to know whether the witness had seen those natural kinds of things in the appropriate arrangement. One does not require knowing what the witness conceives a man, a horse, and a dog to be. Consequently, if we understand 'leading us to conception of the things which underlie our utterances' to signal an achievement, the recognition of things referred to in speech, then definition is useless—hence Sextus' objection. The school Sextus objects to found definition to be useful only because they took the emphasis upon 'conception of the things which underlie our utterances' to be psychological and intensional, exploring how we conceive the things we talk about.

What makes this obscure little passage of Sextus so interesting is that it sketches out two fundamentally opposed attitudes toward semantic definition, and for that matter the nature of empirical enquiry. From the point of view of the school Sextus attacks *ennoiai* determine what it is we mean to refer to and definition becomes all important as a prerequisite for enquiry, no matter how these *ennoiai* themselves are engendered from experience. The objection Sextus employs emphasizes that knowledge is of what is, pure and simple. Consequently, having some preconceived definition is otiose, because the world itself comes divided into natural kinds of things and our task is simply to recognize them. The difference between a man, a horse, and a dog is not a difference we impose on the world but a feature of the world itself and the different kinds of things in it. Acts of speech label these differences and occasion communication. When my companion yells 'Tiger!' upon the approach of thè ravenous beast, his speech names that animal, neatly sorting it out from all the other kinds of animals therè are, and at the same time triggers my recognition of the same thing. If there be any time for definition it is subsequent to the empirical confrontation between man and beast.

It is time to unveil the cast of characters. We know from such sources as Galen that the school Sextus is objecting to are the Stoics.[2] And we know from the anonymous commentator

---

[2] Cf. *SVF* ii, 224–9; also Frede (1983).

on the *Theaetetus* that the objection Sextus employs was familiar to the Epicureans.[3] The commentator, who incidentally does not agree with Epicurus and defends against him the objection Sextus gives, remarks: 'Epicurus says that words are clearer than definitions.' This is a theme which is familiar enough in the Epicurean doxography, but its importance has rarely been appreciated, the discovery of *peri Phuseos* XXVIII notwithstanding. Words are clearer, because words label states of nature, whereas definitions merely relate words among themselves. The important things for Epicurus are the states of nature, or *pragmata*, which underlie our utterances, which settle disputes and solve problems. And this emphasis distinguishes the Epicureans from the Stoics. Now there are two competing kinds of *ennoiai* in the Sextus passage: one representational, the other recognitional; one Stoic, the other apparently Epicurean. Judging from the objection Sextus gives, Epicurean *ennoia* is merely designatory, the fruition of an act of attention when an individual comes to think of some feature in the world. By contrast, Stoic *ennoia* is completely intensional, a conceptual content which fashions what an individual can fathom about the world, the conceptual starting point for vision and investigation. Both kinds of *ennoia* are psychological, in the broadest sense of the term as the cognitive acts of some agent, but only the Stoic *ennoia* is psychological in the strict sense of being a mental representation: that is to say, having a content which may or may not be in tune with the world and which at best captures one aspect of reality—namely, the way it seems to the subject that the world is. Apparently the Epicurean 'conception of the things which underlie our utterances', on the other hand, only co-ordinates a psychological act of recognition seizing upon the appropriate stimulus in the world, without the mediation of some added significance which one gives to the experience to characterize one's state of mind and to represent the world. Instead, one simply responds to and recognizes a man on a horse leading a dog.

I have been dwelling on this passage, because it serves as

---

[3] Cf. Diels and Schubart (1905): col 22. 27–23. 8. I am grateful to Myles Burnyeat for first pointing out this passage to me, but see now Asmis (1984).

a handy prolegomenon to the study of Epicurean *prolēpsis*.
If the objection Sextus brings against the Stoic defender of
definitions is Epicurean, then this is embarrassing for the
*consensus omnium* of scholars who will not distinguish
between the conceptual character of Epicurean *ennoiai* and
the Stoic variety, whereas it seems that the two stand at
cross-purposes to each other. And just as Epicureans and
Stoics apparently differ about *ennoiai*, so it might just well
be that the two schools were not of one mind with respect
to *prolēpseis* either, despite the nearly unanimous consensus
of scholars that the Stoics simply appropriated Epicurean
*prolēpsis* for their own, a most unlikely turn of events, if one
stops to think about it.

Unfortunately there are precious few texts which can provide reliable information about Epicurean *prolēpsis*. From
what has survived of Epicurus' own writings there are just
three or four explicit illustrations of *prolēpsis*, examples
which are only mentioned but not discussed, in connection
with our knowledge of the gods, of justice, of responsibility
perhaps, and of time—with the last being a case where
a *prolēpsis* is said not to be relevant. There is the single
extant mention of *prolēpsis* in *peri Phuseos* XXVIII, where
the context is fragmentary and interpretation controversial.
In the theoretical section opening the *Letter to Herodotus*
scholars generally agree that *prolēpsis* is being discussed, but
that term is conspicuously absent from the discussion.
Among Epicureans, Lucretius provides not even a mention
of *prolēpsis* in the epistemic section of book IV nor does he
give us any examples elsewhere, unless we translate 'notitia'
in that way, which policy cannot be adopted uniformly or
without prejudicing the question. The helpful Diogenes of
Oenanda is apparently not at all helpful here. And Philo-
demus raises more difficulties than he solves, because Philo-
demus is an apologist for Epicureanism in the debates with
the Stoics and is consequently prone to using Stoic vocabulary, which is especially evident in his *Rhetorica* and *de Signis*.
Worst of all, what the doxographical sources have to say
about Epicurean *prolēpsis* is almost always from a Stoic
perspective, even when the author (Cicero, Diogenes Laertius)
is trying to be fair, which is not always the case, as with

Plutarch and Sextus. Indeed, the only explicit discussion of the character of Epicurean *prolēpsis* comes from these same Stoicizing sources. Even so, this little argument in the *Outlines of Pyrrhonism* on the uselessness of definition provides at least a clue, suggesting that Epicurean *prolēpsis* may not be the conceptual device it is represented to be by Stoics, doxographers, and scholars alike. At the same time we do know that *prolēpsis* plays some role in Epicurean doctrine because of *peri Phuseos* XXVIII: 'all human error is exclusively of the form that arises in relation to *prolēpseis* and appearances (*phainomena*) because of the manifold conventions of language.'[4]

### The doxographical representation of *prolēpsis*: Diogenes Laertius

Diogenes Laertius' report of Epicurean *prolēpsis* is painfully groping, looking for the right expressions to describe the device: 'By *prolēpsis* they mean a kind of *katalēpsis* (apprehension) or right opinion or concept (*ennoian*) or universal thought (*katholikēn noēsin*) stored in the mind—that is, the memory of a frequent appearance from the outside' (Diogenes Laertius (D.L.) X. 33). It is clear that this represents an analysis on Diogenes Laertius' part concerning what the Epicurean doctrine amounts to. One thing that infects this analysis is Diogenes' describing the Epicurean position in terms of well-known Stoic conceptual categories—*katalēpsis*, *ennoia*, *katholikē noēsis*. Another is Diogenes' ambiguous portrayal of the function *prolēpsis* is to serve: 'What primarily underlies every word is evident and we should not have started out to seek what is sought had we not already recognized it.' One wants to know whether *prolēpsis* is supposed to underlie language the way meaning underlies

[4] *peri Phuseos* XXVIII fr. 12. III. 6–12 (tr Sedley). On the interpretation of these lines see Long (1971*b*), Sedley (1973), and Glidden (1983*a*). Let me take this opportunity to extend my thanks to David Furley for first showing me the profound problem of Epicurean *prolēpsis* in 1968, to audiences at Philadelphia (Society for Ancient Greek Philosophy, 1982) and at the University of California at San Diego and at Stanford (1984) who heard portions of this paper, and to Jonathan Barnes, Tony Long, and Mike Wigodsky for their incisive criticisms of an earlier version.

language, providing the intensional *ennoiai* our words first signify, or whether *prolēpsis* is supposed to underlie language the way what our words refer to fundamentally underlies language, providing those real things we can name with our speech. On the first alternative, 'man' signifies some conception of man, enabling us to make sense of the sounds we speak. On the second alternative, 'man' names some perceived form, some sort of thing which we have found in the world and which our speech then names. Diogenes continues with this ambiguity:

Nor would we have ever been in a position to have named anything had we not first learned by *prolēpsis* the type of thing it is (μὴ πρό-τερον αὐτοῦ κατὰ πρόληψιν τὸν τύπον μαθόντες). *Prolēpseis* are, then, evident, and what is believed depends on some prior evidence (ἀπὸ προτέρου τινὸς ἐναργοῦς) by reference to which we say, for example, how we know if that is a man.

Diogenes adds that in contrast to *prolēpsis* the Epicureans say that *doxa* is a kind of judgment, or interpretation (*hypolēpsis*), which can be true or false.

On the one hand Diogenes' analysis suggests *prolēpsis* is a sort of intensional device, ranging between individual concepts and whole claims. But whatever *prolēpsis* encompasses, it would then do so willfully, establishing the mental categories (simple or complex) by which we can apprehend any thing or any fact. Although Diogenes goes on to suggest that these *prolēpseis* are themselves the children of experience (προηγουμένων τῶν αἰσθήσεων), such an epistemic role would seem to ignore this heritage. Instead, one can perceive only what one can expect to see. One can understand only what one can first conceive.

On the other hand, Diogenes' illustrations of *prolēpsis* suggest a rather different view, that *prolēpseis* are only temporally intermediate, subsequent to the sensory experiences which formed them, yet prior to any particular situation where a judgment is called for, requiring the kind of evidence only a *prolēpsis* can provide. In this way *prolēpseis* are temporally prior without being preconceived. In other words, by considering this passage from Diogenes Laertius one can on the one hand understand *prolēpsis* to be a conceptual device, encompassing both single concepts and complexes of concepts, or else one can alternatively understand *prolēpsis* to be a kind of *aisthēsis*, or perception, reporting on some state of the world. On the former view *prolēpseis* serve the psychology of knowledge, providing the semantic primitives, or concepts, with which the knower can describe his sensory experience and which circumscribe his view of the world generally. On the latter view *prolēpseis* emerge from *aisthēseis*, when accumulative perceptions enable one in time to recognize persistent features in the world, the *morphē* of a man or a horse, or even a man on a horse leading a dog.

This competition becomes transparent once we consider Diogenes' final stab at clarifying what the Epicureans take *prolēpsis* to be: 'that is, the memory of a frequent appearance from the outside' (τουτέστι μνήμην τοὺ πολλάκις ἔξωθεν φανέντος). Those who consider Epicurean *prolēpsis* to be some sort of conceptual device take Diogenes' remark as delineating merely the genealogy of *prolēpseis*, how such ideas are formed in the psychology of humans. Another way of taking the remark is as a statement of identity, not a statement of genealogy. Here *prolēpseis* just are habitual, remembered recognitions, where to remember anything requires one be successful at naming the original experience and in this case the experience named is some regularity in nature, or at least some appearance nature regularly presents. In this way *prolēpseis* are epistemic achievements, rather than psychological episodes with a prehistory dating back to childhood. It is not that *prolēpseis* do not enjoy this prehistory; it is just that Diogenes' claim concerns something else, something ontological: that one can remember accumulated *phainomena* and apply such memory in evaluating further appearances and making claims about the world.

There are elements in Diogenes' opening summation that do suggest the genealogical interpretation of the role memory plays in the formation of *prolēpseis*: that is, when Diogenes describes *prolēpsis* itself as *ennoia* and *katholikē noēsis*. And for this reason scholars uniformly give a psychological reading to Diogenes' last remark about memory and *prolēpsis*, preferring instead to emphasize *prolēpsis* as a conceptual device with a universal scope, understanding *katholikē* in this way.[5] But I take Diogenes' final clarification to be his last word on the subject, laying down the historical basis for his own analysis of the term, where *prolēpsis* is identified with 'the memory of a frequent appearance from the outside', providing an epistemic connection between perceivers and observed regularities in nature, thanks to the mechanism of memory. And there are elements corresponding to this representation of *prolēpsis* as a recognitional achievement also to be found in Diogenes' summation, when he describes Epicurean *prolēpsis* as a kind of *katalēpsis* or correct opinion, singling out the success of a *prolēpsis* in recognizing some fact or feature of the world.

Unfortunately, the phrase 'the memory of a frequent appearance from the outside' is one which has echoed through the ages, from Aristotle to Galen, and consequently it lacks any peculiarly Epicurean resonance. Aristotle, in looking back at Plato and the Presocratics, uses something similar to describe the consolidation of experience, or *empeiria*, where many memories of the same thing can constitute a single experience. And in words which seem to haunt the Epicurean letters Aristotle writes: 'ἐκ πολλῶν τῆς ἐμπειρίας ἐννοημάτων μία καθόλου γένηται περὶ τῶν ὁμοίων ὑπόληψις'.[6] Separate bits of information are accumulated in the mind's memory and when they come to be assimilated together the result is an interpreted experience of a single kind of thing. Prior to the willful formation of any interpretation, or *hypolēpsis*, this description coincides almost exactly with the way in which the empiric physicians, generations after Epicurus, came to characterize experience.

In the course of a lifetime of medical practice the cases the empiric physicians witnessed would accumulate and observations organize themselves more elaborately into new associations of observed symptoms, at an ever-increasingly higher level of generality. The physician would further

---

[5] Cf. Sandbach (1971); Long (1971*b*); Manuwald (1972) 4-10, who recognizes the possible Stoic corruption of the passage; Sedley (1973); Striker (1974), 68-73; Juerss (1977); Goldschmidt (1978); Asmis (1984).

[6] Aristotle, *Metaphysics* 980b25-981b10; cf. *Posteriora Analytica* 100a3-9 and Asmis (1984) ch IV. Like Epicurus, Aristotle used the term *ennoēma* sparingly, but I take it that both authors designate the same thing with the expression: namely, something brought to mind through perception.

184   *David K. Glidden*

expand his experience to include the clinical observations of other empirics, and in this way entire case histories would appear, even associating collections of symptoms with various diseases and treatments. For the experienced physician clinically trained in this way, seeing particular symptoms in one patient would trigger the memory of similar conditions in other patients, and the physician would automatically categorize such conditions within even larger groupings of symptoms extending across time. From the particular instance under inspection, then, the empiric physician would arrive at the accepted clinical observation and treatment. Yet the important point for the empirics was that no inferential reasoning or interpretation would be involved: experience teaches and habitual association alone effects the education of the physician. The assimilation of separate perceptions into kinds of symptoms was something perceptual habit would do at the behest of nature, rather than something the mind would impose on the world. So the empirics distinguished themselves from the so-called philosophic physicians, who theorized about the hidden causes of disease and used inference where the empirics simply used familiarity.[7]

This empiric strategy was distinct from Aristotle's approach to *empeiria* since Aristotle insisted upon something more than just the collection of similar experiences in the memory; what was also required was some cognitive understanding of the kind of similarity which binds those particular experiences together, what Aristotle called 'μία καθόλου . . . περὶ τῶν ὁμοίων ὑπόληψις' or even what the Stoics and Diogenes called *katholikē noēsis*. According to Aristotle and the Stoics, then, experiences may well accumulate but they require the mind to make some response, to come up with some conceptual category to characterize that sort of *empeiria*. Although the memory provides the stimulus for these concepts it does not invent them, and they remain the responsibility of the subject's representation of the experiences they so describe. According to the empirics, as I understand them, nature does all the work and memory continuously assimilates larger groupings of symptoms. The reason why this works as a medical strategy is precisely because these physical symptoms are

[7] Cf. Deichgraeber (1930); Glidden (1983b).

naturally the sorts of things they are, as part of a real causal nexus, and the physician simply learns to read them off the book of nature, seeing the patterns throughout the appearances in addition to recognizing the symptoms individually. He could not do this without the aid of memory, over and above his current observations, but he does not require cognitive representations as well.

It would be nice if we could take Diogenes' remark 'the memory of a frequent appearance from the outside' as providing a link between empiric practice and Epicurean *prolēpsis* and in this way distinguishing Epicurus' historical position from Diogenes' analysis of what that position amounts to in misleading Stoic terms. Unfortunately, the historic connections between ancient medicine and Hellenistic philosophy are too confused and complex to justify this synthesis, as striking as it may be. It could just as well be the case that empiric practice developed as a retrenchment against the Stoic position, cutting back to the level of *empeiria* before the application of *ennoiai*: 'Whenever many memories come about which are similar in form (ὁμοειδεῖς), at that point we say one has *empeiria*, for *empeiria* just is the multitude of appearances which are similar in form (τὸ τῶν ὁμοειδῶν φαντασιῶν).'[8] And the difference between Stoic *ennoia* and memory is obscure enough already: 'they define conceptions (νοήσεις) as sorts of conserved notions (τὰς ἐννοίας ⟨ἐν⟩αποκειμένας τινας) and memories as abiding and stable impressions (μνήμας δὲ μονίμους καὶ σχετικὰς τυπώσεις).'[9] But even if the connection between empiric practice and Epicurean *prolēpsis* is at best a coincidence, then so much the worse for Diogenes' final clarification as well as our effort to extract the historical doctrine from Diogenes' analysis of what that doctrine amounts to. In this case nothing in Diogenes' summation would remain above suspicion or unambiguous.

Yet there are also Diogenes' illustrations of *prolēpsis*: 'Take for example 'such and such is man' (τοιοῦτον ἐστιν ἄνθρωπος): as soon as man is named (ἅμα . . . τῷ ῥηθῆναι ἄνθρωπος), straightaway because of *prolēpsis* his *tupos* is

[8] Cf. *SVF* ii, 83 (Aetius), discussed by Asmis (1984), ch IV.
[9] Cf. Plutarch, *de Communibus Notitiis* 1085a.

thought of (καὶ ὁ τύπος αὐτοῦ νοεῖται), with the senses leading the way.' And again, 'for example, the thing standing in the distance is either horse or cow, but we must have, at some time or other, been in the position to recognize because of *prolēpsis* the form (*morphē*) of horse and cow.' As Diogenes says, if we are ever to name anything (ὠνομάσαμεν τι) we must first learn its *tupos* and *prolēpsis* accomplishes this. The trouble is, these illustrations perpetuate the very same ambiguities of reference. On the one hand, we can understand 'his *tupos* too is thought of' intensionally as a mental representation and in this way take Epicurean *prolēpsis* to be something like a Stoic *ennoia*. Here *tupos* would be something like a sense impression stamped on the memory, and *prolēpsis* would provide the conceptual interpretation with which to classify impressions of that sort. So Epicurean *prolēpseis* would be representational concepts. On the other hand, we can understand the point of reference (ἐφ᾽ ὃ ἀναφέροντες) not to be a mental representation at all, but rather the shape (*morphē* or *tupos*) real things naturally happen to have. The Epicurean perceiver, after the fashion of the empiric physician, not only perceives discrete appearances but after repeated experiences is in a position to recognize natural kinds of things as well, such as a man or a horse. Here *prolēpsis* just is the memory of those similar experiences, leading to the recognition of natural kinds. And Epicurean *prolēpsis* becomes an extended form of habitual perception, of the sort the empirics later called *empeiria*. On this view *prolēpseis* are *enargeis*, not because they are analytically clear as Cartesian concepts would be, but because they are similar to *aisthēseis*, providing perception of the world at a higher level of generality by recognizing natural kinds of things. Since language typically operates at this general level, singling out kinds of things with general terms in preference to proper names, it is not surprising that Diogenes Laertius would want to make a connection between *prolēpseis* and general terms for horse or cow or man. What is surprising to me is that Diogenes failed to fathom the difference between the empiric character of recognized general features in nature and the intensional character of representational concepts.

The doxographical representation of *prolēpsis*: Cicero

When compared to Diogenes, Cicero is a more careful historian of philosophy, although he writes in a style which tends to obscure the precision of his remarks. All the same, what Cicero says about Epicurean *prolēpsis* has difficulties of its own, difficulties I find particularly instructive. I have no quarrel with Cicero's remark that Epicurus named something new with the word *prolēpsis* nor even that one such *prolēpsis* informs us that the gods are blessed and immortal ('deos beatos et inmortales').[10] After all, Epicurus says much the same thing about the gods in his *Letter to Menoeceus* at 123-4. What is puzzling is that in his discussion of Epicurean theology Cicero seems to conflate the Epicurean apprehension of the gods through *epibolē tēs dianoias* with the apprehension of their nature through *prolēpsis*.

Velleius' representation of the Epicurean position together with Cotta's counterarguments largely constitute book I of the *de Natura Deorum*. Both presentations place firmly together two distinct metaphysical claims alongside a third, psychological one: that there are gods, that the gods are blessed and immortal, and that these facts are known by the universal consensus of mankind. Although it is said that the latter claim can also be rationally defended,[11] its authority primarily derives from a physiological process—that is to say, the way we all think about the gods is forced upon us by a chain of atomic events linking our material minds to the matter of the gods, yielding what Velleius calls 'primas notiones'. That there are gods nature herself impresses on the mind ('. . . esse deos, quod in omnium animis eorum notionem inpressisset ipsa natura', I. 43), and this explains the universality of the conception. Similarly, Velleius goes on to insist, nature engraves on our minds the fact that the gods are blessed and immortal: 'Quae enim nobis natura informationem ipsorum deorum dedit, eadem insculpsit in mentibus ut eos aeternos et beatos haberemus' (I. 45). The very same process

---

[10] Cf. Cicero, *de Natura Deorum* (*ND*) I. 44–5; cf. Hirzel (1877), i, 4–190.

[11] Cicero, *ND* I. 46–9, which contrasts with Lucretius V. 1161–240, where Lucretius emphasizes instead the human foibles of faulty reasoning about the gods' character. Cf. Sextus, *adversus Mathematicos* (*M.*) IX. 25–6, which backs up Lucretius' contrast.

impresses two facts upon us concerning the gods' existence and their character, and Velleius calls this process Epicurean *prolēpsis*: 'id est anteceptam animo rei quandam informationem' (I. 43) or, in other words, an anticipation or premonition of the gods ('sive anticipationem . . . sive praenotionem deorum', I. 44).

Unfortunately, Velleius goes on to describe this process of apprehension in some detail, and the description he comes up with turns out to be exactly what we know to be Epicurus' sixth sense, where the mind itself acts as a sense-organ: namely, *epibolē tēs dianoias*.

Epicurus autem, qui res occultas et penitus abditas non modo videat animo sed etiam sic tractet ut manu, docet eam esse vim et naturam deorum ut primum non sensu sed mente cernatur, nec soliditate quadem nec ad numerum, ut ea quae ille propter firmitatem στερέμνια appellat, sed imaginibus similitudine et transitione perceptis, cum infinita simillumarum imaginum series ex innumerabilibus individuis existat et ad deos adfluat, cum maximis voluptatibus in eas imagines mentem intentam infixamque nostram intellegentiam capere quae sit et beata natura et aeterna.[12]

Over the years this has proved to be one of the most abused passages in Cicero's philosophical writings. Yet some things are plain enough. The process Velleius describes coincides in every point of detail with what we know from Lucretius, Diogenes of Oenanda, and other Epicurean sources to be what Epicurus calls a *phantastikē epibolē tēs dianoias*. In the first place all our sources agree that in addition to the physiological activities of thinking the mind itself is sensitive to flows of atomic *eidola* impinging upon it and which it can singly perceive (hence: 'sed etiam sic tractet ut manu').[13] Furthermore, both Lucretius and Diogenes of Oenanda distinguish this kind of perception, which they say is the stuff dreams are made of, from the apprehension of solid bodies perceived by the other sense faculties (hence: 'nec soliditate

---

[12] Cicero, *ND* I. 49: I suspect 'ad deos' should be emended to perhaps 'ad nos'. For a detailed discussion of the extensive literature on this passage see Manuwald (1972), 11–39 and Asmis (1984).

[13] Cf. Epicurus, *Letter to Herodotus* (*Her.*) 38, *Kuriai Doxai* xxiv; Lucretius IV. 722–826; Diogenes of Oenanda (Diog. Oen.) fr 6, new fr 5–6 (Smith, *American Journal of Archaeology*, LXXV (1971), 357–89).

quadem nec ad numerum, ut . . . appellat').[14] The telling characteristic of such fantastic vision is that the mind selects out and composes the sequence of atomic images it singly perceives (hence: 'in eas imagines mentem intentam infixamque nostram intellegentiam capere') so as to tell a story (hence: 'imaginibus similitudine et transitione perceptis').[15] As a result erotic dreams are experienced ('cum maximis voluptatibus') or visions of a flying Pegasus or in this case a vision of the gods, whose nature is seen to be 'beata et aeterna'.[16]

This must at least be how Cicero understood the Epicurean doctrine, because Cotta's counter-replies directly associate this mental vision of the gods and their character with the Epicurean theory of dreaming. Consequently, Cotta objects, the Epicurean gods, like dream figures, lack the properties of solid objects, having only semblances of such features, and they enjoy human form, because that is the shape the mind is looking for.[17] Referring back to the passage I have quoted from I. 49, Cotta denies that this process of mental vision can testify to the existence and character of the gods, and he argues his case by explicitly attacking the Epicurean *epibolē tēs dianoias*:

Nam si tantum modo ad cogitationem valent nec habent ullam soliditatem nec eminentiam, quid interest utrum de Hippocentauro an de deo cogitemus? omnem enim talem conformationem animi ceteri philosophi motum inanem vocant, vos autem adventum in animos et introitum imaginum dicitis.[18]

In short, from what is presented in book I of the *de Natura Deorum*, Cicero assumes that the very same process of mental vision testifies to the existence and character of the gods, and he calls this testimony Epicurean *prolēpsis*. But we know it to be *epibolē tēs dianoias* as well.

---

[14] Cf. Lucretius IV. 724-43, 762-4; Diog. Oen. fr 7, new fr 6. I. 3-13; cf. Sextus, *M.* VIII. 63.
[15] Cf. Lucretius IV. 768-76; Diog. Oen. new fr 5. III. 6-14. Cf. Asmis (1981).
[16] Cf. Lucretius IV. 1030-6; cf. Dalzell (1974), Clay (1980).
[17] Cf. *ND* I. 75-6, 82-3.
[18] Cf. *ND* I. 105. The contrast between 'motum inanem' and 'introitum imaginum' testifies to the Epicurean zeal to root out all mental invention whatsoever.

Cicero assumes that *prolēpsis* reads off the character of the Epicurean gods by attending to these mental visions. And Cicero takes this to be the basis of an objection against the Epicurean theory: 'Fac imagines esse quibus pulsentur animi: species dumtaxat obicitur quaedam—num etiam cur es beata sit cur aeterna?'[19] Even if one could see these images of the gods, the objection goes, one could not see them to be immortal, and one could not see them to be blessed. Cicero's Cotta denies that what Cicero calls Epicurean *prolēpsis* can obtain the information it pretends to, but this presupposes Epicurean *prolēpsis* pretends to be just a form of perception, not a representation nor an interpretation of such perception. It is not that the mind first perceives these divine forms and then reasons that the gods are blessed, although the mind is free to think this way if it cares to. Rather, the mind just sees both the gods and their character. At the same time Cotta's objection suggests there is a difference between seeing the gods and seeing their character, although Cicero says both are *prolēpsis*.

According to the Epicureans there is a constant and systematic flow of atomic images, called *eidola* or *simulacra*, which assault the sense organs and constitute perception. In the case of vision the eye responds to a sequence of such imprintings so that the perceiver sees something. But when the mind itself responds to the impact of a single atomic image upon a single occasion, the result is an individual *epibolē tēs dianoias*. It is this susceptibility of the mind to any one piece of an infinite amount of atomic particles bombarding it that Cotta finds so ludicrous about the so-called Epicurean perception of the gods ('tota res . . . nugatoria est', I. 108). Judging from the rhetorical questions Cotta puts to Velleius, the trouble seems to be a question of identity, how these separate ephemeral mental visions can be seen to be a vision of one and the same thing. How do we know, Cotta complains, that the dream figure the mind perceives of Homer is the image of Homer or that the visions of the gods are distinct from the visions of fictitious people and places, which the mind also sees, taking particular *eidola* this way?[20]

[19] Cf. *ND* I. 106–7, 107–10, 110–14.
[20] Cf. *ND* I. 107–8; Sextus, *M.* IX. 43–8.

And how do we know, Cotta wonders, that the images I see belong to the same subject as the images your mind perceives? Cotta's complaints suggest that the mental perceptions of the gods, not to mention the perception that the gods exist and that they are blessed and immortal, require something more than individual acts of *epibolē tēs dianoias*. They would seem to require the association of those separate mental visions, linking them together over different occasions as being of the same sort, as another vision of Homer or a vision of the gods. What Cotta questions is how such principles of association could get established on the basis of the experiences themselves, the suggestion being that some interpretation, or *hupolēpsis*, would be necessary to gather together these separate experiences along the lines of similarity. Individual acts of *epibolē tēs dianoias* would not themselves raise such questions of identity, just as seeing a winged horse is distinct from having another vision of Pegasus. Problems only arise when one too has to characterize these individual glimpses of phantom figures as being recognitions of a certain sort. And here too is where our problem of interpretation comes into play, because both *epibolē tēs dianoias* and *prolēpsis* seem to require something more than just the passive presentation of fantastic material—namely, they both seem to require the organization of that material into something recognizable, organization achieved by the active intervention of the mind. Yet it is Cotta's criticism of the Epicureans that they ignore the need for such interpretative organization of raw perceptual experience.

On the one hand, unlike the case of normal perception the mind is sensitive to atomic constructions which lack any real solidity or individual identity. On the other hand, the attentive mind constructs a vision of a divine form from the incessant impacts of atomic *eidola*, so as to think that the gods are blessed and eternal. Lucretius says much the same thing in his description of the same process:

> et quia tenuia sunt, nisi quae contendit, acute
> cernere non potis est animus; proinde omnia quae sunt
> praeterea pereunt, nisi si ad quae se ipse paravit.
> ipse parat sese porro speratque futurum
> ut videat quod consequitur rem quamque; fit ergo.[21]

[*See p 192 for n 21*]

But note that although the dreaming mind recognizes what it expects to see, such recognitions are nothing like what we would call representational preconceptions. The recognitions of our dreams are not effected by acts of rationality (indeed, the dreamer is asleep),[22] but rather they are the manifestations of habit. For this reason, Lucretius says, the habits of our daily lives carry over into the dreams we have. And for this same reason horses dream of races and dogs of chases.[23] What the mind is intent upon, the mind perceives in dreams, but what the mind dreams does not enjoy the authority of reason. It is a case of attention without intention, a case of selective recognition, by happenstance.

Here Cotta's objections are particularly instructive. Although he describes this Epicurean vision of the gods as an 'anticipatum', at the same time he points out that according to the Epicureans nature has taught this ('natura praescripsit', I. 77), which is precisely what Cotta objects to: the Epicureans take as empirical evidence what is actually blind prejudice: 'Non pudet igitur physicum, id est speculatorem venatoremque naturae, ab animis consuetudine inbutis petere testimonium veritatis?'[24] However we are to understand either *prolēpsis* or *epibolē tēs dianoias* as an anticipation and premonition, Cicero's Cotta represents this Epicurean mental vision to be something given to us by nature herself. And Cotta objects that what the Epicureans take to be a *prolēpsis* of the gods turns out to be just *doxa*, and local prejudice at that.[25] In a word Cicero's Cotta takes Epicurean *prolēpsis* to be ill-conceived: it pretends to be a form of perception without interpretation—an empty pretence, according to Cotta.

Habits of the mind organize our dreams and our visions of the gods. One wants to know how these habits are to be distinguished from the intentional representations of the

---

[21] Lucretius IV. 802-6; cf. Cicero, *ND* I. 105.

[22] Cf. Lucretius IV. 765-7, although the point extends to daydreams as well: IV. 973-83.

[23] Cf. Lucretius IV. 962-72, 984-1010.

[24] Cf. *ND* I. 83. Note that this attempt to reduce perceptual *prolēpseis* to purely conventional habits is of a piece with Sextus' strategy regarding *hupomnēstika sēmeia*, but see also *M.* XI. 166 and Glidden (1983*b*).

[25] Cf. *ND* I. 81-4; Sextus, *M.* IX. 25-8.

mind, just as one wants to know the difference between the Epicurean *epibolē tēs dianoias* and Epicurean *prolēpsis*. Taking this latter question first, the evidence from Cicero seems to conflate the two upon the occasion of a mental vision of the gods. At the time when one has a vision of Jupiter, say, the passive presentation of the divine form and the active recognition of Jupiter by a mind intent upon it capture the dual aspects of a mental vision indifferently, whether it be an *epibolē tēs dianoias* or a *prolēpsis*. In both cases habits of recognition are required in order to achieve such mental visions. As Cicero suggests, repeated experiences are necessary to achieve these recognitions: 'hoc idem fieri in deo, cuius crebra facie pellantur animi, ex quo esse beati atque aeterni intellegantur.'[26] Given the infinite amount of atomic particles incessantly bombarding the mind, attentive habits could be acquired in short order, but it may not be the case that *prolēpseis* are as easily acquired as other mental visions. In any case, materially speaking, Cicero sees no difference in kind between the process of *epibolē tēs dianoias* and that of *prolēpsis*. Every *prolēpsis* just is what Epicurus calls a *phantastikē epibolē tēs dianoias*. But it need not follow—and indeed it does not follow—that any *epibolē tēs dianoias* is also an instance of *prolēpsis*.

Although Cicero does not explicitly distinguish the content of *prolēpseis* from the content of other mental visions in book I of the *de Natura Deorum*, one can detect evidence of such a distinction all the same. What concerns Cicero is the Epicurean contention that we have visions of a general character: that the gods exist and that they are blessed and immortal. Cicero calls these specific classificatory visions *prolēpseis* and at the same time he associates them with the physiology of the Epicurean *epibolē tēs dianoias*. Let us assume he was right to do so, but there is a difference none the less in the sheer extent of repeated experience which would be necessary to establish habits of recognition of a more general kind. As one proceeds from a night's vision of Tiberius Gracchus to a vision of the image of Jupiter and then to a vision that the gods exist and that they are blessed and immortal more and more experience would be acquired

[26] Cf. *ND* I. 106; Lucretius IV. 984-6.

to establish the habits necessary for such recognitions. Repeated experiences of mental visions must first become associated together to yield visions of a general sort concerning what it is to be a god—for instance that a god has a human shape: 'quod ita sit informatum anticipatumque mentibus nostris ut homini, cum de deo cogitet, forma occurrat humana.'[27] Similarly, to see that these images are gods that one perceives and to see that these gods are blessed and eternal requires sufficiently more experience so as to entrench the kinds of habits needed for the mind to select the appropriate images displayed to it and organize them so as to exhibit this general character.

It seems that Epicurean *prolēpseis* are a kind of *epibolē tēs dianoias*, distinguished from other mental visions by their generic content. Like any other *epibolē tēs dianoias*, an Epicurean *prolēpsis* acquires its content through habits of association forced upon the mind through repeated experiences. The Stoic and Academic detractors, speaking through Cicero's Cotta, lodge the familiar complaint that these habits of the mind are not something nature forces the mind to see, but rather something the mind willfully manufactures out of prejudice, beliefs, and reasoning. One just cannot see, even with the mind's eye, that gods are blessed and eternal. We can appreciate the difference between these two positions by considering a passage from Cicero's *Academica* concerned with how the Stoic mind organizes sensory experiences:

Mens enim ipsa, quae sensum fons est atque etiam ipse sensus est, naturalem vim habet, quam intendit ad ea, quibus movetur. Itaque alia visa sic adripit, ut iis statim utatur, alia quasi recondit, e quibus memoria oritur. Cetera autem similitudinibus construit, ex quibus efficiuntur notitiae rerum, quae Graeci tum ἐννοίας, tum προλήψεις vocant.[28]

Like the phrase 'conception of the things which underlie our utterances,' this description of the Stoic mind might seem just the sort of thing the Epicureans could say as well. But that cannot be so, and the difference once again is

----

[27] Cf. *ND* I. 76. It may be that the Epicurean point concerns the constraints upon human recognition: i.e. the only gods we can fathom are only those which look like us. Cf. Sextus, *M*. IX. 58.

[28] *Academica* II. 30 with Reid (1885), 212-14.

a matter of emphasis. To be sure, like the Stoics' 'mens construit' Lucretius says that 'mens parat', and Cicero describes Epicurean *prolēpsis* as 'anticipatio', 'praenotio', as 'insitas . . . vel potius innatas cognitiones' presupposing a 'mentem intentam infixamque'.

Yet once we attend to the work done by those various descriptions, none undermines or even qualifies the point that according to the Epicureans, as opposed to the Stoics, it is the uninterpreted process of perception alone (in this case a mental vision) which gives us such information, even when it is of a general sort. What is described is not a matter of intensional representations or cognitive impressions with which we frame our experience. Rather, the Epicureans are concerned with what in the world it is we notice or attend to, because of what we have already experienced. Of course the mind has a role to play in organizing our experience; this has to be so given the nature of Epicurean *epibolē tēs dianoias* and *prolēpsis*. But the mind plays its role in a passive way, letting the habits it has already acquired in experience organize further such subsequent experiences. And so Lucretius allows this process of mental vision to continue during sleep, when the other sense organs have shut down, when reasoning has stopped functioning, when the rational agent is asleep.[29]

One still needs to know, all the same, how such Epicurean habits of organization can be philosophically distinguished from cognitive impressions which structure the reality the subject experiences. In this post-Cartesian era it has no doubt seemed such an attractive way of looking at *prolēpseis* in terms of cognitive representations that the temptation has been inexorable to assimilate Epicurean views to those of the Stoics, especially when one finds such descriptions in the texts as 'innatas cognitiones'. Philosophically such temptations can be tempered once one appreciates that there are at least some animals, such as a spider or a slug, which exhibit complex perceptual discriminations without our requiring them to enjoy Cartesian concepts, even simple ideas of sensation. A spider can look out for what it expects to

[29] Cf. Diog. Oen. new fr 5–6. This specifically blocks the kind of cognitive inference from perceived similarities which so characterizes Aristotelian and Stoic accounts of the organization of experience into interpretative *hupolēpseis*.

catch without having mentally conceived representations. The same can be said of Epicurean *prolēpsis*. It is just a question of acquiring the right habits toward flies or the gods. Historically, we can also resist the temptation to convert Epicurean *prolēpsis* over to its Stoic counterpart, once we compare these Epicurean habits of association which enable the Epicurean to give content to his mental visions with similar habits cultivated by the so-called empiric physicians.

Both the Epicureans and the empirics describe the content of their observations as progressively acquiring a more general character, as the observer's realm of experience expands and evolves. Yet both insist that these expanded observations are simply nature's lessons as opposed to hidden prejudices or dogmas. Even if they are engendered by habits of association, Epicurean *prolēpseis* enjoy authority, the authority of perception and truth. The empiric physicians claim a similar such authority for their established habits of clinical observation. In the case of empiric medicine, by observing enough symptoms in enough patients the physician is said to be able to see things he could not see before—namely, general traits characteristic of different kinds of disease. Habitual observation enables him to recognize these general symptoms, so that he comes to know what to look for in any particular patient. These are acquired habits, not rational inferences or preconceived interpretations, but they owe their authority to the experience of the causal relationships witnessed in disease. For instance, some traits come to be seen as characteristic of pneumonia (such as coughing, lung pain, undulent fever, depression, and disorientation), because the disease, whatever its hidden character (namely, a virus infection), has these kinds of effects on the body. In this way, the empiric is able to identify pneumonia by the general collection of symptoms it manifests, even though he is not in a position to theorize about its microscopic cause. The mind, to be sure, organizes such disparate observations to display a general picture of the disease, but experience and habit teach the physician how to do this, not inferential reasoning or intentional interpretation. Habit succeeds in recognizing the general symptoms characteristic of the disease, precisely because that specific disease causes those symptoms to appear, or so the empirics argue.

Even if it proves impossible to establish actual historical connections between the Epicureans and the empirics, at least the comparison is apposite, for it shows how we are to understand Cicero's description of Epicurean *prolēpseis* as mental acts of perception and at the same time 'innatas cognitiones'. It also shows how we can distinguish the character of Epicurean *prolēpsis* from the fully representational variety, just as the empirics distinguish ingrained habits of general observation from rational conceptions of the character of disease. The premonition of a *prolēpsis* turns out to be the expectation established by general experience that given the specific character of what it is one is about to see (for instance, the specific Jupiter-like shape of a fantastic vision) what it is one sees should enjoy a more general character as well (a vision of an existing god who is blessed and eternal). This is what Diogenes Laertius called, aping the empirics: 'the memory of a frequent appearance from the outside'.

Other difficulties remain with Cicero's account of Epicurean *prolēpsis* in the *de Natura Deorum*: if *prolēpseis* are a form of mental vision, like *epibolē tēs dianoias*, the question arises how these *prolēpseis* can be cognizant of the other five sense faculties, in addition to this sixth sense. One also wonders what the limit of generality might be which distinguishes *prolēpseis* from specific perceptions. An answer to the first question cannot be found in the *de Natura Deorum*, which concerns itself only with the Epicurean mental vision of the gods, but some insight might be gleaned from the passage I have quoted in Cicero's *Academica*, despite its Stoic context. There Cicero says that the mind, which is both itself the source of perception and itself perceptive, arranges some sensory experiences by their similarities and in doing so brings about what the Greeks sometimes call concepts (*ennoiai*) or sometimes *prolēpseis*. Provided that we do not give a Stoic emphasis to this description, wrongly understanding the mind's arrangement as something conceptual, cognitive, and representational, the passage might nevertheless clarify the relation between *prolēpsis* and *epibolē tēs dianoias*, by suggesting that the mind can process and generalize upon the information received by the other sense organs, in addition to the specific information to which it is itself sensitive. In this way we might understand two of Cicero's phrases used to describe Epicurean *prolēpseis* of the gods: 'imaginibus similitudine et transitione perceptis' at I. 49 and 'eamque esse eius visionem ut similitudine et transitione cernatur' at I. 105. Both phrases encompass a process general enough for the 'intenta mens' to arrange other sensory information over and above what the mind itself experiences in its mental visions. So, although *prolēpsis* and *epibolē tēs dianoias* are perceptual activities of the mind, they do not coincide after all. As Cicero's testimony suggests, this fact might well explain an apparent confusion alluded to by Diogenes Laertius on the part of the later Epicureans—namely, whether *epibolē tēs dianoias* played a distinct epistemic role separate from Epicurean *prolēpsis*.[30] According to Cicero, it seems, the answer is yes and no: both are a form of mental vision but they do not both envisage the same kinds of things.

It is, indeed, hard to draw a fine line between proleptic visions and specific perceptions, including specific mental visions. The difference is more apparent in the genealogy of such perceptions than in their content. One requires habitual reinforcement; the other does not. Similarly, the empirics found it easier to distinguish *peira* (specific, individual observation) from *tērēsis* (general, habitual observation) on the basis of circumstance rather than on the basis of what was observed. One must not put too fine a point on it, because the demarcation between the two is only a matter of the degree of experience. For this reason, apparently, Cicero does not distinguish a *prolēpsis* that the gods exist from a *prolēpsis* that the gods are blessed and immortal, although he does distinguish these kinds of mental visions necessary to form a consensus about the gods from the individual visions of specific shapes or figures. But for those like the Epicureans and the empirics who give no more authority to any one perception over any other, the only difference worth talking about is that between what one perceives and what one reasons, and here *prolēpsis* stands firmly on the side of perception.

---

[30] Cf. D.L. X. 31. Perhaps Epicurus' qualification *'phantastikē'* distinguishes an *epibolē tēs dianoias* which is merely perceptive of a specific form from a proleptic *epibolē* perceptive of a general type.

Diogenes Laertius says there are *prolēpseis* of natural kinds like a man or a horse or a dog, while Epicurus himself gives us more abstract examples, that the gods are blessed and immortal and the *prolēpsis* of justice. Perhaps at one time the Epicureans argued that one could just see what it was to be a man or what a god looked like, just as one could see Metrodorus or have a mental vision of Jupiter, and perhaps the Epicureans opposed these specific perceptions to the *prolēpsis* formed by habit and required for perceiving the fortune of the gods or what we perceive justice to be. Perhaps this Platonic dispute never arose among the Epicureans. Yet it really does not matter once the difference between specific perceptions and *prolēpseis* is just a matter of the degree of experience. In this way, one could have both a specific perception of a man and a *prolēpsis* as well, although it takes more time and acquired experience to perceive what human nature consists of than the time required to perceive individual humans, although one sees them as human all along.

We can, at the same time, understand why the instances of *prolēpsis* as Cicero describes them take on what we would call a propositional character (that the gods exist, that the gods are blessed and eternal), while specific perceptions simply take objects, as in seeing Jupiter with the mind's eye or witnessing a man on a horse leading a dog. This syntactic difference is precisely the difference which experience makes, as one comes to recognize the character required to make things what they really are, much as the empiric comes to recognize the symptomatic character of pneumonia. Yet although we might describe the objects of Epicurean *prolēpseis* in terms of propositions, these objects are not cognitive *logoi* or abstract definitions and certainly not intensional entities like the Stoics' *lekta*. They are instead features and facts we come to recognize in the world which persist throughout nature and our experience. This Epicurean world which appears before us does not consist merely of specific individuals, specific clusters of atoms, but it encompasses natural kinds as well: that is, persistent types of atomic conglomerates which exhibit a certain character, as we become familiar with them through *prolēpseis*.

At the same time what counters Cicero's complaint that

such habits lack authority is apparently a conviction the Epicureans share with the empirics, that nature herself makes our perception discriminating. By the activities we are engaged in, by the lives we live, we become selective about what it is we notice, but what it is we notice is always some portion of the way the world is. For this reason, Lucretius tells us, both animals and men alike acquire such perceptual habits:

> Usque adeo magni refert studium atque voluntas,
> et quibus in rebus consuerint esse operati
> non homines solum, sed vero animalia cuncta.[31]

What horses and generals dream of may be selective discriminations, but they are nature's testimony all the same. And the same point would seem to apply to Epicurean perception at large and *prolēpsis* in particular. So understood, Cicero's testimony about the *prolēpsis* of the gods is part and parcel of his general portrait of Epicurean *aisthēsis*, that the Epicureans place all judgments in the senses and that the senses never lie. Cicero, of course, finds such a position ludicrous, but he takes some care in spelling it out.

It is a persistent feature of the doxography that Epicurean *prolēpseis* are said to be indispensable and the same is said of the Stoics as well.[32] Nevertheless, our inspection of the testimonies of Cicero and Diogenes Laertius suggests that although the Epicureans and Stoics come to the same conclusions, they do so for entirely different reasons. The relation of thought to perception, conception to recognition is complex enough certainly to encompass a variety of different theories, whose differences may well have been compressed by the Stoicizing influence of the ancient commentators and further telescoped by time. However we sift and sort the evidence of the ancient doxographers on the question of Epicurean *prolēpsis*, the only result can be informed speculation, since there are no surviving Epicurean texts which exactly circumscribe the nature of *prolēpsis*. At the same time such speculation must respect Epicurean empiricism and Epicurean materialism. The former makes perception alone

---

[31] Lucretius IV. 984-6. I would prefer Lachmann's 'voluptas' to 'voluntas'.
[32] Cf. Usener 255.

the foundation of knowledge. If *prolēpsis* has a role to play in the detection of truth, it is reasonable to assume its role is also perceptual. The latter requires that acts of cognition be material episodes, which notoriously leaves no room for propositions, Cartesian concepts, and other so-called contents of consciousness. So it would seem that *prolēpseis* label states of the world, not states of mind. I believe I have shown that nothing in the ancient doxography need contradict such an account of Epicurean *prolēpsis.*

## The extant Epicurean illustrations of *prolēpsis*

The description Cicero provides for the Epicurean *prolēpsis* of the gods exhibits a tell-tale signature, fashioning a number of disparate contours into a single line: that the gods exist, that the gods are blessed and eternal, that these facts are the common wisdom of mankind, and that this common wisdom is engraved on men's minds by the workings of *prolēpsis.* The line Epicurus articulates in the *Letter to Menoeceus* at 123–4 matches that signature exactly: 'First of all consider god a living being, immortal and blessed, as the common wisdom about god has traced out (ὡς· ἡ κοινὴ τοῦ Θεοῦ νόησις ὑπεγράφη). . . . For there really are gods, because our acquaintance with them is manifest (ἐναργὴς γὰρ αὐτῶν ἐστιν ἡ γνῶσις).'[33] These facts known about the gods are the work of mental recognitions, which enjoy a kind of perceptual authority (hence *enargēs*) because of the way they are produced (hence *hupegraphē*). And so Epicurus goes on to distinguish such perceived facts the mind grasps about the gods from other cognitive considerations, the work of prejudice, opinion, and judgment:

But they [i.e. the gods] are not such as the general populace considers, because people do not keep the gods the way they consider them to be. The impious man is not the one who does away with the gods of the general populace, but rather he who attaches to the gods the opinions

---

[33] Cf. Sextus, *M.* IX. 61–74; Schofield (1980*b*). If the reader accepts my distinction between the perceptual but non-cognitive *prolēpsis* of the Epicureans and the representational *prolēpsis* of the Stoics, it becomes an easy matter to sort out Epicurean and Stoic elements in the doxography.

202    *David K. Glidden*

of the populace. They are not *prolēpseis* but rather false judgments (ὑπολήψεις ψευδεῖς), these popular assertions about the gods.[34]

*Prolēpseis* are to be distinguished from opinions in much the same way that perceptual experience is different from reasoned speculation about the significance of that experience. So Epicurus distinguishes *prolēpsis* from *hupolēpsis* in much the same way that Aristotle distinguished *tēs empeirias ennoēmata* from *hupolēpseis*, although for Aristotle rational consideration was necessary to give form and substance to our accumulated experiences, while for Epicurus such experience is informative in itself.

It is not that Epicurus spurns any and all opinions about the gods. Rather, the only opinions which are reasonable to believe about the gods are those which are required by, or at least consistent with, what we already know from perception alone—strictly speaking, the accumulated experiences which constitute *prolēpseis*. So Epicurus says one must not attach to the gods anything which is foreign to their immortality (τῆς ἀφθαρσίας ἀλλότριον) or inappropriate to their happiness (τῆς μακαριότητος ἀνοίκειον), since the only acceptable opinions are those which preserve their divine character, a character perceived by *prolēpsis*.[35] In this way what Epicurus has to say about the difference between our *prolēpsis* of the gods and any *hupolēpsis* or *doxa* precisely mirrors the strategy of his theory of knowledge in general: that perception is the measure of all things and that whatever opinions we may form about the nature of things must either not contradict our observations or at least be consistent with them. Experience comes before opinion and is the *kanōn* for such opinion. At the same time, like *aisthēsis* in general, *prolēpseis* are just experiences, perceptual discriminations, not cognitive points of view, but rather viewpoints, or vistas, for cognition to peruse.

Not only does this passage from the *Letter to Menoeceus* substantiate much that Cicero says about *prolēpsis*, but it comprehends that remark in *peri Phuseos* XXVIII which is otherwise so hard to fathom: 'all human error is exclusively

[34] *Letter to Menoeceus* (*Men.*) 123-4. Cf. Cicero, *de Finibus* I. 47 and Sextus, *M.* IX. 71 who picks up the term *hupolēpsis*.
[35] *Men.* 123.

of the form that arises in relation to *prolēpseis* and *phaino-mena* because of the manifold conventions of languages.' The ill-founded *apophaseis* of the *Letter to Menoeceus*, like opinions and judgments in general, are ill-founded because they are devoid of experience; they are empty assertions because they fail to label the appropriate state of the world, and they fail to do so because they lack the testimony of nature. The difference between *phainomena* and *prolēpseis* cannot then be the difference between perception and con-ception, since both are forms of experience against which one is to measure one's conceptions and opinions generally. Instead, *phainomena* would seem to be current perceptual apprehensions, what we might call present sensory impres-sions, the way things look right now (what Epicurus terms in the *Letter to Herodotus* τὰς παρούσας ἐπιβολὰς εἴτε διανοίας εἴθ' ὅτου δήποτε τῶν κριτηρίων (38), what the empirics call πεῖρα). And *prolēpseis* turn out to be patterned recognitions, what Diogenes calls the memory of frequent appearances, what the empirics label *empeiria*, what we have found from Cicero to be engrained habits of perception.

At the same time it is easy to understand how Epicurean *prolēpseis* might be misrepresented as conceptual devices when contrasted with *phainomena*, either from the point of view of a Ciceronian critic or a modern Cartesian. Depending on one's psychological proclivities, habits of recognition can be seen as exhibiting a cognitive conceptual framework, so that all such seeing is seen as testimony for some native cognitivism, albeit triggered by experience but also consti-tuting that experience along the lines of its conceptual scheme. The trouble with such a view as an interpretation of Epicurus is that it is plainly incompatible with his brand of empiricism and the contrast Epicurus plainly establishes between opinion and experience. And other models of perceptual psychology are available, no matter how unpopu-lar to disciples of Cartesian intentionality, with which the modern reader can comprehend this ancient doctrine, models concerned with animal behaviour and the physiology of perception. Here, current perceptual discriminations are reinforced over time and become habitual, but they do not thereby become conceptual. Instead, a kitten comes to recognize a mouse upon seeing varieties of shapes and colours in motion. A child comes to recognize a human being. And an empiric physician comes to recognize the symptoms of pneumonia. Besides humans, other animals may not be in a position to think about what it is they perceive, either as single appearances or repeated ones. But what humans use as evidence for their thoughts about the world, Epicurus wants to insist, are these same raw experiences animals are exposed to as well.

Although both animals and people prepare themselves to perceive the fantastic figures they recognize in dreams, what it is we recognize itself takes on a general character, both in our dreams and our *prolēpseis*. We see a flying horse or that the gods are blessed and eternal. And this is recognized by the mind alone. To recognize a kind of thing as the kind of thing it is is the work of imagination and *prolēpsis*, and habit apparently enables the mind to sort out things the way it does. Why these habits of the mind should coincide with the way things really are is a question well worth considering. Epicurus apparently has two answers, corresponding to each side of the requisite template.

On the one hand, the process of imprinting guarantees that the kinds of things there are make their impact on the mind, a causal defense of realism and the testimony of *aisthēsis*. This mechanical process enforces our ability to see things the way they are. To make this defence impregnable the Epicureans went on to insist that anything we can imagine owes its character to a real existence—namely, the shape of some atomic construct striking the mind. To imagine a god or a flying horse or even to see that the gods are blessed and eternal is simply to be exposed to the requisite atomic patterns and in time to come to recognize them. According to Epicurus, it is some such process as automatic as this which makes perception possible and gives it its authority. And the dream figures the mind perceives are of a piece with perception generally, leaving, so to speak, no room for imagination: that is, nothing for the mind to make up on its own or at least no right for the mind to call such inventions *aisthēseis*, when for the Epicureans such cognitive impressions can be nothing more than judgments or opinions which must be tested against the vocabulary of experience, the way things look. Given the connection between *epibolē tēs dianoias* and *pro-lēpsis*, the mind is also said to be able to pick out figures by their sortal nature, to perceive the general character of things. This is all said to be part of the same process and *prolēpsis* is said to enjoy the same sort of epistemic authority as *aisthēsis* in general.

At the same time, the Epicureans appreciate that when things take on a general appearance, it is the mind alone which perceives such facts. The separate glimpses of one sort of atomic conglomerate grasped by the mind's eye testify to some perceived form which all conglomerates of that sort have in common. The separate items of information received by the mind from the other sense organs come to signify to the mind a more systematic phenomenon. All that is required is enough exposure to sufficiently many atomic constructions of the required sort for the mind to recognize them. Such recognitions require allegiance for the Epicureans, because nature herself comes divided that way. It is not merely that there are atoms in motion in the void, but there are also kinds of atomic conglomerates in our world which we can in this way come to recognize, such as a man on a horse leading a dog. On the other hand, the mind must also select out what it chooses to notice from among the streams of atomic images bombarding it from the outside or from what is presented to it by the other sense organs, and it is this which is thought to give *prolēpsis* its proleptic character.

Once a *prolēpsis* has been established by experience, it can then anticipate what it is the mind is about to see, and a particular perceptual act comes to take on a wider significance. Upon seeing the back of Simmias' cloak, we see that it is Simmias wearing it, or we take a certain fantastic vision to be that of a god who is blessed and eternal. An edifice on the hill in the distance is taken to be a tower, provided that it is not so far away that the mind cannot attend to it, lacking the minimal sensory clues needed to trigger the recognition.[36] In this way *prolēpseis* enable the mind to see more than the

---

[36] Cf. Lucretius IV. 354–63, who gives a physiological explanation for in-adequate perceptual clues. Sextus ridicules such physiological causation by illegitimately converting the thesis into an epistemic explanation: *M.* VII. 365–8.

specific information it is on any one occasion exposed to, because the mind comes to each new experience trained in habits of recognition to search out the familiar. As long as each of these habits is grounded in experience, as opposed to, say, pure social conventions, *prolēpseis* remain non-controversially a part of *aisthēsis*, broadly conceived across time. Of course, the range of habitual experiences may vary across individuals with differing skills and interests. So people notice different things. A physician looks out for symptoms which escape the layman. A painter recognizes distinct shades of colour which might otherwise appear roughly the same.[37] Nevertheless, what it is we so attend to remains a portion of reality, for each such habit is brought to us from the world outside, impinging on our bodies. It is just that some individuals have different patterns of recognition, because they are repeatedly exposed to a different portion of reality.

There are some portions of reality all of us are exposed to, yielding up *prolēpseis* all human beings share, establishing a *consensus omnium*. What makes this *consensus* a consensus enjoying the authority of truth is obviously not the mere fact of agreement. Epicurus shows little patience for the popular myths about the gods. It is, instead, a question of the experience it takes to constitute a true consensus through the workings of *prolēpsis*: 'what the common wisdom about god has traced out', as Epicurus says. Now in his discussion of knowledge opening the *Letter to Herodotus* Epicurus placed his emphasis on present sensory experience, *tas parousas epibolas*. It was no doubt prudent to do so in such a brief summary of his doctrine. And Lucretius followed suit in his parallel discussion at book IV in the *de Rerum Natura*. After all, the way things look to a person right now is the starting point of experience. But present appearances alone do not and could not constitute experience, for such appearances build upon each other and continually reconstitute how the world looks to us. So it is not surprising that in *peri Phuseos* XXVIII the authority of experience has been expanded to include remembered habits of recognition as well as present *phainomena*. This enables those who share certain specialized observations to reach a consensus, the way physicians do, for

[37] Cf. Sextus, *M.* VI. 55-9.

instance. It also makes a true *consensus omnium* possible for universal facets of human experience. The foundations of the Epicurean theory of knowledge remain the same, the way things look. It is just that memory and habit come to play a role, concerning what it is we are familiar with and what it is we attend to.

The problem with such a philosophical doctrine of *empeiria* turns out not to be how we can distinguish the specific perception of a man, say of Socrates, from the *prolēpsis* of man, but rather how we can know when the mind has reached such a level of generality that it abandons the assurance of recognized regularities of nature to form opinions and prejudices which must await the testing of their truth. In other words, how can Epicurean *prolēpseis* remain inviolate from the penetration of perception by cognition? Now it is true that simply seeing a man on a horse leading a dog raises exactly this same question for contemporary cognitive psychologists and perceptual theorists, following the lead of their Stoic predecessors. We do see the taint of 'perception penetrated by cognition' colouring Diogenes' Stoicized presentation of the Epicurean doctrine, where it is alleged of Epicurean *prolēpsis* that in order to see a horse one must first have the concept of horse. Yet, over and above the question of how there can be purely perceptual *prolēpseis* for man, beast, or god, we know from the Epicurean texts themselves that Epicurean *prolēpsis* encompassed natures of an even more abstract kind: the character of the gods, the nature of justice, the nature of causation perhaps, and possibly even the nature of truth.[38] These recognized regularities of nature seem barely distinguishable from cognitive judgments concerning the way things are, but apparently they were so distinguished by the Epicureans.

In a passage written into the *Letter to Herodotus* Epicurus says there is no such thing as a *prolēpsis* of time; instead, 'time' need only name something we *conceive* to be a peculiar symptom (ἴδιόν τι σύμπτωμα . . . ἐννοοῦντες, καθ᾽ ὃ Χρόνον ὀνομάζομεν).[39] Here Epicurus draws the line between

---

[38] Cf. Sedley (1983) on Lucretius IV. 478–81, discussed below.

[39] *Her.* 73. Cf. Sextus, *M.* X. 181–8, 219–28, 238–47. Although this passage may possibly have been subsequently added to the letter (cf. Sedley (1973)), it

perception and cognition, but in order to appreciate how this line is drawn, we must first recollect his general theory of properties, encompassing whole natures (*phuseis*, or *naturae*), their permanent properties, or *sumbebēkota* (*coniuncta*), and their incidental features, or *sumptōmata* (*eventa*). The *sumbebēkota* happen to be found in natural kinds of things so long as these respective bodies happen to remain the sorts of things they are. So fire must be hot, and water liquid.[40] Since there are two sorts of corporeal natures in Epicurean physics (kinds of atoms and kinds of visible bodies), both sorts will enjoy permanent properties, although the only *sumbebēkota* we can recognize are those which happen to be seen in visible bodies (atomic conglomerates). Now Epicurus does not seem to be saying that for a thing to retain its nature it must always have exactly the same specific permanent properties, so that a blade of grass must always be green (and never brown) to be that same blade of grass. This may be true of atoms but it will not be true of *horata*, the things we can see. That sort of essentialism is simply inappropriate for substances which are in turn mere conglomerates.[41] What Epicurus is saying, instead, is that for something to be the thing it naturally is certain sorts of properties must belong to it, all of which together give that body its abiding nature.

The important point for Epicurus concerning *sumbebēkota* is that each and every one of these properties is specifically and distinctly perceived (καὶ ἐπιβολὰς μὲν ἔχοντα ἰδίας πάντα ταῦτά ἐστι καὶ διαλήψεις) as a property of the body it belongs to (συμπαρακολουθοῦντος δὲ τοῦ ἀθρόου καὶ οὐθαμῇ ἀποσχιζομένου). It is precisely because these properties are perceived this way that in Epicurean theory we call them *sumbebēkota*, because they are relativized to the entire conception of the body they happen to belong to (κατὰ τὴν ἀθρόαν ἔννοιαν τοῦ σώματος κατηγορίαν εἰληφότος).[42] In addition, then, to our perceiving an individual colour (red)

is nevertheless intimately connected with the Epicurean doctrine of properties and symptoms already present in the letter, as Sextus makes clear.

[40] Lucretius I. 453.

[41] Cf. *Her.* 69; Sextus, *M.* X. 221-3.

[42] *Her.* 69. Cf. Manuwald (1972), 103-9, who seems to confuse an Epicurean *prolēpsis* of a natural kind (e.g. a *prolēpsis* of man) with an Epicurean analysis (hence *ennoia*) of what it is to be an abiding conglomerate in an atomic world.

and an individual shape (round), these properties appear to us as the colour and shape of the apple we are looking at. In this way, I surmise, specific *aisthēsis* grades off into *prolēpsis*. Observed regularities of nature come to identify such bodies as apples or horses, and so *aisthēsis* and *prolēpsis* work in tandem at any one time, although it takes more time for a *prolēpsis* to establish itself than it does to recognize a colour or a shape. Distinguished from this twofold process of perception is a separate process of cognition (hence *doxasteon* at 68), where one considers, for instance, how a particular property is produced by its atomic components, so as to offer an analysis of the abiding character of a thing, as a means of investigating the whole body understood universally.

Presumably one infers from fire always being hot that such an atomic conglomerate in general is composed of exceedingly small smooth atoms. The difference between *prolēpsis* and *hupolēpsis* is in part a difference of background information. One is delimited to collections of apparent properties observed over time. The other incorporates theoretical commitments as well, postulating the hidden causes for such clusters of appearances.

With *sumptōmata*, Epicurus advises, it is different, although such incidental features are always also observed in conjunction with the bodies they are for the time being associated with (κατ᾽ ἐπιβολὰς δ᾽ ἄν τινας παρακολουθοῦντος τοῦ ἀθρόου ἕκαστα προσαγορευθείη, ἀλλ᾽ ὅτε δήποτε ἕκαστα συμβαίνοντα θεωρεῖται).[43] These *sumptōmata* are seen in things, but they are not seen as permanently belonging to the things in which they are seen. They are symptoms of something else, other than the nature of the things in which they are found. They are perceived to have their own characteristic identity, although they are not perceived to be independent of the various bodies they are found in. In the case of permanent properties the observed regularities of *empeiria* testify to the nature of the things which enjoy such *sumbebēkota*. Observed symptoms, instead, testify to the regularity of a condition found in all sorts of things, such as

---

[43] *Her.* 70–1.

war or peace, slavery or freedom, poverty or wealth.[44] Here too there seems to be a twofold process of perception, one addressing specific qualities perceived on any one occasion, the other characterizing those symptoms wherever they occur, wherever they leave the imprint, as it were, of pneumonia or pestilence or war. Such is the difference between *phainomena* and *prolēpsis*. Cognition addresses another issue altogether, speculating upon what is in the nature of things that gives the plague to Athens, war in the Peloponnese, or floods in Thessaly, what hidden secrets make things exhibit the symptoms they do.

*Prolēpseis* would then seem to organize *phainomena* in two different ways, depending on whether the *phainomena* observed are *sumbebēkota* or *sumptomata*. The one yields *prolēpseis* of natural kinds. The other yields *prolēpseis* encompassing persistent conditions, regularities pervading the *phainomena* without coming to identify at the level of appearances natural sorts of atomic conglomerates. So there is a *prolēpsis* of justice as well as of the blissful character of the gods, in addition to the *prolēpsis* of man. But there is no *prolēpsis* for time. Unlike the case of typical *sumptōmata* where one examines the regularity of the situation one is investigating by referring to one's observed *prolēpseis* (ὅσα ἐν ὑποκειμένῳ ζητοῦμεν ἀνάγοντες ἐπὶ τὰς βλεπομένας παρ' ἡμῖν αὐτοῖς προλήψεις),[45] there is no persistent natural condition underlying what it is we call time.[46] Instead, to come up with a conception of what 'time' names, one must engage in various rational procedures (*analogisteon, epilogisteon*) based on the evidence (*enargēma*) of our experiences, reflecting change and duration, such as our observing night following day or the duration and change of our feelings.[47] Unlike other *sumptōmata* which give rise to our *prolēpseis* of them, there is no distinctive sense of time over and above our specific individual experiences of one thing or another: 'nec per se quemquam tempus sentire fatendumst / semotum ab rerum motu placidaqua quiete.'[48] There cannot

[44] Cf. Lucretius I. 455–8.
[45] *Her.* 72.
[46] Cf. Lucretius I. 459–63; Sextus, *M.* X. 219–28, 240–4.
[47] *Her.* 73.
[48] Lucretius I. 462–3.

then be a *prolēpsis* of time, because time as such represents a cognitive creation as opposed to a persistent condition regularly experienced in nature.

I have been assuming that the proper interpretation of *Letter to Herodotus* 69-72 together with its parallels in Lucretius and Sextus, presumes there to be only a conception of time without a corresponding *prolēpsis* to support it. But that may well be too strong an assumption, for all that Epicurus strictly says is that there is no *prolēpsis* of time, ordinarily speaking. Epicurus does not specifically exclude the possibility of there being in this case a special sort of *prolēpsis*, one which discerns a regularity of regularities, a *sumptōma* of other *sumptōmata*, as Sextus reports it. If this were so, one could indeed experience time and have a *prolēpsis* of it, but just not in the way one experiences other *prolēpseis*. One experiences changes of feelings, night following day, and discerns a pattern persisting throughout these changes. Perceiving that pattern just is what it is to experience time and constitutes a special *prolēpsis* all its own. Yet even if there turns out to be something of this sort, such a *prolēpsis* as special as it might be is still to be distinguished from the concept of time, just as having a *prolēpsis* of man or war is distinct from being able to define rationally what it is to be a man or what constitutes a war.

Ontologically speaking, the line between *prolēpseis* and *hupolēpseis* is easy enough to draw. All there is are atoms and void, with the atoms constantly in motion. Since these atoms come together in our world to form persisting conglomerates which we can then observe, all there is that we can see are such natural kinds of things together with the persistent conditions they occasionally find themselves in, the latter being the *sumptōmata* of the former. Such is the natural limit of *prolēpsis*. Anything else must be a conceptual invention (whether true or false). As we have seen, it is this ontological viewpoint which takes precedence with the Epicureans as they examine what underlies our utterances.

Psychologically speaking, the line between *prolēpsis*, or *aisthēsis* too for that matter, and cognition is almost impossible to define a priori. This is the Stoic critic's viewpoint, for the critic wants to know how the Epicurean can experience anything (whether it be a single appearance or a persistent *prolēpsis*) which will distinguish that experience from cognition. That is not Epicurus' concern, who simply maintains that how we know follows upon what there is, rather than the other way around. Epicurus is able to maintain such a view by insisting that perception and *prolēpsis* are each informative without being cognitive; they are each *alogos*.[49] This, in turn, exposes Epicureanism to the ancient objection that without cognitive representation of what we perceive, without cognitive interpretation of what we experience, the person is no wiser than the parrot.[50]

The Epicurean doctrine of *prolēpsis* poses an interesting challenge to cognitive theory, if it can withstand criticism—interesting, in its suggestion that one sort of mental activity (namely, perceiving) can be programmatically sequestered from another (namely, thinking), providing two distinct kinds of information and constituting two distinct forms of physiological activity. The independence from each other of these two materialistic mental modules is what licenses Epicurean empiricism. The programmatic difference between the two is, as we have seen, the difference between recognizing something happening in the world (whether synchronically or diachronically) and conceiving of the world in a rational representational fashion. The former takes place in the demonstrative language of perception; the latter requires the language of definition, demonstration, hypothesis, and verification. What might seem so surprising is how Epicurus conducts such abstractions as justice and possibly even causation into the realm of observation, thereby enriching his empiricism and risking his reputation, the vehicle of *sumptō-mata* notwithstanding.

Epicurus tells us there is a *prolēpsis* of justice, which is no

---

[49] Cf. D.L. X. 31 which admits Epicurean *aisthēsis* is *alogos* but seems to suggest that memory (and hence *prolēpsis*?) would not be *alogos*. Yet I would not conclude from this passage that *prolēpsis* is here said to be cognitive and rational the way Stoic *lekta* are, as Liebich (1954) argues. Rather, Epicurus maintains that *prolēpsis*, like *aisthēsis* in general, is *alogos* as well. Epicurus distinguished the associative mnemonic habits of *prolēpsis* from the cognitive memory of thought: hence Lucretius IV. 765-7 argues that in dreaming *epibolē tēs dianoias* is active but cognitive memory is not.

[50] Cf. Glidden (1983*b*), 238-44.

less a *sumptōma* than the Trojan War or the wealth of Croesus. There was once a Platonic Form by that name and the two (*prolēpsis, eidos*) are not that dissimilar, since on both accounts justice is a structural feature of reality, as opposed to a purely human conception. But Plato thought we could discover justice only by a kind of mental recognition, which would require preliminary reasoning and the repression of the senses. Epicurus even agrees that it is a kind of *epibolē tēs dianoias* which grasps what justice is, but (unlike Plato) this is to be a kind of sensual vision, not a kind of visionary *logos*, or definition.

We can and do recognize a man on a horse leading a dog, without first having among ourselves agreed upon conceptions of what it is to be a man or a horse or a dog. And dogs and horses can do this too. We humans can also recognize a war when we see one or poverty or justice, because we are familiar with such symptoms among ourselves. What we care to think about such human conditions, Epicurus suggests, is altogether a different matter. But can we so rigorously distinguish how things look from what we think about them? The empiric physicians, and the methodists too for that matter, thought we could, and they built their practice of medicine around the difference. Indeed, the 'general symptoms' recognized by the methodists are strikingly similar to Epicurean *prolēpseis*, in that both concern persistent conditions varying widely from place to place, without always indicating the same hidden causes. The empirics even thought we could perceive symptoms and their antecedent causes without having to speculate about the hidden mechanism: we could just see that a puncture wound in the heart caused the death of the patient.[51] Now David Sedley has recently and heroically gleaned from Epicurus' *peri Phuseos* (possibly the papyrus for book XXXV) the following phrase, standing in a brief section between two lacunae: 'τὴν τῆς αἰτίας πρό[λη]ψιν', which suggests an Epicurean *prolēpsis* for causation.[52] This does not surprise me as long as the causation involved is something we can observe, as the empirics thought it was (much to the indignation of the Pyrrhonists). We do seem to see causes persisting in nature, regardless of

[51] Cf. Sextus, *M.* V. 104.     [52] Sedley (1983), 19-31.

our philosophic theories: the sun melts the snow, the man
leads his dog. So antecedent causes may well have their place
in the perceptual module of the mind.

What limits the content of *prolēpseis* are the limits of what
we can observe, present and persistent appearances. Since
Lucretius invariably uses 'notitia' to circumscribe thoughts
and theoretical conceptions whose subject matter would not
present such appearances, the way justice or war, for instance,
can be seen as opposed to the way 'time' must be conceived
instead of being perceived, 'notitia' cannot then be Lucretius'
translation for *prolēpsis*. More likely, it is his translation for
*ennoia*. So there is no need to postulate a *prolēpsis* of truth
corresponding to Lucretius' 'notitia veri':

> Invenies primis ab sensibus esse creatam
> notitiem veri neque sensus posse refelli.
> nam maiore fide debet reperirier illud,
> sponte sua veris quod possit vincere falsa.[53]

Rather, Lucretius' point is that our conception of truth and
our theory of knowledge in general should be derived from
and be conceived of as a consequence of our perceptual
experience, the way we conceive of time, for instance. Yet
conceptions such as these are not identical to our perceptual
experiences: the two are programmatically distinct. It goes
without saying, however, that conceptions too must label
reality the way it is, on pain of being empty conceptions,
empty utterances, false *hupolēpseis*.

We are free to conceptualize and theorize about anything
at all, about the movements of atoms, about the authority of
experience. But our starting point and the measure of the
truth of everything we have to say must remain the way
things look, the present and persistent appearances of *phainomena* and *prolēpseis*. This guarantees that whatever we think
about always attaches to some portion of reality. It is worth
savouring the irony that this is a strategy which would
appeal more to a Skeptic than a Stoic, for by completely
isolating present and persistent appearances this way from
the cognitive constructions of reason, the Epicurean perceiver
has only the way things look to go by, the way things appear

---

[53] Lucretius IV. 478-81; cf. IV. 476. Cf. Burnyeat (1978), Sedley (1983), 27-8.

without representation, without interpretation. The Epicurean bravely vows to pull knowledge of reality up from this well of raw experience. The Skeptic from Aenesidemus to Hume goes this far in the company of the Epicureans. But when it comes to working at the well and coming up with something known, the Skeptic holds back and takes his rest.

*University of California, Riverside*

# BIBLIOGRAPHY

Ashworth, E. J. (1981): ' "Do Words Signify Ideas or Things?" The Scholastic Sources of Locke's Theory of Language', *Journal of the History of Philosophy*, XIX, 299-326.

Asmis, E. (1981): 'Lucretius' Explanation of Moving Dream Figures at 4. 768-76', *AJPh* CII, 138-45.

Asmis, E. (1984): *Epicurus' Scientific Method* (Ithaca).

Burnyeat, M. F. (1978): 'The Upside-Down Back to Front Sceptic of Lucretius IV 472', *Philologus*, CXXII, 197-206.

Burnyeat, M. F. (1983): *The Skeptical Tradition*, ed M. F. Burnyeat (Berkeley).

Burge, T. (1977): 'Belief *De Re*', *Journal of Philosophy*, LXXIV, 338-61.

Clay, D. (1980): 'An Epicurean Interpretation of Dreams', *AJPh* CI, 342-65.

Dalzell, A. (1974): 'Lucretius' Explanation of the Doctrine of Images', *Hermathena*, CXVIII, 22-32.

Deichgraeber, K. (1930): *Die Griechische Empirikerschule* (Berlin).

Fodor, J. (1981): 'Methodological Solipsism Considered as a Research Strategy in Cognitive Psychology', *Representations* (Cambridge, Mass.), 225-53.

Frede, M. (1983): 'Stoics and Skeptics on Clear and Distinct Impressions', in Burnyeat (1983), 65-94.

Glidden, D. K. (1983*a*): 'Epicurean Semantics', in *SUZETESIS* (1983), 185-226.

Glidden, D. K. (1983*b*): 'Skeptic Semiotics', *Phronesis*, XXVIII, 213-55.

Goldschmidt, V. (1978): 'Remarques sur l'origine epicurienne de la prénotion' in *Les Stoiciens* (1978), 155-70.

Hirzel, R. (1877): *Untersuchungen zu Ciceros Philosophischen Schriften*, vol i (Hildesheim, Olms reprint, 1964).

Juerss, F. (1977): 'Epikur und das Problem des Begriffes (Prolepse)', *Philologus*, CXXI, 211-25.

Kim, J. (1982): 'Psychological Supervenience', *Philosophical Studies*, XLI, 51-70.

Liebich, W. (1954): 'Ein Philodem-Zeugnis bei Ambrosius', *Philologus*, XCVIII, 116-31.

Long, A. A. (1971*a*): *Problems in Stoicism*, ed A. A. Long. London: Athlone.

Long, A. A. (1971*b*): 'Aisthesis, Prolepsis and Linguistic Theory in Epicurus', *Bulletin of the Institute of Classical Studies*, XVIII, 114-33.

Manuwald, A. (1972): *Die Prolepsislehre Epikurs* (Bonn).

Putnam, H. (1979): 'The Meaning of Meaning', *Mind, Language and Reality: Philosophical Papers Volume 2* (Cambridge), 215-71.

Reid, J. S. (1885): *Cicero. Academica* (Hildesheim, Olms reprint, 1966).

Reid, J. S. (1925): *Cicero. De Finibus Bonorum et Malorum Libri I-II* (Hildesheim: Olms reprint).

*SVF*: Arnim, J. von (ed) *Stoicorum Veterum Fragmenta*, 4 vols (Dubesque, Brown reprint of 1903).

Sandbach, F. H. (1971): '*Ennoia* and *Prolēpsis* in the Stoic Theory of Knowledge', in Long (1971*a*), 22-37.

Schofield, M. (1980*a*): *Doubt and Dogmatism*, ed Malcolm Schofield, Myles Burnyeat, and Jonathan Barnes (Oxford).

Schofield, M. (1980*b*): 'Perception, Argument, and God', in Schofield (1980*a*), 283-308.

Sedley, D. N. (1973): *Epicurus, On Nature, Book XXVIII* in *Cronache Ercolanesi*, III, 5-83.

Sedley, D. N. (1983): 'Epicurus' Refutation of Determinism', in *SUZETESIS* (1983), 11-51.

*Les Stoiciens* (1978): *Les Stoiciens et leur logique* (Paris).

Striker, G. (1974): 'Kriterion tes aletheias', *Nachrichten der Akademie der Wissenschaften in Göttingen*, II, 47-110.

*SUZETESIS* (1983): *SUZETESIS: Studi sull' Epicureismo Greco e Romano Offerti a Marcello Gigante*, vol i (Naples).

# LOGIC AND OMNISCIENCE: ALEXANDER OF APHRODISIAS AND PROCLUS*[1]

Mario Mignucci

## I

Let us consider a proposition such as 'Socrates is sleeping' or, if you prefer something more delightful:

(1) Luciano Pavarotti is singing.

The predicate of this statement 'is singing'—as well as 'is sleeping' in 'Socrates is sleeping'—contains an implicit reference to time. Let us call singular propositions in which there is such an implicit temporal reference 'indefinitely tensed statements'. An obvious question arises about these sentences. Are they really propositions? If a Fregean semantics is adopted, an affirmative answer to this question is not straightforward. As is well known, Frege distinguishes the sense of a proposition, its propositional content, from its meaning (*Bedeutung*) or denotation, which is its truth-value.[2] If the truth-value of a proposition constitutes its extension, it cannot be the case that two utterances of one and the same proposition have different truth-values. If $P$ uttered at $t_1$ had a truth-value different from the truth-value of $P$ uttered at $t_2$, $P$ at $t_1$ could not be the same proposition as $P$ at $t_2$,

* © Mario Mignucci 1985.

[1] I am indebted to many friends and colleagues for helpful suggestions and criticisms they addressed to former drafts of this paper. I would like warmly to thank Enrico Berti, Fernanda Decleva-Caizzi, Pierluigi Donini, Giancarlo Movia, Carlo Natali, and Giovanni Reale among ancient philosophers and Pierdaniele Giaretta and Paolo Leonardi among logicians. I also took advantage of a seminar I gave on this subject at the University of Catania and at the University of Trieste in spring 1983. But I am especially grateful to Richard Sorabji, Anthony Lloyd, and Jonathan Barnes who made me aware of many problems and difficulties while discussing a version of this paper I had the opportunity of reading at the Institute of Classical Studies in London in March 1983.

[2] Cf. G. Frege, 'Über Sinn und Bedeutung', in *Kleine Schriften*, hrsg. von I. Angelelli (Darmstadt, 1967), 149–50 (34–5).

because they do not have the same extension. Now, (1) is true only if the event $A$ to which (1) refers occurs. But $A$ sometimes does not occur: Luciano Pavarotti is not always singing. Therefore the truth-value of (1) depends on the time in which (1) is uttered and consequently in one case it can be true and in another case it can be false. The conclusion is that (1) is not a proposition. But in the everyday language we use phrases such as (1) with reference to truth and falsity. It is therefore convenient to find some device in order to reduce these expressions to propositions. The simplest way of doing this is to consider (1) as an incomplete proposition, which can be restated as a complete proposition when an explicit temporal reference is introduced, for instance a date. Thus (1) can be reduced to the proposition:

(2)  Luciano Pavarotti is singing at $t_k$

where '$t_k$' is a temporal constant. In (2) 'is singing' no longer contains a temporal reference and (2) does not change its truth value according to the time at which it is uttered. (2) becomes something like:

(3)  Luciano Pavarotti's singing occurs at $t_k$

where there is no implicit temporal reference any more than there is in a mathematical statement. Willard Van Orman Quine and Nelson Goodman have notoriously defended this treatment of the indefinitely tensed statements by which they could be eliminated.[3] There are of course other ways of considering them, in which no reduction to atemporal statements is worked out.[4] But we will not examine these approaches here, since they can hardly be reconciled with the assumption that a changeless entity which is all-knowing exists, in so far as they are based on the idea that tensed statements cannot be detensed.[5] We will consider below some

[3] Cf. W. V. O. Quine, *Word and Object* (12th edn, Cambridge, Mass., 1981), 191–5; N. Goodman, *The Structure of Appearance* (3rd edn, Dordrecht and Boston, 1977), 261–72.
[4] The distinction between the two treatments of indefinitely tensed statements is clearly sketched out by N. Rescher and A. Urquhart, *Temporal Logic* (Wien and New York, 1971), 23–30. See also R. Sorabji, *Necessity, Cause and Blame. Perspectives in Aristotle's Theory* (London, 1980), 91–103.
[5] Cf. P. Grim, 'Some Neglected Problems of Omniscience', *American*

doctrines in which the existence of such an all-knowing entity is presupposed.

## II

I have insisted on describing the modern way of treating indefinitely tensed statements because I wish to emphasize its difference from the approach that most of the ancient authors had to this subject. Aristotle, for instance, in *Categoriae* V. 4a21–b2 says rather crudely that one and the same *logos*, that is one and the same proposition, can be sometimes true and sometimes false, and he repeats the same point in *Metaphysics* Θ. 10. 1051b9–17. This latter passage allows us to determine better the class of propositions that, according to Aristotle, can change their truth-value. In any proposition the verb 'additionally signifies time' (*de Interpretatione* (*de Int.*) III. 16b6–7). For instance 'recovers' additionally signifies that *now* someone is getting better (16b8–9). It apparently follows from this definition that any proposition in which its verb is not specified by an explicit temporal reference is an indefinitely tensed statement, even if any other temporal token reflexive is taken away from the proposition. But one could ask whether a mathematical statement has really an implicit temporal reference according to Aristotle. Does

(4) Every triangle has the sum of its inside angles equal to two right angles

additionally signify time? If an affirmative answer to this point is thought to be the right one, then (4) means that every triangle always has the *2R*-property; otherwise, (4) simply means that every triangle has the property at issue atemporally. I do not wish to discuss this difficult and controversial problem here.[6] My point is simply that indefinitely

*Philosophical Quarterly*, XX (1983), 272–4; R. Sorabji, *Time, Creation and the Continuum. Theories in Antiquity and the Early Middle Ages* (London, 1983), 258–60.

[6] J. Hintikka, *Time and Necessity. Studies in Aristotle's Theory of Modality* (Oxford, 1973), 82–4, is in favour of the omnitemporality of mathematical statements. See also Sorabji, above n 5, 125–7.

tensed statements which are said to change their truth-value are not mathematical statements such as (4). They must fulfil at least two requirements. Firstly, they must contain an implicit temporal reference. Secondly, they must be contingent statements, that is propositions which can be true and can be false, and mathematical propositions are not contingent. These two conditions are satisfied by the majority of the statements whose subjects denote individuals (individuals of the sublunary world of course) and which do not contain an explicit temporal reference. Note that not only propositions in which a phasal property (or relation) is attributed to an individual are to be counted among the indefinitely tensed statements, but also many propositions in which a permanent property is truly attributed to an individual. According to Aristotle a statement like

(5) Luciano Pavarotti is a man

becomes false after Luciano Pavarotti's death (*de Int.* XI. 21a22-3). Therefore even propositions which express non-phasal and essential properties of individuals are not always true. This probably depends on the fact that individuals of the sublunary world, after they have disappeared, cannot maintain the features they possessed throughout their existence. However, it has to be pointed out that according to Aristotle it is not always the case that the death of an individual implies that no property can truly be attributed to him. We can truly say that Homer is a poet after his death (*de Int.* XI. 21a25-8). At any rate, the majority of the propositions referring to individuals of the sublunary world are in the precarious situation of our 'Luciano Pavarotti is singing', independently of the question whether the property which is said to be true of the subject is phasal or not.

A similar view can be ascribed to the Stoics. The best evidence comes from Alexander of Aphrodisias. In a passage reported by Simplicius (*in Aristotelis Physica commentaria* 1299. 36-1300. 10 = *SVF* II. 206) he considers the conditional statement

(6) If Dion is alive, then Dion will be alive

and he attributes to the Stoics the view that (6) is not always true, since in the instant immediately preceeding the death of

Dion its antecedent is true and its consequent is false. Therefore one and the same proposition after having been true for
a certain time becomes false because the event to which it
refers changes.[7] A particular case of propositions which
change their truth-values according to time is given by the
statements called 'corruptible propositions' by the Stoics,
that is by statements which after having received a truth-
value for a given time are destroyed in the sense that they do
not possess a truth-value any more and therefore they cease
to be propositions. The example discussed by Alexander of
Aphrodisias (*in Analytica Priora* (*in APr.*) 177. 25 ff = *SVF*
II. 202a) against Chrysippus is the following:

(7) If Dion is dead, this (man) is dead

where 'Dion' admits an anaphoric reference, but 'this (man)'
does not. Before Dion dies, (7) is true since its antecedent is
false. When Dion dies, its antecedent becomes true. Against
all expectation the same does not happen to its consequent,
because the latter loses any truth-value, nothing being the
reference of 'this (man)' in 'this (man) is dead'. Apart from
the acceptability of such a doctrine, what interests us is to
emphasize that according to Chrysippus one and the same
proposition can become false and even lose its truth-value
from being true.

The semantics which seems to be naturally associated with
this view about indefinitely tensed statements makes truth-
values properties of propositions which do not contribute
to identifying them. If (1) can change its truth-value without
losing its identity, its being true and its being false cannot be
taken as distinctive features of it. From this point of view
true and false have to be considered on the same footing as
phasal properties of individuals. The man who is now bald is
the same man who had long hair twenty years ago. He is the
same man even if twenty years ago he had a property that he
does not possess now any more. The property of having long
hair (or being bald) does not affect the identity of the man at

---

[7] Whether this view is consistent with the doctrine of the eternal recurrence
held by the Stoics (e.g. *SVF* ii. 625) is a question which cannot be answered
here. Cf. also J. Barnes, 'La doctrine du retour éternel', *Les Stoïciens et leur
logique*, Actes du colloque de Chantilly, 18–22 septembre 1976 (Paris, 1978), 3–20.

issue any more than the property of being true (or false) affects (1). Using the Aristotelian terminology, one could say that true and false are accidental properties of indefinitely tensed statements. Let us call 'thesis (T)', or more simply '(T)', precisely the view that admits that one and the same statement can change its truth-value and that true and false are accidental properties of propositions in the sense described.

It is sensible to conclude that Aristotle and the Stoics adopted thesis (T). Practically, almost all knowledge we have of the individuals of the sublunary world falls under (T), in as much as it is concerned with individuals and events which change continually, come into being, and pass away.

III

That the ancient philosophers had a view about indefinitely tensed statements different from the modern standard one has been repeatedly observed. First noticed by Peter Geach, this point has been discussed and developed by Arthur Prior, and Jaakko Hintikka has recently tried to show how it is linked with some deep epistemological patterns of ancient Greek culture.[8] The consequences that the admission of thesis (T) has for the development of philosophical ideas in areas different from logic have not been widely studied yet, as far as I know. I would like to examine here some aspects of the role that thesis (T) plays in the difficult and controversial discussion on the nature and limits of divine knowledge in post-Aristotelian philosophy. That there is a link between thesis (T) and the way of conceiving divine knowledge can easily be seen. As is known, Aristotle in his famous chapter 9 of *Metaphysics* Λ attributes to the first unmoved mover a very poor knowledge of our world. According to some interpreters he has no knowledge at all of what is different from him, while others think that he knows at least the general principles which constitute all things.[9] However,

---

[8] Cf. P. T. Geach, 'Review of J. Weinberg, Nicolaus of Autrecourt. A Study in 14th Century Thought', *Mind*, LVIII (1949), 238–45; A. Prior, *Past, Present and Future* (Oxford, 1967); Hintikka, *Time and Necessity*, 62–92.

[9] D. Ross, *Aristotle* (London, 1923), 182–3, is the champion of the thesis by which the first unmoved mover knows only himself. The opposite view is held by R. Norman, 'Aristotle's Philosopher-God', *Phronesis*, XIV (1969), 63–74 (also in

the splendid isolation of Aristotle's god was bound to fail even among his followers.[10] The idea that the world is ruled by provident gods became more and more familiar to a large number of Hellenistic philosophers. The Stoics, for instance, had made divine providence one of the relevant points of their system. According to them, the natural idea that every man has of god is an idea of a provident divinity and the best way of justifying divination is by admitting that the gods exist and are provident towards man.[11] The existence of a provident divinity was therefore founded on very common and uncontroversial cultural patterns which no philosophical school could easily disregard. But, if god is provident, he must know the things towards which he exerts his benevolent influence. In particular, he must know the individuals and the events which constitute the elements and the history of the world. Hence the problem: god is normally conceived as immutable; but he knows the individuals and the events of this world. By thesis (T) such a knowledge is a changeable knowledge, being sometimes true and sometimes false. Therefore if the gods know the world, they must change, since they must modify their knowledge in order that it remain true. The immutability of the gods, their knowledge of changing individuals and thesis (T) are inconsistent. Post-Aristotelian theology had to face this problem, and I will try to illustrate some of its solutions, namely Alexander of Aphrodisias' view on the one hand, and Proclus' on the other.

## IV

Full light has not yet been shed on the works traditionally attributed to Alexander of Aphrodisias.[12] Unfortunately part

*Articles on Aristotle*, IV: *Psychology and Aesthetics*, ed J. Barnes, M. Schofield, and R. Sorabji (London, 1979), 93–102.

[10] See for instance *de Mundo* 6. 397b24 ff; Diogenes Laertius V. 32. Cf. P. Moraux, *D'Aristote à Bessarion. Trois exposés sur l'histoire et la transmission de l'aristotélisme grec* (Montreal, 1970), 54 ff. I follow Professor Owens's warning in avoiding capitalizing 'god': J. Owens, *The Doctrine of Being in the Aristotelian Metaphysics* (2nd edn, Toronto, 1963), 171 n 47.

[11] Cicero, *de Divinatione* I. 82–4 = *SVF* ii. 1192. For an analysis of the Stoic reasons in favour of the existence of divine providence see M. Dragona-Monachou, *The Stoic Arguments for the Existence and the Providence of the Gods* (Athens, 1976).

[See p 226 for n 12]

of those which are relevant for our enquiry are not certainly by him, but probably come from his pupils.[13] It would be safer to speak here of an Alexandrinist doctrine of providence. Hereafter when I name 'Alexander', I will mean 'Alexander and his pupils'.

Alexander develops a rather original position. On the one hand he is ready to distance himself from Stoicism. Let us quote an example which is interesting:

> It seemed right to me to be against the view held by the Stoics accord-
> ing to which the intellect, being divine, is even in the most ordinary
> things and there is an intellect and a purposive providence in the things
> of this world.    (*de Anima Mantissa* (*de An. Mant.*) 113. 12–15)

Alexander does not deny that there is a providence. His criticism affects the way in which the Stoics thought that god was provident. On the other hand, he maintains that only things of the sublunary world are liable to fate, since eternal things and regularly recurrent events of the upper world are exempt from it (*de An. Mant.* 181. 6–22). If what Alexander says here about fate can be extended to providence,[14] one could see a polemical allusion to the view held by some former Peripatetics echoed in *de Mundo* VI. 397b24 ff and Diogenes Laertius V. 32 in his point. Besides, even if it is not true that things of our world are the intended result of the providential activity of the gods (*Quaestiones* (*Quaest.*) II. 21. 69. 1–31), it cannot be inferred that the gods are provident towards things of the lower world in an accidental way only (*Quaest.* II. 21. 66. 25–67. 2), since an accidental providence, being an inconsistent notion, is no providence at all (*Quaest.* II. 21. 65. 32–66. 2).

More specifically, Alexander holds that the movements of the stars lead and master the things which are bound to generation and corruption (*Quaest.* II. 19. 63. 22–8). This regulation is thought to be the result of the activity of

---

[12] The announced third volume of Paul Moraux's *Der Aristotelismus bei den Griechen* dedicated to Alexander will surely solve these problems.

[13] That is the case particularly for the *Quaestiones*. Cf. for instance R. B. Todd, *Alexander of Aphrodisias on Stoic Physics. A Study of the De Mixtione with Preliminary Essays, Text, Translation and Commentary* (London, 1976), 19.

[14] R. W. Sharples, *Alexander of Aphrodisias: de Fato* (London, 1983), 26, is in favour of this extension.

a force (*dunamis*[15]) which constitutes and preserves the different kinds of things (*Quaest.* II. 3. 48. 15-22) and, in particular, makes the forms of the individuals persist (*Quaest.* I. 25. 40. 30-41. 4, II. 19. 63. 22-6). This point is confirmed by a fragment of the unfortunately lost *de Providentia* quoted by Cyrillus of Alexandria, where it is said that the god's providence preserves the forms of individuals.[16] These passages have led scholars to think that according to Alexander, although divine providence reaches the sublunary world, it does not directly concern individuals.[17] This interpretation is confirmed also from the Arabic translation of the lost *de Providentia* edited some years ago by Hans-Joachim Ruland.[18] When criticizing the Stoic view, Alexander puts forward several arguments (14. 7 ff (Ruland)) against the thesis according to which the gods are provident towards individuals of this world. At the same time, the Arabic translation allows us to solve some doubts that the remaining Greek works are not able to eliminate. In the Greek works the conception of providence as a force which gives order to the cosmos prevails. The naturalism implicit in this view engenders the suspicion that providence is not coupled with any knowledge or, better, that it does not correspond to the fulfilment of an intended project planned by the gods. As far as

[15] On this term cf. P. Moraux, 'Alexander von Aphrodisias Quaest. 2. 3', *Hermes*, XCV (1967), 160 n 2 and G. Reale, *Aristotele: Trattato sul cosmo per Alessandro* (Napoli, 1974), 79 ff.

[16] *Contra Julianum*, PG 76, 625B-C (emendations in I. Bruns, 'Studien zu Alexander von Aphrodisias, 3.: Lehre von der Vorsehung', *Rheinisches Müseum für Philologie*, NF VL (1890), 234-5).

[17] Cf. P. Moraux, *Alexandre d'Aphrodise exégète de la noétique d'Aristote* (Liège and Paris, 1942), 197-200; H. Happ, 'Weltbild und Seinslehre bei Aristoteles', *Antike und Abendland*, LIV (1968), 81-3; F. P. Hager, 'Proklos und Alexander von Aphrodisias über ein Problem der Lehre von der Vorsehung', *Kephalaion. Studies in Greek Philosophy and its Continuation, offered to Professor C. J. De Vogel*, ed J. Mansfeld and L. M. de Rijk (Assen, 1975), 172-5; Todd, above n 13, 213; P. Donini, *Le scuole, l'anima, l'impero: la filosofia antica da Antioco a Plotino* (Torino, 1982), 213; Sharples, above n 14, 25-6.

[18] Cf. H.-J. Ruland, *Die arabische Fassungen von zwei Schriften des Alexander von Aphrodisias: Über die Vorsehung und Über das liberum arbitrium* (Saarbrücken, 1976). On the Arabic translation of the *de Providentia* see also P. Thillet, 'Un traité inconnu d'Alexandre d'Aprodise dans la Providence dans une version arabe inédite', *L'homme et son destin d'après les penseurs du moyen-âge*, Actes du premier congrès international de philosophie médiévale, Louvain and Bruxelles 28 août-4 septembre 1958 (Louvain and Paris, 1960), 313-24. My translations of this work are from Ruland's German version.

I know there is no evidence in Alexander's Greek texts that is able to disconfirm this hypothesis.[19] But a plain declaration against a mechanistic conception of providence can be found in the Arabic version of the *de Providentia*. Alexander says:

At any rate the view according to which god does not know what is generated through him is absurd. Thus it is necessary that the gods know better than anyone else that their specific nature makes good things. But if they know that, they must also know what depends on such a nature.                                                    (66. 9-13 (Ruland) )

It is therefore clear that a kind of knowledge is presupposed by divine providence. The gods know themselves and the things depending on them. This passage does not clarify the precise nature of the relationship which there is between the knowledge that the gods have of themselves and their knowledge of this world. However, their being provident is not the result of a blind force deprived of knowledge.

Luckily enough, there is another fragment preserved from the Arabic tradition which gives us some new information on the way in which the link between the gods and our world was conceived by Alexander. Averroes quotes a fragment of Alexander's commentary on book Λ of Aristotle's *Metaphysics*[20] where Alexander is supposed to have said:

Alexander says that the worst mistake is made by those people who maintain that providence concerns all individuals, as the men of the tent do. Providence could flow from the celestial powers only if they possessed knowledge, as has been said before. But how is it possible that they have a knowledge of individuals which is always renewed and besides which is infinite?                               (fr 36 (Freudenthal) )

Freudenthal points out that the expression 'men of the tent' by which the Stoics are meant and the reference to a previous

---

[19] See the discussion of Greek evidence in Moraux, above n 17, 200-2.

[20] As is known, the commentary to the books E-M of Aristotle's *Metaphysics* that the tradition has attributed to Alexander is not by him (cf. Moraux, above n 17, 14-19). The true commentary of Alexander is lost except for some fragments preserved by the quotations of Averroes in his own commentary to the *Metaphysics*. These fragments have been collected in a German translation by J. Freudenthal, 'Die durch Averroes erhaltenen Fragmente Alexanders zur Metaphysik des Aristoteles untersucht und übersetzt. Mit Beiträgen zur Erläuterungen des arabischen Textes von S. Fränkel, *Abhandlungen der königlichen Akademie der Wissenschaften zu Berlin,* aus dem Jahre *1884* (Berlin, 1885), 1-134. Freudenthal has shown that Averroes was normally accurate in quoting Greek commentators known by him through Syrian versions.

discussion raise the suspicion that Averroes is not quoting Alexander literally.[21] Nevertheless he thinks that the passage corresponds to Alexander's doctrine, as is confirmed by the fact that what is stated in it does not match Averroes' views.[22] If this fragment can be trusted, a fundamental step towards the understanding of Alexander's position can be made. Alexander denies that the gods may be concerned with all individuals and his argument is *ex impossibili.* Suppose that the gods were provident towards all kinds of individuals. Therefore they must know all individuals. But such a knowledge is impossible, because it should be renewed again and again and should be infinite. Let us leave out the problem that a divine mind cannot know an infinity of things and consider the other reason given by Alexander: if the gods knew all individuals, then their knowledge would have to be renewed again and again. I assume that the renewing which is in question here has something to do with the changing of individuals and events of our world. In our world it happens that what is now a bearer of a property did not exist before and will not exist in the future. The knowledge of such individuals must change correspondingly, if we do not admit that it becomes false. If $a$ is $F$ at $t_1$ it is true to say at $t_1$ that $a$ is $F$. But suppose that at $t_2$ $a$ is not $F$ any more; then at $t_2$ it is not true to say that $a$ is $F$, being true that $a$ *was* $F$. The knowledge of $a$ has therefore changed from $t_1$ to $t_2$. According to this interpretation the function of thesis (T) in our text is fundamental. Individuals of our world, being liable to change, cannot be known by an immutable mind such as god's mind.

To be cautious, one might say that Averroes' passage could be interpreted in such a way that there is no need of thesis (T). Suppose that one assumes that every statement concerning the future does not have a truth-value before the event (or events) it denotes happens (happen). When one posits that

---

[21] Cf. Freudenthal, above n 20, 112 n 7 and 60.

[22] For instance in the *Tahafut al Tahafut* (*The Incoherence of the Incoherence,* tr from the Arabic with Introduction and Notes by S. Van Den Bergh, 2 vols (London, 1969)) Averroes discusses and rejects the theses according to which god would have only a general knowledge of individuals. He says that divine knowledge cannot be qualified either as universal or as particular, being a creative act (462, I. 280–1 Van Den Berg).

(i)   There will be a sea-battle

what one says can be neither true nor false. Therefore (i) is not a proposition and there is nothing to know when one utters it. On the other hand the past is fixed and immutable. Once a sea-battle occurs, the proposition

(ii)   There was a sea-battle

is definitely true. Thus one could think that god's knowledge increases in the sense that new propositions are always being known by him, namely the propositions that become true or false according to the flux of events. In this way there is a change in the knowledge of the individuals without propositions about them changing their truth-values. No recourse to thesis (T) is demanded.

This interpretation is not very convincing. First of all, it is doubtful that Alexander maintained that propositions such as (i) have no truth-value at all. He does not say it in the *de Fato*[23] and the text which comes closest to this position simply states that (i) is not definitely true (or false), and not that it has no truth-value (*Quaest.* I. 4. 12. 13–17). Besides, it is by no means clear that a proposition concerning the past cannot change its truth-value. Suppose that no sea-battle has taken place near Salamis before 480 BC and that someone says in 481 BC:

(iii)   There was a sea battle at Salamis.

This proposition is about the past. Therefore it has a truth-value and it is false by hypothesis. But it is difficult to deny that if it were uttered in 479 BC it would be true. Therefore (iii) changes its truth-value according to (T).

One could reply that according to Alexander (e.g. *de Fato* 197. 11–15) and the majority of ancient philosophers[24] propositions about the past do not change their truth-values. Therefore the argument—one could conclude—even if it is sound in principle, cannot be applied to Alexander. But what is meant by ancient logicians in general, and by Alexander in particular, is not that every proposition about the past

---

[23] Cf. Sharples, above n 14, 11–12.

[24] The most notable exceptions are supposed to be constituted by Cleanthes and Antipater (Epictetus, *Dissertationes* II. 19. 2 = *SVF* i. 489).

cannot change its truth-value, but that a proposition which truly asserts that a past event has happened is necessarily true, because the past cannot be changed. That is the same as saying that every true affirmative proposition about the past does not change its truth-value. This claim is plausible: once (iii) becomes true, it remains always true. But this point does not imply that a proposition which truly denies that an event has occurred always keeps the same truth-value. (iii) is false before 480 BC and true after, and

(iv)  There was not a sea battle at Salamis

is true before 480 BC, and becomes false after this date. Even if Alexander did not explicitly consider this difference (as far as I know), from the mere fact that he says that a proposition such as (iii), if it is true, is always true, it cannot be concluded that he asserts that every proposition about the past cannot change its truth-value. However, the same point can be made about statements concerning the present, such as (1). Even if it is admitted that propositions about the future have no truth-value at all, (1), being about the present, has a truth-value and this truth-value changes according to whether the event it refers to occurs or not at the moment in which (1) is uttered. If Luciano Pavarotti is singing at the moment in which (1) is uttered, (1) is true, and it is false if Luciano Pavarotti is not singing at that time. Two different utterances of (1) can be easily imagined in one of which (1) is true and false in the other. It follows that (1) changes its truth-value. The moral of the story is that even if one is led to think that every statement about the future is non-defined with respect to its truth-value, there are propositions about the present and the past which change their truth-values. If the interpretation I am trying to contrast were accepted, one would have to conclude that the knowledge of individuals which is mentioned in the passage reported by Averroes refers only to future individual events. It may be that Alexander also considered this kind of knowledge, but it seems to me to be arbitrary to maintain that he had only this one in mind. If he refers to any kind of knowledge of individuals, then his claim that knowledge of individuals is always renewed can reasonably be explained by appeal to thesis (T).

*De Fato* XXX, a chapter that Alexander dedicates to the problem of the divine foreknowledge of future events, can be interpreted in a way that makes this text consistent with (and even confirm) the point I am trying to defend. I cannot offer here a detailed analysis of this rather controversial and difficult text, nor do I claim that my interpretation is the only possible one. Things could be put as follows. What Alexander wishes to refute is that one can infer that everything is by necessity from the fact that the gods are supposed to have foreknowledge of any future event (200. 12-15). Let '$A$' stand for any proposition about a future (allegedly) contingent event and the argument attacked by Alexander can take this form:

(P1)  For every $A$: if the gods have foreknowledge of $A$ then $A$ is necessary;
(P2)  for every $A$: the gods have foreknowledge $A$;
(C1)  for every $A$: $A$ is necessary.

According to some interpreters Alexander's refusal of the argument would have led him to affirm that the gods are provident towards everything in the world and that they know everything: what is necessary as necessary and what is contingent as contingent.[25] I do not think that this interpretation, which is claimed to be founded on *de Fato* 201. 16-18, is really warranted by this text. Alexander develops a rather complex argument there and our passage takes on a different meaning if it is considered in its context. A first step of his reasoning is contained in 200. 15-201. 1 which intends to assert that (P1) implies

(P3)  For every $A$: if $A$ is contingent, the gods cannot have foreknowledge of $A$.

My claim is that Alexander's next step is directed to refuting (P2). Let us expand it as follows. In order to conclude that

    [25] Cf. G. Verbeke, 'Aristotélisme et Stoïcisme dans le *De Fato* d'Alexandre d'Aphrodise', *Archiv für Geschichte der Philosophie*, L (1968), 97. Sharples is much more cautious. Cf. his 'Alexander of Aphrodisias, *De Fato*: Some Parallels', *The Classical Quarterly*, NS XXVIII (1978), 260: "He [Alexander] does however suggest—though only hypothetically, his concern being to refute his opponents rather than to establish a position of his own—that the gods have foreknowledge of the contingent in a sense, foreknowledge of the contingent *as contingent*'. The same point is made in his *Alexander of Aphrodisias: de Fato*, 165.

there is no contingent proposition, something like (P2) must be assumed or, at least,

(P2') For every $A$: the gods can have foreknowledge of $A$.

That means that the gods have the possibility of knowing everything. But this is precisely the point that is disproved by (P3), if one assumes that there are contingent propositions. If $A$ is contingent, then the gods cannot know it. According to Alexander (201. 1-6) (P3) simply states that the gods do not possess the power of knowing everything. Putting things in a slightly different way, the argument Alexander tries to refute shows that (P1), (P2), and the negation of (C1) cannot be true together. That simply means that one of them has to be refuted. Therefore to deny the negation of (C1) does not depend on the argument itself, but from other assumptions that have to be proved. Alexander insists on his point. If (P2') had to be admitted, one should conclude that the gods can know everything, and therefore, among others, what is impossible to be known, as, for instance, the measure of the infinite (201. 6-13). Furthermore, if $A$ denotes by hypothesis a future contingent event, then $A$ must be foreknown as a proposition about a future contingent event, that is, as a contingent proposition, and that is ruled out by (P3) (201. 13-21). Alexander concludes his refutation by proposing a dilemma: either one says that what is impossible becomes possible for the gods; in this case (P2') becomes true, but (P3) cannot be admitted any more; or one maintains that what is impossible is impossible also for the gods; then (P2') has to be proved independently before being put as a premiss of the argument (201. 21-8).

Alexander stops his discussion in *de Fato* XXX with a quite unexpected remark:

We therefore do not do away with prophecy or with the god's foreknowledge by saying that they make predictions about things in accordance with the way the things naturally are.[26]

Whatever the meaning of this rather obscure sentence may be, it is hard to believe that Alexander legitimates here the possibility that the gods have a real foreknowledge of *all*

[26] *de Fato* XXX. 201. 28-30 (tr Sharples).

contingent events. Actually the simple admission of thesis
(T) does not rule out that some predictions can be made.
Suppose for instance that someone truly predicts that

(F1) If John has a mole on his cheek, then John will not
be a luteplayer.

It is easy to find a reasonable semantics according to which
(F1) is always true.[27] One can think that before John's birth
and after his death the antecedent of (F1) is false. Therefore
when John is not alive, (F1) is true. But the same holds
during his life, because the consequent of (F1) will never be
false, since the prediction is by hypothesis a true one. Therefore (F1) never changes its truth-value. Thus (F1) cannot be
ruled out from what the gods know by recourse to thesis (T).
I do not claim that Alexander had exactly this point in mind
when he attributes some kind of foreknowledge to the gods.
His attitude towards prophecy is not very clear: he never
explains how it could be possible nor does he even say clearly
that he accepts it.[28] However, if the statement I have quoted
has to be taken to express Alexander's own view, and not as
a mere dialectical move, it could be reconciled with the use
that is made of thesis (T) with reference to divine knowledge by restricting the set of the propositions about sublunary individuals that the gods cannot know. There are
propositions about individuals which are predictive and
which do not change their truth values. Knowledge of such
propositions can safely be attributed to the gods, while
propositions which change their truth values are out of their
reach. At any rate it remains that thesis (T) has an essential
function in limiting the domain of divine knowledge: the
gods are not omniscient. At this price the gods can still be
admitted to be immutable.

# V

We have seen up to now how thesis (T) has an influence on
theology in the sense that its acceptance contributes to the

---

[27] This semantics is not inconsistent with the assumptions Alexander makes in
his *In APr.* 177. 25 ff against the Stoics.
[28] Cf. Sharples, above n 14, 18–19.

assigning or denying of certain attributes to the gods and also to the precise interpretation of the nature of their knowledge. Late Neoplatonism is perhaps an interesting example of the reverse influence. Proclus for instance will modify the traditional semantics of singular propositions and abandon to some extent thesis (T) in order to keep divine immutability and omniscience. To understand how this goal is reached, we need to describe briefly Plotinus' view. According to him, being provident towards our world is an activity not of the One or the Intellect, but of the Soul. His providence is explained by the fact that our world is produced by the Soul in its contemplation of the ideas which constitute the Intellect (IV. 3. 11. 8-21). Plotinus is aware that the attribution of providence to the Soul could be thought to imply the attribution to it of a kind of knowledge of the contingent individuals and events of this world. He meets this difficulty when analysing the problem whether the Soul has memory. According to him neither the Intellect nor even the Soul has memory, otherwise they would change, since one remembers something which was present before and which is not any longer (IV. 3. 25. 10-20, 27 ff). But if the Soul and the Intellect do not change—Plotinus continues—how can they know changing things? In particular, does the Soul change when registering and knowing the changing things towards which it is provident? (IV. 3. 25. 20-7, IV. 4. 9. 1-9). Even the way in which the problem is stated shows the influence of thesis (T). Plotinus' answer is no less dependent on (T). He denies that (T) does not apply to divine knowledge. He says:

But what prevents such a being (from possessing memory in the sense of) perceiving, without variation in itself, such outside changes as, for example, the cosmic periods? Simply the fact that following the changes of the revolving Cosmos it would have perception of earlier and later: intuition and memory are distinct.

(IV. 3. 25. 20-4; tr S. Mackenna, 281)

The idea that a divine being can have an immutable knowledge of things which are mutable is ruled out. Positively, Plotinus maintains that Zeus, that is the ordering power of the world, to be identified with the Soul (IV. 4. 10. 1-4), is such because he embodies an immutable knowledge which comes to him from the everlasting contemplation of the

Intellect (IV. 4. 13. 17-25). As things of this world reflect and grow out of one and the same nature which permeates them (IV. 4. 11. 9-11), so the world order depends on the everlasting vision of the intelligible world. This way of thinking is at work for instance in IV. 4. 10. 9-15:

> Yes: for what must be stands shaped before the Cosmos, and is ordered without any setting in order: the ordered things are merely the things that come to be; and the principle that brings them into being is Order itself; this production is an act of a soul linked with an unchangeable established wisdom whose reflection in that soul is Order. It is an unchanging wisdom, and there can therefore be no changing in the soul which mirrors it, not sometimes turned towards it and sometimes away from it—and in doubt because it has turned away—but an unremitting soul performing an unvarying task.   (tr S. MacKenna, 295)

The knowledge that the Soul has of the world depends on the knowledge that it has of its archetypes. It is difficult to press Plotinus with more precise questions. For instance, does Zeus know individuals distinctly? In Plotinus' system the question turns out to be: is there a distinct knowledge of individuals in the knowledge that Zeus has of the archetypes which form the substance of the Intellect? This issue connects with the debated question about the existence of the forms of individuals.[29] I will not discuss here these difficult problems. However we suppose that Plotinus solved these issues, the influence of thesis (T) on his view is evident. If no distinct knowledge of contingent individuals is admitted on the part of god, this happens precisely because of thesis (T). On the other hand, let us suppose that Plotinus recognized that god has a distinct knowledge of individuals. Then the consequences of thesis (T) are exorcized only if one thinks that the knowledge of individuals is given to god, so to speak, a priori in their archetypes. In this way god's immutability is saved. But one could ask at what price his omniscience is preserved. What the Soul knows is not individuals but their forms. Now, either individuals are the same as their forms or there is some difference between them. If the first case is chosen, divine omniscience is rescued, but the distinction

---

[29] The *status quaestionis* of this problem can be found in A. H. Armstrong, 'Form, Individual and Person in Plotinus', *Dionysius*, I (1977), 49-68 (now also in *Plotinian and Christian Studies* (London, 1979), No 20).

between the material and the intelligible world vanishes, and, at the very end, the possibility of attributing a certain degree of reality to our world. On the other hand, if the second alternative is preferred, the sensible world can be distinguished from the intelligible one, but god is not omniscient any more. He does not know individuals of this world, but their immutable and never changing forms. Individuality, mutability, temporality are all precluded to god.

# VI

Plotinus' approach to the problem of omniscience is in fact not very different from Alexander's solution, apart from the metaphysical context in which it is embedded. It is only with the late Neoplatonists that a new position is sketched out. I will consider Proclus as the reference point for describing this change of view. As is known, Proclus attributes the job of being provident to the superior gods, the Henads, entities which are intermediate between the One and the intelligible world.[30] What is peculiar to Proclus is that gods take care of individuals and even the most negligible aspects of reality (*Platonic Theology (Theol. Plat.*) I. 15 (69. 10-12, 70. 22-5, 74. 9-16 Saffrey-Westerink)). That implies that the gods must know not only what is universal and eternal, but also what is particular and contingent up to the minimal details of individuals (*Theol. Plat.* I. 21 (98. 5-12 Saffrey-Westerink); *Institutio Theologica* 124 (110. 10-13 Dodds);*Decem Dubitationes (Dub.*) II. 6-23 Isaac). Proclus insists on this point. When discussing how the gods know this world, he affirms that he is surprised that many Platonists, in order to justify god's omniscience, put the intelligible models of individuals and bad things in the divine mind (*Theol. Plat.* I. 21 (98. 16-20 Saffrey-Westerink)). A criticism of Plotinus' view could be seen in this remark, if one is willing to attribute to Plotinus admission of the existence of intelligible forms of individuals.

To recognize that the gods know individuals and contingent

---

[30] Cf. *Institutio Theologica (Inst.)* 114, 120 Dodds. On the origin of the doctrine of the Henads see J. M. Dillon, *Iamblichi Calcidensis in Platonis Dialogos Commentariorum Fragmenta*, ed with translation and commentary (Leiden, 1973), 412-16.

events of this world entails the usual difficulty: divine knowledge changes according to the way in which the corresponding things vary. Proclus gives a new answer to this question. He does not give up the immutability and omniscience of the gods, but he prefers to modify thesis (T). His argument has several steps. A first one is a general epistemological point. Since to know is an activity of a knowing subject, the modalities of knowledge depend not on the nature of the object known, but on the nature of the knowing subject. This thesis can be found in its more general form in *Decem Dubitationes* II. 7. 1–29 (Isaac) and it is ascribed to Jamblicus by Ammonius, a pupil of Proclus (*in Aristotelis de Interpretatione commentarius* (*in Int.*) 135. 12 ff). In the major works of Proclus this view is applied to divine knowledge. Let us consider the following passage of *Institutio Theologica* 124 (110. 14–23 Dodds):

> For if the gods have all their attributes in a mode consonant with their character as gods, it is surely manifest that their knowledge, being a divine property, will be determined not by the nature of the inferior beings which are its object but by their own transcendent majesty. Accordingly their knowledge of things pluralized and passible will be unitary and impassive: though its object be a thing of parts, yet even of such the divine knowledge will be undivided; though its object be mutable, itself will be immutable, though contingent, necessary, and though undetermined, determinate. For the divine does not get knowledge extraneously, from its inferiors: why then should its knowledge be restricted by the nature of its objects?          (tr Dodds)

This text gives us an idea of what, according to Proclus, was a modality of the knowledge depending on the nature of the knower. Knowledge is necessary or contingent, mutable or immutable, undetermined or determined according to the nature of the knowing subject. For instance, the knowledge of a contingent thing is contingent if the knowing subject is contingent, but it is necessary if the knowing subject is necessary. Let us concentrate on the modality of the immutable.[31] According to Proclus then the gods know immutably the

[31] By the way, it is interesting to remark that the pair determined–undetermined is used by Proclus (*de Providentia* 63–6 Isaac) and by Ammonius (*in Int.* 136. 1 ff) in order to explain divine foreknowledge of contingent future events and to avoid determinism.

things which are mutable. One writer has judged this position a vain effort to conciliate the two requirements from which Proclus himself had started: to guard the real contingency of the world on the one hand and to secure the omniscience of the gods on the other (*Dub.* II. 6. 1-20 Isaac). In other words Proclus would fall into Plotinus' difficulty. From a logical point of view he should either give up divine omniscience, or eliminate contingency and mutability from the world.[32] But I think that Proclus is free from this difficulty. First of all, it must be noticed that Proclus does not say that some properties of the objects of knowledge change according to the fact that these objects are known by us and by the gods. What is contingent and mutable does not become necessary and immutable for a divine mind. If it were so, the gods would be mistaken, since, according to Proclus, contingent things are really contingent. What he underlines is that the *knowledge* of what is contingent is not necessarily contingent and that the *knowledge* of what is mutable is not necessarily mutable. The modality of the objects known is not in question here, but the modality of their knowledge. Secondly, Proclus insists that the gods, being transcendent, know in a unified way what is manifold and what is stretched out in time. Besides *Inst.* 124, which we have already quoted, the following passage of *Platonic Theology* I. 21 (99. 6-9 Saffrey-Westerink) is worth keeping in mind:

For, since the gods transcend things which are eternal and things which are in time, they keep gathered in themselves the truth of each and every thing in a single and unified truth.

In the light of these remarks I propose to interpret Proclus' point as a question of semantics. Let us consider again the statement we started off with—

(1) Luciano Pavarotti is singing

and let us imagine that (1) could be the content of an act of divine understanding. (1) was traditionally conceived as

---

[32] This is the view of R. T. Wallis, 'Divine Omniscience in Plotinus, Proclus and Aquinas', *Neoplatonism and Early Christian Thought*, ed H. J. Blumenthal and R. A. Markus (London, 1981), 227. It would be unfair to underline my disagreement from him without saying how much I owe to his learned article. A similar point is made by Hager, above n 17, 179.

a proposition which changes its truth-value when the event denoted by it changes. Proclus does not deny this fact, but he interprets it in a way that does not affect the immutability of divine knowledge. A possible way of explaining how this is possible is to assume that the semantics for statements like (1) is different from the semantics which is implied by (T). In (T) the truth value of (1) is not embedded in its meaning in opposition to Frege's view. We can guess that Proclus comes back to Frege—if one could say so—but with the difference that the meaning of the proposition is not given by a single truth-value, namely the truth-value that the proposition takes at the time of its utterance, but is determined by the sequence of the truth-values that the proposition takes in time. Using standard mathematical jargon, according to this view (1) becomes a function which associates truth-values to instants. Let us assume that Luciano Pavarotti is really singing at $t_j$ and $t_k$ and that he is not singing any more at $t_m$ (where $t_j < t_k < t_m$). Then (1) associates the truth-value *True*—say '1'—to $t_j$ and $t_k$ and the truth-value *False*— let us call it '0'—to $t_m$. Therefore the extensional meaning of a proposition, being a function, is given by a set of ordered pairs whose first member is an instant and whose second member is 1 or 0. In our example the meaning of (1) is a set of pairs among which there are those containing $t_j$, $t_k$, and $t_m$, that is:

$$(1) = \{\ldots, <t_j, 1>, <t_k, 1>, \ldots, <t_m, 0>, \ldots\}$$

Let us call '*a*' the set which defines (1).

It is evident that *a* can be conceived differently according to the ways in which we consider how function (1) is defined. Suppose that the life of Luciano Pavarotti is comprised between $t_i$ and $t_p$ (a long span I hope!). In this interval (1) will probably be sometimes true and sometimes false. Therefore *a* will contain pairs whose second members are 1 or 0. But what about the instants before $t_i$ and after $t_p$? There are several possibilities which look familiar to people acquainted with modern temporal logic:

(*a*) Nothing prevents us from thinking that function (1) is not defined before $t_i$ and after $t_p$. If Luciano Pavarotti does not exist, it is meaningless to say that he is singing. 'Existence is a presupposition for truth-values' could be the slogan of this view. Therefore (1) has to be conceived as a partial function which associates truth-values only to a finite set of instants, namely the set of instants comprised between $t_i$ and $t_p$.

(*b*) It is also sensible to think that (1) is defined over all instants. To say something true or false about Luciano Pavarotti does not presuppose that Luciano Pavarotti exists. Of course, when Luciano Pavarotti is not alive, it is false to say that he is singing. Function (1) will have 0 as its value until $t_i$ and the same will happen after $t_p$. In the interval between $t_i$ and $t_p$ 1 and 0 are its possible values. Since instants are infinite, according to this view $a$ will be an infinite set of pairs.

(*c*) Let us consider a third hypothesis. It is also reasonable to assume that function (1) is not defined before $t_i$ and that it is always defined after $t_i$. Before Luciano Pavarotti was born it was meaningless to state something about him, but after his birth, any proposition concerning him is true or false, even if it is uttered after his death. Of course, saying that Luciano Pavarotti is singing after his death will always be false. In this case $a$ will be an infinite set and the sequence of the values of (1) will be constant after $t_p$.

If we limit ourselves to considering the values of (1) in the interval $t_p$ -$t_i$ we can abstain from deciding between the three possibilities (*a*), (*b*), and (*c*) just examined, because their differences become relevant only if the instants before $t_i$ and after $t_p$ are considered. Let us take this route. It is now clear in what sense Proclus may say that our knowledge of (1) is different from the divine knowledge of it. Since (1) denotes a contingent event, $a$ cannot be conceived as a law-like sequence in the interval $t_p$ -$t_i$. Whichever partial stretch of the interval may have been covered, it cannot be forecast how the succession will be completed up to $t_p$. From the fact that Luciano Pavarotti was (or was not) singing in an instant included among $t_p$ -$t_i$ it cannot be inferred that he will (or will not) be singing in the following instants up to $t_p$. Therefore our knowledge of (1) in the interval $t_p$ -$t_i$ can change significantly. $a$ is increased step by step by new pairs which are not necessarily the same as the preceding ones and the development of the resulting sequence cannot be fixed in advance. On the other hand, let us assume that there is a divine mind which is outside time. Such a mind is able to know every pair of the interval $t_p$-$t_i$ altogether. Then his knowledge of (1) does not change in time, but is fixed and stable since it is all given in a kind of eternal present. This mind does not pass from an element of $a$ to another and in this sense it has a full knowledge of what a human mind knows only partially and step by step.

An objection can be raised against this interpretation. There is a difference between the human and the divine way of knowing (1) in the interval $t_p$-$t_i$. My knowledge of the fact that Luciano Pavarotti is singing develops and increases along with his life, while no such development takes place in the divine knowledge. But is there still a difference when a human mind considers (1) after Luciano Pavarotti's death? When the history of Luciano Pavarotti is accomplished, the knowledge of the fact that he was singing is something stable that a human mind can grasp in a way which is similar to the divine way of knowing the same event. In other words, one could say that after Luciano Pavarotti's death (1) is always false or that it does not take a defined truth-value. Consequently the sequence of pairs forming $a$ either becomes constant after $t_p$ or it stops at $t_p$. Therefore a human mind which considers (1) after $t_p$ can, at least in principle, have a knowledge of it as complete as the knowledge that the gods have. As Proclus himself says, the indeterminacy of what is contingent depends only on its being put into the future (*Dub.* III. 14. 22-5 Isaac).[33] It follows that with respect to

[33] Luca Obertello, 'Proclus, Ammonius and Boethius on Divine Knowledge', *Dionysius*, V (1981), 136-7 interprets this passage differently. From *Dub.* III. 14. 22-8 (Isaac) he infers that according to Proclus what is undetermined is the same as what is contingent. Since to be present, past, or future depends on us to a certain extent, the same will hold also for what is contingent or necessary. I assume that this point could be proposed by Obertello as a justification of the thesis that the gods have a necessary knowledge of what is contingent. But one could ask whether this way of making the notion of contingency relative entails the impossibility of what Proclus himself admitted to be the starting point of his enquiry, namely that contingency is a real modality of things, 'natura quaedam in entibus' as he says (*Dub.* II. 6. 16). Besides, the notion of contingency that

a past event there is no indeterminacy and a human mind can get the same degree of certainty as the divine mind. This objection can be reinforced by supposing that time is not dense and that the interval $t_p$-$t_i$ is constituted by a finite set of instants. If the hypothesis $(a)$ is preferred, $a$ will be formed by a finite number of pairs which can be grasped by a human mind considering $(1)$ after $t_p$. But also in the case of $(b)$ or $(c)$ the infinity of $a$ is not such that it prevents a human mind from knowing $(1)$ completely. According to $(c)$ $a$ is constituted by a sequence of pairs which becomes constant after a certain point. In the case of $(b)$ we have a sequence which is constant up to $t_i$ and which becomes constant again after a finite interval. This kind of infinity does not represent a problem for a finite mind. If I know that $a$ was born at $t_i$ and that he died at $t_p$, I can say that all the values of $F(a)$ before $t_i$ and after $t_p$ (if any) are 0, without needing to inspect them one by one. Therefore the objection concludes that the semantics attributed to Proclus is not able to justify the distinction he states between the divine and the human knowledge of this world.

Against this difficulty two lines of defence are possible. First, it is not plain that according to Proclus time is discrete.[34]

Obertello attributes to Proclus, making him an ideal pupil of Diodorus Cronus, cannot be drawn from *Dub.* III. 14. 20–4, as he claims. In this passage that Obertello quotes in the translation of Isaac Comnenus Proclus says: '$(a)$ ὅτι μὲν οὖν πᾶν $(b)$ καὶ τὸ ὁπωσοῦν ἀόριστον ἐν τῷ μήπω εἶναι τὸ ἀόριστον ἔχει $(c)$ καὶ τοῦτο ὃ φασιν ἐνδέχεσθαι, . . . $(d)$ καὶ οἱ στοχασμοὶ δηλοῦσιν'. Obertello takes τοῦτο in $(c)$ as referring to τὸ ἀόριστον of $(b)$ and he implies ἐστι after this pronoun. The passage could be read in another way. One could take τοῦτο as proleptic of the relative pronoun and co-ordinate $(c)$ to τὸ ἀόριστον of $(b)$. In both ways the sense of the passage will be that what is undetermined takes its indeterminacy and contingency from the fact of not yet being. To be future becomes the same as to be contingent. But neither of these interpretations seems to me to be sensible because of the καὶ in $(b)$ which has the καὶ introducing $(c)$ as its natural correspondent. The same link can be found in the Latin translation of Guillelmus of Moerbeke on which the version of Isaac Comnenus depends: 'quod *quidem* omne qualitercumque indeterminatum in nondum esse indeterminationem habet *et* hoc quod aiunt contingere' (22–5). The meaning of the passage becomes the following. What is undetermined *and* what is contingent have their indeterminacy in the fact that they do not yet exist. In other words being future is the reason, not of an event's being contingent, but of its being undetermined, that is of the fact that the proposition which expresses this event cannot be said to be true or false before the event occurs. What predictions confirm is not that the only contingent thing is the future, but that there is a link between indeterminacy and future.

[34] Flowing time is said to be continuous (*suneches*) by Proclus (e.g. *In Tim.*

If it is conceived as dense, then the interval $t_p - t_i$ contains infinite instants. Therefore the sequence of pairs forming *a* in the interval $t_p - t_i$ is infinite and the human mind cannot grasp them completely, even if it considers (1) after $t_p$. It has to be remembered that the sequence of the values of (1) in the interval $t_p - t_i$ cannot be determined in its future development from any partial stretch of it, since (1) denotes a contingent event.

This first answer, on the one hand, points to the limits of the human mind, but, on the other hand, it could lead one to think that it attributes powers which are too high to the divine mind. If the gods know (1) completely, they must know an infinity of things, namely the infinite pairs which form *a*. But is it correct to confer such a power to the gods? Alexander of Aphrodisias found in the impossibility of grasping an infinity a reason for denying that the gods know all individuals (*in Aristotelis Metaphysica* (*in Metaph.*) Λ fr 36 Freudenthal). Plotinus, although he maintained that the One and the other hypostases are infinite since they have unlimited powers (VI. 9. 6. 10-11, IV. 3. 8. 35 ff), states that the ideal forms cannot be infinite (VI. 5. 8. 39-42). What the Intellect knows is a finite number of forms.[35] Does Proclus deviate from this well-established line of thought? If we are inclined to think that he followed Amelius, one of Plotinus' pupils, who would not have hesitated to admit that ideal forms are infinite,[36] then we can conclude that the semantics for (1) we have sketched out together with the hypothesis of dense time are sufficient to establish the radical difference of the divine mind from the human one. If on the contrary Proclus has to be put in the Plotinian tradition, we must give up the idea that time is dense and retire to the second line of defence we have spoken about before.[37] With inessential

III. 27. 2 Diehl). On his conception of time cf. S. Sambursky and S. Pines, *The Concept of Time in Late Neoplatonism* (Jerusalem, 1971), 17-18, and Sorabji, above n 5, 42, 184-5.

[35] Cf. A. H. Armstrong, 'Plotinus's Doctrine of the Infinite and its Significance for Christian Thought', *The Downside Review*, LXXIII (1954-5), 51 (now also in *Plotinian and Christian Studies* (London, 1979), No 5).

[36] Cf. Syrianus, *in Metaphysica commentaria* 147. 1-6 = fr 45 Zoumpos.

[37] But it is difficult to refuse to the gods a knowledge of an infinity of things, if they are supposed to know individuals of this world with their histories all together.

modifications this argument can be coupled with the preceding one if this latter is supposed to be valid, as a further coordinate answer to the difficulty we are discussing. It can be admitted that a man may attain a knowledge of (1) as perfect as the divine. Nevertheless our knowledge is always lower than the divine one. The human knowledge of an individual is always a posteriori, that is *post factum*, while the gods, who are beyond time, know the same individual *ab aeterno* and therefore even *ante factum*. From the point of view of men the future is always obscure. It ceases being hidden only when it ceases being future. That implies that although men are in principle able to obtain, step by step, a complete understanding of past events, they cannot hope to know all events, otherwise they would be at the end of time and time has no end. For a divine mind the future is plain as much as the past, because there is a future and a past only with respect to things which are in time.

If this interpretation is accepted, Proclus has to be put in a different position not only from Alexander but also from Plotinus. Plotinus as much as Alexander could not really explain divine omniscience, since he was pressed on the one hand by the admission of thesis (T) and, on the other hand, by the idea that the gods are immutable. It is only by Proclus that the immutability and omniscience of the gods can be reconciled to a certain extent with the contingency of the world, because he implicitly adopts a new semantics for indefinitely tensed statements.[38]

Even if this enquiry is far from being complete and satisfactory I have to limit myself to two final remarks. First, the interpretation I proposed of Proclus' position contributes (I hope) to explaining the extraordinary success that this view had in Christian culture without casting trivial doubts on the philosophical capacities of its supporters.[39] Secondly

[38] Of course not all problems of divine omniscience are solved by Proclus. Some of them are connected with the so-called essential indexicals. See N. Kretzmann, 'Omniscience and Immutability', *The Journal of Philosophy*, LXIII (1966), 409–21; Grim, above n 5; M. J. White, 'Time and Determinism in the Hellenistic Philosophical Schools', *Archiv für Geschichte der Philosophie*, LXV (1983), 40–62.

[39] Proclus' solution was anticipated by Saint Augustine (*de Civitate Dei* XI. 21. 339. 12 ff; *ad Simplicianum* II. 2. 2) and restated by Boethius (*Consolatio*

I would like to emphasize a point of method. We have seen that a logical doctrine, namely the semantics of indefinitely tensed statements, is connected with a theological problem, affecting the question about the nature of divine knowledge. The thesis that logic because of its formalism has nothing to do with ontology is false not only from a conceptual but also from a historical point of view.

*University of Padua*

*Philosophiae* V. 3. 7, V. 6) through Ammonius (*in Int.* 132. 8 ff) or its Neoplatonic source (on the dependence of Boethius on Ammonius see L. Obertello, *Severino Boezio*, 2 vols (Genova, 1974), i, 522–44, esp. 540–2). A path not yet well explored is its reaching Thomas Aquinas (e.g. I. 14. 13–15, esp. 15 *ad 3um*) and other medieval masters (cf. Wallis, above n 32, 227–32. For the whole problem see also Sorabji, above n 5, 253–67.

# PROFESSOR VLASTOS'S ANALYSIS OF SOCRATIC ELENCHUS*

## Ronald M. Polansky

Professor Gregory Vlastos has recently offered students of Greek philosophy an elaborate and provocative interpretation of Socrates' elenchus.[1] In his view, the cross-examinations in Plato's early dialogues aim not only to test the moral beliefs of Socrates' interlocutors but also to discover universal truth. Professor Vlastos claims that with but one exception, *Protagoras* 352d–358a, the method of elenchus is Socrates' only means for uncovering moral truths.[2] Understanding the logic of the elenchus, then, is crucial for appreciating this vital centre of the Socratic enterprise. Consequently, Professor Vlastos devotes himself to tracing the logic of the elenctic method and pays special attention to the *Gorgias*, which alone makes it explicit. I think, however, that there are grave difficulties in his account of the working of the method.

## I

According to Vlastos there are four components of the 'standard elenchus', that form of the elenchus which dominates the early dialogues. This standard elenchus differs from another less common form—employed, for example, in *Republic* 333-4 and *Euthyphro* 6c-8a, but solely to 'rough up' the interlocutor—in that it uses as premisses only propositions other than the original proposition to be investigated (39).[3]

* © Ronald M. Polansky 1985.
[1] 'The Socratic Elenchus', *Oxford Studies in Ancient Philosophy*, vol i (Oxford, 1983), 27-58.
[2] See 38 n 29 and 44 n 47. I indicate a problem for Vlastos's claim in the next note.
[3] The non-standard elenchus, which uses the refutand as a premiss in its own refutation, must be devalued by Vlastos precisely because 'Socrates is not himself committed to the truth of the whole of the premiss-set from which he deduces the negation of the thesis' and so it cannot establish the falsehood of the thesis (39). We may observe some difficulty for Vlastos in regard to this 'indirect' or

The four characteristic components of, or stages in, the standard elenchus are:

(1) An interlocutor makes a statement or assertion that gives Socrates a target for refutation;

(2) Socrates begins the refutation by introducing propositions which are not argued for but usually embraced without question by the interlocutor;

(3) these propositions are then used by Socrates as premises in an argument which concludes the negation of the interlocutor's original statement;

(4) Socrates subsequently may speak as if the truth of the negation of the original statement has been demonstrated.

The second and fourth stages thus described are rightly viewed by Vlastos as novel and in need of justification.

In support of his description of the second stage, Vlastos asserts that Socrates is never observed in the early dialogues to argue for any of the premises he employs (40).[4] Interlocutors generally accept the premises Socrates offers them though this eventually lands them in extremely uncomfortable opposition to their original thesis. We might well wonder why these interlocutors so rarely renounce their prior admissions when they discover the problems they cause them. This is an important question and one that we might expect Vlastos to consider. But, in fact, it does not occupy him at all.[5] Instead he concentrates upon determining why

non-standard elenchus, however, in that it can do more than 'rough up' the interlocutor. For instance, Vlastos credits *Republic* (*R.*) I. 347e–354a, with establishing that justice is more profitable than injustice (38 n 29), yet the section 348b–350c, which argues that the just man rather than the unjust is wise and good, is clearly a non-standard elenchus in view of its use in 349d of the refutand as premiss. We may suppose, then, that *Protagoras* 352–8 is not unique in finding a way besides standard elenchus for defending substantive doctrines.

    [4] Richard Kraut, 'Comments on Gregory Vlastos, "The Socratic Elenchus" ', *Oxford Studies in Ancient Philosophy*, vol i (Oxford, 1983), 59–60, responds to Vlastos that Socrates does sometimes offer, within an elenctic argument, empirical support for his premisses. We may see an instance of this in the use of analogy in such passages as *R.* 335b–c.

    [5] Kraut, above n 4, 63–7, suggests that Socrates' interlocutors cannot renounce the premisses Socrates employs because they find them psychologically compelling. Kraut states, 'Socrates is assuming a certain amount of psychological and moral fixity in all his interlocutors: they are all compelled to live with the premisses he uses in his arguments against them' (67).

*Socrates* adheres to these premises as solid reasons for rejecting the interlocutor's thesis and upholding his own. The question about the interlocutor's acceptance of the premises is left at the comment that Socrates 'asks the interlocutor if he agrees, and if he gets agreement he goes on from there' (40). For Vlastos, therefore, it seems that comprehending the way in which the elenchus serves as instrument in the search for universal truth only requires knowing why Socrates can take his arguments as demonstrations (see esp. 39–40).

What then sustains Socrates' faith in his premises and so enables him to believe that he establishes the opposite of his interlocutor's original thesis? Vlastos rejects the possibility that the premises are either self-evident truths or *endoxa*, that is, beliefs held by everyone or at least the most sensible people. Vlastos simply denies there is ever an appeal in the early dialogues to self-evidence (41), but he argues at some length against the view that the premises are *endoxa*, since this was Xenophon's understanding of what transpires in the elenchus and subsequent interpreters frequently follow this line. I shall show, nevertheless, that none of Vlastos's arguments aiming to prove that Socrates cannot rely exclusively upon endoxic premises is effective.

Xenophon states, in Vlastos's translation: 'Whenever Socrates himself argued something out he proceeded from the most generally accepted opinions, believing that security in argument lies therein' (42). Now Vlastos responds that Socrates 'never tells the interlocutor that he must grant *q* or *r* [the premises to be used against his original thesis] because they are self-evident truths nor yet because they are the most generally accepted opinion on the topic' (41). Should we expect, however, to find Socrates pointing out to the interlocutor that the proposed premises are generally accepted (or self-evident)? If, as Vlastos insists, Socrates requires the interlocutor to 'say what he believes', then it would be counterproductive for Socrates to proclaim that the premises are common beliefs. Also, it is unnecessary since, as previously noted, the interlocutor rarely questions the proposed premises or asks why he should accept them. Thus it would be a breach of urbanity and gratuitous for Socrates to harp upon the widespread adherence to the premisses he asks the interlocutor to accept (or their self-evidence).[6]

Still more seriously, Vlastos's further arguments against the view that the premisses are *endoxa* and adhered to for that reason contains a damaging confusion of conclusions and premisses. Vlastos urges that the only time there is an appeal in the dialogues to common belief it is made by an interlocutor only to be rejected by Socrates (41). In the *Gorgias*, for example, Polus contends that his thesis is the one that everybody really believes whereas Socrates defends a terribly incredible view. In response, Socrates dismisses the appeal to what everyone believes at 472b-c and 474a-b. But this dismissal gives no support to Vlastos's point. Socrates merely rejects common opinion at the level of the doctrines under consideration, such as separate Polus and Socrates, but not necessarily as evidence for propositions that may be used as premisses in arguments against those doctrines. I say this because Socrates insists to Polus that, in fact, 'you and I and the rest of the world believe that doing wrong is worse than suffering it, and escaping punishment worse than incurring it' (474b). Now the only means Socrates has for showing that everyone really thinks precisely this way is to argue his view from generally accepted premisses. Accordingly, we find him securing agreement from Polus that doing evil is 'more

---

[6] Vlastos suggests a peculiar understanding of the logic of the elenchus in his n 37. He offers to Norman Gulley the view that 'when the interlocutor is confronted with the inconsistency of his thesis with the agreed-upon premisses the latter will strike him as more "obviously true" than the former', but then complains that 'the obviousness of one or more of the premisses is irrelevant to the logic of the argument', since 'even if those premisses *were* obvious, their obviousness would not be a premiss in the argument'. But who would suppose that the grounds for accepting the premisses need ever themselves serve as further premisses in an argument. This would be a plunge into infinite regress. Surely what discomforts the interlocutor is his having agreed to premisses which entail doom for his original thesis while he remains unable to see any way around the premisses. Socrates does not have to ask the interlocutor to 'concede that your thesis is false because the agreed upon premisses are more "obviously true" than it', but simply that if the premisses are accepted then they do not harmonize well with the original thesis and they in fact entail an opposite conclusion. So long as the interlocutor holds to the premisses while saying what he believes, he thinks the premisses true and what follows from them necessarily true, and consequently his original thesis appears to have been demonstrated to be false. What leads Vlastos away from these easy points is his effort to see the elenchus as a universal demonstration and his previously observed neglect of the interlocutor's motivations.

disgraceful'' or 'baser' than suffering evil (474c), an opinion having hold over Polus because it is conventional. That Polus has succumbed to common belief is later protested by Callicles when he refers to Polus' assent to this premiss and attacks Socrates for resorting to demagoguery and conventional opinion (482e). Thus, even in those contexts in which Socrates questions his interlocutor's too facile reliance upon what is universally believed, Socrates employs premisses that gain acceptance and plausibility precisely because they are in accord with commonly held views.[7] Hence, Vlastos's argument that the premisses of the elenchus are neither self-evident nor common opinions, based upon Socrates' dismissal of appeal to popular opinion, misses the point. Socrates refers to the doctrines that separate him from his interlocutor—doctrines playing the role of conclusions in the elenchus—but the issue is whether Socrates uses *endoxa* for premisses.

But Vlastos has one final argument and a specific instance of non-endoxic premisses. Implicitly acknowledging the difficulty with his previous argument, that it had to do with conclusions rather than premisses, Vlastos contends that though Socrates does use 'endoxic premisses for all they are worth', had Socrates argued merely through endoxic premisses he could never have arrived at such contra-endoxic conclusions as that it is better to suffer injustice than to do it or that one should never harm one's enemies (43). Even if one sets aside the question whether the Socratic paradoxes are ultimately unpopular (on this see, e.g., *Gorgias* 474b, referred to above), one may still reject Vlastos's claim. Quite unusual conclusions, surely, may derive from most ordinary premisses, as can be observed in the *Gorgias* in the refutation of Polus.[8] Moreover, it need not be the case, as Vlastos suggests (43), that were the characteristic Socratic paradoxes

---

[7] We may find strong support for these reflections by considering a passage in *R.* I. 348e where Thrasymachus denies injustice is baser than justice and Socrates comments that were this admission made he could argue *kata ta nomizomena*, which sounds both like a reference to the argument against Polus in the *Gorgias* and an assertion that he uses endoxic premisses. The argument Socrates proceeds to employ against Thrasymachus in terms of overreaching is not what Vlastos calls 'standard', so we need not be concerned whether or not it makes use of non-endoxic premisses.

[8] Kraut, above n 4, 62–3, makes this same point and illustrates it with Arrow's paradox.

to be deduced from *endoxa* that they would necessarily become mere commonplaces and that therefore 'To accept . . . Xenophon's description of Socrates' method of argument . . . is fatal to the elenchus' (44). At least one problem for Vlastos is that he holds too impoverished a conception of *endoxa*. Socrates' frequent appeal to the possibility of a moral expert analogous to the experts in the crafts (see, e.g., *Apology* 25a-c; *Crito* 46-8; and *Laches* 184-6) suggests the availability of endoxic propositions in the moral field which are authoritative because they are the views of the wise, and not just of anyone. Such *endoxa* would be resisted by the mass of men so that conclusions drawn from them would not become commonplaces. There is, indeed, greater value to the elenchus of endoxic propositions than Vlastos allows and his arguments hardly destroy the view that Socrates nearly always depends upon *endoxa*.[9]

The instance Vlastos presents of non-endoxic premisses, *Republic* I. 335b-c, is unconvincing (43 n 41). Socrates extends to men the endoxic premiss about harm to horses and dogs making them worse in their respective sorts of virtue: harming men makes them worse with regard to human virtue. This extension, Vlastos holds, is contra-endoxic. To support this he asks, 'does stealing a man's wallet make him "worse in respect of human excellence"?' In addition, Vlastos regards the following premiss, justice is human excellence, as non-endoxic, if it is taken (as it must) to mean 'that justice is not merely *a*, but *the* human excellence'. Vlastos rightly senses that these premisses only have their full meaning along the peculiar lines of interpretation Socrates would apply to them. Consider first the premiss about harming men. In the immediate context Socrates has distinguished the true from the seeming friend or enemy (334e-335a). This premiss about harming men might, for Socrates, ultimately depend upon a parallel distinction between true and seeming harm. A stolen wallet, Vlastos's example, would be merely apparent harm. Socrates' interlocutor, however, may accept

---

[9] Vlastos might be questioned not only in regard to his narrow conception of *endoxon*, but also for his use of 'self-evident' in reference to Aristotelian first principles. See, e.g., Jonathan Barnes, *Aristotle's Posterior Analytics* (Oxford, 1975), 101.

the premiss even without this distinction. He might tend, perhaps, to the view that man's peculiar function lies in political activity. He would then readily concede that harming men diminishes their capacity to perform their function in much the same way as harming animals diminishes theirs. Without his wallet a man's political functioning is hampered. Thus, taking 'human virtue' along the lines suggested by the context, permits the extension in a popular sense to men of the endoxic proposition about animals. The case is similar for the second premiss about justice being human excellence. For Socrates it rests upon his doctrine of the unity of the virtues, but it also will be affirmed as a commonplace apart from this doctrine. If properly human action lies in the political sphere, justice would be the characteristic human excellence. Meno, we observe, readily embraces the assertion that justice is virtue (*Meno* 73d9-10—only to have Socrates urge that justice is but one of the virtues). Hence, along lines such as these, both premisses might be admitted as popular opinions. Therefore, the instance of non-endoxic premisses that Vlastos has presented may be discounted.

The main concern for Vlastos is Socrates' reason for thinking that the elenctic method enables him to demonstrate moral truth, and the crucial question is what grounds the premisses Socrates employs. Vlastos's denial that self-evidence and *endoxa* provide Socrates his premisses has appeared weak. But let us move on now to the alternative he proposes.

## II

Vlastos's major innovation lies in his account of Socrates' conviction that his premisses are true. Vlastos contends that the logic of the elenchus requires that any interlocutor putting forward an untrue moral thesis will always at the same time have true beliefs which can be used to demonstrate the opposite of the original false moral thesis (49-52). While acknowledging how dubious this may seem, Vlastos has two different ways to defend it. In the main article, he suggests that *Socrates*, as represented in the *Gorgias*, clearly holds this view and arrives at it from his practice of the elenchus. Socrates in fact succeeds in eliciting from every interlocutor premisses that enable him to prove the contradictory of the original assertion (53-4). So, for Vlastos, Socrates has an inductively based confidence that he will always find premisses acceptable to the interlocutor that prove the negation of his assertion. In 'Afterthoughts on the Socratic Elenchus', Vlastos supplies *Plato* a different sort of reasoning: 'if the Socratic theses are universally certifiable by the elenctic method, they should be provable to *anyone*, hence *everyone* must have true beliefs which entail the negation of each of his false moral beliefs' (74). Let us explore these supposed foundations of the Socratic elenchus.

Socrates is thought to believe what Vlastos calls proposition $A$: 'Anyone who ever has a false moral belief will always have at the same time true beliefs entailing the negation of that false belief' (52). But if Socrates does hold $A$, then the question as to how he knows the premisses he uses are *true* is begged. While Socrates may justly conclude from his practice of the elenchus that he is always capable of finding premisses accepted by the interlocutor that lead to refutation through argument to the opposite position, Socrates' practice cannot confirm the truth of these premisses, which is precisely what is at issue.[10] What Vlastos needs to do to overcome this circularity is to remove the word 'true' from $A$, and this he may easily do, since his interpretation does not require it.[11] An alternative approach is that suggested in the 'Afterthoughts'. Plato is not supposed to reflect inductively upon Socrates' experience that his interlocutors always in fact have beliefs available for him to employ in their refutation, but rather that the condition of the possibility of a mutually acceptable demonstration of the negation of the interlocutor's thesis is that the interlocutor have true moral beliefs to serve as premisses (74). Since this is not based upon induction, it avoids the circular reasoning. It would, however, make proposition $A$ completely hypothetical, that is, it must be so *if* the elenchus is to succeed as demonstration. But this

---

[10] The exposure of circularity similar to this is one of the two main points made by Thomas Brickhouse and Nicolas Smith, 'Vlastos on the Elenchus', *Oxford Studies in Ancient Philosophy*, vol ii (Oxford, 1984), 185-95. The criticism was already made by Kraut, above n 4, 68.

[11] The abstract of the elenchus paper which appeared in the *Journal of Philosophy*, LXXIX (1982), 711-14, did not include the term 'true'.

now begs not the truth of the premises but the status of the elenctic argument as demonstration. Vlastos, then, most effectively avoids circularity by allowing Socrates to defend inductively a version of proposition *A* which drops from it the word 'true'.

Vlastos's full interpretation of the reasoning underlying the Socratic elenchus depends upon joining *A* with two additional propositions which he calls *B* and *C*. *B* is the thesis that the set of Socrates' moral beliefs is consistent. Socrates' evidence for this is his experience of victory in elenctic encounter. So long as no one ever refutes any of his moral beliefs, they all must seem to form a consistent set (54–5).[12] Vlastos contends that *A* and *B* taken together—and neither the inclusion nor the exclusion of the word 'true' from *A* affects this—entail *C*, that 'The set of moral beliefs held by Socrates at any given time is true' (55). His argument is that if Socrates were to have any false moral belief then he would also have other beliefs entailing its negation, and hence his set of beliefs would not be consistent, contrary to *B*.[13] Vlastos holds that once Socrates thus gains the confidence that all his moral beliefs are true, he removes 'the problem of the elenchus', for those premises he uses to refute his

[12] On p 55 n 41, Vlastos strangely contends that Socrates must recognize his inductive argument for the consistency of his set of moral beliefs is 'very chancy', since it depends merely upon withstanding the inferior refuting power of his interlocutors. This is strange because on the previous page he argues, based on proposition *A*, that Socrates would refute *himself* if he were to have any false beliefs.

[13] Brickhouse and Smith (above n 10) have rightly argued that *A* and *B* do not necessarily entail *C*, since *A* does not claim that the set of beliefs that will lead to the negation of a false moral belief are themselves exclusively *moral* beliefs and so even a consistent set of moral beliefs might still contain false beliefs. These authors further suggest difficulty either in narrowing *A* to refer exclusively to moral beliefs or in expanding *B* to include any belief, moral or non-moral, employed in an elenctic argument. Their objections to the resort to reformulation of *A* or *B* are not decisive, however, and Vlastos may very well embrace one of these reformulations. Since Socrates does employ non-moral premises in his arguments (e.g. 'one thing has but one opposite', *Protagoras* 332c8–9), it may be difficult to restrict *A* to moral beliefs. It is most likely, then, that Vlastos will modify *B* so that it states, 'All Socrates' elenctically relevant beliefs are consistent', where 'elenctically relevant beliefs' are those moral and non-moral beliefs that enter into elenctic arguments. Socrates might hold that his experience in elenctic encounters gives this modified version of *B* strong inductive support, for where he does use non-moral premises they prove consistent with the moral beliefs he utilizes as the other premises and those moral beliefs that are his conclusions.

interlocutor are his moral beliefs and hence true. This impressive strategy runs, however, into at least three serious problems. The first is that $C$ will still not extend to all the premises Socrates uses; the second is that $C$ already covers what is supposed to be shown; the third is that the strategy will not come into play in much of Socrates' elenctic activity and, even where it might, will have less significance than Vlastos suggests.

Vlastos's first problem is that he has assumed that all the premises Socrates uses in his elenctic arguments (which he has called $q$ and $r$) are moral beliefs and, hence, that they would be confirmed as true if all Socrates' moral beliefs are true. But there are many cases in the dialogues in which Socrates appeals to non-moral premises. For instance, in *Republic* I Socrates gets agreement that the peculiar function or work of anything is what can be done with it alone or best (352e). In the *Euthyphro* we find this very general proposition: 'if anything becomes or is affected, it does not become because it is in a state of becoming, but it is in a state of becoming because it becomes, and it is not affected because it is a thing which is affected, but because it is affected it is a thing which is affected' (10c). In the *Gorgias* itself Socrates employs premises such as: all things are called beautiful either on account of the pleasure they give or their usefulness (474e), and that which is acted upon suffers an effect of the same kind as the agent induces (476d). These premises play crucial roles in their respective arguments. Yet, clearly, they should not be included in Socrates' set of moral beliefs and they certainly cannot be verified by proposition $C$. It could not then be $C$ alone that established the truth of the premises Socrates employs.[14] If Vlastos tries, nevertheless, to defend his approach by expanding Socrates' set of beliefs to include all the premises that are found in any of the elenctic arguments of the early dialogues—that is, all 'elenctically relevant'

[14] Brickhouse and Smith made the more difficult point, based upon the recognition that Socrates frequently uses non-moral premisses, that $C$ will not really follow from $A$ and $B$. I am making the very straightforward point that $C$ will not accomplish what Vlastos thinks it will, i.e., guarantee for Socrates the truth of his premisses. So long as Socrates employs non-moral premisses it will hardly be adequate for him merely to have assurance that all his moral beliefs are true.

beliefs as suggested in note 13 above, only this time for *C* as well as *B*—then Vlastos must abandon his frequently stated view that Socrates is solely a moral philosopher (see e.g. 32–4 and 56). For premises such as I have listed are so general that they get well beyond the moral realm. If *C* were to include as true all Socrates' elenctically relevant beliefs, then proposition *A* would have to be modified so that it read: 'Anyone who ever has a false elenctically relevant belief . . . and so on'. But such an *A* proposition could only be inductively established where Socrates did subject all elenctically relevant beliefs, and not just moral beliefs, to elenctic testing.

The second problem for Vlastos is that his scheme for confirming the premises of the elenctic argument by reference to *C*, which claims truth for the whole set of Socratic moral beliefs, works just as well for the conclusion supposed to be demonstrated. Why need Socrates merely confirm the premises he uses when he could go ahead and confirm that the conclusion he is after also belongs to his set of moral beliefs and must therefore be true? Further, since many of Socrates' premises are not moral beliefs, whereas all of the conclusions he aims for in his standard form elenctic arguments are, there is even better reason for him merely to check the conclusion. Thus, if Socrates really accepts *C*, he has no need to go through the elenctic argument, for in the same way he supposedly confirms his premises he may confirm the conclusion he seeks. Contrary to what Vlastos tells us, then, the elenchus would not be a method of research for Socrates, but merely a means he uses to convey the results of his research to his interlocutors.[15]

It might be claimed that this criticism of Vlastos is unfair since it presumes that Socrates' set of moral beliefs is already complete and that it is rather like a small basket of apples which are all always available for immediate inspection. Only by making such assumptions can we expect Socrates to check

---

[15] In fact Vlastos gives us little evidence that Socrates is engaged in research in the dialogues. If we see Socrates discover or learn something new, it is perhaps only in his autobiographical account in the *Apology* of his realization resulting from elenctic examinations of various Athenians that no man knows anything about virtue. The early dialogues seem to show us a Socrates confirming his moral doctrines to others rather than developing his moral doctrines for himself.

the conclusion he is driving at rather than the premises he might use to get him to it. But if a set of moral beliefs contains beliefs of greater and lesser clarity or certainty— Vlastos distinguishes 'overt' and 'covert' beliefs on page 51 — perhaps Vlastos's approach seems plausible. There is further reason, however, for resisting Vlastos's analysis and it is the third objection I mentioned.

Vlastos takes it that the crucial work for Socrates is done in particular elenctic demonstrations. Yet Socrates' most fundamental moral tenets are never established by a single elenctic argument and could not be so established. The ones I have in mind are the Socratic tenets that we must care for the soul more than the body, that virtue is knowledge, and that he is wisest who is aware of his own ignorance. Socrates does not and could not produce these doctrines as the conclusions of single elenctic arguments, though they may be supported by inductive reflection on all Socrates' elenctic activity. But if these most crucial moral doctrines were established by such induction, then they do not derive from the scheme Vlastos has put forward as the logic of the elenchus. Therefore some moral beliefs, and among them the most important, are not defended along the lines Vlastos proposes. Furthermore, many of Socrates' elenctic arguments refute an interlocutor's suggested definition of a moral concept and so may be said to establish only a negative doctrine. Rather than proving, as he sometimes does, a thesis such as the superiority of suffering to doing injustice, Socrates must often show that justice, courage, temperance, piety, or virtue is not this or that. In these cases should we claim that he not only refutes a faulty view but also establishes one of his own moral beliefs? Must we hold that Socrates', or anyone's, set of moral beliefs prominently includes numerous views as to what virtues are not? And if so, would it be likely that the main line of research into moral truths would serve principally to discover and defend these beliefs as to what virtues are not? There is reason for doubt; we scarcely find Socrates employing such negative beliefs as premises in further elenctic arguments, a tactic we would rightly expect were Vlastos's account of the machinery of the elenchus correct.

This study of Professor Vlastos's explication of the reasoning underlying Socrates' elenchus has exposed several difficulties. It seems that a different account of the logic of elenctic enquiry is required.[16]

*Duquesne University*

[16] I wish to thank the National Endowment for the Humanities for its support of a seminar in which I began work on this topic. Also I am grateful to Alan C. Bowen for his suggestions.

# Review Articles

## THE BEAUTIFUL AND THE GENUINE*

A discussion of Paul Woodruff, *Plato, Hippias Major.
Translated with Commentary and Essay*[1]

Charles Kahn

This is a welcome book for many reasons. It facilitates access
to a dialogue which many scholars believe to be Platonic by
offering us a lively translation and a detailed commentary. It
also deals at length and in an open-minded way with the
question of authenticity. And Woodruff's general essay on
the dialogue goes beyond the question of authenticity to
make an important contribution to our understanding of the
Socratic search for definitions.

In 1919 Wilamowitz's rejection of the *Hippias Major* as
un-Platonic may have represented the prevailing view, but
there were always strong voices on the other side: Raeder,
Apelt, Ritter, etc. In the 1920s Tarrant's attack on authenticity was more than balanced by Grube's defence: the
dialogue was gaining ground. A turning point seems to be
marked by Ross's brief defence in 1951 following Grube, and
then by Marion Soreth's detailed commentary in 1953. Since
then more and more scholars have voted for authenticity:
Gigon (1955), Dodds (1959), Kapp (1959), Guthrie (1975).
In the circle of scholars working with Gregory Vlastos Platonic
authorship seems to have been taken for granted. It is good
then to have a reasoned defence of the dialogue by a member
of that group, the first full discussion of this question in
English since 1929. After a brief description of the contents
of W.'s book and some critical remarks on translation and

* © Charles Kahn 1985.
[1] Paul Woodruff, *Plato, Hippias Major. Translated with Commentary and
Essay* (Hackett Publishing Co., Indianapolis and Cambridge, 1982), xvii + 211;
£19.50.

commentary, I will deal at length with (*a*) the question of authorship and (*b*) W.'s treatment of Socratic definition. A short Introduction (xi–xiv) summarizes the claims of the long Essay (93–190). The Translation aims to render the dramatic vigour of the dialogue 'without loss of philosophic clarity' and is largely successful. The line-by-line Commentary (35–89) discusses problems of style, characterization, historical background, logic of argument, textual difficulties, etc. The Essay consists of eight chapters. The first is concerned with authenticity. Chapters 2–4 deal with the sophistic milieu, the characterization of Hippias, the plot and humour of the dialogue. Chapters 5–8 discuss philosophical issues: Socrates' method in asking the what-is-it? question, the priority of definition, the principles governing Socratic definition, the question of ontology in the dialogues of search, and philosophical results concerning the fine and the good. There is a useful Bibliography and an Index Locorum.

The translation is readable and in most places reliable. The decision to translate *kalos* and its derivatives throughout by 'fine' (and similarly for other Greek terms subject to word-play) gives good results. I have noted the following defects in the translation.

288b8: W. misses Kapp's elegant emendation of Ἠλεία for θήλεια (*Hermes*, LXXXVII (1959), 130): 'Isn't a fine Elean mare a fine thing?' (instead of 'isn't a fine female horse a fine thing?' as in the MSS). The correctness of Kapp's reading is guaranteed by Hippias' response: 'The god was right to say that we breed very fine mares in our country'.

296a3: 'The finest thing of all is to be able politically in your own city'. W.'s decision to translate *dunatos* throughout as 'able' conflicts here with his goal of producing speakable English (xv). The reference is surely to political power, not to political ability.

297b2–3: 'the good should come to be *from* the fine' mistranslates ὑπό. Read 'the good will be produced *by* the fine'.

298d2: 'could easily be seen' mistranslates τάχ' ἂν φανείη. Read 'might perhaps be seen'. Philosophically important because Socrates leaves open the possibility that such *kala*

are perceptible only for the sake of the argument. He implies
that these examples would defeat the definition (as *Symposium* shows in the ladder of love).
   300b1: ἄλλως ἀμφότεραί γε . . . καὶ ἑκατέρα. Read
‹You don't suppose› that both would be fine in a different
way from each?’ W.’s rendering ‘I don't suppose there's any
other way they would both and each be fine’ is less relevant;
it misses the comparative construction of ἄλλως καί (reinforced here by Burnet's γε).
   302b2–3: ‘Whatever is true of both and each is true of
each and both as well’. Syntax and logic are both misrepresented. Read ‘whatever is true of both is also true of each,
and whatever is true of each is also true of both’. The correct
version is guaranteed by 302c1–2, etc.
   304e8: ‘The proverb says, “What's fine is hard”.—I think
I know *that*’ mistranslates ὅτι ποτὲ λέγει. Read ‘I think
I know the meaning of the proverb, “Hard is the fine”’
(or ‘‘What's fine is hard”).

## Commentary

W.’s comments are an excellent guide to philosophical argument and literary structure in ‘Plato's most comic dialogue’
(61). He conscientiously points out those features of the
dialogue which have been the basis for so many attacks on its
authenticity: the oddities of thought and language, the striking parallels to other Platonic dialogues, and the gross ridicule
to which Hippias is subjected. Why does Hippias accept
Socrates’ obviously false account of the Seven Sages as
refusing to engage in politics? How can he fail to perceive the
irony in Socrates’ proof of the superiority of modern over
ancient sages by their making so much money (281c–283b)?
W. has an answer. ‘Hippias probably does appreciate Socrates’
irony, but makes the best of a bad situation by not responding to it’ (35). When given a choice between agreeing to
something preposterous or moderating his professional claims,
‘Hippias always agrees. He was professionally intent on
agreeing with people’ (36). What is the unifying link between
this initial concern with Hippias as man and teacher and the
sustained attempt to define *to kalon*? Why is Hippias the

subject of a personal attack 'unparalleled in Plato's work' (131)? The long introduction serves to illustrate Hippias' versatility (35): he is 'a mathematician in Athens, but an antiquarian in Sparta' (130). In his flexibility and superficiality he is 'a living metaphor' for the philosophical subject of the dialogue, the term *kalon*. He illustrates corrupt tendencies in the word that Socrates wants to overcome, 'its facile and superficial use in ordinary language'. So Socrates' personal attack on Hippias parallels his attempt to reduce the versatility of this word of commendation 'to a single referential meaning' (131).

Such is the ingenuity and spirit of charity that animates W.'s interpretation. Why does Hippias (unlike other Socratic interlocutors) refuse to distinguish the question 'what is *the* fine?' from a request to identify *something* fine, and why does he offer three definitions in a row that suffer from the same defect of not being general enough to qualify even as a candidate? Answer: Hippias is not being stupid, he is being sly. He 'probably knows better' (46); 'he substitutes *kalon* for *to kalon* merely as a debating tactic' (49). He tries not to answer Socrates' question but to avoid it by designating something that is undeniably fine (48 ff). We are perhaps not always persuaded by W.'s display of hermeneutical generosity, but we are at least provoked into thinking again about something that had seemed obvious, namely, that the author of the dialogue was not a first-rate writer. W. succeeds in making the figure of Hippias appear considerably more interesting and intelligent than the impression of him we had received from the text.

The principle of charity also operates in the philosophical exegesis. W. gives a clear picture of the seven[2] successive definitions and shows how they fall into two distinct groups: the first three offered by Hippias and the last four, quite different and more adequate, provided by Socrates himself or by the unnamed Questioner by whom Socrates claims to be tormented (46). The first three definitions illustrate Hippias'

---

[2] Why is the eighth and final proposed definition (harmless and best, or beneficial, pleasures at 303e4–304a1) omitted in W.'s enumeration, although he recognizes this as 'the last fresh start' (87 n 190)? Apparently he counts this only as a variant of proposal 6, the beneficial.

versatility in evading questions (48), but they also explore different aspects of the fine and 'three ways in which sentences of the form "*a* is fine" may be incomplete' (59 f). The last four attempts give us 'an exercise in the logic of Socratic definition'; we learn more about the rules of definition than about the fine (62).

W.'s analysis of the arguments is generally convincing. Occasionally the charity wears thin, as when he would defend Hippias' third definition by shifting the reference of an ambiguous dative (62, with n 102 on 60), or when he would derive a subtle philosophical point from a corrupt text (66 f n 122). The star example of misplaced charity is W.'s attempt to salvage Socrates' argument against the sixth definition (*to kalon* as the beneficial, the cause productive of something good) at 296d–297d. Against most commentators who recognize the argument as fallacious (as he dutifully reports), W. presents an account that he himself describes as 'speculative' and as relying heavily on 'the pragmatic principle of charity' (71). Socrates argues that, according to the proposed definitions, the fine produces the good as a father produces a son. But since (*A*) the father is not (the) son, and the cause is not (the) effect, similarly (*B*) the fine will not be good, nor the good fine (297c). (The two definite articles, required here for idiomatic English, are not present in the Greek.) Now result (*B*) is unacceptable to both participants. Hence the definition fails. Why was (*A*) accepted? The most natural reading is to take (*A*) as claiming that two things are distinct, that the relation between them is not reflexive: the father is not *his own son*, though he may be the son of someone else, as the cause is not *its own effect*. Here 'is not' is read (roughly) as a denial of identity. But (*B*) is unacceptable on a quite different reading, because 'is not' is taken as predicative, denying the attribute. In order to avoid this fallacy (which is surely good enough to fool Hippias) W. proposes to read 'the *F* is *G*' in Plato as meaning 'that the *F* is a logical cause of being *G*' (75), so that (*A*) denies that being a father *makes* you a son, that is, 'to be a father is not to be a son' (76 n 147), and (*B*) becomes 'to be fine is not to be good', that is, 'fine things are not made good *by being* fine' (76 n 148). Here W.'s logic has now taken him far afield from the dramatic action of the dialogue. Few readers will recognize in Hippias a man able to follow such distinctions, nor can we see why Socrates (or Plato for that matter) should waste such fine logic on him. The suggested reading of 'the *F* is *G*' may be appropriate for the *Sophist* but surely not for the *Hippias Major*.

In my judgment the most unsatisfactory feature of W.'s Commentary is a surprising *lack* of charity in his analysis of the last major argument, Socrates' refutation of the claim that the fine is 'what is present through sight and hearing'. Here Socrates' argument seems to me sound and straightforward; W.'s criticism is basically off target. He is probably right to say that the principle of unity of definition begs the question against any attempt at a disjunctive or Gorgianic definition, the sum of several partial definitions (78 f). But that is a relevant objection to Socrates' argument only if Hippias or some imaginary interlocutors were prepared to challenge the principle of unity, and of such a challenge there is no trace. Hippias agrees that all cases of 'is fine' must be explained in the same way.[3] The defect with the conjunctive definition 'pleasant through sight *and* through hearing' is that it cannot apply *either* to visible things that are not audible *or* to audible things that are not visible.[4] Hence what is probably the most striking philosophical idea of the dialogue, the recognition that some terms apply to two things taken together without applying to either one alone,[5] is not strictly required for the argument at all. It is introduced only to disarm Hippias' objection to the conclusion, namely, his claim that there cannot be an attribute that is true of both without being true of each (300b6-8). The long logical

[3] This point may be missed as a result of W.'s mistranslation of 300b1 (see above, 263), which should read: 'For I don't suppose that both pleasures would be fine in a different way from each?' to which Hippias agrees.

[4] So 299e2-300b5, 303d1-4. W. seems to miss the point, since he thinks that if the author of the *Hi. Ma.* had been clearer 'he would have revised the refutandum to read ". . . through hearing *or* sight" ' (80 n 152a). But in that case the principle of unity would still be violated; only there could have been no refutation relying on the concept of 'both'.

[5] This point is a clever development of a thought that is implied at *Theaetetus* (*Theaet.*) 185b: a colour and a sound are 'both two, but each is one'; a further power is required in order to reveal 'what is common (κοινόν) to all' of these. I suspect that this is the Platonic inspiration for our author's reasoning.

parenthesis on 'both' and 'each' (300c–302b) does not provide a premiss for the argument, as W. supposes; it serves only to show that the conclusion is plausible, since there certainly *are* terms of this kind.

W. construes the issue first as 'the problem about how a whole can have different properties from its parts' (82), and then as a division of attributes into two categories based upon a mistaken analysis of the logic of 'both' (83). But the notion of two categories is an over-interpretation of the two lists given for terms that do and do not illustrate the feature in question. Socrates does not claim, and it would be irrelevant to the argument to claim, that this is a feature every attribute must either have or lack. What W. calls Socrates' 'general rule governing "both" and "each" ' (80), namely that they entail one another for a certain set of attributes, does not figure as a premiss in the argument at all. That the attribute *being fine* has this feature is not inferred from any rule but accepted on its own merits as a fact (303c3–7). The only general principle needed as a premiss for the argument is the requirement of unity: that the definiens must specify something that is *one and the same* in every case of the definiendum. For that is what the proposed definition cannot do.

## Authenticity

The *Hippias Major* shares with the *Seventh Epistle* the dubious privilege of being the only works in the Platonic corpus on whose authenticity competent opinion is still seriously divided, after more than 170 years of critical debate.[6] Given the record so far, it is highly unlikely that a consensus will ever be established for either work, though for quite different reasons. The difficulty with the *Seventh Epistle* is that it is a unique document, for which no appropriate comparative tests are available. The *Hippias Major*, on the other hand, is a highly typical text, for which comparisons abound. The problem here is that if, as I believe, the dialogue

---

[6] I ignore here the question of the *Eighth Epistle*, whose claims to authenticity probably stand or fall with those of the *Seventh*. Belief in the Platonic authorship of the *Epinomis* seems to be generally abandoned, in my opinion rightly. See L. Tarán, *Academica: Plato, Philip of Opus, and the pseudo-Platonic 'Epinomis'* (Philadelphia, 1975); also Guthrie, *History* (Cambridge, 1962–81), v, 385.

was not written by Plato, its author was an intelligent student of Plato's work, whose familiarity with the dialogues was comparable, say, to that of Guthrie or Vlastos, and who aimed to produce a work that would be as much like Plato's as possible. As a result we can find no 'mistakes' of the egregious sort that would stamp the dialogue as clearly un-Platonic. I confess that I share the reflex of the Oxford don who remarked (in after-dinner conversation) that 'anyone who doubts the authenticity of the *Seventh Epistle* has no ear for Greek'. I am inclined to assert, with like effrontery, that anyone who takes the *Hippias Major* for a work of Plato's has no sense for the art of the greatest prose writer of antiquity. But when I review the authorities ranged on the other side (including in this case my own teacher, Ernst Kapp), I despair of conveying in any persuasive way my conviction that the voice of Plato, which is clearly to be heard in the *Seventh Epistle*, is nowhere recognizable in this work of 'low comedy' (W. 106) and wooden philosophy. The grounds for my judgment are very much those expressed by Wilamowitz (cited by W. 97): 'it has no Socratic *ethos*; it lacks Platonic wit and Platonic charm'. (To which I will add: and it makes no contribution to our understanding of Plato: see below.)

W. distinguishes such 'subjective grounds' for judging authenticity from what he calls matters of 'fact': parallels in Aristotle and Xenophon, lexical oddities, and philosophical content. He dismisses the former considerations as irrelevant and admits that the latter are indecisive, but he claims that they point towards authenticity. His Commentary and Essay taken together, by answering the familiar factual and artistic objections, constitute a sustained argument for Platonic authorship.

This reviewer differs from W. in believing that, in the case of the *Hippias Major*, the subjective grounds are the only ones that really count. If the author was not Plato, he was a philosopher so much in love with Plato's work that he paid him the compliment of faithful and intelligent imitation, within the limits of his inferior talent. He was perhaps not a forger in the sense of someone who aims to have his product mistaken for an original. But in its deceptive success his work is comparable to those Etruscan warriors which stood until recently on display in the Metropolitan Museum. I knew a distinguished historian of Etruscan art who said that he would presume them authentic until the contrary was proved. Well, in that case the forger became impatient of fame and produced photographs of the unfinished statues in his workshop. We cannot hope for such 'objective' confirmation in the case of the *Hippias Major*. So those of us who are confident that the dialogue is not by Plato will remain firm in our disbelief until (to borrow an image) Plato himself should stick his head up from below to inform us that he *did* write this piece after all! In the mean time, no serious philosophical harm will be done to scholars and students who take the work for Platonic, so cleverly has the author done his job.

Still, there are a few 'objective' signs of non-Platonic authorship that deserve mention before this topic is dropped. First of all, W. asserts that 'both sides agree to date the *Hi. Ma.* during Plato's lifetime' (xi–xii). I emphatically disagree. I do not believe that anyone would presume to compose such a piece—a scrupulously faithful but pale rival to the genuine dialogues—while Plato himself was alive and writing. The meticulous attempt to reproduce Plato's *early* style and thought suggests a Hellenistic or Roman date, when the dialogues have become enshrined as classical models. (What a fourth-century imitator would be more likely to produce can be seen from the *Epinomis*.) And the first few items in the following list strongly point in the direction of a post-Aristotelian author.

(1) W. notes (99) that the use of συρφετός for a single person at 288d4 cannot be paralleled before Roman times. Similarly for the Homeric use of γεγωνεῖν in prose (at 292d4).

(2) The same is true for ἀρχαιολογία as 'ancient history' at 285d8; LSJ lists no parallels before the first century BC. (Thucydides uses the verb ἀρχαιολογέω at VII. 69. 2, but not in the technical sense of 'history'.)

(3) The conception of a school of philosophers 'around Milesian Thales, and those later down to Anaxagoras' (281c5–6) presupposes Aristotle's account of Ionian philosophy in *Metaphysics* A. 3. Plato never refers to a Milesian school.

(4) The dialogue repeatedly uses οὐσία (301b6, b8, 301e4, 302c5) as a frozen technical term, as in Aristotle or even later. The second occurrence (ἡ πάθος ἢ οὐσίαν at 301b8) could be inspired by *Euthyphro* 11a7–8 (and cf. *Protagoras* (*Prt.*) 349b4). The fourth (302c5, τῇ οὐσίᾳ τῇ ἐπ᾽ ἀμφότερα ἑπομένη . . . τῇ δὲ κατὰ τὰ ἕτερα ἀπολειπομένη) might perhaps be paralleled in late Plato or Aristotle. But the first (301b6, οὕτω μέγαλα . . . καὶ διανεκῆ σώματα τῆς οὐσίας πεφυκότα) and third (301e4, διανεκεῖ λόγῳ τῆς οὐσίας) are hard to make sense of, much less find parallels for. Grube renders 301b6 as '⟨Therefore you fail to perceive that⟩ such large *bodies of being* are also by nature continuous' (*Classical Quarterly*, XX (1926), 147). What are 'bodies of being'? Such 'confused and sometimes obscure terminology' (Grube) is not to be found in Plato, where the role of οὐσία as nominalization either of veridical εἶναι or of the τί ἐστι question is normally clear from the context, as in *Euthyphro* 11a7, *Phaedo* 65d13, 76d9, etc. (See *Phronesis*, XXVI (1981), 109–11, 119 ff.)

(5) The construction of ὀνομάζων with an adverb (καλῶς) instead of an accusative at 282b1 (to mean 'using words in a fine manner') is unparalleled in Plato and rare in any classical author. (Tarrant cites a parallel from Demosthenes *de Corona* xxxv.) Similarly for ὀνομάζειν οὕτω ('to use words in this way', 284e2); which is less striking only because here we have the illusion of an accusative object. Even φαῦλα ὀνόματα ὀνομάζειν at 288d2 is not standard Platonic usage, since the accusative normally refers to the thing named, not to the words used in naming.

(6) The reference of σοφισταί at 281d5 to include the Seven Sages and Presocratic philosophers conforms to the use of the term by Herodotus, Xenophon, etc. but not to Plato's: for Plato σοφιστής means a sophist who teaches for pay. The author has been misled by *Protagoras* 316d3, where Protagoras is defending his τέχνη by claiming Homer, Orpheus and other worthies as his predecessors.

(7) 283c4, εἰς ἀρετὴν βελτίους ποιεῖν: I find no Platonic parallel to such redundancy with ἀρετή. At 283e3 εἰς ἀρετὴν ἐπιδιδοῖεν is more normal. Compare *Protagoras* 318a9 ἐπὶ τὸ βέλτιον ἐπιδιδόναι.

(8) Has no commentator ever compared the passage on a teacher who does not make money in Sparta (283b ff) with *Laches* 183a? (This is not in W.'s list of Platonic parallels on p 104.) To make this comparison is to see what Wilamowitz meant by looking in vain in the *Hippias Major* for Platonic wit and charm.

(9) That the author took his cue from the *Hippias Minor* (together with *Protagoras*, etc.) seems clear from a comparison of the following passages:

| *Hippias Major* | *Hippias Minor* |
|---|---|
| 286b5–7 (Eudikos son of Apemantos) | 363a–b |
| 285b–e (the arts in which Hippias excels) | 366c5, 367d6, e9, 368b–369a (with *Prot.* 315c, 318e) |
| 301b, 304a5, b4 (protest against Socrates' method) | 369c1 |

On the other hand, the characterization of Hippias is *not* consistent with that of the shorter dialogue. In the *Hippias Major*, as W. shows, the sophist is ready to agree with everything, no matter how preposterous (until he sticks on a mistaken point of logic at 300b). In *Hippias Minor*, by contrast, he is an honest man of good common sense, who stubbornly refuses to concur in Socrates' paradoxes (369b–c, 370e5–9, 371d8–372a5, 375d3–6, 376b7).

This list of un-Platonic features could be lengthened indefinitely. But that would not settle the issue. For despite this mass of circumstantial evidence *against* authenticity, there are a few points which must remain embarrassing for anyone like myself who denies Platonic authorship. The two items that give me most pause are (1) the apparent echoes of the *Hippias Major* in the *Topics*, especially the critique of 'pleasing through sight or through hearing' as a definition of *to kalon* at *Topics* VI. 7. 146a21 ff (and see also the definition of the fine as τὸ πρέπον at *Top.* 102a6 and 135a13); and (2) the fact that the author must not only have known the dialogues extremely well but must have had a clear enough sense of the difference between the middle dialogues and earlier works to produce a dialogue of search that avoids the terminology and metaphysics of the middle dialogues while anticipating one or two of their doctrines. Such a quasi-historical perception may seem surprising in an ancient author. But it is comparable in principle to Aristotle's statement that Socrates did not separate the Forms, which I take to reflect Aristotle's own recognition of the difference between the middle dialogues and Plato's earlier, more 'Socratic' works. Item (1) is more troublesome, since the parallels in the *Topics* would be quite naturally explained if the *Hippias Major* were authentic, whereas they are rather puzzling if it is not. (The hypothesis of a different author contemporary with Plato would be convenient here; but that seems to me quite implausible.) What the parallels in the *Topics* show is that two of the seven definitions proposed in the *Hippias Major* were circulating in the early Academy. Where they came from, I cannot say. The author of the *Hippias Major* may have got them either from the *Topics* or from some common source.

Among a thousand *subjective* reasons for recognizing that this author is not Plato, let me mention only one. W. frankly admits the 'central oddity in the *Hi. Ma.*—that it holds the person of Socrates' interlocutor up to uniquely sharp ridicule' (100). As we have seen, W. explains this by construing the character of Hippias as a personal symbol for the unprincipled use of *kalos* in ordinary language (130 f). This is an imaginative interpretation that has, as far as I can see, occurred to no reader before W., nor does he point to any visible hint of this connection in the text. So we are left with the unexplained fact of personal ridicule levelled against Hippias, whose intensity is 'without parallel in Plato' (108) and which (for any reader before W.) has no detectable philosophical motivation other than a generalized animosity against the sophists. If the dialogue were genuine, Hippias would be safely dead, or at least extremely aged, at the time of composition. So why should he be treated with a 'gratuitous cruelty' (120) that is never directed against Callicles or Thrasymachus, nor even at Euthydemus and Dionysodorus, much less at Protagoras or Gorgias? (It is also not directed against Hippias himself either in the *Protagoras* or in the *Hippias Minor*.) W. is well aware of the anomaly and has done his best to justify it. Those of us who are suspicious of the author on other grounds will recognize here the lack of that exceptional taste and balance that is the mark of Plato's art. Finally, what is at issue besides the name of the author? What could we learn from this dialogue if it were a genuine work of Plato? Apart from the depiction of Hippias and the account of his diplomatic and commercial success (which is of some historical interest, and more likely to be reliable if the author is Plato), the four most interesting features of the dialogue are these: (i) an extreme statement of the principle of priority of definition; (ii) exploration of the relativity of terms like *kalon* whose applicability varies with the comparison class, and of similarly 'incomplete' predicates like *useful* and *appropriate*; (iii) the contrast between being and seeming in connection with the objects of definition; and (iv) recognition of the logical peculiarity of terms like *both* that apply to two subjects taken together but to neither one separately. I discuss these features in connection with the philosophical section of W.'s book.

### The theory of definition

Chapters 5–7 of W.'s Essay present a unified account, perhaps the best we have, of Plato's theory of definition in the pre-middle dialogues. (By 'pre-middle' I mean dialogues earlier than the *Symposium*, *Phaedo*, and *Republic*.[7])

W. begins by distinguishing definition-testing arguments from other elenctic or 'purgative' arguments. In the latter all premisses stand on the same footing; their only authority comes from being accepted by the interlocutor. But in definition-testing arguments certain premisses are privileged; they express the principles or criteria against which any

---

[7] W. cites me (180 n 16) as challenging the division into early and middle dialogues', but that is misleading. What I challenge is (*a*) the assumption that the dialogues of search (like the *Laches* (*La.*) and *Euthyphro* (*Eu.*) ) and inconclusive dialogues (like the *Prot.* and *Lysis* (*Ly.*) ) must be earlier than the more dogmatic *Gorgias* (*Grg.*), and (*b*) that these dialogues are primarily designed to depict the historical Socrates and were written shortly after his death. I prefer the term 'pre-middle' to 'early' or 'Socratic' because it recognizes the well-established division into two classes (before and after the neo-Eleatic metaphysic of Forms) without claiming to specify *when* or *why* the earlier dialogues were written.

proposed definition is to be measured, and thus they articulate the meaning of Socrates' what-is-it? question. The most valuable part of W.'s Essay is the careful formulation of these principles (in Ch 6).

First, however, he discusses the epistemic priority of definition and defends Socrates against Geach's charge of fallacy. It is easy to show that Socrates does not commit the naïve Socratic fallacy of 'supposing that a person cannot use a word correctly unless he can define it' (139). W. undertakes the more ambitious task of defending against vicious circularity what he takes to be the Socratic claim that knowing the definition of $X$ is prior to knowing of anything that it is $X$ (140). How can one test a proposed definition of $X$ against alleged counter-examples unless one knows that the example is or is not $X$? It is worth noticing that the principle in this form is attested (or plausibly implied) only in the *Hippias Major* (286c–d, 304d–e). A rather different principle of priority emerges from the genuine dialogues, and most clearly at *Meno* 71b: knowing the definition of $X$ is prior to knowing of $X$ that it is or is not $F$.[8] Plato is careful, as the author of the *Hippias Major* is not, to avoid formulating the principle in a way that invites the charge of circularity in the search for definitions. (This is the one case where accepting the *Hippias Major* as authentic might affect our philosophic interpretation of Plato's work, and affect it negatively.) When Plato is ready to deal with the issue of circularity he does so expressly, in the paradox of enquiry at *Meno* 80d.

Regardless of how the principle of priority is formulated, the charge of circularity can be avoided if we assume that the propositions required for the search are available on the basis of true belief (as Irwin and others have suggested) or 'tested opinion' (to use a concept introduced by W. in a slightly different context). But if belief or opinion can serve both for dialectic and for practical decisions in life (140, 143), why are the elusive definitions so important? Because they would give you what Socrates calls *technē*, the mastery of a subject matter that not only makes you an authorized judge but

---

[8] See also *Meno* (*M.*) 86d–e; *La.* 189e–190e; *Prt.* 360e7–361c; *Republic* (*Rep.*) 354c. It is not clear that Plato means to assert this principle for every value of $X$ and $F$.

enables you to teach others.[9] This is the sense of knowledge implied by Socrates' avowal of ignorance (141-3). There are, however, some things Socrates must know in order to pursue his search. These are the principles of definition, the 'guiding properties' that an adequate definition must have (149 ff). W.'s exposition of these principles is specifically adapted to the *Hippias Major* and does not fit the genuine dialogues so well. I follow a different order beginning with the *Laches*, which I take to be Plato's earliest exploration of the topic of definition. The three dialogues *Laches-Euthyphro-Meno* can be seen as a trilogy on definition, designed to be studied in that order. We begin with the most elementary principle.

## 1. *Coextensivity*

The definiens must be true of all and only those cases which are cases of the definiendum. The refutation of Laches and Nicias is a systematic exercise in the application of this principle. Laches' first definition in terms of hoplite courage is too narrow: we want to specify 'what is the same in all these ⟨cases⟩' (191e10), what runs 'through them all' (διὰ πάντων, 192c1). In the rejection of Nicias' proposal the extensional principle is made explicit: his definiens is inappropriate because it designates 'not a part of virtue [as courage was said to be] but the whole of virtue' (199e). In the *Euthyphro* Socrates mentions the extensional criterion early (5d1, 'piety is the same in every action') and then discusses extensional relations at length: all the pious is just but it is not the case that all the just is pious (11e); the pious is a part of the just (12d) as reverence is a part of fear and odd is a part of number: in each case the latter term 'reaches further' than the former (ἐπὶ πλέον, 12c5). So in the *Meno* justice is said to be *a* virtue (ἀρετή τις) not virtue simply, because there are other virtues as well, as the round is *a* figure but not 'simply figure' (73d-e). In the *Meno* we are looking

---

[9] How could we achieve definitional *Knowledge* on the basis of belief or opinion? *M.* 85c-86a, 98a suggests how true opinion is to be turned into knowledge by the dialectical process itself. Unlike W., I doubt whether any account of how the *knowledge* of definitions is possible, even in principle, can be extracted from dialogues earlier than the *M.*

not for a part but for the whole, the one form which runs through all the virtues (διὰ πάντων, κατὰ πάντων, 74a9–b1; cf. ἐπὶ πᾶσιν, 75a4, a8). Phrases like 'the same in all these ⟨cases⟩' are sometimes cited as evidence for the 'immanence' of forms in the pre-middle dialogues (see W. 166, citing Ross). But the parallel phrases with other prepositions (διά, κατά, ἐπί) show that Plato's focus is on extension and universality rather than on immanence.

It is striking that the extensional criterion, which is so conspicuous in the *Laches–Euthyphro–Meno*, is not articulated as such in the *Hippias Major*. (It is also not articulated in the *Charmides* or *Protagoras*, but these dialogues are less directly concerned with the logic of definition.) Hippias' three attempts to define *to kalon* (a pretty girl, gold, a Solonian life) are all too narrow, but the objection that they lack the universality required for *to kalon* is never directly formulated. Socrates seems to be working towards the extensional principle when he points out that not only a pretty girl but also a fine mare, a fine lyre, and even a fine cooking pot can all be 'something fine' (288b–e); but he does not go on to ask Hippias to specify 'what is the same in all these', as in the trilogy of genuine dialogues on definition. Instead he slides into a quite different principle: that the girl is not really beautiful at all, since she would be ugly in comparison with a goddess. As a result of his focus on the *Hippias Major* W. does not list coextensivity as such among his principles of definition but includes it under another principle.

## 1A. *The unity requirement*

'The fine must be *one* and the same in every case of fineness' (150, W.'s emphasis). The unity of the definiendum is entailed by Plato's version of the coextensivity principle: we are looking for what is common to all the cases, the one over the many that is 'the same in all'. The *Hippias Major* develops a new thought: the definiens must reflect this unity in its logical structure. It cannot take the form of a conjunction (or disjunction) of partial or 'Gorgianic' definitions. That is one way to see what is wrong with 'pleasant through sight and through hearing' as a definition of the fine (*Hi. Ma.* 299–303). The closest parallel to this point in the

*Laches-Euthyphro-Meno* trilogy is the rejection of the cumulative definition of virtue at *Meno* 71e ff with a request for 'that in which they do not differ but are all the same', 'the single form which they all have' (72c2, c7). But to say that the form to be defined is *one* is not yet to say that the definiens itself must be unified in a formal way. That point seems to be made only in the *Hippias Major*.

## 2. The explanation requirement

In the *Euthyphro* we are introduced to a principle of definition that was not mentioned in the *Laches* (though it might be seen as implicit there) and which will be taken for granted in the *Meno*. Euthyphro's second proposal, 'what is pleasing to the gods is pious, what is not pleasing to them is impious' (6e10), passes the extensional test once the possibility of a disagreement among the gods is eliminated.[10] The objection to this proposal invokes a new condition: it does not explain *why* a particular action is pious. (Euthyphro has agreed at 10d-11a that the gods love an action *because* it is pious, not conversely.) The explanatory requirement is silently assumed

---

[10] It was Euthyphro who insisted that the gods quarrel. (Socrates by implication doubts that they do, and so for him this problem does not arise.) But if the gods disagree, the same action will be both pious and impious, which makes the definition incoherent. It becomes coherent if we limit its application to those cases where the gods are unanimous (9d1-3), thus bringing Euthyphro's position into line with Socrates.

Following Soreth, W. claims that this objection to Euthyphro's second definition conflicts with the doctrine of *Rep.* V (479a6-8; cf. *Phaedo* (*Ph.*) 74b8) that particular actions can never be pious without qualification; only the form *F* is such that it is never *non-F*. The claim is that, if this doctrine had been formulated when the *Eu.* was written, Socrates could not have made this objection (W. 177 f). I agree that the *Eu.* shows no sign of the doctrine in question, but the notion of a conflict seems to be a mistake (so rightly Malcolm, in the article cited below in n 14). If an action such as Euthyphro's is pious in one respect, impious in another (and impious overall, as Plato no doubt believes), that is a problem for Euthyphro but not for Plato. (To this extent the objection is *ad hominem*.) But the attribute itself as distinct from its possession by particular subjects remains unqualified and non-relativized, in the middle dialogues as before. The flaw in Euthyphro's unrevised definition is that (on his own theological assumptions) it does not give a determinate, unambiguous content *to the attribute piety itself*. In W.'s terms, the unrevised definition fails to satisfy the requirement of unity, unless 'pleasing to the gods' is a unified notion. 'Pleasing to Zeus or to Hera or to Kronos, etc.' is no more acceptable as a definition than 'pleasing through sight and through hearing'. So Socrates' objection is entirely compatible with the doctrine of the middle dialogues.

in the *Meno* (72c8, in a context which echoes *Eu.* 6e) and elaborated at length in the safe αἰτία of *Phaedo* 100b ff. The language of the *Phaedo* is closely paralleled in the *Hippias Major*.[11]

On this requirement W. remarks: 'An expert on fine things must know what it is that makes them fine, so he can explain their fineness to those who doubt it, and predict the fineness of things unseen' (151). It is precisely because they provide knowledge of explanatory causes that Socratic definitions are essential for the capacity to teach and to make authoritative judgments on the relevant subject matter. Such causes give us some insight into the nature of things: '[they] are had by, or occur in, other things, and impart their nature to these other things' (152). On the other hand W. follows Vlastos in sharply distinguishing these 'logical causes' from other types of causation, in particular from *productive* causes which produce another item of the same ontological level, as a father begets a child. The distinction is important, but it is drawn in such a way as to suggest no link between the two kinds of causation. Given the context in which Plato introduces this theory of causation in the *Phaedo* as a 'second best' after giving up on cosmological causes in the style of Anaxagoras, and given the fundamental role of formal paradigms in the *Timaeus* account of demiurgic productivity, it is natural to suppose that, from Plato's point of view, there must be some kind of *deep* connection between logical causes and an adequate theory of physical production. W. implies the contrary by comparing the paradigm function of logical causes (*Eu.* 6e, *M.* 72c) to what an apprentice is looking for when he asks an expert 'what it is that makes antiques valuable, so that knowing in general what to look for he may set a proper value on each piece he sees' (153). This is misleading, since the value of antiques is entirely external and

---

[11] Compare *Hi. Ma.* 287c8–d1, τὰ καλὰ πάντα τῷ καλῷ ἐστι καλά, with *Ph.* 100e2; *Hi. Ma.* 288a10, δι' ὅ . . . καλά, with *Ph.* 100c5, οὐδὲ δι' ἕν ἄλλο καλὸν εἶναι, etc.; *Hi. Ma.* 290d6, τοῦτο καλὸν ποιεῖ ἕκαστον, with *Ph.* 100d4–5, οὐκ ἄλλο τι ποιεῖ αὐτὸ καλόν; *Hi. Ma.* 299e4, τὸ αἴτιον καλῇ εἶναι with αἰτία in *Ph.* 100b4, b7, c10, 101b5, c4. The first formula appears in *Eu.* 6d11, the second in *M.* 72c8; only the *Ph.* has all four, as in the *Hi. Ma.* These parallels will count either as anticipations or as echoes of the *Ph.*, depending on one's views concerning authenticity.

conventional; there is no intrinsic *nature* that accounts for their price, and only a very indirect connection with the causes that produced them. For natural kinds, on the other hand, there will normally be an essential connection between logical and productive causes. (As Aristotle says, in natural change the efficient cause and its product must be the same in kind; that is, they will have the same formal cause.) And it is clear that Plato conceives of the virtues (and other targets for definition, such as *to kalon*) after the pattern of natural rather than conventional entities. The *Laches*, in introducing what is perhaps the earliest literary search for a definition of virtue, motivates this search by the claim that a *technikos* who is able to improve people's psyche must know what virtue is *in order to know how to produce it* (189e–190b). W. has ignored this fundamental link between the definition and the production of virtue in the dialogues. Useful as it is, then, the notion of logical cause is only a first step towards understanding Plato's conception of the explanatory function of Socratic definition.

## 3. *The self-predication requirement*

'What makes things fine must be strictly fine itself; that is, it must in no way or circumstance be foul' (150). W. introduces a helpful notion of *strict predication* to elucidate the content of self-prediction. The many fine things are fine only under restrictive qualifications; the fine itself is fine in every respect and from every point of view. (This is the distinction which Plato later tries to capture by a contrast between 'to be' and 'to become' or 'to have a share in' (154).) W.'s notion of strict predication is useful precisely because it preserves the formal notion of self-predication ('The $F$ itself is $F$') while respecting the type distinction between Forms and particulars (since the latter are never *strictly F*) and thus avoiding self-predication in the vicious sense (taking the Form both as an attribute that other things have and as a subject that has this attribute). How are we to interpret strict predication and thus give some positive content to the notion of self-predication? W. suggests a reading that I would describe as reinforced Pauline predication. If $F$ is the definiendum and $G$ the definiens, then a proposed definition of the form 'The

*G* is (the) *F*' is to be read as 'things are *F* insofar as they are *G*' (155); for example 'things are pious insofar as they are pleasing to the gods'. This is 'probably all Socrates wants from self-predication. [In asking 'what is the fine?] Socrates wants . . . a test for fineness'. He wants to be sure that whatever satisfies the definition 'will have its share of fineness' (ibid).

This is unobjectionable but disappointing. For 'The fine itself is fine' it gives us the empty reading: 'things are fine insofar as they are fine'. This seems to me a case of over-kill in salvaging Plato's theory: in the effort to avoid absurdity, self-predication has been made insignificant. In fact we expect strict predication to tell us something about the *nature* which makes things what they are. A minimally explanatory reading of self-predication would be: 'the fine itself is what makes other things fine'; that is, things are fine *because* the fine is what it is, and because of their relationship to it. W.'s phrase 'are *F* insofar as they are *G*' has the dubious advantage of hovering uncertainly between a weak extensional criterion and the stronger requirement of explanatory causality. As explicated by W., the self-predication formula contains no uneliminable reference to a form of fineness. This fits with W.'s tendency to see the explanatory requirement in purely epistemic, non-causal terms and his eagerness to minimalize ontological commitment in the pre-middle dialogues.

## Ontology

In Chapter 7 W. argues against the view, prominently defended by R. E. Allen, that the *Euthyphro* and other pre-middle dialogues (including *Hi. Ma.*) presuppose or imply some ontological theory behind the pursuit of the what-is-it? question. In discussing what Allen calls Plato's 'earlier theory of Forms', W. distinguishes two questions: (1) is the *Hippias Major*, and by implication is any pre-middle dialogue, concerned with ontological theory? and (2) 'how much of Plato's mature theory of Forms shows up in the *Hi. Ma.*', and more generally in the dialogues of search (162)? The two questions are connected because (beyond the special problem as to how the *Hi. Ma.* is to be fitted into an account of Plato's development) we want to know 'from what beginnings Plato's ontology grew, and how far it had grown when he wrote the dialogues of search' (161).

The first question is answered in the negative: the concerns of the pre-middle dialogues are logical rather than ontological. The three principles we have discussed are introduced simply as 'working constraints on definition' arising from 'the needs and practice of the elenchus itself' (170). The search for definition is not ontologically motivated, but it 'invites ontology by making a distinction that will grow into Plato's separation of Forms' (161). But this question seems to me badly posed, as if it admitted a yes-or-no answer. Surely the problem whether a philosopher has reflected upon the onto-logical implications of his practice and doctrine is a matter of degree. The *Euthyphro* and the *Meno* are more explicitly ontological than the *Laches* and *Charmides*—that is, they tell us more about the nature of definienda—but less explicitly ontological than the *Symposium* and *Phaedo*. (The *Lysis* is in some respects more ontological than the *Meno*; we may not have a linear ordering.) Where we recognize the first appearance of ontology in such a gradation is more a question of how we define ontology than a substantive issue about Plato's doctrine. The second question, concerning the 'begin-nings' of Plato's development, is also naïvely posed, as if we could read off Plato's intellectual biography from the way he chooses to present Socrates in the dialogues. What we *can* say if we consider the relevant dialogues in approximately chronological sequence, from the *Laches* to the *Republic*, is that Plato's presentation of definienda as Forms becomes more and more ontologically articulated. But the relative avoidance of ontological commitment in the earlier state-ments seems to me to show more cunning than innocence.

On question (2) W. has nevertheless made a substantial contribution by providing a precise measure of the extent to which the pre-middle dialogues anticipate certain aspects of the doctrine of Forms (162 ff). As W. clearly shows, what is *lacking* in dialogues earlier than the *Symposium–Phaedo* is the neo-Eleatic opposition between stable Being and variable Becoming, with the corresponding epistemic contrasts

between knowledge and opinion, noetic and sensory apprehension (163, 165). There is no full-strength metaphysical
contrast between Forms and sensible particulars until these
dichotomies are introduced in the *Symposium* and developed
in the *Phaedo*. What remains in dispute is how far this metaphysical contrast is prefigured by a clear type distinction
between Forms and particulars in the *Euthyphro* and in other
pre-middle dialogues such as the *Lysis*. W.'s position is
systematically deflationary. Let me briefly call attention to
two passages whose implications he seems to have under-
estimated.

In *Euthyphro* 6d–e actions, that is, the many pious things,
are said to be correctly called 'pious' only to the extent to
which they resemble the *paradeigma*, the one form itself 'by
which all pious things are pious'. Here we have in three
sentences (*a*) a prefiguration of the eponomy relation of
*Phaedo* 78e2, 102b2 (things are named after Forms), in close
connection with (*b*) the one-over-many principle and (*c*) the
principle of explanatory causation, together with a clear
suggestion of (*d*) a similarity-relation between particulars and
the Form. What is lacking here (but implied later, on one
reading of 8a11) is (*e*) self-predication for the Form. If now
we turn to *Lysis* 219c ff we find (*a*) eponymy and (*b*) one-
over-many both instantiated by the relation between 'that
primary *philon*', which alone is 'truly *philon*', and all other
things that are said to be dear. Here (*e*) self-predication is
repeatedly affirmed in the most dramatic way (219e7–d1,
d4, 220b1–2, b4): only the primary Dear is truly (i.e. intrinsically) dear; when other things are called dear it is
only derivatively so, because of their relationship to the
primary case. (Thus self-predication is logically presupposed by eponymy, which was not clear from the *Euthyphro* passage.) Furthermore, the explanatory relation (*c*)
is given in a new form: other things are dear for the sake
of, because of their relationship to, the primary case. The
notion of *paradeigma* does not appear, but (*d*) the similarity relation is hinted at in the suggestion that other dear
things may deceive us into taking them for truly dear, 'being
as it were images (εἴδωλα) of it' (sc. of the primary Dear,
219d3).

The *Lysis* must be later than the *Euthyphro*,[12] and its ontology is more explicit. But it shows no trace of the Being–Becoming or noetic–sensory contrasts, and on this criterion it is definitely a pre-middle dialogue. The *Lysis* is not seeking a definition; it focuses instead on a different aspect of (pre-middle) forms: their role as source of value. But the *paradeigma* terminology of the *Euthyphro* and the *eidōla* terminology of the *Lysis* complement one another perfectly in foreshadowing the participation-as-imitation doctrine of the *Republic* and *Timaeus*. We are told so little about 'forms' in dialogues earlier than *Symposium–Phaedo* that it is surely significant that one of Plato's central metaphysical doctrines should be anticipated in this way. In view of this complementary fitting-together of the *Euthyphro* and *Lysis* passages, it seems more plausible to read them both proleptically, as prefigurations and (in the case of the *Lysis*) mysterious hints of things to come, rather than as the depiction of a Socrates who is 'not yet aware of the allurements of ontology' and hence can 'innocently examine proposed criteria' (165). Whatever Socrates may be up to, the author of these two dialogues is obviously concerned with more than extensional criteria for definition. We cannot know nor even guess, on the very limited evidence of the passages just discussed, how far he had already thought through the metaphysics of the middle dialogues. What we can be sure of is that when he is ready to expound this doctrine in *Symposium–Phaedo*, the preparations for it have been carefully put in place in the *Euthyphro*, *Meno*, and *Lysis*.

### *Hippias Major* as transitional dialogue

Following Soreth and Malcolm, W. sees the *Hippias Major* as playing an important transitional role in this preparation, on three grounds. I consider a fourth as well.

---

[12] In some respects the *Ly.* seems later even than the *M.* In addition to the εἴδωλα terminology it contains a preliminary version of the ἐκεῖνο ὅ ἐστι formula (at 219c7, d4) which becomes a technical expression for the Forms in the middle dialogues. See *Phronesis*, XXVI (1981), 107, 110, 114 f, 127 ff. For the way in which εἴδωλον at *Ly.* 219d3 alludes to a doctrine it does not state, compare the occurrence of the same term in *Symposium* (*Symp.*) 212a4.

1. 'Only the *Hi. Ma.*, among dialogues earlier than the
*Phaedo*, treats forms explicitly as causes and as self-predicating'
(177). As we have seen, the full causal terminology of the
*Hippias Major* is paralleled only in the *Phaedo*, but the dative
construction is found in the *Euthyphro* and the δι' ὅ phraseo-
logy in the *Meno*. Self-predication is strongly asserted in the
*Lysis*. So here the *Hippias Major* adds nothing to what we
know from other dialogues.

2. 'Only the *Hi. Ma.* gives a full-dress argument against
a set of partial definitions' (ibid). This is the argument against
'pleasant through sight and through hearing' as a definition of
the fine. As we have seen, this argument is an ingenious combination of the principles of unity and explanation: the
proposed definition cannot point to any *single* feature,
common to the two cases,[13] which would explain why these
pleasures (and these alone) are *kalon*. Furthermore, the argument introduces an intelligent discussion of terms that apply
to two things together but not to each singly. This section of
the dialogue shows the author at his philosophical best: he is
thinking here on his own. But he is only thinking through the
implication of principles that are clearly enunciated in other
dialogues.

3. It is the third item above all that W. regards as a philosophical innovation pointing ahead to the middle dialogues:
'the *Hi. Ma.* first observes the deficiency of some of the
things that are not forms' (177). In emphasizing that a pretty
girl is ugly compared to a goddess, that a life which is fine for
most men would be impious for one whose parent was divine,
and that in general the value of functional terms is relative to
their function, the *Hippias Major* prepares for a central argument for the Forms in *Republic* V. 476e ff. This argument
'leaves a gap'; it presupposes 'that any of the many fine
things will be seen to be foul (479a). The missing point is
argued in the *Hi. Ma.* for some fine things.' 'Without the
*Hi. Ma.* we could not explain why Plato leaves the gap; with

---

[13] 300a10, 'τὸ κοινὸν τοῦτο'. This usage of κοινόν is familiar to us from Aristotle (Bonitz, *Index* 399b18 ff) but, as far as I can see, unparalleled in Plato in
connection with definition. The closest Platonic use is probably *Theaet.* 186c,
which I have suggested on other grounds as a likely source for this development
on 'both' and 'each' (above n 5).

it, we can reasonably suppose that Plato thought the point too well-known to require argument' (178).

This is a persuasive claim because it reflects a very accurate sense for the way in which Plato in one dialogue builds upon results developed in an earlier work. But although persuasive the claim is false. We can fill the gap without the *Hippias Major* if only we recall, as W. in this connection does not, that the *Symposium* is probably (to my mind certainly) earlier than the *Republic*. For the *Symposium* declares in the most memorable terms that the Form of the Beautiful alone is beautiful in every respect (211a ff). The *Phaedo* makes the same point more briefly for the Equal itself (74b–c) and extends it to the Beautiful and other Forms (75c10–d1). (And a very similar point was prepared in the *Lysis* by the claim that only the primary Dear is truly dear.) So there is no gap for the *Hippias Major* to fill. There is only a point made dramatically and somewhat dogmatically in other works which the author of our dialogue has taken pains to develop in a more patient and pedestrian way. In all probability, he has indeed presented these arguments as a preparation for the doctrine of *Republic* V, as W. suggests. But he has done so by developing the hints of *Symposium* 211a and *Phaedo* 74b.[14]

4. Another anticipation of the type distinction of the middle dialogues, which W. does not discuss, is the use made of the being–seeming contrast in *Hippias Major*. In several key passages of the *Phaedo* and *Republic*, with one occurrence in the *Symposium*, the verb φαίνεσθαι serves to describe the imperfect or incomplete possession of an attribute $F$ by one of the many $F$s, in contrast to strict predication of $F$ for the Form (*Phaedo* 74b8, c1; *Rep.* V. 476a7, 479a7, b2, b4, d1; cf. φαντασθήσεται at *Symp.* 211a5).[15] Our author has noticed this use and attempted to reproduce it in a non-metaphysical way, but he has done so rather clumsily. He begins by using φανεῖται for the relative and incomplete possession of beauty

[14] See also J. Malcolm, 'On the Place of the *Hippias Major* in the development of Plato's Thought', *Archiv für Geschichte der Philosophie*, L (1968), 192 f. For the anticipation of *Rep.* 479a in *Symp.* 211a-b, see G. Vlastos's article 'Degrees of Reality in Plato', reprinted in *Platonic Studies* (2nd edn, Princeton, 1981), 66-7.

[15] See the discussion of this point by J. A. Brentlinger, 'Particulars in Plato's Middle Dialogues', *Archiv für Geschichte der Philosophie*, LIV (1972), 124-30.

by visible objects (other than the gods) in contrast to the form, fineness itself (289b3, b5, d3, d8, e5-6). The type distinction is then *verbally* expressed in the same terms by Hippias: you are looking for the beautiful which is such as 'never to appear ugly anywhere to anyone' (291d3, a transparent echo of *Symp.* 211a). And Hippias correctly shifts from 'seeming' to 'being' when he formulates what he takes to be the affirmative case: 'what *is* (εἶναι) the finest thing always and everywhere and for everyone' (291d10). The answer he gives, however, in terms of the Solonian life, shows that Hippias has missed the point. The type contrast between being for the Forms and seeming for sensible particulars turns out to be presupposed by Socrates but not actually articulated in this passage after all. And when the being–seeming opposition is exploited in the next argument (294a1-e9) it is used to reject 'the appropriate' as definiens (since that serves to make things *seem* fine, not to *be* fine) without reference to the type distinction. What we have, I believe, is an extended but crude attempt to imitate the genuinely Platonic anticipations of later terminology in the *Euthyphro* and *Lysis*.

### The Fine, the Good, and the Beneficial (Chapter 8)

W.'s study closes with an excellent discussion of the Socratic conception of *to kalon* as presented in the *Hippias Major* and other pre-middle dialogues. Although he does not wholly resist the temptation to reconstruct fifth-century history from Plato's fourth-century fictions (as when he discusses potential disagreement between the Socrates known from the dialogues and 'his most famous pupil' (185) ), W.'s conclusions in this chapter concerning the pre-middle dialogues are essentially independent of the question of the historical Socrates and independent also of the question of authenticity for the *Hippias Major*. W. shows convincingly that the Platonic Socrates assumes that the fine and the good are extensionally equivalent, even if neither term can be used to define the other. He also shows how, if 'all good things are beneficial' (*M.* 87e; cf. *Grg.* 499d), fine things too can be beneficial without becoming subordinate or merely instrumental goods (185).[16] The Socratic search is in every case a pursuit of something that is fine, good, and beneficial: 'why else would he pursue it?' (182). And these terms figure among the guiding properties for any definition of the virtues. But if virtue itself is fine it must be *strictly* fine, for anyone and under any circumstance. W. concludes with an elegant demonstration that the logical requirements of Socratic elenchus tally perfectly here with Socrates' ethical conception of the virtues (187 f).

*University of Pennsylvania*

[16] Some readers will regret that W. has not dealt in this connection with the *Ly.* and with Irwin's claim that in that dialogue Socrates denies that anything could be both good in itself and good for its consequences (*Plato's Moral Theory* (Oxford, 1977), 85).

# NATURE AND REGULARITY IN STOIC ETHICS*

A discussion of Anna Maria Ioppolo, *Aristone di Chio
e lo Stoicismo Antico*[1]

Nicholas White

Philosophical views are best understood when they can be
contrasted with views in opposition to which they were
formed and advocated. There are several reasons for this. One
is that an important stimulus to philosophical thought, and
certainly to philosophical self-expression, is disagreement
with ideas that one meets. Another is that when what a philosopher says is obscure, one can make out at least something
of it by knowing what the philosopher is trying to avoid
saying. We can be fairly sure that even if we had all of the
writings of the early Stoics we would still find their views
unclear in important ways. But since we know so little about
what they said, we need all the help we can get from knowing
what was said by those with whom they differed. We rely
a great deal for this on the Epicureans and especially the
Sceptics. And thanks to the present book, we can now use
Aristo of Chios in the same way much more effectively than
we did before. But we have to be careful. We cannot blithely
assume that Aristo was a critic of Stoicism. Perhaps he was
primarily that, but perhaps he was rather an adherent, not
even a very unorthodox one. On one account, to which
Ioppolo subscribes, he was a would-be Stoic who shared
with Zeno, or at least Zeno's earlier stage, a fairly close
affinity to the Cynics, but was later driven from the Stoic
school by Chrysippus.[2] Whether one believes this account
or not, it is hard to tell whether the disagreements between
Aristo and what we now think of as orthodox Stoicism were

* © Nicholas White 1985.
[1] Anna Maria Ioppolo, *Aristone di Chio e lo Stoicismo Antico* (Bibliopolis,
1980), 374; 16,000 lire.
[2] See, e.g., John Rist, *Stoic Philosophy* (Cambridge, 1969), 63-80.

about central issues or superficial ones. So we cannot play the Stoics off of Aristo as directly as we might like. Still, the comparison and, where appropriate, the contrast between the two is shown by Ioppolo's book to be well worth exploiting.

Of the many issues about Aristo that can be raised, three seem to me to be philosophically the most illuminating about Stoic lines of thought. All of these issues are treated by Ioppolo, but as will emerge, my emphasis is rather different from hers. One of the issues has to do with Aristo's rejection of the study of physics (in the broad Greek sense of the study of nature) and logic (*SVF* I. 351-7),[3] which the Stoics generally insisted on. Another has to do with his rejection of what Seneca calls *praecepta* and the activity of *praecipere* (*parainein*; see I. 358-9 and in general *Epistolae Morales* (*Ep. Mor.*) 94 *passim*, and also 95 *passim*). The third concerns his claim that not only is nothing good or bad except for *aretē* and *kakia*,[4] which is a standard Stoic view, but there are no other distinctions of value among other things at all, contrary to the standard Stoic doctrine that of the things that are neither good nor bad, that is, the so-called *adiaphora* or indifferents, some have 'worth' (*axia*) and are 'preferred' (*proēgmena*) and some have 'unworth' (*apaxia*) and are 'dispreferred' (*apoproēgmena*). Aristo apparently maintained that the end, the *telos*, is to live in accordance with the realization that there is no distinction of value at all among indifferents, or in accordance with the attitude of indifference reflecting this realization (I. 351, 360). On each of these three issues Aristo seems to disagree with the usual Stoic view. We would like to know why, and what is at stake in the disagreement.

Starting with the third issue seems to me the best way of making sense of things, since Aristo's position on it seems to have the most wide-reaching implications. Here I disagree

---

[3] 'In spite of its disadvantages, I shall use many references to J. von Arnim, *Stoicorum Veterum Fragmenta* (Stuttgart, 1905), by the abbreviation *SVF*, but sometimes only with the Roman volume number and the Arabic fragment number.

[4] I resist translating these terms by 'virtue' and 'vice'. The defects of these translations for interpreting Aristotle are generally appreciated nowadays, but I think that they are equally great in the case of the Stoics. I do not have space, however, to give the explanation that would be required to explain any other translation.

with Ioppolo, who appears to me to make far too little of this matter.[5] Why did Aristo hold that nothing except *aretē* and *kakia* has any sort of value at all, and that the notion of preferredness has no application? Evidently for a reason analogous to the Stoics' reason for holding that nothing except these two things is in the strict sense either good or bad. By their argument, everything that can be either well or badly 'used' must itself be neither good nor bad, but can have value only relative to the circumstances (III. 117, 122, 123). Clearly the things in question are types or classes of things or actions. Since the Stoics thought that the terms 'good' and 'bad' ought to be reserved for things whose value is not relative in this way,[6] and maintained that *aretē* and *kakia* could never be used otherwise than well or badly, respectively, they concluded that only these two things are, respectively, good or bad. To judge by Sextus Empiricus, Aristo went them one better (I. 361 = *adversus Mathematicos* XI. 63–4).[7] By any criterion for specifying which indifferents are preferred, he said, any specification of a class of putatively preferred things would turn out to contain some instances that would clearly be dispreferred.[8] For example, although health is generally preferred, under some circumstances ill-ness is so instead. In general, he contended, there is no possibility of an informative specification, not subject to uncontroversial counter-examples, of any class of things having either positive or negative value. According to Seneca, he admitted very general philosophical theses about value, *decreta philosophiae* (*Ep. Mor.* 94. 13, 31; cf. 95. 60–4), but these would not be of themselves informative specifica-tions of what is preferred. We shall have to look further into this distinction between *decreta* and what I am calling

[5] This is not to say that she does not discuss it: see esp. 188–207 (here and elsewhere I use Arabic numerals alone to refer to pages of Ioppolo's book).

[6] For some observations pertinent to this point see A. A. Long, *Hellenistic Philosophy* (New York, 1974), 179–84; for further discussion see my paper, 'The Role of Physics in Stoic Ethics', forthcoming in the *Southern Journal of Philosophy*.

[7] See Rist, above n 2, 75–6.

[8] See J. Moreau, 'Ariston et le Stoïcisme', *Revue des Etudes Anciennes*, L (1948), 27–48, and my 'Two Notes on Stoic Terminology', *American Journal of Philology*, L (1978), 111–19, esp. 111–15.

'informative specifications', but let us leave it vague for the moment until more is on the table.

Given Aristo's views about the impossibility of differentiating degrees of preferredness among indifferents, it is not too hard to see how the other two issues might reasonably be handled. If 'precepts' are some sort of non-trivial rules about which actions are appropriately performed in which sorts of circumstances (Seneca (Sen.), *Ep. Mor.* 94. 5, 8-9 = *SVF* I. 359), then one would expect Aristo to deny that any rule could be given that would not be subject to exceptions.[9] This move is perhaps not quite as automatic as it seems. Precepts have to do with what the Stoics called 'appropriate' actions (*kathēkonta*). But 'appropriate actions' and 'preferred things' are not coextensive, in the Stoic view (indeed, the relation between them is complicated and not easy to make out in all its details), and there is no reason to think that any corresponding coextensiveness would hold in Aristo's view.[10] Still, there are plainly close connections between the two (see, e.g., D.L. VII. 107, 108, or *SVF* III. 135, 494, and the connection there between the two via the notion of *phusis*), and it is easy to see that the same sort of argument that Aristo raised against the notion of preferredness would hold equally for the differentiations that precepts embody, and from Seneca it is clear that Aristo used it there too (94. 14-15).[11] As for the first issue, the objections to studying physics and logic would arise merely from their inability to provide general standards of conduct or evaluation, at least of an informative sort, as most Stoics thought they could.[12]

This outline of the disagreement on these points between Aristo and other Stoics is basically right, I believe, though it needs to be refined a good deal. The crucial point of dispute is over whether certain sorts of general specifications can be given of the things and actions, aside from *aretē* and *kakia*,

---

[9] See Rist, above n 2, 74-8.

[10] Rist, above n 2, 69, equates these two things unjustifiably; but there clearly is a close connection, which needs to be carefully disentangled (see Rist 97-111, and Diogenes Laertius (D.L.) VII. 107-9).

[11] See I. G. Kidd, 'Stoic Intermediates and the End for Man', in *Problems in Stoicism*, ed A. A. Long (London, 1971), 150-72, esp. 164, quoted by Ioppolo 124 n 80.

[12] See White, above n 6.

that have some sort of value. It seems to me to be a very deep disagreement, but to be sure we shall have to look more closely into it, and also into the consequences, for Aristo and the others, of responding to it one way or the other.

Ioppolo's tendency is to try to take most disagreements between Aristo and Zeno, and some of those betwen Aristo and other Stoics, to be relatively superficial, and usually a matter of pedagogy (e.g. 110-15, 127, 131, 133, 141, 142, 159, 160). I do not think that this general interpretative approach is correct. Leaving aside for the moment Ioppolo's belief that Zeno's views evolved, I think we know that at least for a substantial period, Zeno distinguished between preferred and dispreferred indifferents, and indeed originated the use of these terms for these notions (III. 128). He also originated the use of the term *kathēkon* for 'appropriate' action (I. 230). So it is clear that he made distinctions of value among indifferents (97), and thus did not subscribe to Aristo's argument against doing so. (This holds even if Ioppolo is right, at 99, to say that Zeno used the word *kathēkon* to include *katorthōmata*, namely, actions actually done out of a virtuous state of soul.) Nor do we have any reason at all to think that Zeno opposed precepts or general specifications of types of appropriate action. Seneca tells us that Cleanthes thought that the part of philosophy consisting of precepts was useful (as long as it 'ab universo fluit', and 'decreta ipsa philosophiae cognovit', *Ep. Mor.* 94. 4—on which see below), but says nothing about any objection to it from Zeno. If there had been such an objection Seneca would surely have had to try to disarm it, since he is trying to portray Aristo as unorthodox. And there is no sign anywhere in the tradition that Zeno aligned himself with Aristo's actual argument, which we saw from Sextus, against distinguishing among indifferents.

That this issue is not superficial, and not mainly concerned with pedagogy, we shall soon see, but we should note here that Seneca does not take it to be so. It clearly has consequences for pedagogy (since if exceptionless informative rules do not exist, attempts to use them in teaching must be cautious at least) and Seneca duly takes them up (cc. 5-12). But he also clearly reports the issue of principle, of whether there are any determinate specifications of appropriate actions that the mind can comprehend (cc. 14-17).

It also seems clear that Zeno and Aristo were divided on whether one could appeal to the notion of nature, *phusis*, as some sort of guide in one's evaluations. Zeno approved of physics, and the fragments show that he did quite a lot of it (I. 85-77, with Ioppolo 78). Ioppolo is one of those who believe that in his description of the *telos*, Zeno meant to be recommending not some sort of conformity with the nature of the universe, which she thinks was mainly Chrysippus' idea, but a kind of consistency which she takes to be equivalent to conformity with human nature (143). I doubt this account of Zeno's view, and the alleged equivalence seems to be doubtful, but we may leave these matters aside. The point here is that even if Zeno thought of the *telos* as conformity with human rather than universal nature, there would *still* be the question whether that sort of conformity could be formulated in informative general rules or not. So we still have the same substantial disagreement between Zeno and Aristo that we have already seen.

We could mitigate the disagreement if we accepted with Ioppolo (90, 151-2) the view, advocated by Rist and others, that Zeno underwent a change in position, from a time in which he was mainly influenced by the Cynics and denied any distinctions of value among things other than *aretē* and *kakia*, to a time when he took over ideas from Polemo and started to hold that nature, in some sense, could provide a criterion of what things are preferred and what actions are appropriate. It seems to me that the evidence for this hypothesis is very weak,[13] and what Ioppolo adds does not seem to me to strengthen it.[14] The hypothesis would not, of

[13] See for example Rist, above n 2, 64-72. Although Rist accepts the hypothesis, I do not see that the evidence he gives supports it; indeed, most of the evidence he gives seems to me to lead to the conclusion that Zeno was in substantial ways non-Cynic from the start.

[14] The following seem to me to be the main weaknesses of her argument. (1) She cites *de Finibus* (*de Fin.*) IV. 54, 56 (150 n 16). But in the first place, this is a highly contentious description of Zeno's view by a convinced opponent, who is anxious to show a conflict between ideas that the Stoics thought perfectly consistent (see III. 22). In the second place, the words *in prima constitutione* (c. 54) and *postea* (c. 56) do not prove a distinction between early and late works, and in fact do not even show that we are dealing with separate parts of the

course, allow us to eliminate by any means all disagreement between Aristo and Zeno, but only that between Aristo and Zeno in his hypothesized early period, perhaps only the period of the *Politeia*, generally supposed to be a quite early work.[15] Most of what we know of Zeno's views shows them to conflict with Aristo's, particularly, as Ioppolo recognizes (90, 127-8, 151-2, 154-5), on the three issues on which I am focusing here, that is, the study of physics, the possibility of formulating precepts, and the existence of evaluative distinctions among things other than *aretē* and *kakia*. So even if Ioppolo were right about Zeno's evolution, the split between Aristo and what became known as orthodox Stoicism does not begin with disagreements between Aristo and Chrysippus. Ioppolo presents evidence that Aristo had tried to operate within the Stoic school under the headships of Zeno and Cleanthes, and was then forced out by the hostility of Chrysippus to his views (33-8). But even if the academic politics of the Stoa, so to speak, was as she maintains, nevertheless operating within the Stoic school is, as she also says in citing the 'freedom of research' permitted within the Stoa (35), not the same thing as agreeing with Zeno, and it is entirely likely, it seems to me, that Aristo did a good deal of the former without, at least much of the time, doing very much of the latter.[16] However instrumental Chrysippus may have been in causing Aristo to be regarded as heterodox by

same work, since they can equally well indicate Cicero's own logical progression of thought, rather than any progression in Zeno. (2) The fact that we do not have an attested use of *proēgmenon* in Zeno's *Politeia* (151) shows virtually nothing about the ideas or even the terminology contained in that work, given how little of it we have. (3) Ioppolo cites *de Fin.* IV. 70 as showing that Zeno insisted that there is no distinction among indifferents (151 n 20). But she neglects to quote the whole passage, cc. 68-71, which seems to me to be clearly and explicitly *contrasting* Zeno with Aristo on just this point. The other passages that she cites there attribute to Zeno simply the doctrine that only virtue is good, which is of course compatible with his having held the whole while that some indifferents are preferred. (4) Rather than supporting her account of Zeno's development (149-50 with n 16), *de Fin.* IV. 45, if it indicates anything at all about the chronology of Zeno's views (which I doubt), suggests an original adherence by Zeno to Polemo's notion of the *prōta kata phusin*, which Ioppolo rightly ties to a distinction of value among indifferents (146-9, esp. 147).

[15] See Rist, above n 2, 64.

[16] *SVF* I. 39 seems to me to carry no weight at all for saying that Aristo agreed with Zeno on the issues in question here. It is simply too vague. (Cf. Ioppolo 38, 167.)

our sources among later writers (37)—and here Ioppolo
seems to me quite correct—we have seen that there were
what look to be substantial disagreements between Aristo
and Zeno by, at the latest, the time when Zeno's views had
taken the form that most of our sources allow us to see. So it
seems to me a bit misleading to say even that her arguments
have shown that '[t]he philosophies of Aristo and of Chrysippus represent . . . two possible developments, even if diver-
gent, of the doctrine of Zeno' (38). The 'doctrine of Zeno' in
question would have to be the earlier one, and one would
have to add that the later Zeno might well have wished
to demur.

But let us now see a bit further what the disagreements
were between Aristo and the orthodox Stoics, and try to
confirm the suspicion that they were not superficial but
central.

First of all, we have seen that Aristo denied that the study
of physics had a role to play in ethics. (He also denied a role
to logic, as we have noted, but although the roles of the two
cannot be fully separated in Stoic thought, the issues concerning physics are easier to get at, and I shall confine myself
to them.[17]) But this does not mean that the notion of nature
has no role to play in his ethical views, as Ioppolo sometimes
seems to suggest (but not always; compare 90 and 108 with
145). All that it need mean is that nature cannot provide us
with any *general rules* governing conduct or evaluation.
Nevertheless the actions that are done out of *aretē*, in particular those performed by the good man or Sage, can perfectly
well be held to accord with nature, even if there is no informative general specification of any type that they have
to belong to in order to do that. Moreover both Sextus and
Seneca record Aristo as having used the term *phusis* in such
a way as to imply that being in accord with nature is a commendation of a thing (I. 361, 359). In particular, Seneca
represents him as holding that the happy life is the one that
is *secundum naturam* (I. 359; Sen. *Ep. Mor.* 94. 8), and,
further, that we should bravely accept everything that 'the
necessity of the universe commands' ('quae . . . mundi

---

[17] Ioppolo distinguishes different periods in Zeno's attitude to logic also
(72 n 36).

necessitas imperat', 94. 8). Aristo's point is evidently just that the universe does not issue its commands in the form of general specifications of what to do, not that it does not issue commands or fix what is appropriate to do. Seeing this fact allows us to cope with a difficulty felt by Ioppolo (97), in the explicit evidence from Seneca (94. 5) that Aristo employed the concept of *officium*, or *kathēkon*, which she thinks ought to be eschewed by anyone who does not accept evaluative distinctions among indifferents. She tries to deal with the problem by arguing that Aristo meant by *kathēkon* what was later meant by *katorthōma*, namely, an appropriate action that is actually done out of *aretē* (III. 517, 516, 500, 494); and she argues that Zeno himself used the term *kathēkon* to include *katorthōmata*, not having developed the latter term himself (96–101). But since Aristo allowed that individual actions can be dictated by nature, there is no reason to doubt that he used the word *kathēkon* for them. (Ioppolo is averse to this idea because she makes the mistake of thinking that the word *kathēkon* connotes *not* being a *katorthōma*, i.e. not being done out of *aretē* (98). But the passage she cites, *SVF* III. 495, does not say this, so far as I can see, and the quotation from Stobaeus just preceding it in *SVF* contradicts it, by making *katorthōmata* a sub-class of *kathēkonta*, that is, the ones that are *teleia*. So rather than being a peculiarity of Zeno's early terminology, the use of the word *kathēkonta* to cover *katorthōmata* is standard.) This designation does not apply to them *as* done out of a good state of soul, but there is nothing in that fact against Aristo's having used it.[18]

We can go even further, I think, and say that according to

---

[18] There is a complication here that I cannot explore. Whereas *kathēkonta* can be thought of as either types of acts or as particular token acts, *katorthōmata* need to be thought of as particular token acts, except when they are specified by a description that indicates that they are done out of *aretē*. The type, honouring one's parents, is *kathēkon* (III. 495); every token of parent-honouring is also *kathēkon* as such (see III. 512); if a token of parent-honouring is actually done from *aretē*, then it is a *katorthōma* (III. 494; it is apparently also a *teleion kathēkon*, which requires further explanation); but no general expression picks out a type of *katorthōma* unless it connotes the doing of something out of *aretē*, though of course it might pick out a type of action that is *aei kathēkon*, which clearly is a different matter (though the example of an *aei kathēkon* in III. 496, discussed below, seems also to be a type of *katorthōma*).

Aristo, someone who possesses *aretē*, and performs a certain action because of it, must know that that particular action is the right one to perform, and that it is in accord with nature and is what the *necessitas mundi* commands. This might seem to conflict with the fact that for Aristo, the judgements of what to do are irreducibly particular, and the fact that Cicero reports him as having said that the Sage, rather than using any rule as a criterion of action, will do 'whatever comes into his mind' ('quodcumque in mentem incideret', or 'quodcumque tamquam occurreret', *de Fin.* IV. 43 = *SVF* I. 369). These facts might make it seem as though the appropriateness of the Sage's action is *constituted by* its being what he takes it into his head to do, that is, that he *makes* it appropriate by taking it into his head to do it. It seems to me that the evidence speaks clearly against this interpretation.[19] Aristo's descriptions of the Sage, *aretē*, and *kakia* are consistently cognitive, to the point that he identifies *aretē* with the knowledge of goods and bads, which can be exercised in various spheres of action (I. 374-6). The conclusion seems inevitable that the appropriateness of a certain particular action is an objective fact which the Sage *recognizes*, rather than being a fact that the Sage creates by deciding on his action. So what the Sage does is to recognize, without recourse to general rules of an informative kind, those actions that are in accord with nature.

On their side, why did orthodox Stoics think that general rules were possible, or that the study of nature might help us find them? For Aristo's argument against them was one that the Stoics seemingly had to take seriously, since as we have seen it appears to be merely an application of their own argument for saying that *aretē* is the only good. The usual account says that in admitting evaluative distinctions among indifferents, and in using conformity to nature as a guide to them, the Stoics were being less 'rigorous' or 'strict' than people like Aristo and perhaps the Cynics, or were making concessions

---

[19] I was mistaken on this point in my 'Two Notes on Stoic Terminology', above n 8, 115. It is unclear to me what Ioppolo's position is on this question; she seems to me to write ambiguously with regard to it on, e.g., 178, 181-3. On a related point about the orthodox Stoics, see A. A. Long, 'The Logical Basis of Stoic Ethics', *Proceedings of the Aristotelian Society*, LXX (1970-1), 85-104, esp. 102.

to the needs of everyday life. Ioppolo accepts this sort of account (151-2, 90). Advocates of this account generally have in mind that the Stoics wished their doctrine to be something that non-Sages could use as a genuine guide for action (152, 'l'uomo medio', and 194). This of course cannot be the whole truth, since the Stoics thought that the Sage too would be aware of what is preferred, what is appropriate, and what is in accord with nature (*de Fin.* III. 59; cf. *SVF* III. 613-14).[20] Rather, I think it is clear that the Stoics, especially Chrysippus, thought that apart from any need we may have of a guide for action, the very notion of *aretē* itself would turn out to be in some sense empty, if it were not possible to make distinctions of preferredness and appropriateness concerning actions that are, nevertheless, indifferent with respect to goodness and badness. This is the crucial fact that treatments of Stoicism have missed. It is that in their view, distinctions among indifferents are *necessary* to give content to the notion of *aretē*, and this consideration is pressing for them even prior, logically, to any attempt to say just how the distinctions are to be drawn.

The point can be seen if we consider the problem that Aristo faces when he says that the only good is *aretē*, and that *aretē* is the knowledge of what is good and what is bad (I. 374). If this is all we have to go on, then if we want to know either what *aretē* is, or what the good is, then we are caught in a tight circle, which is not broken or even significantly expanded by being told that the *telos* is a state of indifference (*adiaphoria*) toward everything that is neither *aretē* nor *kakia*. Plutarch gives us a slightly tortuous version of this difficulty advanced by Chrysippus against Aristo (III. 26 and also *de Communibus Notitiis* 1072a; see Ioppolo 166-7). We can find out from Aristo that the end is a state of indifference toward everything other than attaining the end or the lack of it, but that is not much to be told. Chrysippus insists that we be told more, on pain of having left the

---

[20] It seems to me that Kidd, above n 11, 165-6, is mistaken if he means to be denying this. Cicero, *de Officiis* III. 15 does not support it (n 134), nor does Sen. *Ep. Mor.* 94. 30. The latter cites a particular need that non-Sages have for *praecepta*, but does not imply that Sages do not register distinctions among indifferents. The former says that *officia* are not peculiar to Sages but are common to them and everyone else.

concept of *aretē* contentless. This, I would argue, is the gist of much of the discussion of these matters in Cicero's *de Finibus*, though it tends to be mixed in with other points (see esp. II. 43, III. 12, IV. 46, 69). (One of these other points, interesting in its own right, is the Stoics' claim that if *aretē* is not substantially linked to indifferents, then there will be no possible explanation of the genesis of *aretē* in us; one of the main reasons why *de Finibus* III says so much about human development is its attempt to show that Stoicism admits such an explanation (see esp. III. 20-2, IV. 47-8).) One reason for this may be that Zeno himself probably did, as Ioppolo says, object to Aristo's view on the score of its failure to provide a practically usable guide for action (this seems clear from IV. 70; cf. Ioppolo 151-2). But even if this was Zeno's motive, or one of them, for distinguishing among indifferents, it seems that the other, logical issue about the content of the notion of *aretē* also arose, and the objection recorded by Plutarch and the discussion in the *de Finibus* are manifestations of it.[21]

The fact that the Stoics thought they needed an evaluative distinction among indifferents was of course no guarantee that they could get one. They were working in a milieu where many people found it congenial to think that nature could be a source and criterion of value, and so it is hardly surprising that they turned in that direction. But they still had to answer Aristo's argument that any general specification of a class of putatively valuable things is bound to contain exceptions, and so to be ruled out as a piece of knowledge (Sen. *Ep. Mor.* 94. 15-16). It looks as though they simply denied his claim that there are no exceptionless informative generalizations about the value of indifferents. Certainly this seems so for the case of *kathēkonta*. For according to Diogenes Laertius, they maintained that some things are *aei kathēkonta*, always appropriate, as opposed to things that are not always appropriate (VII. 109 = *SVF* III. 496). On the other hand, the example given of something always appropriate is

---

[21] There is a deeper issue here, which may or may not have been raised. It is that the idea that *aretē* does indeed *have* content *might* be argued for on the ground that it will be useless if it does not. But that is a different point, at a different level (concerned explicitly with what concepts are allowable).

disappointingly uninformative: living in accordance with
*aretē*.[22] But other examples, whereas they have the look of
rules of thumb, are certainly not wholly trivial (e.g. III. 495,
498, 501), and Seneca holds against Aristo that certain
precepts are self-evidently correct (94. 43), his examples
being 'Nothing to excess', 'Greed is never satisfied', and
'Expect from others what you do to them'. Something
similar can be said about the practical maxims given toward
the end of Cicero's *de Finibus* III, in cc. 60–71. And of
course one must also add the various important remarks
about laws, such as *SVF* I. 62, II. 1003, III. 314, 315, 520,
613–15, 623. At the end of *de Finibus* III, though, the Stoic
Cato says, 'No one can judge truly concerning goods and bads
unless he knows the whole plan of nature (*ratio naturae*) and
of the life of the gods, and whether or not the nature of man
is in accord with universal nature' (c. 73). He then goes on to
say that without physics no one can see the meaning (*vis*) of
the old precepts of the wise, such as 'Follow the occasion'
and 'Nothing to excess'. This suggests that we cannot have
fully satisfactory rules unless we have complete knowledge of
the pattern of nature, but that we can have such rules if we
do have such knowledge. And finally and most clearly, at
*Epistolae Morales* 94. 35, when confronted with the suggestion
by Aristo that *praecepta* are *infinita*, Seneca just flatly denies
it (*falsum est*). And he goes on to say, just as flatly, that not
only are precepts not *infinita*, but that although they are
subject to minor qualifications (this seems clearly the force
of *differentias*; cf. *diaphora* at *SVF* II. 378) required by
times, places, and characters, general precepts can be given
⟨to cover⟩ these too (*his quoque dantur praecepta generalia*).
So he is saying that we can include enough qualifications in
our rules to make them immune to exceptions.

---

[22] On the classifications of different kinds of *kathēkonta*, see my 'Two Notes
on Stoic Terminology', above n 8, 111–15. On 202–3 Ioppolo says that *kathēkonta
peristatika* are to be identified with *katorthōmata*. This seems to me quite impossible. *Kathēkonta peristatika* are types of actions that are appropriate only in
difficult and exceptional circumstances (see my article, above n 8, cited by
Ioppolo 203), whereas *katorthōmata* are actions that are actually done out of
*aretē* (see above n 18). Sages will of course always perform *kathēkonta peristatika*
when they are in the appropriate circumstances, but plainly not all instances of
*kathēkonta peristatika* need be performed by Sages, since someone not a Sage
might perform such an act out of some state of soul other than *aretē*.

If we look directly at Stoic physics, we seem to find a belief that the understanding of nature is in principle formulable in regularities without remainder, along with an understandable hesitation about stating just what those regularities are. The Stoics held that when all conditions are the same, the result must invariably be the same too (II. 943-4).[23] Cicero seems to be reflecting Stoic views when he says that if one knew all of the causes, one could predict everything without error, but that since no one could do this but a god, a human being must use *signa* (*de Divinatione* I. 127 = *SVF* II. 944; cf. III. 605). And of course we see generalizations given for the same kind of example, like the one in *de Fato* 12 (*SVF* II. 954) to the effect that no one born under the Dog Star will die at sea. When Cicero says, however, that gods but not human beings could predict everything, it seems likely that the Sage would fall into the former class, not the latter. For the Stoics were accustomed to say that the Sage is divine (III. 606), and specifically that the Sage has no mere opinions and is without ignorance (*mēd' agnoein mēden*, III. 548). I think that there is real uncertainty in the evidence about whether the Sage is really supposed to be omniscient, and to know regularities that have absolutely no exceptions (for one contrary indication, see *SVF* III. 564-5). But there seems to be no reason to deny that the Stoics thought that such regularities held, whether a human Sage would know them or not.

It is too bad that we do not have more evidence about this debate over the possibility of general regularities concerning preferredness and appropriateness, but I think we have enough to tell us one more important thing about it. Recall the distinction we saw in Seneca's reports of both Aristo and his opponents, between *decreta philosophiae* and *praecepta*.[24] In it, I suggest, we can see reason to think

---

[23] See Richard Sorabji, 'Causation, Laws, and Necessity', in *Doubt and Dogmatism*, ed M. Schofield, M. Burnyeat, and J. Barnes (Oxford, 1980), 249-82, esp. 253-4.

[24] It might be argued that this distinction is late, but I think it clearly goes back to Chrysippus and possibly earlier. Showing this requires argument, of course, but for now I simply point to the uses of *theōrēma* at III. 214, 278, 295. As pointed out in the next paragraph, there was necessarily disagreement over the nature of the distinction.

that what Aristo and the Stoics disagreed about here was the possibility of giving *factual* conditions, or something very close to that, for the correctness of evaluative claims. By this I mean the following. Two forms or precepts are given by Seneca: (1) 'Behave in manner *M* toward a friend' (94. 11), and (2) 'You will do *X* if you want to be temperate' (95. 66). Precepts of the second type are said to be equivalent to *descriptiones*, which are of the form, 'He who does *X* is temperate' (95. 66). The spaces occupied by '*M*' and '*X*', it is clear from his examples, are meant to be filled by non-evaluative expressions, such as could be determined to apply by either sensation or memory (95. 61). Precepts accordingly say that if a certain factual condition obtains, then such-and-such an evaluative claim holds ('He is temperate') or such-and-such an imperative is to be issued ('Do so-and-so'). What Aristo denied is that any replacement of '*M*' or '*X*' by a finite factual expression will guarantee exceptionlessly correct results (94. 14–16). The Stoics, on the contrary, asserted that some such replacements do yield exceptionless truths (94. 35). This is what I meant when I said earlier that Aristo denied that we could give 'informative' generalizations about the value of indifferents. That is, he denied that we could determine by straightforwardly factual investigation when a given evaluative term is applicable. (I think that this is, at bottom, why he denied that giving someone precepts could move him if he were not already so inclined (see 94. 11); but that is another story.)

The nature of the contrast between *praecepta* and *decreta* becomes itself entangled in the disagreement. The Stoics think that the contrast is merely between general and more specific injunctions, that is, that *decreta* are really just *praecepta* of a general sort (94. 31), though they admit that there is a further difference with respect to clarity and accessibility to sensation (95. 60–1, 64). Aristo thinks that the contrast is much greater.

If one steps back and looks at the Stoic position in ethics, one sees that it is not surprising that they should have become involved in disputes of this sort. With one proviso, we can say that their view of ethics is naturalistic, in the modern sense of holding that evaluative conclusions can be validly derived from factual premisses, and that evaluative notions can be given factual definitions. The proviso is that the Stoic notion of what is 'in accord with nature' be admitted to be a factual one (which of course some will deny).[25] For statements about what is in accord with nature provide the stock of premisses and definitions that they use for deriving and explaining evaluative claims (such as the usual Stoic accounts of the *telos*, most obviously, but see also D.L. VII. 107-8, e.g.). Now even aside from Humean problems and Moorean open-question arguments, it is notoriously difficult to produce adequate factual explanations of evaluative notions and convincing cases of entailments of evaluations by factual premisses, and it was just these difficulties that Aristo tried to exploit. The Stoics thought he failed. They certainly would think so. They believed that statements about the overall structure of the universe entailed evaluative claims.[26] Precepts and ascriptions of preferredness were for them, as we saw (Sen. *Ep. Mor.* 94. 31), merely derivations of evaluative conclusions from factual descriptions of narrower circumstances supposedly part of the broader overall structure of nature.[27]

But if the Stoics were defending a naturalistic position, it would be wrong to think that Aristo was a straightforward

---

[25] In a sense more traditional than the modern one, naturalism is the doctrine that evaluative conclusions can be derived from premisses explicitly about nature or what is natural, and that evaluative notions can be explained by means of 'nature', 'natural', and other such expressions. (These two conjuncts are separable, but we may pass over that here.) If 'nature' and the like are factual terms, then a doctrine is naturalistic in the modern sense if it is naturalistic in the traditional sense, but not necessarily vice versa. If 'nature' and the like are not factual terms, then a doctrine is non-naturalistic in the modern sense if it is naturalistic in the traditional sense. (I recognize that many would reject this distinction between 'factual' and 'evaluative' terms, but whatever its difficulties it still seems useful for these classificatory purposes.)

[26] See Long, above n 19, and my article, above n 6.

[27] Why, one might ask, is something not *good* if it is exceptionlessly in accord with nature, or *aei kathēkon*? After all, as we saw, the Stoics argued that things that are sometimes well used but sometimes badly used cannot be good. But in fact there is more than this to the distinction between the good and the merely appropriate or preferred, which I have not been able to go into here, but which is discussed at some length in my 'The Role of Physics in Stoic Ethics', above n 6. The fundamental point is that even if a type of action, say, is always *kathēkon*, nevertheless its value derives from its place within a wider context, and thus is a form of contributive value rather than the sort of intrinsic value for which the Stoics reserved the word 'good'. See also Long, above n 6, 179-84.

anti-naturalist. If an anti-naturalist is, for example, one who thinks there are no factual definitions of evaluative terms and no factual conditions for evaluative conclusions, then Aristo indeed seems to have been that. But there is clear evidence, we have seen, that he thought that appropriate actions are in accord with nature, just as the Stoics did, even though this accord could not be expressed in *rules* giving factual sufficient conditions for evaluations. Thus he thought a Sage would know that a *particular* action was appropriate, there being a *particular* fact of the matter to know. He evidently believed that *decreta* could be applied by the Sage to yield judgments about particular situations, without the intermediary of more specific precepts (94. 5, 10, 12). We have no record of any account he gave of how the Sage could do this, and plainly Zeno (*de Fin.* IV. 70) and Chrysippus were not satisfied by whatever account he did give, if he gave any. In any case, his view seems to be naturalistic about the existence of particular facts about what particular actions are appropriate, but not about the existence of factual explanations of evaluative terms, and naturalistic about the possibility of correctly determining the applicability of general evaluative principles to particular situations, but not about the possibility of giving rules of inference from factual general conditions to evaluative statements.

This difference of view between Aristo and the Stoics amounts to what I would call a deep difference, and seems to me to be at the centre of the split between them. I would not want to hold that absolutely all of the other disagreements between them arise from this one—and Ioppolo helpfully discusses quite a number of others—but still this one and its consequences deserve extensive study in our efforts to understand the issues involved in Stoicism.

*The University of Michigan*

# DEMARCATING ANCIENT SCIENCE*

A discussion of G. E. R. Lloyd, *Science, Folklore and Ideology: the Life Sciences in Ancient Greece*[1]

James G. Lennox

Perhaps more than any other historian of ancient science on the contemporary scene, Professor Geoffrey Lloyd has sought to use the documents of ancient science to explore issues in the philosophy and sociology of science. In particular, Lloyd's writing displays a sensitivity to the lessons of this material for the question of 'demarcation' between science and other forms of human cognitive activity; and to questions of the influences of traditional modes of thought, popular culture, folk beliefs, etc., on those among the ancients whom we recognize as formative figures in the history of Western science.

These are important questions. The answers we give to them will have ramifications for our interpretation of a thinker, and for our evaluation of that thinker's place in 'the scientific tradition'. Furthermore, asking them of the documents which form the very well-springs of that tradition is especially important and interesting. As Professor Lloyd notes (14), it can teach us much about the requirements of rational enquiry, its origins, and the extent to which its originators were able to stand outside of the various traditional elements of their culture.

In its fundamental concerns and motives, *Science, Folklore and Ideology* can be seen as a continuation of the work of *Polarity and Analogy*, *Magic, Reason and Experience*, and a variety of papers exploring the nature and extent of the 'rationality' and 'empiricism' of ancient medicine, astronomy, psychology, botany, and zoology.

In this instance, however, Professor Lloyd's methodology

* © James G. Lennox 1985.
[1] G. E. R. Lloyd, *Science, Folklore and Ideology: the Life Sciences in Ancient Greece* (Cambridge, 1983), xi + 260; hardback £49.50, paperback £16.95.

is somewhat more self-conscious and carefully controlled. *Science, Folklore and Ideology* consists of three self-contained studies, each focused on a specific subject matter with quite specific questions in mind. None the less, as we are told in the introduction, there are two unifying themes. In each study, Lloyd's starting point is the hypothesis that:

Ancient science is from the beginning strongly marked by the interplay between, on the one hand, the assimilation of popular assumptions, and, on the other, their critical analysis, exposure and rejection . . .  (1)

Given this starting point, a number of questions naturally arise concerning 'the extent and the limits, of the critical scrutiny undertaken by ancient writers' (1). In particular, to what extent did they accept, reject, or support prevailing cultural norms, beliefs, and attitudes?

A critical review of such a work must operate at two levels. As we explore each of Professor Lloyd's case studies we will need to evaluate both his interpretation of the texts from 'the life sciences', and his attempts to establish relationships between these texts and specific elements of the 'folklore' and 'ideology' of their culture. These two aspects of Professor Lloyd's project are not, of course, without their points of intersection. Anachronistic interpretation can tear a text from its cultural fabric altogether; extreme cultural determinism will predispose an interpreter to read each text as *post hoc* window dressing for a culturally dominant point of view. Happily, Professor Lloyd sails nicely between these extremes.

The breadth of Professor Lloyd's learning in this arena surely extends beyond the bounds of any one reviewer's competence. In my own case, I shall restrict my comments on Part III of *Science, Folklore and Ideology* to a brief summary of its contents and the philosophical issues it raises, and leave it to the scholars of Pliny, Rufus, and Soranus to give it the careful and critical evaluation it deserves. My critical remarks will be restricted primarily to Parts I and II.

1. The development of zoological taxonomy

The first study focuses on Aristotle's zoological treatises. Lloyd, relying on recent social anthropology in the structuralist tradition, draws our attention to three common tendencies in Greek culture: (i) to description of animal behaviour in human, social terms, (ii) to anthropocentricity, and (iii) to fascination with marginal or 'boundary crossing' animals. Lloyd's question, of course, is the extent to which Aristotle's 'zoological taxonomy' reflects and is (perhaps only implicitly) influenced by these traditional tendencies.

This discussion is divided into some introductory remarks on Aristotle's 'zoological taxonomy' (14–18) and three studies focused respectively on Aristotle's discussions of animal social behaviour (18–26), his use of Man as a model for the investigation of animals (26–43), and his interest in 'dualizers' or 'boundary crossers' (44–53). He concludes from these studies that Aristotle's work is the first recognizably scientific animal taxonomy in the Greek world; self-consciously systematic and empirical, critical of its sources, concerned to formulate a language appropriate to its subject. And yet 'he [Aristotle] still thinks about animals in human terms, assuming a parallelism between the animal series and the moral one'; 'he uses taxonomy to convey value judgments about man's place in nature . . .'. 'In each of these three areas the influence of earlier patterns of thought— not so much on particular points of detail as on the fundamental presuppositions with which taxonomy is undertaken—is stronger and more persistent than might be supposed' (55).

Evaluation of this conclusion ultimately depends on the strength of his case in the detailed studies intended to support it. But it is worth noting that the paragraph following that from which these quotations are drawn points to the role of Aristotle's teleology and conception of natural form as partial support (cf. 214–15). Does Professor Lloyd suppose that these quite idiosyncratic philosophical tools are evidence of the influence of the folklore or ideology of classical Greece on Aristotle's taxonomy? This seems to be an implication we are expected to draw, but I am unable to find good grounds for doing so. That Aristotle's classifications and methods of classification reflect his agonizingly worked out theory of the unity of matter and form in organisms or his causal (teleological) theory why organisms are structured or behave as they do, suggests the influence of his own philosophizing on his classifying, perhaps. Let us see if Lloyd's three areas of focus suggest more.

(a) 'Suspicion, the off-spring of fear, is eminently characteristic of most wild animals. Courage and timidity are extremely variable qualities in the individuals of the same species . . .'. Aristotle? No, Charles Darwin in *The Descent of Man and Selection in Relation to Sex*.[2] Until behaviourism got a strangle-hold on the subject, suggesting such language be 'reduced' to terminology appropriate to *là bête machine*, it was common within the evolutionary biological community to see animal behaviour as on a continuum with our own, and springing from similar though not identical cognitive dispositions. Indeed Darwin rested his hopes of an explanation of man's 'higher functions' on the evolutionary existence of such a continuum. With the timely demise of behaviourism, this viewpoint is currently staging a vigorous revival, as a glance at recent issues of *Behavior and Brain Science* reveals.

I say all this to offset a tendency some of us may have, when away from our pets, to view the attribution of beliefs, desires, or emotional dispositions to animals as inherently pre-scientific, an element of folklore. Most of Lloyd's analysis of Aristotle's discussions of the social behaviour of animals consists of a clear, careful, and straightforward presentation of the claims Aristotle makes, necessarily so in view of the general lack of familiarity with these texts.[3] Yet one feels a good deal of tolerant winking going on between the lines, as if the mere presentation of such ideas were enough to establish their indebtedness to folklore and popular culture.

The crucial texts here are those which show Aristotle to have a self-consciously theoretical stance toward the use of the language of virtue, emotion, intelligence, and social relationships in application to animals other than humans. Lloyd *mentions* that *Historia Animalium* VIII–IX both open

---

[2] Charles Darwin, *The Descent of Man and Selection in Relation to Sex* (London, 1871), 39.

[3] Along with Lloyd, Balme, and Pellegrin, *La Classification des Animaux chez Aristote* (Paris, 1982), 65–9, I will operate on the assumption that there are no compelling grounds for treating *Historia Animalium (HA)* IX as inauthentic.

with such texts, but does not do them justice. *Historia Animalium* VIII. 1, which applies the analysis of similarity and difference to actions and behavioural dispositions which I. 1 had applied to parts, is the other side of the *Nicomachean Ethics* distinction between the natural and moral virtues. *Nicomachean Ethics* tells us that it is by metaphor that beasts are called self-controlled or self-indulgent (1149b31-6). *Historia Animalium* VIII. 1 allows other animals 'traces' of such dispositions, saying that some animals differ from us and one another by more and less, others by analogy. As he does in the *Nicomachean Ethics*, he here allows the other animals a *natural capacity akin* to intelligence and crafts-manship (*HA* VIII. 588a25-6). Again like the *Nicomachean Ethics* the familiar analogy between children and wild beasts is made, which 'is not unreasonable, if some of these traits are the same, others not very different, while others are analogues of those in other animals' (*HA* VIII. 588b1-3). Given this explicit argument at the beginning of *Historia Animalium* VIII sanctioning the discussion of animal behaviour in language common in the human context; given the common sense of doing so which only Cartesian dualism (or its mind-less offspring, radical behaviourism) would wish to deny; much depends on quite *detailed* evidence of *precise* borrow-ings from folklore. Lloyd gives us precious little evidence at all, and none of it of the specificity required.

(*b*) Lloyd next considers 'man as model' in the zoological writings. Lloyd here wishes to review claims in the zoology about man's uniqueness and the influence of 'the anthro-pocentric perspective on Aristotle's zoology more generally' (27). Here we must ask what relevance this discussion has on Lloyd's overall theme, for he admits that '[t]he pervasive theme of man as model or as supreme, paradigmatic animal, is not an idea that Aristotle can be said to have taken over from previous popular beliefs or folklore (42). The best Lloyd can do is see it as a 'translation of a popular pre-occupation with animals as related to man'. Yet, as Lloyd himself points out, given that 'man *is* an *animal*', and the organizer of zoological information, it is to say nothing about Aristotle in particular, or his culture in particular, to note that *his* zoology is concerned, in part, with 'man's place in nature'.

Lloyd's review of the evidence establishes that at *Historia Animalium* I. 6. 491a15-26 Aristotle provides reasons for beginning the entire investigation with a top to bottom review of the external organs of man. These passages make it *very* clear, however, that this is *not* because man is superior or a paradigm in any way—it is simply because in a comparative study the obvious place to begin is with the familiar. As Lloyd himself points out, when we move on to the internal organs and to the study of generation, man is said to be an inappropriate starting point. Professor Lloyd now looks for evidence of man's priority 'derived from his [Aristotle's] doctrine of man's essential nature' (27). Here he reviews those texts asserting man's share in the divine, his possession of higher intelligence relative to other organisms, his various anatomical and physiological differences. He reaches three conclusions: that at least some of these claims are empirically well-founded; that some show the influence of Aristotle's theoretical preconceptions on his generalizations; and that he is 'preoccupied' with this question of man's priority (35).

A review of the material mentioned by Professor Lloyd reveals a number of texts in various treatises which, at least on first glance, contradict each other, and raises acutely the issue of what sort of evidence Aristotle would use in establishing some of them, given that he virtually never tells us precisely how he grounds comparative claims about such things as the relative amounts of sperm produced in a species. How one takes the further step of establishing that a specific 'theoretical preconception' is responsible for any of these claims is not, as far as I can see, discussed by Lloyd.

Further, two caveats must be made. Contradictions are not easily established in such comparative material. One must be sure that when Aristotle says 'man alone has *P*' in one place and '*S* (*S* ≠ man) has *P*' elsewhere, the implied reference class is the same. The propositions 'Man alone among the viviparous quadrupeds has variable numbers of offspring' and 'Some of the birds have variable numbers of offspring' do not contradict one another. But it is often difficult to decide how extensive the comparisons in the zoological works are intended to be.

Second, the precision of such claims is crucial. Lloyd notes two texts which state that humans alone have 'anomalous' gestation periods (*HA* 584a33, *de Generatione Animalium* (*GA*) 772b7 ff) and two (both referring to dogs (*HA* 545b6, 574a20)) which note a gestation period varying from 60–63 days in dogs. Do these texts conflict? Is a three-day variation considered a fluctuating gestation period by Aristotle, or a uniform one?

One final point is worth mentioning. Contradictions *may* suggest tensions in a thinker's work due to theoretical preconceptions. But this is not the only, or even the most obvious, source. They may on the contrary suggest an openness to new data. David Balme has suggested that the *Historia Animalium* is a 'layered' treatise, with a good deal of gathered but 'undistributed' and 'unassimilated' material within its covers.[4] The very contradictions Lloyd discusses may, until we have a method for sorting these issues out, count just as well as evidence of a refusal to let guiding preconceptions dictate the gathering of data.

Professor Lloyd now tries to nail down some of these 'guiding assumptions'. Those he works on are that the main animal groups form a hierarchy (35–7); that anatomical and physiological theories about lower groups are determined by what Aristotle thinks about higher ones (37–40); and that certain *groups* are maimed, stunted, or deformed with respect to others (40–3). Once more the review of the evidence is in the main clear, encyclopedic, and judicious. But does this review reveal 'guiding assumptions', or hard-won theoretical results? Though I incline one way on this question, Lloyd another, I do not raise this question rhetorically but rather to isolate it as the basic question raised by Professor Lloyd's work.

Here I found Lloyd's discussion of Aristotle's search for analogues of organs found in the blooded organisms among the bloodless most enlightening. As he points out, in certain

---

[4] David Balme, 'The place of biology in Aristotle's philosophy' forthcoming in *Philosophical Issues in Aristotle's Biology*, ed A. Gotthelf and J. G. Lennox (Cambridge, 1985).

ca$\acute{s}$es this leads to remarkable identifications, but perhaps left Aristotle unprepared for radically anomalous structures. Aristotle's notion of 'natural deformities' is reviewed without mentioning what to my mind are the two crucial points— that there is a *developmental theory* underlying this doctrine,[5] and that the deformity is always *relative* not just to a closely related kind, but to a wider kind.[6] The blind mole, for example, is a deformed viviparous quadruped, and *due to* a developmental anomaly which prevents the eye's development. Lloyd supposes (40 n 155) Aristotle's remark that lobster's claws are used not for prehension but locomotion suggests an implicit comparison 'with hands, not the forefeet of quadrupeds'. Yet the comparison is clearly with the *claws* of all other members of the γένος of clawed crustaceans made up of the καρκίνοι and κάραβοι ('έν τῷ γένει . . . τῷ έχοντι χηλάς', 684a35) which all of them have 'instead of hands, relative to grasping and holding' (683b34). It is crucial to identifying this organ as a deformity (684b1) that the lobster be a member of the clawed γένος and that its claws be irregular (άτάκτως) with respect to the claws of the γένος.

Man is surprisingly absent from most of this discussion— it will be recalled we are discussing 'man as model'—and in his one conspicuous appearance I think Lloyd misses Aristotle's point. Lloyd refers to Aristotle's claim that 'in man alone the natural parts are in their natural positions' (*de Partibus Animalium* (*PA*) II. 656a10). Lloyd remarks

'Nature' is here equated not with what happens always or for the most part in the animal kingdom, but with what applies exclusively to man, and the whole animal kingdom is, in a way, a decline from man. . . .                                                                                          (42)

In the passages cited by Lloyd (*PA* 656a10; *HA* 494a26 ff) Aristotle asserts that the *biologically* up and down corresponds

[5] Cf. esp. *HA* VIII. 2. 589b29–590a11.

[6] This is convincingly argued in Allan Gotthelf, 'Notes towards a study of substance and essence in Aristotle's *Parts of Animals*', II–IV, forthcoming in *Aristotle on Nature and Living Things: Philosophical and Historical Studies, presented to D. M. Balme on his 70th birthday*, ed Allan Gotthelf (Pittsburgh, 1985). Professor Gotthelf has also drawn to my attention *Metaphysics* V. 22. 1022b25-7 (on privation) which contrasts privation according to the thing itself with privation κατὰ τὸ γένος. A blind man is deprived of sight *qua* man; the mole is *not* blind *qua* mole, but rather κατὰ τὸ γένος, i.e. compared to the kind of which the mole is a form (perhaps viviparous quadruped).

perfectly with the cosmological up and down only in man. He defines the place wherein nutrients enter as biologically 'up'. As he explains in *de Incessu Animalium* (704a30-2) 'this distinction is based on function (ἔργον), and not merely on position relative to the earth and the heaven. For where the intake of nourishment and growth is for each, there is up . . .'. Plants, therefore, have their functional 'up' cosmologically 'down' (*de Incessu Animalium* (*IA*) 705b4-7; *PA* 683b22-3). In all these passages κατὰ φύσιν is *explicitly* spelled out as 'relative to the cosmologically up and down' ('πρὸς τὰ τοῦ παντὸς ἄνω καὶ κάτω', *HA* 494a29; 'πρὸς τὸ τοῦ ὅλου . . . ἄνω', *PA* 656a12). Thus, far from setting up man as a standard by reference to which everything else is a decline, Aristotle is merely noting that in man the functional 'up' corresponds to cosmological 'up'—that is, man walks upright. Indeed, it seems likely the two uses of φύσις in this passage, to modify parts and to characterize their arrangement, correspond to the functional nature of the parts and their positioning in man according to what is cosmologically natural. It is worth stressing this point, for Professor Lloyd uses his interpretation of these passages to reinforce his conclusions about Aristotle's treatment of dualizers (52-3) and character differences between the sexes (99, 104, 211, 214-15).

On the whole, then, I find rather little support in Lloyd's discussion for the view that Aristotle uses humans as a model by which to judge or evaluate other animals. Aristotle tends to evaluate each group on its own terms, relative to its own life. The 'monstrous' and 'deformed' are not so judged by reference to a human model, but by reference to their proximate wider kind. And while there are various rankings imposed on the animal kingdom, these are biological rankings and cannot be *assumed* to reflect the uncritical adoption of ideological preconceptions.

(*c*) The question of dualizers is next on Lloyd's list of possible 'popular' or 'pre-scientific' influences on Aristotle's zoology. This is a technical notion for Aristotle, though with clear Platonic roots (cf. *Republic* 479b–d), referring to animals which possess two characteristics which are normally

316    *James G. Lennox*

associated with distinct animal groups. While viviparous
quadrupeds have tails but no buttocks, and viviparous bipeds
have buttocks but no tails, apes lack *both* buttocks and tails
(*PA* 689b13-15). Cetacea receive and expel air like land
creatures, yet are footless and live and receive nourishment in
the water. And so on. The typical pattern is the simultaneous
possession by one animal of features which are strongly
(indeed, often *causally*) associated with distinct groups, but
within this pattern the variations are many and important.
Often a single feature is 'ambiguous'—the ostrich's feather
(bird) is hair-like (quadruped); the bat's forelimb (quadruped) is wing-like (flyer—note the care; not bird, but
flyer); the seal's rear feet (land animal) are fin-like (water
animal). On other occasions (the first two examples above)
two features consequent on being one or another sort of
animal are conjoined.

Here again I find the evidence for 'folk' influence on
Aristotle's thinking virtually non-existent. Lloyd provides
only two or three references to pre-Aristotelian texts, and
these do not stress 'boundary crossing'. That an animal
group which *Aristotle* treats as 'tending in both directions'
is occasionally *discussed* in Greek literature is not nearly
enough to allow Lloyd's conclusion that 'it can hardly be
doubted that he [Aristotle] was to some extent influenced
by such beliefs [popular lore about boundary crossers]'.

Indeed, Lloyd's careful survey of the Aristotelian texts
leaves him precious little room to meet this conclusion, in
that it becomes clear how central is Aristotle's consideration
of these cases to his critique of Platonic division and the
development of his own multiple differentiae method. This is
the thrust of David Balme's discussions of 'dualizers',[7] which
(surprisingly) is not discussed by Lloyd.

Lloyd has provided a masterful account of Aristotle's
zoological discussions of animal behaviour, human nature, and
'dualizers'. Where Part I of *Science, Folklore and Ideology*
fails to convince is regarding its thesis that these discussions

[7] David Balme, 'Aristotle's use of differentiae in zoology', (revised) in *Articles
on Aristotle I Science*, ed J. Barnes, M. Schofield, and R. Sorabji (London, 1975),
189-92.

are in any interesting way indebted to the 'folklore' of Aristotle's culture. This failure in no way detracts from its being a lucid and suggestive study of some central issues in Aristotle's zoology.

## 2. The treatment of women

Lloyd's second set of studies (58-111) concerns the medical treatment of, and biological theories about, the female sex in the fifth and fourth centuries. Taking the belief in the inferior status of women and the superiority of the male in the Greek culture of this period as a given, Lloyd attempts to ascertain the extent to which this 'ideology' was taken for granted in the medical treatment of women and in biological theories of sex. His chief sources are the Hippocratic corpus and Aristotle's zoological corpus. Once more we have a brilliant review of an enormous body of material, including many Hippocratic treatises on the medical care of women not yet in English translation (perhaps due to some unchallenged preconceptions of English-speaking historians of the life sciences!). And again, I find it difficult, when all is said and done, to say what the material presented has to say on the place of a specifically male-dominant ideology either on practice or theory.

Briefly, let us consider just four areas of the Hippocratic corpus which Lloyd attempts to bring to bear on his question. Lloyd begins by claiming that the main surgical treatises are directed primarily to the treatment of male patients. Yet he notes that the masculine patient references are adequately accounted for by the fact that ἄνθρωπος (human being) is a masculine noun. He then notes that while patients are often categorized, they are seldom categorized along lines of gender. But this, combined with the first point, only establish a *lack* of sexual distinctions in the treatises, *not* a male orientation. The same is true of Professor Lloyd's next point, that these works do not mention how women in particular might react to the pain involved in certain treatments. I cannot help thinking that if such a point *had* been made, it would have counted as male condescension to the 'weaker sex'. The evidence Lloyd brings to bear from the surgical treatises, then, seems inconclusive.

In the *Aphorisms* and *Coan Prognoses*, on the other hand, there *are* sections devoted specifically to women. Here Lloyd says,

> . . . in both cases, little attention is paid to differences between men and women until we reach the section devoted to women's complaints.   (65)

But this comes dangerously close to being tautological. Lloyd notes that the more theoretical treatises spend much time discussing sexual differences, that anywhere from 25–45 per cent of the case histories discussed are of female patients, and that these evidence as careful consideration of the patient as those of males (64–7). Lloyd provides a most interesting and balanced discussion of the evidence relating to the male doctor/female patient relationship from the Hippocratic Corpus. The evidence indicates, for example, that sometimes doctors personally examined the vagina and/or womb of the patient, while on other occasions either a female assistant or the patient herself did so. The result?

> . . . we can do no more than guess the precise factors that weighed with these doctors in deciding when to examine personally and when to delegate this to others.   (73)

Likewise Lloyd's evidence for male bias in discussions of the causes of sterility is less convincing once one realizes that much of it is based on a general absence of discussion of causes of male sterility in *On Sterile Women*. In a footnote (n 102), Lloyd notes that, even in the gynaecological treatises, there are occasional discussions of how males can increase their fertility.

The evidence for specific ideological influence, then, is once more underwhelming. The last two sections of Part II of *Science, Folklore and Ideology* concern theories of the female seed, and Aristotle's account of sex differences. Lloyd begins the first of these by remarking that 'it was commonly supposed that the essential contribution to reproduction and to heredity was that of the male parent' (86). Again, however, his review of the evidence fails to establish this as more than one competing view. Indeed his discussion clearly establishes the variety of theories defended, and casts doubt on the view that at least by the fifth century, there were any 'common suppositions' regarding the relative contributions of the male and female to reproduction. Aristotle on the female sex is an emotionally charged issue. I do not believe the discussion in *Science, Folklore and Ideology* has helped. Lloyd quotes the usual phrases: 'the female is defined by an incapacity', 'the female is a natural deformity', 'the female provides the matter for the offspring', 'the female is cooler than the male', and so on. But he is very quick to *assume* that these ideas *derive from a priori* assumptions of male superiority (95, 98, 101, 104) —even though he notes that Galen held just such assumptions, and held a completely *different* theory of the female contribution to generation (109-10). What Aristotle clearly holds is that the male's generative contribution—σπέρμα— is a hotter and more concocted form of the same stuff out of which the female generative contribution—καταμένια— is formed. Actually, Aristotle considers both of them σπέρμα (*GA* 725b3, 728a26, 728b22, 737a28, 750b4, 766b14), and both contribute motions responsible for development (*GA* 737a28, 741a24, 767b37, 768a14, 768b1, b8), but the male supplies heat *alone*, no matter. And, in sexually differentiated organisms this heat appears to be required to *complete* the development (cf. *GA* I. 21, 22). Wind eggs are his favourite evidence for this, for while the female has sufficient heat to produce the egg, she needs the male's fertilization to have the egg develop to maturity. As he holds that all the characteristics of the male parent including his primary and secondary sexual ones are somehow 'represented' in his heat, and likewise in the heat of his σπέρμα, he deduces that, should his heat completely actualize its potentialities, the offspring will be male. Animal nature is for good reason so arranged, however, that many fertilizations will not have this result.[8]

Aristotle's arguments for his specific views of 'the male' and 'the female' are extremely complex, are a response to a variety of alternatives he successfully refutes, and are invariably supported by an appeal to evidence. How does one determine either that the theories themselves, or the

[8] *GA* IV. 3. 767b8 ff.

use of evidence to support them, are biased by a prior set of specific ideological beliefs, especially in terrain as foreign to us as classical Greece? Take a couple of specific examples. Lloyd is not the first to be shocked by Aristotle's claim that, in four species including humans, males have more teeth than females, while in others he cannot say, 'for observations have not been made' (501b19 ff) (102). Lloyd footnotes the Harig and Kollesch[9] paper which points out in how many ways this apparently 'a priori' remark could have been based on careful (if non-randomized) observation. And note how strange it would be *not* to have based it on observation, given Aristotle's explicit refusal to generalize a priori. More to the point, what would be at stake for a male-dominant ideology here? If Aristotle is willing to say that females generally are better learners and more clever than males (*HA* IX. 608a27-8), would he really be ideologically motivated to deny them more teeth in the face of contrary evidence?

Or take Lloyd's reference to the 'unfortunate discussion of the sex of bees' (102). Why unfortunate (beside the complexity and difficulty of the Greek)? As Lloyd sees it, Aristotle takes a theory well-supported in large familiar animals —nature usually does not provide defensive organs to females—and applies it here, reaching the conclusion that worker bees cannot be female.

But as the passages quoted by Lloyd (101) show, Aristotle does not see this as a reliable generalization, and at any rate it is one side of a plausibility ($\epsilon\upsilon\lambda o\gamma o\nu$) argument which also provides evidence *against* worker bees being *male* (they tend the offspring)—again not certain evidence, for Aristotle allows that males of a few kinds do tend the young (cf. Lloyd 99). This is surely why Aristotle himself, in a passage Lloyd refers to elsewhere ('but cf. 760b27': n 162) but does not discuss, insists that his discussion is all based on $\lambda o\gamma o\varsigma$ and opinion, and the facts of perception must decide which theory we ultimately adopt.[10]

---

[9] G. Harig and J. Kollesch, 'Neue Tendenzen in der Forschung zur Geschichte der antiken Medizin und Wissenschaft', *Philologus*, CXXI (1977), 114-36.

[10] Cf. G. E. R. Lloyd, *Aristotle: the Growth and Structure of his Thought* (Cambridge, 1968), 76-9; *Magic, Reason and Experience* (Cambridge, 1979), 137-8.

Given all these problems, Professor Lloyd's sweeping conclusions come as a surprise.

> Yet even if his research had been more comprehensive, careful and exact, his preconception of the superiority of the male sex would have survived intact—at least as long as he accepted the ideological presuppositions of his contemporaries concerning the differences between men and women. The firmer the evidence for aspects of the superiority of females among other animals, the greater would have been his commitment to the view that in this, as in other respects, man is the only truly natural creature. Meanwhile those ideological presuppositions acquired some ostensible colour—and reinforcement—from the biological arguments that Aristotle mounted in their support.
>
> (104–5; cf. 211, 214-15)

If I understand Professor Lloyd, this supplies Aristotle with the following argument, based on two ideological and unargued assumptions: (1) humans are the only truly natural beings; (2) women are obviously inferior to men; (3) thus this is the 'natural' way for things to be; (4) where it is not, this is degenerate and contrary to nature. But by (1) Aristotle means only that man's 'biological' up and down is aligned with cosmological up and down (cf. above 314–15); (2) is never stated in this bald way—the female (not women particularly) is typically less hot and is unable to complete by herself an offspring; and is *different* from the male in various anatomical, physiological and behavioural ways (not all, or even most, of these differences suggest 'superiority' in either direction); therefore (3) cannot be his view; and (4) is contrary to what is often taken to be most central to his biological perspective: '. . . nature makes nothing at random, but always the best from among the possibilities for the being *of each kind of animal*' (*IA* 704b15-17, 708a10-12; emphasis added). To assert the principle Lloyd persistently gives Aristotle (that only man is truly natural, other kinds being degenerate by comparison) one must attribute a supernatural teleological standard to him, according to which we may make such judgments. This is quite out of spirit with his delight in how anatomically well-adapted *each* kind is to *its* life. It may be (though I am inclined to the view that more argument is needed here as well) that Aristotle held, and even defended, quite conventional social attitudes toward women. It remains to be shown that his biological theories and generalizations about sexual differentiation either were supported by, or lent support to, these attitudes.

### 3. Later developments

Part III consists of a number of case studies, somewhat artificially organized around the subjects of pharmacology, anatomy, and gynaecology. The first examines the respective attitudes of the Hippocratics and Theophrastus toward the ῥιζότομοι and φαρμακοπῶλαι (root-cutters and drug-dealers) (119–35); the second illuminates the strategic use of sources in Pliny's *Natural History* (135–49); the third is a study of the barriers in the way of the development of a uniform anatomical vocabulary, much of it focused on Rufus of Ephesus (early second century AD), *On the Naming of the Parts of Man* (149–67); the last two are sympathetic studies of Soranus as a critic of traditional folk elements in gynaecology (168–82) and as a revisionist in the methodist 'school' of medicine (182–200).

Here the common threads woven throughout these case studies are insufficient to unify them to the extent of Parts I and II—but this merely reflects the richness and diversity of the materials. Assuming the emergence of a tradition of critical methodologically guided research in medicine and biology in the fifth and fourth centuries, Lloyd seeks to measure its inertia and, assuming this is not linear and uniform, the constraints on further progress. In addition, he sees this as fruitful territory within which to test J. Goody's ideas on the central place of literacy in the development of critical rationality. Some highlights here include a careful textual comparison of Pliny's *Natural History* XXV and Theophrastus' *Historia Plantarum* IX, aimed at determining what motivated Pliny's work and to what extent it maintains the critical research orientation of the texts it relies on; a reading of Rufus' work which clearly identifies the *methodological* importance of its subject and the institutional and sectarian barriers to a uniform anatomical dictionary; and an account of Soranus' gynaecological works which deftly brings into relief its epistemological foundations in Methodism and the tensions between these foundations and the requirements of clinical practice. In terms of Professor Lloyd's own views on the primary constituents of the scientific spirit, Soranus cannot help being a sympathetic figure in *Science, Folklore and Ideology*. On Lloyd's telling even the principles of his own 'method' give way to his consistently critical attitude; while traditional beliefs and practices are consistently rejected if they conflict with medical experience or cause needless pain and suffering for the patient.

*Science, Folklore and Ideology* shares a number of virtues of its immediate predecessor, *Magic, Reason and Experience*. Professor Lloyd's literary style is elegant, graceful, and uncluttered. He has the art of the footnote mastered—scholarship is neither sacrificed nor allowed to interfere with the flow of narrative; it is banished to the fine print at the foot of the page, where it belongs. As such, the book is (as I learned by experience with *Magic, Reason and Experience*) a suitable teaching aid for (bright and eager) non-specialists. The bibliography, *index locorum*, and general index are prepared with characteristic care. Indeed the entire volume exudes the careful art of the current regime at Cambridge University Press.

The life sciences are often studied with the prejudices of those who take mathematization and predictive power to be the hallmarks of science. The same can be said of the medicine and biology of classical and Hellenistic Greece. Geoffrey Lloyd sees clearly that the achievements of Aristotle in zoology, Theophrastus in botany, and Galen or Soranus in medicine must be studied on their own terms and without prejudice. When we do so, Lloyd tells us, the common components of 'the Greek achievement' emerge: critical debate over principles; the development of systematic research strategies; concern for the empirical adequacy of explanations. The chief claim of the book, of course, is that certain popular assumptions stubbornly resisted critical scrutiny and indeed became crucial assumptions of research in some cases.

The chief concern of my discussion has been to suggest the difficulty of making out this case. But the crucial importance of Lloyd's work is that it asks so many of the right questions about this subject. His work brings a subtlety and precision to the issue of the emergence of rational enquiry in the ancient world which it deserves, and seldom receives.[11]

*University of Pittsburgh*

[11] I take this opportunity to thank Allan Gotthelf for comments on an earlier draft of this discussion.

# INDEX LOCORUM

**Aeschylus**
*Agamemnon*
553-4: 91 n 2
928: 91 n 3

**Alexander of Aphrodisias**
*de Anima Mantissa*
113. 12-15: 226
181. 6-22: 226

*de Fato*
177. 3 ff: 49
197. 11-15: 230
200. 12-15: 232
201. 6-13: 233
201. 13-21: 233
201. 16-18: 232
201. 21-8: 233
201. 28-30: 233 n 26

*de Providentia*
14. 7 ff Ruland: 227
66. 9-13 Ruland: 228

*in Aristotelis Analytica Priora*
10. 15 f: 81
11. 17: 78
177. 25 ff (= *SVF* II. 202a): 223, 234 n 27
184. 10 ff: 62 n 48
400. 34: 43

*in Aristotelis de Interpretatione commentarius*
135. 12 ff: 238
136. 1 ff: 238 n 31

*in Aristotelis Metaphysica*
80. 14: 149 n 43
85. 22: 149 n 43
97. 18-19: 131 n 13
Γ: 43
fr 36 Freudenthal: 228, 244

*in Aristotelis Topica*
183. 24: 43

*Quaestiones*
I. 4. 11. 9 ff: 44
I. 4. 12. 13-17: 230
I. 4. 12. 13 ff: 45 n 26

I. 4. 13. 2-8: 63
I. 25. 40. 30-41. 4: 227
II. 3. 48. 15-22: 227
II. 19. 63. 22-6: 227
II. 19. 63. 22-8: 226
II. 21. 65. 32-66. 2: 226
II. 21. 66. 25-67. 2: 226
II. 21. 69. 1-31: 226

**Ammonius**
*in Aristotelis de Interpretatione*
128-31: 42
130. 23: 45 n 26
130. 23-4: 45
130. 27: 49 n 34
130. 28: 43
131. 3-4: 42
131. 25 ff: 38
132. 8 ff: 246 n 39
139. 2: 43
139. 29: 43
140. 17-21: 43
140. 19: 43
141. 16: 43
141. 31 ff: 43
143. 15-20: 43
154: 45
154. 16-20: 40
154. 33 f: 75 n 70

**[Anon]**
*Dissoi Logoi*
6. 1: 2
6. 3: 12 n 26
6. 4: 12 n 26

**Aristo**
*[SVF]*
I. 351: 290
I. 351-7: 290
I. 360: 290
I. 374: 299
I. 374-6: 298

**Aristotle**
*Analytica Posteriora*
A. 13. 32b18-20: 62
71a13: 79 n 77
72a11: 81 n 79

73b23: 79 n 77
75a1–37: 54 n 38
77a22: 79 n 77
77a30: 79 n 77
79a21: 67 n 56
87b22: 67 n 56
88b1: 79 n 77
93a13: 134 n 19
97b15–26: 122 n 38
100a3–9: 183 n 6

*Analytical Priora*
I. 3: 62 n 47
25b4: 67 n 56
I. 13: 62 n 47
32b10: 67 n 56
32b18–20: 62
34a12: 71 n 65
34a14: 70 n 62
34a25–9: 48
38b21: 81 n 79
43b33–6: 67 n 56
48b3: 39
49a6: 39
52a32: 39
57a35–40: 48

*Categoriae*
1a24: 134 n 19
1a24–5: 164, 168, 173
3a21: 154 n 54
3b36: 154 n 54
4a21–b2: 221
4a21 ff: 34 n 8, 35 n 10
6a36: 40
6b28: 40
7b22 ff: 39
7b27: 38
8a13: 154 n 54
8a31: 154 n 54
8a33–b19: 42 n 23
8b21: 154 n 54
12b26 ff: 42 n 23
12b39: 42 n 23
13a12: 38
13a37: 81 n 79
13b6: 57
13b21 ff: 57 n 41
14b12: 39
14b14: 39
14b27: 39

*de Anima*
403b6: 134 n 19
403b10: 154 n 55

406a17: 154 n 54
412a22–8: 113
413b14: 154 n 55
413b14–15: 130 n 8
415b11: 154 n 54
416b24: 134 n 19
429a11–12: 130 n 8
429a12: 154 n 55
432a20: 130 n 8, 154 n 55
433b25: 154 n 55

*de Caelo*
278a11: 134 n 19
I. 12: 54 n 39, 63, 69 n 59
281b2 ff: 48
281b6: 62
281b16: 70 n 62
283a11: 69
283b6 ff: 34 n 8
283b8–11: 70, 72
293b15: 154 n 54
302a1: 134 n 19
305a17: 134 n 19

*de Divinatione per Somnia*
463a28: 41 n 20

*de Generatione Animalium*
715b29: 134 n 19
725b3: 319
728a26: 319
728b22: 319
I. 21: 319
I. 22: 319
731b34: 154 n 54
736b22: 131 n 13
736b26: 134 n 19
737a28: 319
739b30: 134 n 19
741a24: 319
750b4: 319
760b27: 320
766b14: 319
767b8 ff: 319 n 8
767b37: 319
768a14: 319
768b1: 319
768b8: 319
772b7 ff: 313

*de Generatione et Corruptione*
316b3: 146 n 37
317b11: 146 n 37
317b28: 126 n 4
317b33: 146 n 37

320a34-b9: 134 n 19
320b12-14: 130 n 8
320b24: 130 n 8
320b28: 134 n 19
321a34: 154 n 54
321b24: 112
322a28: 112
322a29: 113
324b19: 134 n 19
327b17-22: 146 n 38
337a34: 41
II. 11: 50

*de Incessu Animalium*
704a30-2: 315
704b15-17: 321
705b4-7: 315
708a10-12: 321

*de Interpretatione*
16b6-7: 221
16b8-9: 221
16b33: 78
17a4: 57
17a24: 70
17a25: 77
17a26 ff: 70
17b2: 70
17b18: 54 n 39
17b24 ff: 34
17b27-30: 54 n 39
17b29: 34 n 8
17b36: 34 n 8
18a3: 45
18a19 ff: 78
18a28-33: 34
18a28-18b25: 33 ff
18a29-31: 47
18a30: 54 n 39, 71 n 65
18a34-b8: 36
18a34-b9: 35
18a34-b16: 72
18a35: 71
18a37: 35 n 10
18a38: 37
18a38-b3: 71
18a39: 47
18a39-b1: 37
18a39-b3: 37
18a39 ff: 35 n 9
18b1-2: 37
18b1-3: 40
18b2: 37, 47
18b2-3: 37

18b3: 37, 48
18b4: 35 n 10
18b5-9: 66
18b6-9: 46
18b7: 47
18b8: 71 n 64
18b9: 64 n 53, 66
18b9-16: 35, 51
18b10: 47
18b10-12: 48
18b14: 71 n 64
18b15: 71 n 64
18b15-16: 66
18b17-25: 57 n 41, 71 n 63
18b18: 57 n 41
18b24: 66
18b26-31: 57
18b26-19a22: 57 ff
18b26-19a23: 57
18b27: 79 n 77
18b29: 35 n 10
18b29-30: 66
18b30 ff: 71 n 64
18b31-3: 57
18b35: 71
18b36-19a1: 35 n 9
19a1-5: 71 n 65
19a3-6: 71 n 64
19a9: 57
19a9-11: 57, 61 n 46
19a12: 63
19a12-16: 57
19a13: 71
19a16-22: 58
19a17: 61, 71 n 64
19a18: 64, 66
19a18-22: 64, 72
19a19: 64 n 53
19a19-21: 47
19a20-1: 66
19a23: 67, 69, 70, 71, 72
19a23-7: 68
19a23-b4: 68 ff
19a23 ff: 38 n 14
19a25-6: 72
19a26: 69, 70
19a27: 74, 77
19a27-32: 37, 68
19a27-8: 73
19a28: 71
19a28-32: 73
19a29: 45, 74
19a31 ff: 37

19a32–3: 46
19a32–9: 68, 75, 77
19a33: 64 n 53, 75
19a35: 77
19a36: 76
19a38–9: 47, 66, 76
19a39: 43, 76
19b2: 35 n 10
19b9: 35
21a22–3: 222
21a25–8: 222
21b20: 79 n 77
22a14 ff: 62 n 47
22b12: 80 n 77
22b21: 37

*de Juventute*
469a21: 134 n 19

*de Longitudine*
465b15: 146 n 37

*de Motu Animalium*
703b22: 148 n 42

*de Partibus Animalium*
644b29: 148 n 42
644b31: 148 n 42
654b4: 148 n 42
654b8: 148 n 42
654b10: 148 n 42
656a10: 314
656a12: 315
683b22–3: 315
683b34: 314
684a35: 314
684b1: 314
689b13–15: 316

*de Sensu*
439a24: 134 n 19
446a12: 134 n 19
446a18: 134 n 19

*de Xenophane*
980b11: 134 n 19

*Eudemian Ethics*
1215a10: 100 n 16
1215a12–19: 94 n 9
1215a13–19: 102
1217b2–16: 137, 159, 160, 161 n 11,
    172 n 9
1218a2 ff: 131 n 13, 170
1218b7–12: 95 n 10
1219a35: 95 n 10

1219b4–7: 95 n 10
1219b4–8: 103
1219b34: 134 n 19
1219b36: 154 n 54
1232b9: 122

*Fragmenta*
147 Ross: 122 n 38

*Historia Animalium*
I. 1: 311
491a15–26: 312
494a26 ff: 314
494a29: 315
501b19 ff: 320
507b36: 134 n 19
545b6: 313
555a16: 134 n 19
574a20: 313
584a33: 313
VIII. 1: 311
588a25–6: 311
588b1–3: 311
589b29–590a11: 314 n 5
608a27–8: 320

*Magna Moralia*
1182b13: 149 n 43
1182b15: 149 n 43
1185a5–9: 103
1. 1. 12. 2: 134 n 19
2. 12. 10. 2: 134 n 19

*Metaphysics*
A. 3: 269
980b25–981b10: 183 n 6
989b2–4: 146 n 38
989b3: 146
990b22–991a8: 149 n 44
991b1: 126 n 4
991b3: 126 n 4
996a3: 154 n 54
996a15: 134 n 19
996b26 ff: 79 n 77
998a9: 134 n 19
998a18: 134 n 19, 154 n 54
1002a4: 154 n 54
1002a28: 154 n 54
1005b19: 80 n 78
1006a3: 80 n 78
1007b18: 80 n 78, 82
1007b26–9: 82
1008a4: 80 n 78
1008a12 ff: 82
1008a18–20: 74
1008a34: 80 n 78

1009b10: 65
1009b14: 48
1010b24: 54 n 39
Γ. 7: 65
1012b10: 79 n 77
1015a35: 64
Δ. 6: 140, 141 n 30
1015b36-1016a17: 140 n 29
1016a33-b7: 154 n 56
1016b8: 154 n 55
1016b32: 128 n 5
1017a31: 39
Δ. 11: 136
1019a1-4: 131 n 13
Δ. 12: 48, 141 n 30
1019b23 ff: 48
1022b25-7: 314 n 6
1023a8 ff: 153 n 53
1023a11-13: 135 n 22
1023a12: 152
1023a23: 134 n 19
1024 ff: 39
1025a15: 67 n 56
1025a20: 67 n 56
1025b28: 154 n 55
1025b30 ff: 155
1026a15: 134 n 19
1027b20: 73 n 68
1027b25-8: 39
1028a23: 146 n 37
1028a31-b2: 136
1028a32: 126 n 2
1029a2: 152
1029a22-33: 152
1029a28: 125, 126 n 4
1029a29-30: 153 n 51
1029a31-2: 153 n 51
1030a7-10: 78 n 74
1030b23: 134 n 19
1030b25: 154 n 55
1031a1-2: 126 n 2
1031a10 ff: 126 n 2
1035b15: 154 n 54
1035b23: 148 n 42
1036a32: 134 n 19
1036b4-7: 134 n 19
1037b6: 152
1038a19: 154 n 54
Z. 13: 150 n 46
1038b12: 154 n 54
1038b21: 154 n 54
1038b28: 145
1038b29: 146 n 37, 154 n 55

1038b32: 134 n 19
1039a3: 153 n 50
1039a3-4: 145
1039a7: 145, 148 n 2
1039a17: 145
1039a27: 134 n 19
1039b1: 134 n 19
1039b16: 154 n 54
1040b7: 148 n 42
1040b28: 125, 126 n 4
H. 1: 126, 152 n 48
1042a25-32: 152
1042a29: 125, 154 n 55
1042a30: 129, 154 n 56
1042a31: 130 n 9
1045a12: 78 n 74
Θ. 3: 68, 82 n 80
Θ. 3-4: 69
1047a17 ff: 61 n 45
1047a24: 62
Θ 4: 62, 63 n 49, 68
1047b4: 63
1047b13: 48
1047b35 ff: 72
1048a6: 72 n 66
1048b14-15: 130
1050b7: 154 n 54
1050b8: 61
1050b10-12: 62
1051b1 ff: 39
1051b7-9: 39
1051b9-17: 221
1051b13: 35 n 10
1051b13-16: 34 n 8
1051b16: 54 n 39
1051b23: 66 n 54
1052a25-8: 140 n 29
1052a30-4: 154 n 56
1060b16: 134 n 19
1060b25-8: 134 n 19
1062a24: 65
1064a24: 154 n 55
1064a25: 134 n 19
1065a23-7: 134 n 19
1068b26: 130 n 10, 134 n 19
1070b36: 126 n 4
1071a2: 131 n 13
1071a3: 131 n 13
1073a4: 130
1074a6: 130
Λ. 9: 224
M. 1-2: 135 n 20
1076a33: 134 n 19

1076b3: 134 n 19
1077a31: 154 n 55
1077a36–b11: 131 n 13
1077b3: 126 n 4
1077b7: 126 n 4
1077b15 ff: 134 n 19
M. 3: 134 n 20
1077b32: 129 n 7
1078a17: 154 n 55
1078a22: 154 n 55
1078b31: 149 n 43
1080a1: 126 n 4
1080b1: 134 n 19
1085a26: 134 n 19
1086a35: 149 n 43
1086b16–19: 125, 127
1086b17: 126 n 4
1086b19: 126 n 4
1087a23: 126 n 4
1087b1: 147 n 39
1088a23: 154 n 54
1090a24: 134 n 19
1090a30: 134 n 19

*Meteorologica*
327b27: 41 n 20

*Nicomachean Ethics*
1095b25: 97
1095b31–1096a2: 94
1095b32: 95 n 10
1097b6–21: 94 n 9
1097b8–11: 118
1097b8–13: 93
1097b8–21: 93
1097b16–20: 93 n 8, 100 n 15
1097n20: 93 n 8
1098a18: 94 n 9
1098a18–20: 103
1099a31–b8: 94
1099a32–3: 95
1099a32–b2: 95
1099b2–6: 96
1099b18–25: 94 n 9
1099b20–1: 102
1099b25–1100a4: 89
1099b27–8: 95
1099b32–1100a3: 104
1100a4–9: 89, 104
1100a9: 104 n 22
I. 10: 100 n 16
1100a11–12: 90
1100a34 ff: 106 n 24
1100b2–7: 91

1100b8: 102
1100b8–11: 102
1100b11–22: 97, 101, 102
1100b12–22: 112
1100b23–35: 98
1100b25–8: 95
1100b27: 100
1100b31–3: 120
1100b32–3: 109
1100b33–1101a11: 100 n 16
1101a6–11: 104
1101a12–13: 104
1101a16–21: 106 n 24
1101a17: 106 n 24
1102a26: 134 n 19
1102a28–31: 130 n 8
1104b32–3: 112
1110a4–8: 119 n 36
1117b18–20: 121
1121b21–8: 119
1122b19–23: 120
1123a19–27: 120
1123b15–24: 95
1123b32: 120
1123b34–6: 95
1124a12–20: 120
1124a19: 120
1124a20: 120
1124a20–6: 120
1124b5: 122
1124b23–6: 121
1124b31: 120
1125a9–10: 120
1129b1–4: 95, 96
1139b7–9: 48
1149b3–6: 311
1153b14–25: 94
1153b17–25: 95 n 11
1153b19–21: 94 n 9
1154a22–5: 89
1156a7–9: 113
1156a10–19: 113
1156a16–24: 113
1156b9–12: 113
1165b20–36: 113
1166a29: 109
1167b4–16: 112
1171a15: 92 n 5
1172a9: 112
1173b25–8: 117
X. 6–8: 101 n 18
1178a26: 95
1179a1–17: 100

*peri Ideon*
149 n 43
fr 5 Ross: 131 n 13, 138 n 25

*Physica*
185a31: 126 n 4, 139, 149
186b21: 154 n 55
186b22 ff: 134 n 19
188a6: 146 n 37
192b28-30: 134 n 19
193a10: 154 n 54
193b4: 134 n 19, 154 n 55
193b4-5: 130 n 8
194a1: 154 n 55
196b11 ff: 67 n 56
200a15 ff: 38 n 14
201b23: 146 n 37
203a6: 134 n 19
209b24: 134 n 19
210a20: 152
IV. 3: 135, 164, 172
210a20-1: 135 n 22
210b3: 148 n 42
210b4: 134 n 19
212b6: 148 n 42
216b6: 127
216b7: 127
217a24: 127
225b11: 154 n 54
V. 4: 140 n 29
235b15: 80 n 77
242b72: 62
257b31: 148 n 42

*Poetics*
1451a30-5: 105 n 23

*Politics*
1260a20-8: 11
1276b20-35: 122
1323b24-9: 94 n 9, 102

*Protrepticus*
fr 5, p 32 Ross: 131 n 13

*Rhetorica*
1360b14-17: 91
1360b28-9: 91, 105
1392b33-1393a8: 41 n 20
1418a3-5: 48

*Sophistici Elenchi*
165b30-4: 9
166a3: 70 n 62
166a18: 129 n 7

166a23-31: 70 n 62
171b3: 79 n 77
172b18: 79 n 77
174b38: 79 n 77
181a38: 79 n 77
181b23: 79 n 77
181b36: 134 n 19

*Topica*
102a6: 271
135a13: 271
146a21 ff: 271

**[pseudo-Aristotle]**
*de Mundo*
397b24 ff: 225 n 10, 226

**Augustine**
*ad Simplicianum*
II. 2. 2: 245 n 39

*de Civitate Dei*
XI. 21. 339. 12 ff: 245 n 39

*de Magistro*
40: 26

**Averroes**
*Tahafut al Tahafut*
462, I. 280-1 Van Den Berg: 229 n 22

**Boethius**
*Consolatio Philosophiae*
V. 3. 7: 245 n 39
V. 6: 245 n 39

*in Aristotelis de Interpretatione commentarius*
II. 125. 15: 44 n 25
4. 9-14: 32
200. 11 ff: 45 n 26
200. 22: 45 n 26
208. 1: 45
208. 7 ff: 76
208. 17: 45 n 27
246. 2: 45 n 26
246. 14 ff: 45 n 26
247-8: 45 n 26

**Cicero**
*Academica*
II. 30: 194 n 28

*de Divinatione*
I. 82-4 (= *SVF* II. 1192): 225 n 11
I. 127 (= *SVF* II. 944): 302

*de Fato*
III. 21: 79
XII (= *SVF* II. 954): 302
XIII: 63 n 49

*de Finibus*
I. 47: 202 n 34
II. 43: 300
III. 12: 300
III. 20-2: 300
III. 22: 294 n 14
III. 54: 294 n 14
III. 56: 294 n 14
III. 59: 299
III. 60-71: 301
III. 73: 301
IV. 43 (= *SVF* I. 369): 298
IV. 45: 295 n 14
IV. 46: 300
IV. 47-8: 300
IV. 54: 294
IV. 56: 294
IV. 68-71: 295 n 14
IV. 69: 300
IV. 70: 295 n 14, 300, 305

*de Natura Deorum*
I. 43: 187, 188
I. 44: 188
I. 44-5: 187 n 10
I. 45: 187
I. 46-9: 187 n 11
I. 49: 188 n 12, 189, 198
I. 75-6: 189 n 17
I. 76: 194 n 27
I. 81-4: 192 n 25
I. 82-3: 189 n 17
I. 83: 192 n 24
I. 105: 189 n 18, 192 n 21, 198
I. 106: 193 n 26
I. 106-7: 190 n 19
I. 107-8: 190 n 20
I. 107-10: 190 n 19
I. 108: 190
I. 110-14: 190 n 19

*de Officiis*
III. 15: 298 n 20

**Demosthenes**
*de Corona*
xxxv: 270

**Diogenes Laertius**
V. 32: 226
VII. 107: 292
VII. 107-8: 304
VII. 107-9: 292 n 10
VII. 108: 292
VII. 109: 300
X. 31: 198 n 30, 212 n 49
X. 33: 180

**Diogenes of Oenanda**
fr 6: 188 n 13
fr 7: 189 n 14
new fr 5. III. 6-14: 189 n 15
new fr 5-6: 188 n 13, 195 n 29
new fr 6. I. 3-13: 189 n 14

**Epictetus**
*Dissertationes*
II. 19. 2 (= *SVF* I. 489): 230 n 24

**Epicurus**
*Kuriai Doxai*
24: 188 n 13

*Epistula ad Herodotum*
38: 188, 203
68: 209
69: 208 n 41, 208 n 42
69-72: 211
70-1: 209 n 43
72: 210 n 45
73: 207 n 39, 210 n 47

*Epistula ad Menoecum*
123: 202 n 35
123-4: 187, 201, 202 n 34

*peri Phuseos*
XXVIII: 178, 179, 180, 202, 206
XXVIII fr 12. III. 6-12: 180 n 4
XXXV: 213

**Euripides**
*Andromache*
96-103: 91 n 3

*Heraclidae*
863-4: 91 n 3

*Iphigenia at Aulis*
161-3: 91 n 3

*Trojan Woman*
505-10: 91 n 3

**Fragments**
*SVF*
I. 39: 295 n 16
I. 62: 301
I. 358–9: 290
I. 359: 296
I. 361: 296
II. 83: 185 n 8
II. 224–9: 177 n 2
II. 378: 301
II. 943–4: 302
II. 1003: 301
III. 26: 299
III. 117: 291
III. 122: 291
III. 123: 291
III. 214: 302 n 24
III. 278: 302 n 24
III. 295: 302 n 24
III. 314: 301
III. 315: 301
III. 494: 297, 297 n 18
III. 495: 297, 297 n 18, 301
III. 496: 297 n 18
III. 498: 301
III. 500: 297
III. 501: 301
III. 512: 297 n 18
III. 516: 297
III. 517: 297
III. 520: 301
III. 548: 302
III. 564–5: 302
III. 605: 302
III. 606: 302
III. 613–14: 299
III. 613–15: 301
III. 623: 301

*Usener*
255: 200 n 32

**Herodotus**
I. 30–3: 90
III. 106. 2: 3

**Hesiod**
*Works and Days*
293–4: 26 n 45

**Homer**
*Iliad*
XXIII. 276: 3
XXIII. 374: 3

**Hypereides**
*Epitaph*
41: 4

**Isocrates**
*Antidosis*
186–92: 3 n 11
274–5: 3 n 11

*contra Sophistas*
14–18: 3
21: 3

**Lucretius**
*de Rerum Natura*
I. 453: 208 n 40
I. 455–8: 210 n 44
I. 459–63: 210 n 46
I. 462–3: 210 n 48
IV: 179
IV. 354–63: 205 n 36
IV. 476: 214 n 53
IV. 478–81: 207 n 38, 214 n 53
IV. 722–826: 188 n 13
IV. 724–43: 189 n 14
IV. 762–4: 189 n 14
IV. 765–7: 192 n 22, 212 n 49
IV. 768–76: 189 n 15
IV. 802–6: 191 n 21
IV. 962–72: 192 n 23
IV. 973–83: 192 n 22
IV. 984–6: 193 n 26, 200 n 31
IV. 984–1010: 192 n 23
IV. 1030–6: 189 n 16
V. 1161–240: 187 n 11

**Philoponus**
*in Aristotelis Analytica Priora*
376. 35: 43
436. 6: 43

**Pindar**
*Nemean Odes*
III. 41: 3

*Olympian Odes*
II. 86–8: 3

**Plato**
*Alcibiades*
105d ff: 14
118c–119a: 11 n 25
124b1–c2: 14 n 27
135d–e: 14

*Apology*
25a–c: 252
41c–d: 107 n 27

*Charmides*
157e7–159a3: 5 n 17

*Crito*
46–8: 252
48b9–10: 107 n 27

*Euthydemus*
275d3–4: 8
276b4–5: 8
276c6–7: 8
276d7–8: 8
277a8–b4: 9
277c6–7: 9
277e3–278b2: 9
282c1–8: 2
295e–296d: 19

*Euthyphro*
5a3–b7: 14
5d1: 275
6c–8a: 247
6d–e: 282
6d11: 287 n 11
6e: 278
6e10: 277
8a11: 282
9d1–3: 277 n 10
10c: 256
10d–11a: 277
11a7: 270
11a7–8: 270
11e: 275
12c5: 275
12d: 275

*Gorgias*
448e–449a: 19 n 33
449b4–c7: 19 n 33
451a3–c9: 19 n 33
452a1–a4: 19 n 33
455a8–e5: 19 n 33
457c3–458c8: 19 n 33
472b–c: 250
474a–b: 250
474b: 250, 251
474c: 251
474e: 256
476d: 256
482e: 251
499d: 286

*Hippias Major*
281c–283b: 263
281c5–6: 269
281d5: 270
282b1: 270
283b ff: 271
283c4: 270
283e3: 270
284e2: 270
285b–e: 271
285d8: 269
286b5–7: 271
286c–d: 274
286c8–d2: 6 n 17
287c8–d1: 278 n 11
288a10: 278 n 11
288b–e: 276
288b8: 262
288d2: 270
288d4: 269
289b3: 286
289b5: 286
289d3: 286
289d8: 286
289e5–6: 286
290d6: 278 n 11
291d3: 286
291d10: 286
292d4: 269
294a1–e9: 286
296a3: 262
296d–297d: 265
297b2–3: 262
297c: 265
298d2: 262
299–303: 276
299e2–300b5: 266 n 4
299e4: 278 n 11
300a10: 284 n 13
300b1: 263, 266 n 3
300b6–8: 266
300c–302b: 267
301b: 271
301b6: 270
301b8: 270
301e4: 270
302b2–3: 263
302c1–2: 263
302c5: 270
303c3–7: 267
303d1–4: 266 n 4
303e4–304a1: 264 n 2
304a5: 271

304b4: 271
304d-e: 274
304d4-e3: 6 n 17

*Hippias Minor*
363a-b: 271
366c5: 271
367d6: 271
367e9: 271
368b-369a: 271
369b-c: 271
369c1: 271
370e5-9: 271
371d8-372a5: 271
375d3-6: 271
376b7: 271

*Laches*
183a: 271
184-6: 252
185a1: 13
185a6: 13
186a5-6: 13
189d-190a: 14
189e-190b: 279
189e-190e: 274 n 8
190b8-c2: 5 n 17
191e10: 275
192c1: 275
199e: 275

*Lysis*
219c ff: 282
219c7: 283 n 12
219d3: 282, 283 n 12
219d4: 282, 283 n 12
219e7-d1: 282
220b1-2: 282
220b4: 282
223b4-8: 5 n 17

*Meno*
81a1-4: 2
71a5-7: 5
71a6: 5
71b: 274
71b4: 5
71c5-d5: 11
71e1-72a5: 11
71e ff: 6, 277
72c: 278
72c2: 277
72c7: 277
72c8: 278, 278 n 11
73a1-5: 6

73c ff: 6
73d1: 6
73d-e: 275
73d9-10: 253
74a9-b1: 276
75a4: 276
75a8: 276
76b ff: 6
78a1-9: 100 n 17
79a7-e4: 6
79c7-80b3: 6
79d5: 6
79e4: 6
80b4: 6
80d: 274
80d1-3: 7
80d3-4: 8
80d5-9: 1
80d8: 23
80e1-5: 9
80e3-5: 23
80e5: 23
81a5-86c2: 2
81d2-3: 17
81d4-5: 17, 22
82a1-2: 17
82b6-7: 17
82b9-83e3: 20
82c7-8: 18
82d1-2: 18
82d8-e2: 18
82e4-6: 17
82e5-6: 18
82e11-12: 21
82e14-84a2: 21
83c8-d1: 18
83d4-5: 18
84a3-4: 21
85b8-9: 21
85c-d: 22
85c-86a: 275 n 9
85c2-7: 21
85c6-7: 16
85c9-d1: 17, 21
85c10-11: 22
85d3-4: 21
85d3-7: 17
85d6-7: 22
85e-86b: 29 n 50
86a7-8: 22
86d-e: 274 n 8
87c5-6: 2
87e: 286

89e–96b: 11
91c1–92c5: 11
92e ff: 5 n 15
93b–94e: 11
95a–b: 11
95b–c: 11
95c–96a: 12
96a6: 26
96a6–b1: 11
95b1–3: 11
96d ff: 23 n 40
97a–b: 27
97a9–11: 7
97d6–98b5: 7
97e–98a: 17
98a: 275 n 9
98a3–4: 22
98a3–5: 7
98a4: 22
98a4–5: 22
100b4–6: 5 n 17

*Phaedo*
65d13: 270
74b: 285
74b–c: 285
74b8: 285, 277 n 10
74c1: 285
75c10–d1: 285
76d9: 270
78e2: 282
100b ff: 278
100b4: 278 n 11
100b7: 278 n 11
100c5: 278 n 11
100c10: 278 n 11
100d4–5: 278 n 11
100e2: 278 n 11
101b5: 278 n 11
101c4: 278 n 11
102b2: 282
118a16–17: 15

*Protagoras*
313a1–314c2: 12
313c4–5: 12
313c7: 12
313d1–3: 12
313d3–5: 12
313d8–31: 12
313e1–2: 12
313e2–5: 12
314a3–b1: 13
314b1–4: 13

315c: 271
316d3: 270
318a6–9: 13
318a9: 270
318d7–e5: 13
318e: 271
319e–320b: 11 n 25
320c2–4: 18
332c8–9: 255 n 13
349b4: 270
352–8: 248 n 3
352d–358a: 247
360e7–361c: 274 n 8
361c3–6: 5 n 17
371a5–b3: 2 n 8

*Republic*
333–4: 247
334e–335a: 252
335b–c: 248 n 4, 252
345b3–c3: 6 n 17
347e–354a: 248 n 3
348b–350c: 248 n 3
348e: 251
349d: 248 n 3
352d–354a: 3
352e: 256
354c: 274 n 8
476a7: 285
476e ff: 284
479a: 284, 285 n 14
479a6–8: 277 n 10
479a7: 285
479b2: 285
479b4: 285
479b–d: 315
479d1: 285
518b6–7: 28

*Symposium*
211a: 285, 286
211a–b: 285 n 14
211a ff: 285
211a5: 285
212a4: 283 n 12

*Theaetetus*
185b: 266 n 5
186c: 284 n 13
202d5: 27

**Pliny**
*Natural History*
XXV: 322

**Plotinus**
*Enneads*
IV. 3. 8. 35 ff: 244
IV. 3. 11. 8–21: 235
IV. 3. 25. 10–20: 235
IV. 3. 25. 20–4: 235
IV. 3. 25. 20–7: 235
IV. 3. 25. 27 ff: 235
IV. 4. 9. 1–9: 235
IV. 4. 10. 1–4: 235
IV. 4. 10. 9–15: 236
IV. 4. 11. 9–11: 236
IV. 4. 13. 17–25: 236
VI. 5. 8. 39–42: 244
VI. 9. 6. 10–11: 244

**Plutarch**
*Alcibiades*
16. 3: 92 n 5
23. 4–5: 92 n 5

*Alcibiades et Coriolanus*
1. 3: 92 n 5
2. 1: 92 n 5
3. 2: 92 n 5
4. 5: 92 n 5
5. 1: 92 n 5

*de Communibus Notitiis*
1072a: 299
1085a: 185 n 9

*Solon*
3. 2 (= fr 4. 9–11 Diehl): 102 n 20

**Proclus**
*de Providentia*
63–6 Isaac: 238 n 31

*Decem Dubitationes*
II. 6–23 Isaac: 237
II. 6. 1–20 Isaac: 239
II. 6. 16 Isaac: 242 n 33
II. 7. 1–29 Isaac: 238
III. 14. 20–4 Isaac: 243 n 33
III. 14. 22–5 Isaac: 242
III. 14. 22–8 Isaac: 242 n 33

*Institutio Theologia*
114 (120 Dodds): 237 n 30
124 (110. 10–13 Dodds): 237
124 (110. 14–23 Dodds): 238, 239

*in Platonis Timaeum commentarii*
III. 27. 2 Diehl: 243 n 34

*Platonic Theology*
I. 15 (69. 10–12, 70. 22–5, 74. 9–16
Saffrey–Westerink): 237
I. 21 (98. 5–12 Saffrey–Westerink):
237
I. 21 (98. 16–20 Saffrey–Westerink):
237
I. 21 (99. 6–9 Saffrey–Westerink): 239

**Seneca**
*Epistolae Morales*
92. 22: 100 n 17
94: 290
94. 4: 293
94. 5: 292, 297, 305
94. 5–12: 293
94. 8: 296
94. 8–9: 292
94. 10: 305
94. 11: 303
94. 12: 305
94. 13: 291
94. 14–15: 292
94. 14–16: 303
94. 14–17: 294
94. 15–16: 300
94. 30: 299 n 20
94. 31: 291, 303, 304
94. 35: 301, 303
94. 43: 301
95: 290
95. 60–4: 291
95. 60–1: 303
95. 61: 303
95. 64: 303
95. 66: 303

**Sextus Empiricus**
*adversus Mathematicos*
V. 104: 213 n 51
VI. 55–9: 206 n 37
VIII. 63: 189 n 14
IX. 25–6: 187 n 11
IX. 25–8: 192 n 25
IX. 43–8: 190 n 20
IX. 61–74: 201 n 33
IX. 71: 202 n 34
X. 181–8: 207 n 39
X. 212–28: 207 n 39
X. 219–28: 210 n 46
X. 221–3: 208 n 41
X. 238–47: 207 n 39
X. 240–4: 210 n 46

338   *Index Locorum*

XI. 63–4: 291
XI. 166: 192 n 24

*Outlines of Pyrrhonism*
II. 211–13: 176
II. 212: 175

**Simplicius**
*in Aristotelis Categorias commentarium*
195: 43
407. 12–13: 44

*in Aristotelis Physica commentaria*
1299. 36–1300. 10 (*SVF* II. 206): 222

**Sophocles**
*Antigone*
583–92: 91 n 2

*Oedipus Tyrannos*
1186–96: 91 n 2
1204: 100 n 17
1524–30: 91 n 3

*Trachiniae*
1–3: 91 n 3

**Syrianus**
*in Aristotelis Metaphysica commentaria*
147. 1–6 (= fr 45 Zoumpos): 244 n 36

**Theophrastus**
*Historia Plantarum*
IX: 322

**Thucydides**
I. 2. 4: 3
I. 138. 3: 92 n 6
II. 65. 6: 92 n 6
VII. 69. 2: 269

**Xenophon**
*Memorabilia*
III. 9: 3

**Zeno**
*SVF* I. 85–77: 294
*SVF* I. 230: 293
*SVF* III. 128: 293

## Notes for Contributors to Oxford Studies in Ancient Philosophy

1. All contributions should be typed, double spaced, and on one side of the A4 page only. Ample margins should be left.

2. Two copies of all articles should be sent to the editor.

3. Footnotes should be numbered consecutively and typed together on a separate page or pages, in double line spacing. They will be printed at the foot of each page. Wherever possible references should be built into the text.

4. Contributors are asked to minimize the use of Greek, substituting transliteration where possible; but Greek will be printed in the text and footnotes wherever it is indispensable for the argument. The Greek *must* be typed in contributions.

5. In references to books, the first time the book is referred to—

   it is normally desirable to give at least the first name or initial of the author, and the place and date of publication, thus:

   T. Irwin, *Plato's Moral Theory* (Oxford, 1977).

   The volume number of the periodical should also be given.

6. Where the same book is referred to on subsequent occasions, it is acceptable to use op cit and omit the author's first name or initial (op cit is printed in Roman not italic and without abbreviation stops), thus:

   Irwin, op cit, 164

   or to use an abbreviated reference to the title, thus:

   Murdoch, *The Fire and The Sun*, 47

   or to refer back to the footnote giving the complete references, thus:

   Irwin, above n 8, 49 (omitting the abbreviation stops after 'n').

   In a long article, or where the references to the same work are separated by several pages, the last method is preferable.

7. Titles of books are always printed in italics and should therefore be underlined in the typescript.

8. Titles of journals will be printed in italics and should be underlined in the typescript. The name of the journal should be given for the first citation, with the abbreviation to be used in subsequent citations given in brackets:

   *Proceedings of the Aristotelian Society* (*PAS*), LXXXII (1982), 97

   Use the abbreviations suggested in the journal itself for subsequent citations.